Dedication

To the glory of God with thanks to him for the gift of Lisa—my wife, best friend, and partner in what's been an amazing adventure. My deepest gratitude goes to my heavenly Father. The mystery of your amazing love and grace continue to baffle me.

Acknowledgments

If God hadn't allowed my life's path to cross many others, the pages of this book would be blank. As with everything that I am and do, this book reflects the investment that numerous mentors, influencers, coworkers, and friends have made in my life. While I only have the space to thank a few here, there are many more who deserve recognition.

My deepest gratitude goes to my heavenly Father. The mystery of your amazing love and grace continue to baffle me.

Second, I thank those God has brought into my life. My wife Lisa has been a faithful friend, encourager, and supporter. More than anyone else, she's helped me maintain priorities and perspective since the day we began our life together. Thanks for loving me. Caitlin, Josh, Bethany, and Nate, it's been a joy to watch you grow. I pray that God will continue to use both the joys and sorrows of life to shape and mold you into the image of Christ.

I thank my parents, Dr. and Mrs. Walter Mueller, Jr. for passing on the valuable inheritance of faith.

To the staff, board, and supporters of the Center for Parent/Youth Understanding, I'm grateful for your part in working out the mission and vision of CPYU. Thanks for your partnership and commitment. To our present staff—Cliff Frick, Doug West, Chris Wagner, Lisa Mueller, Derek Melleby, and Paul Robertson—working with you is a joy. The fruit of your labors and support are woven in and through the pages of this book.

To the folks at Youth Specialties, I'm grateful for all you've done to promote and expand the ministry of CPYU over the years. I'm grateful to Tic Long, Michelle Fockler, Mark Oestriecher, and the rest of the YS team for giving us a place to meet and equip youth workers year after year. Jay Howver, Jen Howver, Roni Meek, Holly Sharp and the rest of the YS/Zondervan publishing team—I thank you for your valuable help in making this book a reality. Special thanks to Dave Urbanski—you've been the kind of editor who not only makes my writing look so much better than it is, but you've also helped me sleep more soundly during the editing process.

I'd also like to thank a few of the people who've shaped my thinking through their teaching, example, and investment in my life. While I was growing through the sometimes difficult and always exciting years of my own adolescence, there were four men who took an interest in me and modeled the redeeming love of Christ: Phil Douglass, Mike Barbera, Chuck Wiggins, and Lowell Meek. I hope that this book will influence and help countless thousands of other men and women to influence teenagers for the Kingdom in the way that you did me. And my thanks to those thinkers who taught me a love for understanding the Word as well as the world—Dr. Russell Heddendorf, Dr. Dean Borgman, Dr. Dan Jessen, Dr. Richard Peace, Dr. J. Christy Wilson, Dr. Gary Pratico, Dr. Royce Gruenler, Dr. Francis Schaeffer, and Dr. John Stott (and many others), as well as three institutions that have done the same—Geneva College, The Coalition for Christian Outreach, and Gordon-Conwell Theological Seminary.

To the thousands of youth ministry coworkers who I've had the privilege of meeting over the years—thanks for your constant encouragement. To my colaborers in training youth workers—Duffy Robbins, Marv Penner, Doug Fields, Chap Clark, Rich Van Pelt, and others too numerous to mention here—I treasure our friendships.

And finally, to the scores of teenagers I have met and talked to during my three decades in youth ministry, thanks for allowing me the opportunity to have access into your lives and world.

—*Walt Mueller, Center for Parent/Youth Understanding, May 2007*

To access additional information on today's youth culture, visit the Center for Parent/Youth Understanding at www.cpyu.org. The site is updated daily. To access regularly updated and categorized supplemental resources for *Youth Culture 101*, go to the CPYU site and click on the book's supplemental resources section. You can also sign up to receive weekly youth culture updates via email and CPYU's quarterly journal of youth culture, *ENGAGE*.

contents

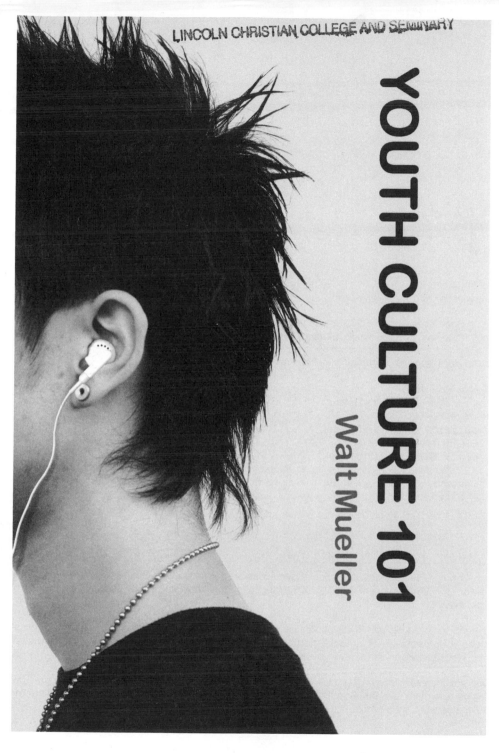

YOUTH CULTURE 101

Walt Mueller

ZONDERVAN®

ZONDERVAN.com/
AUTHORTRACKER
follow your favorite authors

youth
specialties

Youth Culture 101
Copyright © 2007 by Walt Mueller

Youth Specialties products, 300 South Pierce Street, El Cajon, CA 92020, are published by Zondervan, 5300 Patterson Avenue Southeast, Grand Rapids, MI 49530.

Library of Congress Cataloging-in-Publication Data

Mueller, Walt, 1956-
  Youth culture 101 / Walt Mueller.
      p. cm.
  Includes bibliographical references.
  ISBN-10: 0-310-27313-7 (pbk.)
  ISBN-13: 978-0-310-27313-4 (pbk.)
  1. Christian teenagers—Religious life. 2. Parent and teenager—Religious aspects—Christianity. 3. Church work with teenagers. I. Title. II. Title: Youth culture one hundred one. III. Title: Youth culture one hundred and one.

  BV4531.3.M845 2007
  277.3'0830835—dc22

                                                                          2007005986

Web site addresses listed in this book were current at the time of publication. Please contact Youth Spe-cialties via e-mail (YS@YouthSpecialties.com) to report URLs that are no longer operational and provide replacement URLs if available.

Interior design by Mark Novelli, IMAGO MEDIA
Cover design by SharpSeven Design

Printed in the United States

07 08 09 10 11 12 • 10 9 8 7 6 5 4 3 2

introduction

Why I Wrote This Book

It all began in 1988 with a simple question from a group of concerned parents, to me, a thirty-something youth pastor who'd been hired to minister to their kids: *We feel like we are increasingly out of touch with our kids. You spend a lot of time with them. Would you help us understand them by helping us understand their world?*

What motivated them was a widening cultural-generational gap that needed to be closed. They stood on one side, bewildered by the rapidly changing and confusing world of their teenagers; on the other side stood their children—and they longed for parents and other significant adults who'd help them through the confusing maze of youth culture and lead them to a spiritually and emotionally healthy adulthood. It was a gap nobody—teens or adults—wanted.

While initially hesitant, I took the challenge and immersed myself in a three-month process of gaining a deeper understanding of youth culture and then communicated information and analysis on what I discovered to the parents for an hour every Sunday morning. The parents eagerly embraced what they were learning. They said it was transforming their relationships with their kids. Much to my joy, their kids said the same thing. To make a long story short, it all led to the birth of the Center for Parent/Youth Understanding in 1990. I've been studying youth culture ever since. It's my passion, and something I believe is a necessary task for anyone called to minister to teenagers or raise children.

Here are two important things to keep in mind regarding youth culture: 1) Its rate of change is speeding up, not slowing down—and if we hesitate, stand still, and don't stay on top of the rapid changes, we'll be left in the dust; 2) Not only are there more voices taking up space in youth culture all the time, but they're also getting louder, more attractive, and more convincing. The question a concerned father asked me 15 years ago rings truer every day: "How can I expect my son to hear the still small voice of God with all those other voices screaming in his ears?"

As the father of four kids myself and a culture-watcher, I wrote Youth Culture 101 to help you—and me—answer that question.

This book is for all of you who recognize that being a youth worker, parent, pastor, or educator is a cross-cultural missions venture. This book is for all of you who desire to cross the generational gap and help the youth you know and love to hear the God who still speaks. It's my hope that this book will open your eyes to the cultural realities our kids—from the time they're born—live with in today's world. And it's only by facing and understanding these realities that we can truly break through the cultural barriers, walk with them in their world, and share God's unchanging, life-giving story in ways they'll understand and respond to. But if we don't know their world, our efforts to speak God's truth to them may fall on deaf ears. So it's my hope that this book will help you become like "the men of Issachar, who understood the times and knew what Israel should do" (1 Chronicles 12:32).

Who Do I Want Reading This Book? (And How Should They Read It?)

Parents. Because your God-given responsibility is to nurture your kids toward a deep Christian faith that's integrated into all of life, you need to know their culture and world. You need the knowledge to affirm culture's positives and counter its negatives. But where do you begin? If you feel out of touch and confused by your teenagers' world, please know you're not alone! It's my hope that this book will provide you with the information necessary to navigate what's often youth culture's perplexing maze.

But also keep in mind that *Youth Culture 101* is not a book on parenting. While I share some anecdotes and principles from my (and many others') experiences, this book is focused on helping you understand your children's world so you can parent them more effectively. As a fellow struggler in the parenting journey—still with one child left in high school—believe me, I'm reading along with you!

Youth workers. I hope the information and analysis included in the forthcoming pages increases your ministry effectiveness by deepening your understanding of the issues facing your kids every day—and your ability to address those issues with relevance—and proves a valuable reference you'll pull from your shelves over and over. What's more, it's my hope that you'll share the information in *Youth Culture 101* with the parents of your students. They're hungry to understand their kids and their world—and they're looking to you to fill in the blanks. So...use the text in parents-of-teenagers classes or discussion groups; place it in parents' resource libraries; and pass on tidbits of information from this book through your newsletters and Web sites.

Educators. I trust the information (and considerable research gathered) within these pages proves foundational for your classrooms as you teach youth culture and the principles of walking alongside and mentoring young people.

Pastors. I pray this book will be a ready guide as you build your understanding of the complex interplay between the cultural forces molding and shaping the values, attitudes, and behaviors of the kids in your congregations—and that it provides hundreds of windows into new sermons and teaching.

Bible college and seminary students. This book is as much for you as it is for the other groups of people listed. Because if you're preparing to embrace the wonderfully satisfying calling of ministry to students, you'll need a resource that not only will communicate helpful information, but also will build in you the resolve to fulfill your calling with a passion for Scripture and for having a ready answer about the culture in which you will communicate God's truth.

Finally I hope *Youth Culture 101* will open many eyes to the real world of today's teenagers—a world we often choose to ignore or simplify. And then so armed with that understanding, as well as a growing, vital faith in the God who calls us to minister to the young, we can work together to help youth hear and respond with an emphatic "yes" to Christ's life-changing invitation: "Come, and follow me."

* mid-life

Good News: There's a Teenager in Your Life!

1

It is time for us to reject the wholesale cynicism of our culture regarding adolescence. Rather than years of undirected and unproductive struggle, these are years of unprecedented opportunity... These are the years of penetrating questions, the years of wonderful discussions never before possible. These are the years of failure and struggle that put the teen's true heart on the table. These are the years of daily ministry and of great opportunity.

—PAUL DAVID TRIPP IN *AGE OF OPPORTUNITY*[1]

When I got to the point where I had been given all I could humanly handle, I never once doubted that God in his grace would give me all I needed to continue on and handle whatever was to come.

—MOTHER OF A TEENAGE SON LOCKED IN THE STRUGGLES OF ADOLESCENCE

It's a commonly held notion that raising or ministering to teenagers is always difficult. I'm here to tell you that for me, it's been an incredible ride marked by some amazing ups and a few challenging downs. I spent the first 16 years of my adult life working with teenagers in a variety of youth ministry positions. I've spent the last 17 years studying teenagers, their lives, and their culture. In the midst of all that, I've spent 23 years raising four kids of my own. Three have already passed through their teenage years. One's still smack dab in the midst of adolescence.

For the most part, my incredible ride's been marked by amazing sights and scenery that have put a big smile on my face. Teenagers are lots of fun, and mine have brought great joy to my heart. But there have been some periods during my journey—periods that have coincided with my own kids' adolescent years—that have been quite bumpy. When I look in the rearview mirror and see the years that have flown by far too quickly, I see there have been times when I've missed a turn, fallen asleep at the wheel, or even wrecked altogether. There have been times when my kids have done the same. But through it all and by the grace of God, I've never once regretted the ride or wished I'd never set out on the journey in the first place. Whether you're a parent of or someone working with teenagers, I hope that when all is said and done, it's the same for you.

But let's face the truth: We're adults; they're teenagers. Although we may share a roof and DNA, a cultural-generational gap will exist. And if adults don't make an effort to love teenagers by working to close that gap, it *will* only continue to widen. What should parents do when they experience the highs and lows of parenting in a rapidly changing world? What should youth workers and others in relationships with teenagers do to close the gap and become more effective at fulfilling their unique callings? How can we avoid being overwhelmed by the normal feelings of confusion, frustration, and misunderstanding that go with the teenage years? Is there anything constant we can grasp? Yes, there is.

Finding Your Way Through the Maze of Their Adolescence

Our search and experience has yielded some distinct patterns and approaches consistently present when parents and youth workers and the teenagers they love have worked together well to find their way through the maze of contemporary adolescence. As you read through the remainder of this book, I trust you'll understand even more the unique pressures, problems, choices, and issues facing our teenagers in today's fast-paced and rapidly changing world. In order to be prepared to respond to these issues in a hope-filled, positive, compassionate, and productive manner, it's important that you understand and embrace several truths for yourself and your family and your youth ministry. I know from experience that if you take them to heart, they can radically transform your life and the way you approach the valuable years you spend with your kids.

Kids Are God's Gifts to Us

Our widespread cultural cynicism regarding teenagers and these exciting years of their lives is unjustified and must cease. The psalmist writes, "Don't you see that kids are God's best gift? The fruit of the womb his generous legacy? Like a warrior's fistful of arrows are the kids of a vigorous youth. Oh, how blessed are you parents, with your quivers full of kids!" (Psalm 127:3-5, *The Message*). It's a big mistake to think of kids as liabilities; they're rewards from God, given to us as a sign of God's favor. Because God values them so highly, so must we. They're not inconveniences or nuisances—whether they're in your home or in your youth room. Even during difficult times, the kids God's given me as gifts *remain* gifts.

No One Ever Said It'd Be Easy

I learned a shocking lesson shortly after Caitlin's birth, and I've been relearning it ever since. No matter how much time and effort I put into preparing for parenthood, there will always be surprises. Some of those surprises can seem paralyzing. Raising and relating to kids is difficult for everyone, and it tends to become more so as kids reach the teenage years. The situation grows more complex for parents who raise more than one child since each child brings a unique personality and set of experiences.

Each of us will experience highs and lows, jolts and joys, thrills and spills. If you're struggling as a parent, rest assured you're not alone. I've made efforts, but I've also made mistakes, struggled with feelings of inadequacy, and grappled with rebellion in my kids. I've known sickening dread, sleepless nights, rage, bitterness, frustration, shame, futile hopes being shattered, and the battle between tenderness and contempt. (If you're a youth worker, you know a bit about this, too!)

If you've raised a teenager and been totally spared all of these experiences, it's only by the grace of God. The reality is that it's not easy. But we can approach our parenting as a glorious challenge and opportunity. Dr. Paul Tripp reminds us that "the teenage years are often cataclysmic years of conflict, struggle, and grief. They are years of new temptations, of trial and testing. Yet these very struggles, conflicts, trials and tests are what produce such wonderful parental opportunities."[2]

There Are No Perfect Kids...or Parents...or Youth Workers

The root of problems in our families and homes and youth ministries is the sinful, selfish nature of kids and adults. It can be difficult to coexist peacefully. Parents must strive to raise healthy, well-adjusted kids. But it's unrealistic to expect perfect kids and perfect families. To embrace such expectations only burdens parents and their kids with never "measuring up."

We must never forget that we're all imperfect, finite beings touched by sin and incapable of perfection—not with our parenting, our ministries, or our homes.

The World Is More Than Happy to Raise Our Kids for Us

In recent years, adolescents have had fewer opportunities for times of interaction and communication with their parents and other adults. Many families have experienced divorce; and in those families where Mom and Dad still live together, members get busier all the time thanks to schedules full of meetings, activities, clubs, and sports. The other extreme is also occurring in a growing number of families, where members may all be at home in the evenings, but everyone retreats to the "aloneness" of their own rooms to interact "solo" with the TV, computer, or any number of media outlets that fill their personal spaces.

All of these factors keep families from eating together on a regular basis, and these realities have certainly contributed to the fact that when teenagers need advice, they're more likely to turn first to a friend (55 percent), followed by Mom (44 percent), a boyfriend or girlfriend (23 percent), and then Dad (20 percent).[3] When push comes to shove, American dads and moms are devoting less time to bringing up their sons and daughters, thereby allowing someone or something else to raise their kids for them.

As a result of his research on the lives of mid-adolescents (ages 14 to 18), Chap Clark concludes "many if not most mid-adolescents have been set adrift by parental and familial authorities, and they are operating as if they are on their own."[4] This sad reality has been developing for years. Back in the early 1990s, I attended a presentation on a new reading program at our local elementary school. While I applauded our school district's efforts in teaching kids to read, I was concerned about the social problems it cited for the existence of the program known as HOTS (Higher Order Thinking Skills). The goal of HOTS is to help kids who consistently fall behind at school learn how to think for themselves through the use of computers and "controlled floundering." Dr. Stanley Pogrow, the founder, explains: "Traditionally, we learn to think by sitting around the table, being questioned by parents, and talking as a family. Today, who has time for sit-down meals? Yet, this critical stage of development cannot be bypassed...So what is the solution?...Bring dinner table conversation to school. That's what HOTS does!"[5]

Sadly, the HOTS program exists to fill a void left by parents who no longer see the importance of spending time together as a family. When parents give up these responsibilities, no matter what the age(s) of their kids, others—by default—take over. In today's rapidly changing youth culture, we hand over the parenting reins to a variety of institutions, including the school, church, media, advertising, coaches, and so on. Sure, some of these institutions are well intentioned and they really do care for kids. But they can never replace the role parents must play in the lives of their teenagers.

In the same way God gives parents the gift of kids, he gives kids the gift of parents who will love and nurture them. Scripture clearly states that parents are to exercise their parental responsibilities by spending time with their kids, and that includes teaching them God's will and way (Deuteronomy 6:6-7). Raising teenagers requires a diligent and unwavering investment of *all* our resources. And lest parents should fall into the trap of thinking teenagers don't *want* their investment of time, guidance, and direction—they should think again. Teenagers can be viewed as distinct lumps of clay that God has entrusted us with, and he has an individual plan for each one. Like the lumps of clay spinning on a potter's wheel, no two start out alike. And by the time the potter is finished, each will become a unique cup, vase, plate, pot, or bowl.

I've had the privilege of watching my own four lumps of clay grow and take their unique shapes over the years. When they were little, I wondered what they'd end up like when all was said and done. Yet, in the midst of that wondering, I knew God had chosen my wife and me to be stewards of this sacred trust. As parents, we have the awesome task of cooperating with God to mold and shape those lumps under his guidance.

A potter is committed to shaping that lump of clay. If she makes a mistake, she reworks the clay, rather than giving up on it. What would happen to the clay if the potter decided she didn't want to work with it any more and suddenly threw it out the window? Its destiny would vary, depending on where it landed. It could land in the street and be run over, flattened and forgotten. It could land in the grass, only to be pounded and eroded by the elements. It could bake in the sun until all of its pliable properties disappeared. Dried and hardened, it could never be worked again. All too often, teenagers meet such fates due to parental neglect. It's as if they've been thrown out the window and left to whatever fate befalls them. I know this is true because I've met far too many of these abandoned lumps of clay over the years.

But when the potter keeps the clay in her hands, working and reworking it with tender care, it eventually turns into a beautiful and unique piece of pottery. So it should be with our kids. They must grow up knowing Mom and Dad are loving, hands-on kind of people who eagerly fulfill their God-given responsibilities to raise their kids.

Any Kid, Anywhere, Anytime

During a youth culture seminar I was leading a few years back, I made an effort to help parents and youth workers see that a variety of factors combine in our world to make the voice of the culture far more compelling and attractive to kids. I told them it doesn't matter where they live, whom they live with, or what kind of school they go to. Any kid living anywhere can be influenced by the negative and dangerous aspects of our culture at any time. No church, school, family, or child is immune. To my surprise, many in the audience protested this message and refused to believe it was true.

In November 2005, a friend called me to ask what role, if any, the Center for Parent Youth Understanding was playing in the unfolding story of a double murder that had occurred on a quiet Sunday morning in Lancaster County, Pennsylvania. A local 18-year-old had allegedly shot and killed the parents of his 14-year-old girlfriend. Then the pair took off to get married and start a new life, only to be caught a day later in Indiana. The story was loaded with the kind of dramatic twists and turns that make news producers and networks drool. They told the story over and over in typical soap opera fashion: a forbidden love affair, a double murder, a kidnapping, access to the kids through their online blogs, their "religious" backgrounds, a multistate manhunt, and their history as homeschooled kids. Nonstop news network coverage featured the "expert" pontificators speculating, as usual, in a manner that told the story long before the story was even known.

"We're not involved," I replied.

"Well, what do you think of it all?" he asked.

I answered, "Sad, but not surprising." I didn't know the families, nor did I know enough about their backgrounds to make comments on the tragedy. However, this situation and the specifics as we knew them prompted some thoughts that have continued to evolve as I study the Scriptures and observe our Christian subculture. For years we've been challenging Christian parents to stay in touch with teenagers and their world. To believe our faith somehow insulates them from the realities of the world is both pragmatically and theologically wrong. Like it or not, we live in the culture and that culture influences and affects us all. There's no escaping it. And there isn't supposed to be a way out. Like it or not, God doesn't want us circling the wagons or living in some kind of a bubble in an effort to keep ourselves pure. Jesus prayed the will of the Father the night before his death—that his disciples in all times and in all places would be in the world (living as salt and light) while not living as though they're of the world (John 17). That's not only how we should be living, but it's how we should be preparing our students to live every day of their lives.

Believe it or not, to assume you've somehow made kids immune to the influence of culture just by shielding them from culture might just produce the opposite effect. In other words, by not preparing them to engage the culture with minds and hearts saturated by a biblical world and life view, we actually make them more vulnerable to the negative cultural forces they face both now and for the rest of their lives. Both we (parents and youth workers) and our kids need to be wise to the Scriptures and streetwise about our culture. Just like he did with his son Jesus, God has made us all particular types of people who do his particular work in the particular time and place where he's placed us.

Over the years I've been questioned by a growing number of pastors and youth workers who are dealing with a segment of Christians who resist this approach and even believe it's morally, ethically, and biblically wrong. Sorry, I don't see it. I feel even more sorry for their kids. I love what theologian John Stott says about every Christian's call to become a double-listener: "Christian witnesses stand between the Word and the world, with the consequent obligation to listen to both. We listen to the Word in order to discover ever more of the riches of Christ. And we listen to the world in order to discern which of Christ's riches are needed most and how to present them in their best light."[6]

This is our calling as parents and youth workers, and, consequently, it's also the calling of our kids. When it comes to teenagers and their culture, what we don't know (or don't want to know or refuse to know) *can* hurt them.

They Long for God

Blaise Pascal described a universal hole in the soul as a God-shaped vacuum. Alister McGrath describes Pascal's model as "a God-shaped emptiness within us, which only God can fill. We may try to fill it in other ways and with other things. Yet one of the few certainties of life is that nothing in this world satisfies our longing for something that is ultimately beyond this world."[7]

Teenagers are no different from anyone else. Their great need is to have this God-shaped emptiness filled by God. If you listen and look closely, you'll see and hear that their music, films, books, magazines, and very lives are crying out for spiritual wholeness.

Over the years I've had the privilege of working with thousands of teenagers. I can't remember a single one who didn't exhibit this thirst for God. Each of us can look directly into the eyes of the teenagers we know and love and be certain this is their reality, too. Even when they don't recognize it as such, we can rest in the assurance their hunger is for heaven. John Stott reminds us that even when they're running away from God, they know they "have no other resting-place, no other home."[8] This fact should spur us on to constantly and consciously serve as signposts, pointing them to the cross that leads them to their true home.

Your Teenagers Are in Process

Now that three of my children have moved out of adolescence, I'm realizing they didn't come equipped with a switch or button that can be tripped or pushed to make them accept, embrace, and believe everything I tell them. Instead, I need to allow them to grow just as I was allowed to grow. Their intellectual, physical, and spiritual development are all ongoing processes. They don't happen instantaneously or overnight. Our role is to consistently model and speak truth into their lives. Then we must allow the Holy Spirit to do the work that only he can do. We serve to guide and direct. God's Spirit works to bring about change and growth at just the right time, and does so over the course of time. We can't do what only God can do.

A couple of years ago, my then-17-year-old daughter Bethany was struggling with a friendship issue in school. Aware of the problem, I stepped in to make a few fatherly pronouncements that I thought served as a good perspective and great advice. In fact, I remembered saying the same things to my older daughter, Caitlin, when she faced a similar problem at age 17. I shouldn't have been surprised by what seemed to be Bethany's rejection of my perspective and advice. Caitlin had reacted the same way just a few years before. But I was encouraged when I later overheard Bethany sharing her problem with Caitlin and soliciting her older sister's advice. What advice did Caitlin give her? Amazingly, it was the same advice I'd given to Bethany. In fact, it was the same advice Caitlin had seemingly rejected just a few years before.

While I hate cheesy bumper sticker sayings, there's one that speaks to all of us who love and work with teenagers: "Be patient. God isn't finished with me yet." Never stop speaking and living truth into teenagers' lives. But don't be surprised if they don't immediately care to hear or embrace what you're saying. Always remember they're in process. Prayerfully expect God to open their eyes at just the right time, a time that may, in fact, be pretty far down the road.

Helpless Is a Good Place to Be

The words of Psalm 13 came to have deep and significant meaning for me over the course of several dark and seemingly endless nights. One of my kids had made a series of poor choices. Now that child's world was shattered and a deep price was being paid. Feeling as though I'd just survived a horrible train wreck, my mind was filled with questions. *How could this happen? Why did this happen? Have I done anything to cause this? God, what are you trying to teach us? God, do you even care? Will my child get through this?*

Helpless might be the best word I can find to describe that feeling. If you're anything like me, you like to be in control. But when that sense of being in control starts to unravel, life spins around so fast that we don't have a clue what to do. The first four verses of Psalm 13 record the words of a helpless person longing for answers and hope:

> How long, O Lord? Will you forget me forever? How long will you hide your face from me? How long must I wrestle with my thoughts and every day have sorrow in my heart? How long will my enemy triumph over me? Look on me and answer, O Lord my God. Give light to my eyes, or I will sleep in death; my enemy will say, "I have overcome him," and my foes will rejoice when I fall.

For several nights, my helplessness allowed me to read only these verses. It wasn't until a few days later that I began to understand in the midst of my helplessness that God was seeking to be my help. Then I was able to join with the psalmist in celebrating God's goodness through the next two verses of Psalm 13: "But I trust in your unfailing love; my heart rejoices in your salvation. I will sing to the Lord, for he has been good to me."

When I look back on the difficult times in my life and in my journey as a parent and youth worker, I sometimes wonder if I could rewind and do it all over again, would I choose to change the circumstances and events so I'd never be reduced to a sense of helplessness? The answer is *no*. You see, in the midst of our help-lessness, God comes to us and reminds us of our need to exercise total dependence on him. He's faithful, promising us the precise measure of grace we need to endure and overcome in times of trial. Suffering and helplessness are redemptive as God does his work in us.

In his encouraging and vulnerable book *Come Back Barbara*, Jack Miller recounts years of helpless struggle as a pastor-father whose compliant and seemingly Christian daughter, Barbara, heads off to college and turns her back on her faith. In the book, Miller tells the heartbreaking story of his struggle to make sense of what was happening in Barbara's life. In the end, Miller and his wife realize Barbara was never a follower of Christ in the first place. She'd simply been outwardly compliant without ever having expe-rienced the rebirth of her heart. Eventually, after years of extreme rebellion against God and her parents, Barbara's life is transformed as she turns to faith and is reconciled with her father.

In hindsight Miller recognizes that Barbara's life wasn't the only one in which God was hard at work. He writes, "So our story comes to its climax with this perception: What seemed to be a tragic defeat for us as parents turned into an unprecedented op-portunity to grow and mature as Christians and to learn extraordi-nary things about God and his ways." [9]

It's inevitable that you'll receive the gift of difficult times. The sixteenth-century English preacher John Fox wrote, "The best teachers are trouble and affliction. These alone give us un-derstanding. How can we feel God's goodness when nothing has troubled us and no danger hangs over our heads?"[10] From a human perspective, these are the times when God does his best work in our lives. The growing up of our children is an opportunity for us to grow up. So if helplessness comes your way—embrace it.

Give the Grace You've Been Given

My heavenly Father has showered me with tremendous amounts of love and amazing grace. I agree with the apostle Paul, who wrote, "But God demonstrates his own love for us in this: While we were still sinners, Christ died for us" (Romans 5:8), and "The grace of our Lord was poured out on me abundantly, along with the faith and love that are in Christ Jesus. Here is a trustworthy saying that deserves full acceptance: Christ Jesus came into the world to save sinners—of whom I am the worst" (1 Timothy 1:14-15). Since I've been the recipient of abundant grace, why have I been far less than graceful with my own kids so many times? When they mess up or do something wrong, I'm quick to jump down their throats, condemning both them and their sins. Then I'm reminded of what Christ has done for me in his mercy and grace, and I'm put to shame.

I once heard an unforgettable lesson from Dr. John White, who was asked how he managed to relate to his own wayward son. White said he'd learned to live his life according to this simple yet profound principle: "As Christ is to me, so must I be to my kids."

When mistakes, difficulty, and rebellion rear their ugly heads—and they will—remember how your heavenly Father has treated you. If you're like me, nothing your kids can do or say to you comes even close to your daily and habitual rebellion against your heavenly Father.

Recently one of our adult children asked to sit down with us. As our child began to speak, we quickly detected some nervousness. God's Spirit had been working on that child's heart for some time, prompting a confession regarding some things that had been done during high school. After sharing those things with us, we all sat together in silence. Amazingly, my mind wasn't focused on the sin that was just confessed. Instead, God filled my mind with reminders of my own sinful rebellion, and I was reminded of my heavenly Father's grace, which he has shown me regularly and abundantly.

Eventually I broke the silence and asked, "How do you expect your mother and me to respond?"

"I think you're going to tell me you're disappointed in me, and you're angry."

As I continued to ponder God's grace in my own life, I could only respond by saying, "I'm neither." A recipient of grace myself, I could do nothing but pour it out on my repentant child.

Never Fear

Parenting teenagers can be scary. One look at their rapidly changing world and all its pressures and choices can make parents and youth workers want to run and hide. An adult once told me that watching kids go through the teenage years is the most effective birth control method around. Yes, the teenage years are difficult for kids, parents, and youth workers. But should we be afraid?

Usually this fear manifests itself in a desire to remove our kids from the world and thereby keep them from harm. Or it immobilizes us, keeping us from fulfilling our God-given roles in our teenagers' lives. While we should be cautious, watchful, and discerning, we cannot allow ourselves to fall prey to fear.

Jesus addresses the former manifestation of fear as he prays the night before his death (John 17). His prayer is not that the Father will remove Christ's followers from the danger of the world, but that he'll protect them from harm while they serve as his ambassadors in the world. We're to be *in* but not *of* the world. John Fischer suggests "we as Christians need to learn to[11] the danger of living in a dangerous world and trust not a safe subculture to protect us, but a praying Savior ...We want to be safe in a safer world; God wants us to be safe in an unsafe world. We want to protect ourselves from danger; God wants to protect us in the middle of danger."[12]

We've Been Given a "Punkuss"

When my son Josh was five years old, I took an extended 10-day trip to speak in the Southeast. Sadly anticipating my departure, Josh started to get antsy the day before I left. As I sat in my recliner and read the morning paper, he ran in a circle from the living room, through the dining room, kitchen, and hallway, and then back to the living room again. Each time he passed by, my paper blew in the breeze. On one of his laps, I looked up long enough to see him stop, get down on his hands and knees, and look frantically under the couch. Not finding what he was looking for, he got up and continued running. My curiosity finally got the better of me, and I asked him what he was doing.

"I'm looking for something, Dad...something I want to give you before you go away on your trip!"

I went back to reading my paper while his frantic search took him upstairs. Soon I heard drawers and closets opening and closing.

"What are you looking for, Josh? Maybe I can help you," I yelled.

"The tire pointer, Dad. You know, that punkuss. I'll find it."

I had no clue what he was talking about. A few minutes passed, and his search brought him back downstairs. Then he yelled with excitement—he'd found the object of his hunt. Seconds later he climbed on my lap.

"Dad, I want you to take this with you when you go on your trip." In his hand was a tiny dime-store compass set in a miniature tire.

"Why do you want me to have this, Josh?"

"Because, Dad, you're going away for 10 days. I want you to keep my punkuss in your pocket so you know where you're from, where you belong, and how to get back home."

Tears filled my eyes. I wasn't scheduled to leave until the next day, and already I felt as though I'd been gone too long. I kept that "punkuss" in my pocket the entire time I was gone.

Life is a mysterious journey. I've been on mine for more than 50 years. And just when I begin to discover the answers to some of my questions, I enter a new phase of the journey with its own set of confusing choices and circumstances. And the questions keep coming. The confusion never lifts.

Whether we're kids, teenagers, or adults, we all look to some higher authority for answers. That authority, be it a friend, parent, spouse, writer, film star, musician, self, or even our changing opinions, becomes our "punkuss" and directs our steps as we try to figure out where we're from, where we belong, and how to get back there.

In a world where there are many "experts" sharing conflicting opinions on the purpose of life, how to live our lives, and how to raise and relate to kids, it's good to know there is a "punkuss" we can trust, one that was handed to us by the One who created life, kids, teenagers, parents, families, and youth workers. That "punkuss" is the Word—both the incarnate Word Jesus Christ and the written Word. Together, the example of Christ and God's revelation of himself in the Bible reveal what we need to know about everything we encounter on the journey.

The words of the apostle Paul to Timothy, a young man who needed encouragement, apply not only to Timothy's life and ministry, but also to us today as we fulfill our God-given ministry in parenting or ministering to kids: "Every part of Scripture is God-breathed and useful one way or another—showing us truth, exposing our rebellion, correcting our mistakes, training us to live God's way" (2 Timothy 3:16, *The Message*).

When each of our kids graduated from high school, we used the space allotted to us in their yearbooks to send them messages, including these words from Proverbs 3:5-6: "Trust in the Lord with all your heart and lean not on your own understanding; in all your ways acknowledge him, and he will make your paths straight." When one of my kids was going through an especially difficult crisis as a late teen, a helper who entered into the crisis communicated these words from Jeremiah 29:11: "'For I know the plans I have for you,' declares the Lord, 'plans to prosper you and not to harm you, plans to give you hope and a future.'" The process of restoring hope and bringing healing had begun.

Prayer Is an Amazing Mystery

Early on in my own life, I viewed and practiced prayer as though I were entering into an arm-wrestling match with God. I believed if I prayed hard enough for something, God would eventually give in and I'd win. As the years have passed, I've now realized prayer is a lifestyle where we constantly enter into the presence of God whether our lives are marked by plenty or want, peace or conflict, joy or sorrow. W. Bingham Hunter describes prayer as "a means God uses to give us what he wants."[13] To believe prayer changes things is to believe that the "things" prayer changes are our own hearts. While the workings of prayer remain an amazing mystery to me, I've experienced the joy of seeing lives—including my own and those of my kids—changed in significant ways through prayer.

Stanley Grenz describes prayer as "the cry for the Kingdom." In other words, "just as the petition 'Your kingdom come, your will be done on earth as it is in heaven' formed the heart of Jesus' praying, so also in every situation the petitions of Jesus' friends ought to be a cry for the in-breaking of God's rulership, God's will, into our world."[14]

As adults helping teenagers into adulthood, we must pray for ourselves, our kids, and our families. These prayers shouldn't come only when crisis or difficulty hits. Instead, we should consistently ask God to unleash his will and way on us. As we pray for teenagers, we must ask God to reveal his will and way to them in a manner that transforms their lives into the image of Christ.

Perhaps sometimes we try to do the work of the Holy Spirit in our kid's lives by trying to control their hearts. But we can't drag our kids screaming and kicking into God's Kingdom. God and God alone changes the heart. May we all rely on God to bring about change, always asking him to move in our teenagers' hearts.

We've Been Given All We Need

During my college years, I loved to watch *Saturday Night Live*. The late Gilda Radner had a repertoire of hilarious characters that included the television commentator Rosanne Rosanna Danna. Somehow Rosanne could always insert her trademark line into every weekly commentary. Maybe she was really speaking for parents whenever she'd say, "It's always something!"

But in the middle of teenage chaos, this fact speaks reassuringly from the pages of God's Word: Although his people often experienced great hardship and difficulty, they were always loved and provided for by a gracious God who never turned his back on them. Read the accounts of Abraham, Isaac, and Jacob. Examine the lives of Noah, David, Ruth, and Joshua. Listen to the laments of the psalmist. Look at the experience of the prophets. Read the words of the Gospel writers and the apostle Paul. Peruse the records of Jesus' encounters with the people of his day. Then think about your experiences raising or working with teenagers. It's good to know God is still active and he makes available all of the resources we need—in the proper measure and time—to guide and raise our teenagers according to his blueprint. I've learned firsthand that if courage and wisdom are needed, God provides it. The key is to seek his will through his Word first, and then conform our thoughts and actions to his will and his way. It sounds almost too simple. Yet, this unexplainable mystery of grace is true.

I've also learned it's easy to forget that I'm a dependent person who was created and is loved by a dependable God. This is why Paul, while talking about his "thorn in the flesh" and other hardships, could enthusiastically say that in the midst of weakness, God's grace is sufficient to meet every need (2 Corinthians 12:9). And while God never promised we'd be immune to life's difficulties, he did promise we wouldn't be overcome by them (Psalm 91).

Getting Personal

Think for a moment about how you handle the trying times parenting throws your way. If you're involved in youth ministry or some other activity with teenagers, think about the hard times you've encountered in that role. Can you say like the apostle Paul: "We proclaim him, admonishing and teaching everyone with all wisdom, so that we may present everyone perfect in Christ. To this end I labor, struggling with all his energy, which so powerfully works in me" (Colossians 1:28-29)? What role do you allow God to play?

I know all too well from my own history and experiences that I sometimes fail to live in total dependence on God. I've tried to parent my teenage children and minister to other teenagers with my own efforts and willpower. When I do, I find myself tired, burned out, and defeated.

I've also made the mistake of "letting go and letting God." After all, if he's in control, what good will it do if I try to help? Let him raise the kids.

And who of us hasn't worked hard to manage our lives and families on our own strength, only to cry out to God, "Lord, help me!" when a crisis hits?

But true total dependence on God requires that we recognize our need to have our lives radically reoriented and reorganized by God. We need God's guidance and enabling every minute of every day in every area of our lives. Entering into God's presence daily to study and meditate on his Word and then seeking his will through prayer allows us to parent in faith with his strength.

I'll be the first to admit that parenting teenagers is hard work and involves many struggles. But through constant, active dependence on the God who never changes, we can live through and embrace the wonder, joy, ups, and downs of parenting through the teenage years. And we can experience the joy of letting God work powerfully in and through us to affect the world—through our teenagers.

2

The Times...
They Are a-Changin'

I never expected to see the day when girls would get sunburned in the places they do now.

—WILL ROGERS

Everything's so different than it used to be. Adults don't have a clue.

—GRETCHEN, AGE 15

When my daughter Caitlin was in first grade, I took her to see my former elementary school. Even though it had been closed for years, my peek through the windows yielded a trip back in time to 1962. I was amazed it still looked the same 28 years later, right down to the alphabet choo-choo train hanging on the wall.

As I lifted Caitlin up to the window so she could see where I'd spent a wonderful year with Miss Wallace, she exclaimed, "I can't believe this is where you went to first grade."

My amazement quickly changed to puzzlement. "Why not, Caitlin?" I asked.

"Because it's in color."

Her answer made me feel pretty old. As a kid, I can remember thinking about what it must have been like for my parents when they lived back in the old days. Somehow all the photographs and eight-millimeter movies left me with the impression that the world must have been black-and-white before I was born. Now my kid was thinking the same thing about her old man.

What Once Was—Isn't

Although the visual colors of the world haven't changed, the world certainly has. And the rate of change isn't getting any slower. A couple of years ago, I was packing up my stuff after spending a day teaching youth workers about the rapidly changing youth culture. After everyone else had left, a young man came to the front of the room to share his gratitude for my time spent with the group.

"Thanks for teaching us all this stuff about teenagers and their world," he said. "I'm currently working with kids at a local high school. I go in after school to help them with their homework and to talk about their lives. Every time I walk onto the campus, I'm struck by how much things have changed since I was there."

I took a long, hard look at him and began to wonder how long it had been since he'd been a high school student. "How old are you?" I asked.

"Nineteen," he said. "I just graduated from that high school 10 months ago."

The rate of change is gaining momentum. Like a snowball that accelerates and grows during its rapid descent down a steep hill, today's youth culture is changing at breakneck speed.

I remember three Norman Rockwell paintings that used to hang on my parents' bedroom wall. My two brothers, Mark and Ken, and I wanted to show Mom and Dad our appreciation for the loving home they'd provided. So we each carefully chose a Rockwell painting that reflected our personal experience of growing up Mueller, and then we gave our parents the pictures on the occasion of their *25th* wedding anniversary.

The first painting showed a nervous young man who was ready to head off to college. He was sitting on the running board of the family pickup, along with his dad and his suitcase, just waiting for the bus to arrive. That was me, the oldest of the three boys and the first to leave home.

The middle painting was of a boy precariously balanced on a pair of homemade stilts. That was my daredevil brother Mark. He was always trying my parents' patience with something new and dangerous, as he spent countless hours walking around on stilts, riding a unicycle, or trying out the tightwire he'd built in the backyard. One time my dad found Mark teaching himself to eat fire in the garage! Mark eventually went off to clown college.

The third painting was of an intelligent, bespectacled young boy standing with a diploma in his hand and receiving pats on the back and praise from his instructor. That was Ken's picture. He was the youngest, so he reaped the benefits of having two older brothers by capitalizing on our school experiences and doing better than we did. This was the kid who read the dictionary while he was still in elementary school.

Every time I see those three pictures, I'm reminded of my childhood, and I'm thankful for the stable home full of love that our parents provided. When Norman Rockwell (perhaps the greatest and most notable period painter of Americana) put his brush on the canvas, I felt as though he'd painted my family.

Granted, life wasn't pretty for every kid back then; but overall, it was a much simpler and more stable time for teenagers. I've often wondered what Norman Rockwell's pictures would look like if he were still alive and painting the American childhood experience today. Maybe he'd paint the family kitchen with only half the members sitting around the table and scarfing down a meal while the others are probably off doing something else. Maybe he'd paint a family hanging out at home during the evening, with each member cloistered in his own room while watching the television, playing video games, or spending time online. Maybe there'd be a picture of a 16-year-old girl driving to school with her books in the front seat and her baby in the back seat. Or a picture of a third grader arriving home from school—with a cell phone in one hand and an iPod in the other—and heading into an unsupervised house for several hours of unlimited TV viewing, video-game playing, and Internet surfing. Sadly, Rockwell might paint students passing through a metal detector as they arrive at school. Yes, times have changed.

What's Up with the Kids?

In the early 1980s, scholars and researchers on family and adolescent issues began asking the question, "What is happening to our kids?" Their answers came through a series of books with discouraging titles such as *The Hurried Child: Growing Up Too Fast Too Soon, All Grown Up and No Place to Go, The Disappearance of Childhood, The Erosion of Childhood,* and *The Rise and Fall of Childhood.* Over the last 25 years, the problems and issues addressed in those books have increased, manifesting themselves in the growing number of negative teenage attitudes, behaviors, and social problems that concern us so much. While there are always glimmers of hope and numerous reasons for optimism, overall trends point to the fact that things aren't getting any better for our teenagers. Now the parenting, family issues, and social science sections in bookstores are expanded to help parents, teachers, and those in the helping professions deal with drug and alcohol abuse, teenage sex, violence, bullying, Internet dangers, self-abuse, and all the other complex issues our kids face every day.

In the midst of these complex problems, we must also acknowledge that there is a *developmental difference* between teenagers and adults. We live in two different stages of the life cycle. Consequently, we think and act in markedly different ways. In this chapter, we will examine a second fundamental truth: There is a *cultural difference* between teenagers and adults. We live in two very different worlds.

A Word on Culture

I like to think of culture as the "soup" in which our teenagers swim around and soak every day. The soup's ingredients include values, attitudes, and behaviors—as well as the media, peer group, language, and so on that express them. To know kids, we must lift the lid on the soup pot and see what's in the mix. "We can't escape the reality that those elements—as strange and frightening as they may seem—shape their worldview and govern their lives. We might even be tempted to close the lid because we don't like what we see."[15] But if we hope to effectively protect our kids from harm, provide for their well-being, and lead them to a vital faith in Christ, we must understand their world...a world that's very different from the world we knew when we were that age. In fact, the "cultural-generational gap" between adults and teenagers widens every day.

While we all share space on the same planet, the world of adults is drastically different from the world of teenagers. Their daily encounters with adults often become like the one I had a few years ago. I was driving a van full of middle school students to a youth group activity. While sitting at a stoplight, I noticed the older couple in the car next to us. They were looking over at my hormonally charged and overactive cargo with curiosity and a bit of mild contempt. A quick glance over my shoulder confirmed my suspicions. This vanload of middle schoolers was acting like, well, middle schoolers. Granted, while their behavior could easily have been construed as immature, socially unacceptable, borderline criminal, and flat-out disgusting, they were just being "normal."

Watching the woman shake her head in repulsion as her husband prepared to speed away as soon as the light turned green, I couldn't resist having a little fun myself. So I rolled down my window and made eye contact with the woman, then I shook my head in disgust as I pointed over my shoulder and said, "Teenagers!"

Today's youth are growing up in a frantic and fast-paced world. When the cultural-generational gap widens, relationships become strained as adults and teenagers find themselves unable to understand each other. And as communication breaks down, the effectiveness of the adult influence decreases. Longing for someone who'll listen to them, teenagers may begin to look elsewhere for guidance, love, and understanding. Even Christian parents may be left reeling by the fact that their kids have bought into a set of values, attitudes, and behaviors contrary to Mom and Dad's.

Certainly there are many kids who fare well on the road to adulthood. But it's alarming to see an increasing number who are adopting self-serving values and ungodly attitudes. Our kids need adults who constantly work hard to stay in touch with the youth culture so they can guide adolescents through the maze of growing up.

I've witnessed something encouraging about today's divide, however. Unlike the generational gap of the 1960s, the older and younger generations aren't standing on opposite sides with no real desire to come together. This is good news because teenagers desperately want and need parents and other adults who will cross the divide by getting to know and understand the cultural soup of their kids. Once we take that step, we can begin to help teenagers swim through the soup and make good choices that reflect God's will and God's way for their lives.

Meet Sarah, an "Average Teenager"

Several years ago I asked teenagers to e-mail me a list ranking the five greatest pressures they face. The results opened my eyes to the changes that have taken place in the cultural soup of teenagers.

One of the kids who responded was Sarah, a 16-year-old only child from New York. Her list was representative of the other lists I received, and I've been reading and rereading her list for years, as it serves as a constant reminder of the realities facing kids in today's youth culture. At number one Sarah listed the pressure for "looks." Like most girls her age, she was preoccupied with her appearance and whether or not her changing body measured up to the prevailing cultural standards. She was consumed with self-conscious worry about her hair, makeup, body shape, complexion, and clothes. Next, she listed "grades for getting into the right college." Third was "drinking," with "sex" and "popularity" ranked fourth and fifth, respectively.

Sarah's list was helpful, but the real eye-opener was the extra, unsolicited information she included in her e-mail: "Walt, I know you didn't ask for this on your survey, but I suffer from a combination of the eating disorders anorexia and bulimia. It is very hard to recover from these devastations, caused largely by the pressure to be thin and to be perfect. I hope I have helped."

Sarah reminded me how much our world is changing. I'd never heard the terms *anorexia nervosa* or *bulimia* until I was 21 years old, and then I had to ask someone what they meant. Over the course of the next 10 years, I was consciously aware of only one person I knew who had anorexia. Not so today. I often ask kids for a show of hands if they know someone—either a friend or perhaps themselves—who is battling anorexia or bulimia. When I'm with middle school kids, nearly all the hands go up in the air. Sarah not only had both, but she also knew about their causes and the difficult road to recovery.

Sarah and I began trading e-mails after that. Perhaps reading her story, written in her own words, will give you the opportunity to look into the cultural soup of the pressures, fears, and choices facing today's teenagers. She writes—

I come from an upper-middle-class home. I'm a straight-A student, class president, and an overachiever in every way. I don't really know why I am anorexic, but I think it's partly because I thought that if I got really sick, people would pay attention to me more and like me. The irony of it is that my father is a psychologist. He doesn't know.

My mother always compares her life to mine, so much that sometimes I feel smothered by her. I cannot talk to my father at all about important things. I never could. My father is home every evening at 6 PM, but my mother is never home. She recently opened a business, so she has to work from 9 AM until midnight. Sometimes she comes home to see me in the afternoons, and sometimes she is around on weekends. Incidentally, my parents do not get along very well.

My mom says if I get therapy, it will go on my record and may keep me out of Princeton or Amherst, the colleges to which I am applying.

I know my parents love me, but they think I am so bright and capable that I don't need help or attention anymore. I just want people to realize I do not have a perfect life, and I am lonely. I want people at school to notice me more and like me. Actually, I'm not at all sure what I want.

I've met many Sarahs over the years, and I continue to meet more of them as time goes by. Although their stories differ in terms of the places, dates, details, and depth of their problems, there are some common threads. Each one is an adolescent who is already dealing with the normal changes that come with growing up. On top of that, each is confused and frustrated by challenging circumstances. Many of them cope and are remarkably resilient. Others struggle to survive. Some self-destruct. Sadly, in the midst of this reality, most adults don't understand that the world has changed. Consequently, they have no idea how it's different and how those differences are affecting kids. Thus, the cultural-generational gap grows wider.

Chap Clark further opens our eyes to the consequences of this reality when he says "systemic abandonment" by adults is the defining issue for today's adolescents, leaving them "to figure out how to survive life on their own."[16] That certainly is the case for Sarah. In order to survive systemic abandonment and still function, vulnerable and confused young people create a separate and highly structured social system Clark calls "the world beneath," a safe place where they find connections—with equally confused and abandoned peers—that help them as they navigate the difficult waters of adolescence. But parents do remain important. Clark says that more than anything else, teenagers want a "relationally focused home where they know they are welcome."[17]

Sarah's harrowing world beneath was largely unknown to her parents, and most likely unknown to the other adults who were also fooled by her surface and viewed her as a well-adjusted young lady who had everything going for her. What Sarah wanted more than anything else was "help" and "attention." Clark concludes that one of the most vital things those of us who are close to kids like Sarah can do is to "understand their world."[18]

During the teenage years, kids are like walking question marks as they seek answers to significant life questions. Today, there are many conflicting voices and they're all screaming answers at our overwhelmed teenagers. The fortunate kids are those who've been blessed with parents and other adults who love them enough to take the time to understand the truth about today's changing world, their cultural soup, and its bewildering mix of changing cultural trends.

The Perfect Storm—Forces and Trends Affecting Teenagers

Several years ago author Sebastian Junger wrote his bestseller *The Perfect Storm*, a book about the violent convergence of three storm systems in the North Atlantic. Junger described how these storm forces combined in a mix that was potentially deadly to the fishermen caught in its fury, as well as their rescuers. In many respects, the convergence of forces and trends our teenagers face in today's world has created a "perfect storm" that's also dangerous and sometimes deadly.

Many American teenagers will get through adolescence with only a few minor nicks and bruises. Their worst crisis might be a bad case of acne, flunking a driver's test, or getting cut from an athletic team. But for an increasing number of adolescents, the pressures of life can be overwhelming. If they're like Sarah, they'll carry some severe scars and handicaps with them all the way through their adult years.

Those who study teenagers are concerned by the rising casualty rate. The National Association of State Boards of Education joined with the American Medical Association to call attention to the declining condition of teenagers in America. Back in 1990, they issued this statement: "For the first time in the history of our country, young people are *less* healthy and *less* prepared to take their places in society than were their parents. And this is happening at a time when our society is more complex, more challenging, and more competitive than ever before."[19]

Around that same time, Senator Dan Coats, a member of the Select Committee on Kids, Youth, and Families, concluded after years of observation and study that the statistics point not to a crisis of teenage behavior but to a deeper crisis of character: "[This] is not a problem that will be solved with money or clinics or medicine. It has deeper roots in hearts and souls. In the mainstream of youth culture, it is deeply disturbing. It leaves a legacy of broken lives. But at the extremes, it is frightening—with kids who seem drained of conscience."[20]

During the years since then, it's not gotten any better. It's been estimated "at least one of every four adolescents in the United States is currently at serious risk of not achieving productive adulthood."[21] When I was invited to Washington, DC, to take part in The White House Conference on Helping America's Youth, we were told the healthy development of young people is increasingly jeopardized by adolescents' health and behaviors, and the social contexts in which they live.

This crisis of character and resulting symptomatic behaviors continue to escalate and manifest themselves in disturbing and frightening ways. Over the last several years I've worked hard to listen to Sarah and the experts. I've observed teenagers and asked them lots of questions. There's no doubt our kids are facing a whole new set of choices, expectations, fears, pressures, challenges, and problems. And they're facing them at younger and younger ages.

In order to deepen our understanding of teenagers, we need to take a look at the major cultural forces and trends that shape their characters, values, attitudes, and behaviors. I believe these particular elements of the soup are at the root of Sarah's cries and the experts' concerns. Many will be dealt with in further detail later in this book. But for now, here's a short summary of some of the main cultural realities.

Families Are Changing

When I began to ask my high school audiences about their family situations, their first-person descriptions, combined with several shows of hands, led me to the conclusion *family* meant something different to many of these kids. Some lived with Dad and Mom. Others lived with Mom. Some with Dad. Some with neither. A few didn't know one or both of their parents. The words *divorce, separation, abandonment,* and *abuse* came up over and over again.

Sadly, those responses are becoming more typical. You and I are living in a period of unprecedented and historic change in family composition, family life, and family experience. This radical shift in family patterns can't help but affect our kids, creating more stress and confusion. This shift is both the result and cause of a growing amount of childhood heartache, pain, and difficulty.

From the beginning of time, God instituted the family to be the place kids are born into, loved, nurtured, and led to a spiritually, emotionally, and physically healthy adulthood. Kids need a mother and father who love God, who love each other, and who love their kids. Anything less, and the family fails to exist and function as it was meant to be. Jack and Judy Balswick suggest the family is to be a place where individuals love and are loved, forgive and are forgiven, serve and are served, and know and are known. As such, it's meant to be a place of covenant, grace, empowering, and intimacy.[22]

While he might not define the functions of the family in the same manner, David Elkind certainly knows the family isn't functioning as it should be. In his book *All Grown Up and No Place to Go*, Elkind uses the term "family permutations" (mutations from the norm that leave a permanent mark on those involved) to describe the increased breakdown of the family. When these rearrangements of existing elements occur, "kids and teenagers tend to lose their special place in the family structure."[23] In the same book, he offers a convincing argument that these changes force teenagers into "premature adulthood." No longer allowed to be kids, what result are stress and its aftermath. It should come as no surprise that Elkind titled his book on changing family relationships *Ties That Stress*. What are some of the disruptions, permutations, and changes taking place in the American family?

The first change is *the increase and acceptance of divorce.* The sexual revolution of the 1960s and 1970s combined with a changing moral climate, rising individualism, and other factors to lower our collective view of marriage, thus leading to a rise in divorce. In 1977 I wrote a paper on the stigma associated with divorce for a social problems class I took in college. At the time, there was plenty of data pointing to the fact that the prevailing view in our culture was that those who divorced were doing something dishonorable. No doubt, there were cases of justifiable divorce at the time, but divorce wasn't viewed or embraced as an easy way out of marriage. In today's social climate, my paper would get a failing grade.

There were 7.8 marriages per 1,000 people and 3.7 divorces per 1,000 people in 2004.[24] "The American divorce rate today is nearly twice that of 1960, but has declined slightly since hitting the highest point in our history in the early 1980s."[25] On the surface, this may seem like a move in the right direction—and in some ways it is. However, during the same time period, the number of cohabiting couples and out-of-wedlock births also increased, which means fewer couples are getting married. (We'll explore this topic further in the next section.)

Although some states no longer tabulate annual divorce statistics, it's estimated there are now between 1 and 1.2 million divorces finalized each year in the United States. Consequently, a million kids will go through an emotional tug-of-war as they watch their parents divorce.[26] "For the average couple marrying in recent years, the lifetime probability of divorce or separation remains between 40 and 50 percent."[27]

In addition, one-third of all births in the United States are to unmarried women. This is an increase from less than five percent in the mid-1960s.[28] It's estimated that up to 60 percent of the kids born in the '90s—today's teenagers—will live in a single-parent home for part of their childhood.[29] All of these statistics add up to this sad fact: The United States has the highest divorce rate and the highest proportion of kids affected by divorce in the developed world.[30] These changes led the Council on Families in America to conclude, "Our nation has largely shifted from a culture of marriage to a culture of divorce. Once we were a nation in which a strong marriage was seen as the best route to achieving the American dream. We have now become a nation in which divorce is commonly seen as the path to personal liberation."[31] Television's Mr. Rogers testified to these changes back in 1990: "If someone told me twenty years ago that I was going to produce a whole week [of shows] on divorce, I never would have believed them."[32]

My one-on-one conversations with and personal observations of kids of divorce have led me to a deeper understanding regarding the toll divorce takes on our kids. God created the family to serve as the basic unit and building block of society. It's the unit into which we're born; and it's where we not only find our identities, but we're also socialized and nurtured. But the increased incidence and acceptance of divorce indicates that, in many cases, this fundamental building block is falling apart.

In her study on the effects of divorce on middle-class families, Judith Wallerstein discovered that divorce hurts kids deeply and for a long time. Regarding children of divorce, she found that—

- Nearly half enter adulthood underachieving, worried, angry, and disapproving of themselves.

- Three in five feel rejected by one or both parents.

- Forty percent set no specific goals as they enter adulthood.

- Many (particularly females) enter adulthood carrying a load of guilt and anxiety that leads to multiple relationships and impulsive, early marriages that end in divorce.

Her study concluded that kids of divorce are also plagued by a variety of other issues including rebellion, depression, discipline problems, grief, guilt, fear, an inability to concentrate, and an inability to trust.[33] She writes,

> National studies show that kids from divorced and remarried families are more aggressive toward their parents and teachers. They experience more depression, have more learning difficulties, and suffer from more problems with peers than kids from intact families. Kids from divorced and remarried families are two to three times more likely to be referred for psychological help at school than their peers from intact families. More of them end up in mental health clinics and hospital settings.[34]

In addition, researchers at the National Marriage Project found that "many of today's youth problems can be attributed, directly or indirectly, to the decline of marriage. This includes high rates of juvenile delinquency, suicide, substance abuse, child poverty, mental illness, and emotional instability."[35] Research also shows that these issues and problems aren't unique to the adolescent years. Kids of divorce carry these problems and their fallout all the way through their adult years. So as our society changes, husbands and wives are becoming more committed to being *uncommitted*. The result is that more kids are suffering.

A second change is *the rise in cohabitation and out-of-wedlock births.* A more negative view of marriage has combined with changing cultural morals and the childhood experiences of a large number of adults who grew up in families where the parents' marriages fell apart. This has resulted in a growing number of people who are ready to live together and have families, but they do so without a willingness to commit to it legally and permanently.

Nearly 36 percent of all births were to unmarried women in 2004.[36] Some of these mothers were living with the child's father;

some were not. Of these 1,470,000 births to unmarried women, 349,000 were to women under the age of 20, and 6,600 of those to girls under the age of 15.[37] Eighteen percent of kids living with single biological or adoptive fathers and 11 percent of kids living with single biological or adoptive mothers also live with their parent's cohabiting partner. Overall, 4.3 million kids lived with a parent or parents who were cohabiting.[38] Since 1970, the number of people living together outside of marriage has increased by more than 1,000 percent.[39]

Not only do these trends affect the well-being of kids as they mature through childhood and adolescence, but they also influence the growing child's personal view of marriage. A Gallup Youth Survey specifically asked teenagers about their views on cohabitation. A significant majority (70 percent) of teenagers said they approve of couples living together prior to marriage. As might be expected, 85 percent of teenagers who don't attend church approve of premarital cohabitation. But alarmingly, 50 percent of teenagers who regularly attend church approve of couples living together before marriage.[40] Clearly, the culture is influencing our kids' values and attitudes.

A third change is *the crisis of fatherlessness.* Tonight, approximately 34 percent of our nation's teenagers will go to bed in a home where their biological father does not live.[41] Some estimate almost 60 percent of the kids born in the 1990s will spend some part of their childhood in a fatherless home.[42] Sadly, a growing number of kids don't even know who their fathers are. Almost 40 percent of kids living in father-absent homes haven't seen their fathers during the course of the past year and 50 percent have never been in their fathers' homes; 26 percent of absent fathers live in different states.[43] Millions of other kids are growing up in homes where their fathers may be physically present but they're spiritually or emotionally detached.

The consequences are grave. We now know that father absence is the variable in the present and future well-being of teenagers. Kids who grow through the difficult, challenging, and formative years of adolescence without their dads have a greater risk of suffering from emotional and behavioral problems such as sexual promiscuity, premarital teenage pregnancy, substance abuse, depression, suicide, lower academic performance, dropping out of school, intimacy dysfunction, divorce, and poverty. It's no surprise to learn that 60 percent of America's rapists, 72 percent of adolescent murderers, and 70 percent of long-term prison inmates grew up without a dad.[44]

A fourth change in the family that affects teenagers is *the increasing number of mothers who work outside the home.* In 1960, 39 percent of mothers with school-age kids were working outside the home. In 1987, 70 percent of mothers with school-age kids had such jobs.[45] By 2001, 78 percent were in the labor force.[46] While the trend has been for more mothers to juggle jobs and families, it appears this trend may now be shifting. A growing number of women are choosing to leave the workforce and come home to spend time with their kids.

A fifth change is *the decreasing amount of time parents are spending with their kids.* Men and women in high-pressure careers often work more than 40 hours a week and bring home the pressures from their jobs, as well as economic worries. Meanwhile, their kids are getting shortchanged. The ongoing myth of "quality time versus quantity time" is often invoked to justify absence from the kids. However, when asked about their wishes for a better life, 27 percent of high school students wanted "more money to buy items such as televisions and cars," 14 percent wished for "a bigger house," but the biggest segment of high school students—46 percent—wished for "more time spent together with family."[47]

Carl Zwerner grew up in a home with a father whose life was his auto-parts business. Swearing he wouldn't make the same mistake with his own family, Carl began a glass-import business. "Like his father, he worked 10- and 12-hour days with little time for his wife and three kids. Home life was a joke, he says. 'Can you picture changing a kid's diaper and all you're thinking about is the next day's paperwork? How much caring can even happen there?' Even on drives to his kids' camp in North Carolina, 'I would stop and see customers on the way.' After 19 years, Mr. Zwerner and his wife divorced. When it comes to business, the long hours may pay off. When it comes to family life, everybody loses."[48]

Sixth, *more teenagers are victims of family violence.* It's frightening to think that much of our nation's child abuse and sexual abuse goes unreported. But the available statistics are frightening enough. It's believed one of every four girls[49] and one of every six boys in the United States is sexually abused by the time they turn 16,[50] and most of this abuse is perpetrated by parents, siblings, or close relatives. In addition, studies indicate that between 3.3 million and 10 million kids are exposed to domestic violence annually.[51] Some of that violence is the direct result of alcoholism in the family.

Kids who are exposed to or victims of family and sexual violence are more likely to become perpetrators of violence themselves. They're also more likely to exhibit a variety of health and behavioral problems as they grow up, including depression, anxiety, suicide, and drug and alcohol abuse.

It's no coincidence that the increasing difficulty of living through the adolescent years parallels an increase in divorce, sexual abuse, violence, alcoholism, and the amount of time parents spend outside the home. Likewise, the decreasing quality of life for teenagers corresponds to decreases in family time, two-parent families, and marital commitment.

Home used to be a place of refuge and a source of much-needed resiliency for kids growing through the normal difficulties of the adolescent years. I remember how great it felt to enter the warmth of my family's house after battling the pressures and expectations of my peers in the war zone known as "school." While my family was by no means perfect, I at least knew that when I got home, I could open the door and walk into never-ending encouragement, acceptance, and love. But many teenagers don't share my experience.

Some time ago I went away with a group of kids on an exciting senior high retreat. During our drive home, I noticed every kid on the bus was asleep except for Meg, who was staring out the window. The tears running down her cheeks told me she was thinking about more than the passing scenery. I thought she might be disappointed the weekend had come to an end, so I asked her if that was the case.

"Sure, I'm sad the weekend is over," she said. "But that's not what I'm crying about. My dad hasn't talked to me or to my mom in weeks. He just sits in his chair and watches TV. My mom's an emotional basket case. Sometimes I feel like I'm her mother. And my brother—he yells at all of us. I don't want to go back home."

Meg's home had become a war zone, and it's only one example of how the changing face of the family is taking a toll on kids. The end result is a hunger for genuine and meaningful relationships so pervasive among teenagers and young adults today that experts now cite "relational deprivation" as one of the marks of today's emerging generations. Our teenagers were created to be in relationship. Humanly speaking, the primary relationship for which they were made is the one with Dad and Mom. Today's teenagers desire real relationships that are characterized by depth, vulnerability, openness, listening, and love—connectedness in their disconnected, confusing, and alienated world.

Outside Influences Are Shaping Teenage Values

After I graduated from high school, I took a summer job with a road construction crew. Shoveling steaming blacktop made an already hot time of the year the hottest summer I can remember. While my stint only lasted three months, most of my coworkers had been at the job all their lives. They were a salty bunch of characters who were a little ragged around the edges, and it was easy to see they'd spent a lot of time with each other.

Each day's conversation was filled with off-color jokes and language that would have turned my mother green. I'd been raised in a home where I never heard my parents utter a single profanity. I'd been taught it was wrong to do so. Therefore, even though I'd heard quite a few swear words during my time in school, I was never tempted to let a blue streak fly. Unfortunately, I spent more time on the construction site than at home that summer, and it wasn't long before I found myself thinking and saying things I'd never thought or said before. Pretty soon a stubbed toe, an impolite driver, or a poor call by an umpire brought out my new vocabulary. While I realize I was ultimately responsible for my words and actions, there was a sense in which I'd been socialized and educated during my time spent with the other crew members. They'd "worn off" on me, so to speak.

The changes I experienced that summer are an illustration of the larger-scale changes taking place in today's youth culture. Traditionally, the home was the institution that exercised the greatest influence on the values, attitudes, and behaviors of teenagers. For the most part, the school and church then shared and reinforced the values that were taught at home. But today the changing face of the family and the pluralistic flavor of our society have weakened the positive influences of the home in the lives of America's teenagers. In fact, home, school, and church don't always agree on issues of right and wrong.

As the traditional influences weaken, the voices of other institutions become more powerful in their ability to educate and socialize teenagers. Then these voices grow louder as they answer teenagers' questions and drown out the voices of parents, school, and church. Although several of these voices will be discussed in the remaining chapters of this book, let this short overview serve as an introduction. Then commit yourself, as a Christian parent or youth worker, to understand and grapple with these competing voices so you can guide teenagers on their way to physical, emotional, and spiritual maturity.

Music, advertising, and other media. This generation of teenagers is the most media-saturated and media-savvy generation of all time. They spend an incredible amount of time interacting with a variety of emerging media technologies as they watch, listen, surf, and so on. The media has become a source of information on everything from sexuality to politics to alternate lifestyles to issues of right and wrong. Many people believe the media, not parents, is parenting kids and teenagers today. (See chapters 3-6 for further information on how to understand the complex world of music, media, and advertising, and for ideas on how to help your child become a safe and savvy media consumer.)

The digital revolution. What was once only a dream that existed solely in the realm of science fiction has quickly become reality for our kids. The growth of computer and digital technologies has changed the face of everything from shopping to studying to communicating to playing to social networking to listening to music. Kids are using music devices, computers, cell phones, and numerous other digital technologies. This rather recent phenomenon has exploded, and it's showing no signs of slowing anytime soon. For our kids, the world is at their fingertips. And with these technologies at their fingertips as well, they can communicate and show themselves to the world. These days, it's unusual to encounter a kid who's *not* carrying or using some sort of new technological device. (See chapters 3 and 5 for more information on how digital technologies are changing our world.)

Peer group. Peer pressure has always been a part of the adolescent experience. While this type of pressure exists for people of all ages, it reaches its zenith during the teenage years. One significant difference between today's peer pressure and the kind that took place 20 years ago is the form it takes. Peer pressure used to manifest itself through an individual or group's verbal invitation to "go ahead and do it," with both the sender and the receiver knowing full well the encouraged behavior is wrong. Typically, there was a sneaky element to the pressure. Now, more often than not, the pressure takes the form of an unspoken expectation to participate in behavior that is generally accepted as normal and right by one's teenage peers and even many adults. As a result, today's brand of peer pressure is much greater than anything I ever knew or experienced. (In chapter 7 there's more information regarding peer pressure and how to help teenagers view it with a healthy and realistic perspective.)

Globalization. Prior generations lived in a world that was extremely diverse, but very segregated. While cultures existed besides our own, they existed largely outside the "ghetto" of those who were not only like-minded, but also from the same racial and socioeconomic group, for the most part. It wasn't until the 1960s that the government began desegregation efforts in the United States. And in the 40 or more years since then, walls of racial and cultural segregation have come crumbling down. "Immigration, emigration, increased mobility, transportation advances, economic opportunity, and the pervasiveness of the global media machine have brought about a major shift in the makeup of neighborhoods, communities, and schools."[52] Our kids' and teenagers' urban, suburban, and rural communities increasingly reflect the multicultural and multiethnic flavor of the world. Even those who have no personal contact with people who are different from them have a multiplicity of cultures at their fingertips through media and the

Internet. This new reality has played a powerful role in shaping the spirituality, ideas, and lifestyles of today's emerging generations.

The postmodern worldview. A few years ago I watched a TV re-broadcast of the Rolling Stone's *Rock and Roll Circus*, a 1968 concert film. One segment featured sixties icons John Lennon and Yoko Ono playing in an all-star band. During one song, Ono did some avant-garde performance art by rolling around inside a black sack in front of the stage. For another number, she wailed and screamed incoherently while the band played. Even guitarist Eric Clapton couldn't help but give her a glance that clearly said, "Lady, what *are* you doing?" This seemed strange back when I was a teenager. But in today's postmodern culture, it hardly seems strange at all.

The world we older folks grew up in was steeped in *modernism*, a worldview that took hold in the eighteenth century, the time of the Enlightenment and scientific revolution. At its roots was the belief that the emerging disciplines of science and reason could lead humanity to truth, solve every problem we face (war, disease, poverty, and so on), and eventually make life on this earth so much better. Although modernist faith trusted human intellect rather than God, there was still a general consensus that right and wrong were absolute, and objective truth could be known.

But something started to change around the late 1960s. The worldview known as *postmodernism* began to emerge on the cultural landscape. Rooted in the belief that there is no such thing as objective and transcendent truth, the postmodern way of thinking and living allows people to discover and invent truth for themselves. Consequently, since no one can truly know what's right, a person is entitled to create and act on his own truth, thereby entitling him to live and do whatever's right in his own eyes. Today, the final court of appeal on religious and moral decisions is personal desire and opinion. In his book *Postmodern Times*, Gene Veith cites the result: "The only wrong idea is to believe in truth; the only sin is to believe in sin.[53]

George Barna asked adults and teenagers if they believe there are moral absolutes that are unchanging or that moral truth is relative to the circumstances.

By a three-to-one margin (64 percent vs. 22 percent) adults said truth is always relative to the person and their situation. The perspective was even more lopsided among teenagers, 83 percent of whom said moral truth depends on the circumstances, and only 6 percent of whom said moral truth is absolute.[54]

Not only are our kids swimming in the postmodern soup every day, but more are inheriting a postmodern view of the world from the adults in their lives. According to Barna, the result is "that numerous decisions are made in a truth vacuum. Sure, teenagers express great interest in having integrity, moral standards and laudable character. But they have thus far avoided the sacrifice of time, energy and image to both consider the foundations of moral truth and its implications for their life."[55]

Very few, if any, kids you know will have consciously adopted a postmodern way of thinking about, viewing, and living life. Most have assimilated it without thought or critique simply because it's part of the cultural soup they've been marinating in for so long. Marva Dawn offers a concise and helpful summary of what we find when we lift the ladle to examine the ingredients in this postmodern soup:

- The Enlightenment project is a bust—there is no such thing as progress.

- Life has no meaning—it's just a game.

- You are the only one who cares about you.

- No story is universally true.

- There is no such thing as truth except what you create for yourself.

- Every claim to truth is a power play.

- Therefore, everything must be mistrusted (or deconstructed).

- There is no order—all is random.

- You only go around once in life, so do it with gusto.[56]

We can reasonably expect we'll see more young people building personal value systems based on a potpourri of ideas gathered from home, peers, teachers, and the media. If you've been wondering about the glaring tendency of those in our culture to say one thing and do another without seeing any inconsistency or feeling any shame, you've been wondering about postmodernism.

Changing Influences Are Leading to New Trends

Sex—no rules. A few years ago I had a conversation with a man who'd been a high school teacher for 30 years.

"How have students changed the most?" I asked.

"That's easy," he replied. "They are so much more sexual today. Both the boys and girls have no problem expressing, talking about, and sharing the secrets of their sexual lives in earshot of anybody."

Our teenagers live in a sex-saturated society. The dominant message they hear from the media is that sex is an appetite to be indulged and enjoyed whenever, wherever, however, and with whomever they like. A growing majority of the population believes that sex before marriage is okay if both people are "emotionally ready." In addition, young people are engaging in a variety of additional sexual behaviors (oral sex) at younger and younger ages, all the while believing that because they're not having sexual intercourse, they're not having sex.

Teenagers who are longing for love and acceptance buy into these ideas and look to have their emotional needs met through a few minutes of sexual intimacy. As more teenagers adopt these attitudes, it becomes increasingly difficult for others to keep their virginity. Many schools add to the pressure by dispensing all the technical information and condoms kids need without ever suggesting abstinence as a possible option. (Chapter 8 will help you understand more about the sexual challenges your teenagers face today and will give you some ideas on how to encourage your teenagers to adopt and live a biblical sexual ethic.)

Materialism—the desirable lifestyle. The dawn of the new millennium has brought increased economic opportunity and wealth into the lives of teenagers. More kids are working long hours, buying cars, and furnishing their rooms with the latest in electronic gadgetry. Many have more monthly discretionary income at their disposal than some adults. As a result, they're the most targeted demographic in the world—a marketing department's dream. They spend their teenage years developing life expectations of having whatever they want whenever they want it. They are, and will continue to be, accumulating debt at never-before-heard-of levels. The possibility looms that at some point, this generation may be in for an economic rude awakening. Regardless of what happens in the future, we know their present situation indicates today's teenagers are building their lives around the desire to possess things. (See chapter 9 on understanding and combating materialism.)

The prevalence of substance abuse. By the time they graduate from high school, three-quarters of all teenagers will experiment with alcohol because they're pressured, bored, depressed, curious, or trying to relieve stress. And for many, it will become an addictive lifestyle. Not only is drinking depicted as fun in alcohol ads, but it's also portrayed as normal. Kids never get to see the consequences of drunken driving, alcohol-related crimes, alcoholism, bad health, and death. And even though alcohol remains the number one drug of choice among teenagers, parents should be concerned about the use of many other illicit drugs. While several recent studies indicate a slight decline in the use of some drugs among teenagers, don't be fooled into believing that drug abuse went out with the sixties and seventies. By the time they graduate from high school, more than half of all teenagers will have tried an illicit drug. (Chapter 10 will give you some up-to-date information on alcohol and drugs so you can help your child hold her own against them.)

Increased risk-taking behavior. While teenagers have always been risk-takers by nature, the extent and frequency of risk-taking has reached unprecedented proportions. By their very natures, teenagers are impulsive because they don't always consider the possible consequences, and they believe they're invincible. But the growing amount of risk-inflicted pain and dangerous behaviors they're choosing indicates some deeper issues as well. More kids are hurting so deeply from relational brokenness that they've become numb. As a result, they may choose to put themselves in dangerous situations where getting a rush allows them to feel *something*. Our culture's decreased value on personhood (abortion, euthanasia, and so on) contributes to a growing sense of lowered self-value and disregard. And, in a postmodern world void of boundaries, kids are more prone to attempt and do things that were previously unheard of.

The rise in teenage violence. The growing epidemic of youth violence extends beyond our cities and into virtually every community, with no regard for socioeconomic status, race, or class. In 1950 the rate of 14- to 17-year-olds arrested was four per thousand. That rate has increased almost 25 times to 97 per thousand. [57] The good news is that those rates were higher in the early 1990s and are now on a downward trend. Still, far too many kids are killing and perpetrating other violence, and far too many are being victimized.

Most adults can remember walking their high school's halls and coming across an occasional fistfight between students. But recent research published by the National Center for Education Statistics reports that during the 30 days preceding the survey, one in six high schoolers (and more than one in four males) had carried a weapon.[58] More than 6 percent had carried a weapon on school property.[59] More schools are installing metal detectors, hiring school resource officers, implementing weapons policies, and conducting regular safety drills in an effort to keep guns out and to learn how to respond if these dangerous weapons do make it inside.

Antibullying programs and campaigns have become part of the school curriculum in an effort to stem the growing tide of students picking on students because of social standing or lack of physical strength. Hazing on athletic teams has led to the implementation of antihazing policies. Forty-two percent of NCAA athletes report they were hazed in high school.[60] Estimates state that 1.5 million high school students are victimized by hazing each year, and half of those victims are athletes.[61]

Kids say guns are easy to buy and can be purchased on the street for as little as $20. Carrying a gun means other kids will "respect me." For some, the gun serves as a personal bodyguard—"I can now protect myself." Triggers are pulled for numerous reasons, some as trivial as someone "giving me a look" in the school hall or "saying something stupid." For others, guns are their weapons of choice as they carry out a premeditated plan in response to harassment, hazing, or bullying.

About 33 percent of this country's high school students had been in a physical fight, and 9.2 percent had actually been assaulted or threatened with a weapon at school.[62] Students aren't the only ones in danger. "Annually...teachers were victims of approximately 183,000 total nonfatal crimes at school, including 119,000 thefts and 65,000 violent crimes (rape, sexual assault, robbery, and aggravated assault)."[63] During one recent school year, 4 percent of public school teachers and 2 percent of private school teachers had been physically attacked by students.[64]

As violent behaviors among teenagers continue to be a part of our cultural landscape, the statistics will continue to be a cause for concern. The National Institutes for Health reports homicide is now the second leading cause of death (after accidents) for 15- to 24-year-olds, and the third leading cause of death (after accidents and cancer) for five- to 14-year-olds.[65]

There are several reasons for the current epidemic of youth violence. The breakdown of the family has left many kids without guidance or support. Feeling as though their lives are spiraling out of control, many teenagers seek refuge in gangs or other assemblies of disenfranchised peers, and these groups become outlets for kids who seek the unity, boundaries, and togetherness they aren't receiving at home.

One common thread seen among offender profiles is the absence of a father and the male support bond. "If we want to learn the identity of the rapist, the hater of women, the occupant of jail cells," writes David Blankenhorn of the Institute for American Values, "we do not look first to boys with a traditionally masculine father. We look first to boys with no fathers." [66] Other research supports this conclusion. "Kids who exhibited violent misbehavior in school were 11 times as likely not to live with their fathers and six times more likely to have parents who were not married. Boys from families with absent fathers and divorced parents are at a higher risk for violent behavior than boys from intact families."[67]

Many kids living in healthy, intact families are influenced by the rash of violent images found in music, film, and television. By the time the average child reaches the age of 18, he has witnessed 16,000 murders and 200,000 other acts of violence on TV alone.[68] Some of the most violent movies playing in theaters today are targeted to teenagers. And then there are the toys. Many of the more violent toys are based on characters from movies and TV shows, and kids will easily spend hours playing in a virtual world where killing equals winning.

If this book had been written 25 or 30 years ago, there would have been little or no mention of teenage violence. But we live in the most violent of industrialized nations. In the days following the 1999 Columbine massacre, I e-mailed several friends around the world to ask them how people in their countries were processing this highly publicized incidence of youth violence. One friend responded, "We're watching very closely. What is happening in your country has not yet happened here. But because we know you're experts at exporting this type of stuff, it's coming our way soon." As adults concerned for kids, we must acknowledge and face this emerging new reality.

The epidemic of teenage depression and suicide. If I had to isolate just a few words teenagers use to describe what it's like to grow up in today's world, they'd include *stress, anxiety,* and *overwhelming.* Kids are juggling the normal changes of the adolescent years with concern over family problems, grades, appearance pressure, popularity, violence, the future, you name it. As a result, more kids are now battling depression, eating disorders, and suicidal inclinations than ever before.

Recent research found that during the prior 12 months, 17 percent of high school students seriously considered attempting suicide, 16.5 percent of students had made a plan to attempt suicide, and 8.5 percent had actually attempted suicide.[69] Suicide is the third-leading cause of adolescent death. Sadly, this fact isn't too surprising, as a growing number of teenagers struggle with clinical depression. In fact, one in eight teenagers suffers from clinical depression.[70] Parents and others who love kids would be wise to remain aware of the discouragement and stress factors in teenagers' lives. (Chapter 11 will help you learn how to guard teens' emotions.)

Smorgasbord spirituality. Generally speaking, today's teenagers are a consciously spiritual bunch. Perhaps more than any other generation in recent time, they're on a deliberate quest to understand and embrace faith. While this is good news, it comes with a set of unique issues related to our culture and times. Because the marinade of our postmodern times is pushing more kids away from a belief in absolutes and transcendent truth, orthodox biblical Christianity is not only not embraced, but it's often looked down upon.

Teenagers struggle with Christianity's exclusivity and ultimately reject Christianity because Christians believe they alone have spiritual truth. In addition, the postmodern emphasis on feelings over and above rationality leads many young people to look for a faith system that's more emotional. Meanwhile, globalization and immigration have opened the door to a variety of previously foreign and unfamiliar faith systems, especially various forms of Eastern spirituality and mysticism, allowing them to find a new home in North American youth culture.

All this has combined to create an environment where young people may step up to the spiritual buffet table and load their plates with personal combinations of elements to create a faith system that satisfies their spiritual palates and hunger. Because each individual has the freedom to choose what he wants for himself, varied day-to-day tastes allow him to change and adapt his preferences on a daily basis. Every plate is custom made by the individual consumer, and no two meals are alike. To more rational and logical observers, the servings on individual plates are often seen to be incompatible with one another. But to postmodern young people, they've been given the freedom to be consistently inconsistent and they see no contradictions.

This individualized, postmodern spiritual journey has had a profound effect on the faith adopted by our self-described Christian teenagers. Christian Smith's groundbreaking research on teenage spirituality reports 84 percent of teenagers in the United States believe in God.[71] At first glance, that encouraging number seems to indicate that efforts to lead young people to faith in Christ have been working. But a closer and more careful look at the study's data indicates we should stop congratulating ourselves and start getting concerned.

Shouldn't we be thrilled that more than eight out of 10 teenagers believe in God? The real question we should ask is *who* or *what* is the God they believe in? The research concludes that their God and their faith aren't the God and faith of the Bible. Rather, it's what Smith labels as "Moralistic, Therapeutic, Deism." In other words, kids believe that to be a Christian means they should strive to be good people. They believe God exists to serve them by helping them to feel good, happy, secure, and at peace. And they believe that even though God made the world, he's only active and involved in our lives when we need him to resolve a problem. In reality, only eight percent of teenagers "believe in God, attend religious services weekly or more often," hold faith to be "important in their lives," regularly "participate in religious groups," and "pray and read the Bible regularly."[72]

The reality of emerging teenage spirituality is that "the majority of American teenagers appear to espouse rather inclusive, pluralistic, and individualistic views about religious truth, identity boundaries, and the need for religious congregation."[73] This explains the rise of teenage interest in New Age mysticism, Buddhism, Islam, Hinduism, Kabbalah, Wicca, and other spiritualities. When it comes to those who claim to be "Christian," that brand of Christianity is becoming distorted and secularized. Smith says, "Christianity is either denigrating into a pathetic version of itself or, more significantly, Christianity is actively being colonized and displaced by a quite different religious faith."[74] More teenagers who've been raised in Christian homes or who've embraced Christianity are adding other spiritual elements to their plates. It's not uncommon to encounter a teenager who believes Jesus is the Son of God, believes in the virgin birth of Christ, believes the Bible is the Word of God, and also believes in reincarnation, reads and follows her horoscope, and sees no contradictions between any of these beliefs. In addition, many who hold to a more orthodox and biblical Christian faith have embraced it as something they do from time to time, rather than someone they are all of the time. Instead of integrating their faith into all of life, they live an unintegrated faith that only touches select parts of who they are. Consequently, their stated beliefs may be kept separate from how they view and respond to authority, how they conduct themselves in dating relationships, who they are as a student or athlete, and so on.

One of the greatest responsibilities of parents and youth workers is to teach kids the difference between right and wrong. But the nature of our culture makes it difficult to instill a set of transcendent godly values when our kids grow up learning to "choose to believe what you want to believe" and "choose to live how you want to live." If we want to reach our kids with the good news, then we *must* survey our changing surroundings with the passion and mindset of a cross-cultural missionary and come to a deeper understanding of the world in which they live. (Consult chapter 12 for strategies to point your teenagers to a life-changing Christian faith.)

Closing the Cultural-Generational Gap: Avoiding the Obstacles

Think about yourself as I describe common "reasons" for allowing the cultural-generational gap to continue to grow. Have any of these excuses found their way into your conscious or unconscious justifications for staying out of touch with your kids? Have these obstacles to family growth opened the cultural-generational gap in your home?

"I'm Scared"

To put it simply, raising and relating to kids is a difficult task that can be quite frightening at times. The fact that we live in a rapidly changing world that often scoffs at our values doesn't make the job any easier.

A Christian mom and dad who love their kids dearly were concerned that a sinful world could exercise a negative influence on them and their kids. So while the kids were still young, the couple, guided by a lifelong conviction and practice of believing that Christian faith is best lived by keeping ourselves "out of the world," made a decision to do whatever was necessary to keep their little ones from being poisoned by the things of this world. They sent their kids to a Christian school (I'm not biased against Christian schools, by the way) and allowed them to go outdoors only when going to and from school or a family activity. The kids never played with the neighbor children. When they were in the house, the kids were not allowed to watch TV or listen to the radio. Like the "bubble boy" whose nonexistent immune system forced him to live in a germ-free plastic bubble, these parents provided a protective shield around their kids. They reasoned that, by separating themselves and their kids from the world, the world would never influence or affect them in negative ways.

Granted, this is an extreme case. But even in less extreme cases, this unrealistic approach—rooted in fear, ignorance, and theological misunderstanding—can be counterproductive. While we might be successful in protecting our kids from the world's influence for a while (and there are elements of the culture from which we should remain separate), sooner or later the bubble will break and the germs will rush in. Or our kids will make a decision to move out of the bubble and into the germs.

Without the protection of a parent-instilled immune system strengthened by years of learning to understand and interact with the world and its potential influence as Christians, their spiritual, emotional, and even physical health could be in jeopardy. In fact, many sheltered kids venture out into the world only to find themselves curiously attracted to what they've never seen before. Without the ability to think critically and biblically about what they've encountered, they can be easily enticed into willing participation in the very things they were shielded from while growing up. And what happens then? How can parents respond to their kids when they don't have a clue as to what their kids are dealing with since they've spent years of living life in a protective bubble themselves?

A better approach would be to realize that, yes, the world is a scary place and we're called not to be involved with obscene entertainment, pornography, sinful behavior, and anything that could be considered idolatry. But there's a tension that exists—a tension that is sometimes very uncomfortable—because God's will is for us to be particular people who live as his people in the particular place in this world where he's placed us. On the night before his death, Jesus prayed the will of his heavenly Father for his followers in all times and all places (John 17). Our place—the place for

Christian parents and the place where they must lead their teen-agers—is in but not of the world.[75] Jesus has called us to be salt and light by learning how to live in the world, while not being of the world. He's also called us to be sheep in the midst of wolves. Scary? Yes. But the Good Shepherd promises protection.

Observing youth culture helps us to understand and relate to our kids while equipping them to relate to the world around them, which is just what Jesus wants them to do. Paul Tripp sums it up when he encourages parents "to raise teenagers who are fully able to interact with their culture without becoming enslaved to its idols."[76]

Something to remember... Observing and learning about youth culture does not imply participation in or acceptance of the un-godly aspects of youth culture. It simply means we want to know as much as we can about kids and their world so we can under-stand them, help them develop a realistic framework for making good choices, and equip them to live as light in the midst of the darkness.

"Not Now. . . I'm Too Busy"

Pushed by a father who is emotionless, busy, detached, dictato-rial, and totally out of touch with his son, Neil Perry of the movie *Dead Poets Society* attends a prestigious prep school to fulfill his parents' dream of his becoming a physician. While at the school, Neil's father directs his every move. On the few occasions Dad visits, it's to remind him that, "I made a great many sacrifices to get you here, Neil, and you won't let me down."

But Neil cries out to a father who never hears him. He tells his classmates, "He's planning the rest of my life for me. He's nev-er asked me what I want." The movie climbs to its tragic climax when Neil disappoints his father by doing what he really wants to do—act. Dragged home by his father and removed from the school after giving an outstanding debut performance in a community theater production, Neil fights back in the only way he knows how. He takes his own life while sitting at his father's desk. Upon find-ing the dead body of his son, Mr. Perry cries out, "Neil! My son... my poor son!" Too little, too late. One has to wonder what would have happened if Mr. Perry had only taken time out of his busy schedule to listen to and understand his son.

We live in a busy and frantic time. We get wrapped up in the demands of work, house chores, social engagements, church activities, community affairs, etc. While many of our pursuits are important, could it be that we're letting even more important pursuits slip through the cracks—such as taking time to understand our kids?

David Elkind, professor of child study at Tufts University and author of *The Hurried Child, All Grown Up and No Place to Go,* and *Ties That Stress,* argues that one result of our busyness and the individualistic thrust of American society is a generation of egocentric parents. They either forget or find it impossible to understand, nurture, and meet the needs of their kids. In effect, they're out of touch and become more out of touch as time goes on.[77] If Elkind and others are right—and I believe they are—then one consequence of parents' self-focus is the current cultural-generational gap.

Something to remember... The task of parenting requires a consistent and concentrated effort at listening, observing, and understanding your child and your child's world. It may demand major changes in your lifestyle and priorities in order to have the time to parent effectively. If you were to take an inventory of how you spend your time, what would you learn about your priorities? What would your kids list as your priorities? Are your kids getting the short end of the stick? Or are you taking the time to get to know them and their world? To help them grow into healthy adults?

"I Didn't Know!"

It happened 20 years ago, and I'll never forget it. A mother came to me and excitedly shared about a "major victory" she'd experienced in her efforts to nurture her 14-year-old daughter in the Christian faith.

"I've finally gotten her to make good music choices. She's listening to Christian music. She loves listening to that guy who wears the cross and who has an album called *Faith*. In fact, she's going to see George Michael in concert tonight!"

I wasn't sure whether to laugh or cry. God bless her. All I know is I almost had to pick the poor woman off the floor after I gave her a copy of the lyrics to George Michael's song "I Want Your Sex": "It's natural, it's chemical (let's do it), it's logical, habitual (hey, we're doin' it), it's sensual, but most of all, sex is something we should do…I want your sex."[78]

I'll never forget the horrified look on her face or what she said to me: "I just didn't know!"

This wasn't a parent who didn't care about her kids. Quite the contrary. She loved her kids dearly and was a fine example of what a parent should be. Yet her naiveté about the unique youth culture in which her oldest daughter was steeped had led to a difficult situation. From that moment on, she committed herself to becoming an informed student of youth culture so she could better understand and guide her own kids.

More than one parent has been caught off guard. A few years ago I read the obituary of a 14-year-old honor student who was found hanging in his bedroom. His mother told me he'd died while "scarfing" (autoerotic asphyxiation: masturbating while limiting the blood flow to the brain by constricting a rope around the neck), an activity that's had some measure of popularity among middle school boys as a way to heighten the sense of sexual pleasure. Still grieving over the death of her son, she told me how she wished someone had warned her about autoerotic asphyxiation so she could have discussed it with her son. In an open letter to other parents that was printed in a local newspaper, this grieving mother writes: "People may not realize that they need to warn their sons about some very dangerous experimentation that may be going on. We are willing to share what little we know with any parent who wants to call us. A beautiful light has gone from our lives forever, and the only way to deal with the pain is by trying to prevent this from happening to anyone else. Information is the only weapon we have in our struggle to protect our most precious treasure—our kids."

Something to remember… Those who don't understand the world of teenagers don't usually make a conscious decision to be naive. More often than not, it's a matter of circumstance. They're loving and caring parents. But all parents should take the time to become informed so they can better help their kids sort through the many muddled messages that bombard them during the turbulent teenage years.

"Who Cares?"

I once asked a group of high school students to break down into small groups to answer this question: *If you knew the world was going to end in five minutes, and you had the opportunity to say one thing to one person, what would you say, and who would you say it to?* The kids were used to questions like this from me, so the discussion started taking off. One group of eight was laughing hysterically at the answers the group was giving, so I went over to listen. But when it came time for Janelle to answer, they all got very quiet. Finally, with an angry look on her face, Janelle shared her answer through gritted teeth: "I would walk right up to my father, look him in the eye, and say, 'Dad, you missed it.'"

Janelle was a wonderful young girl, gifted intellectually and musically. A straight-A student who had the lead role in the school plays, she was the kind of kid you'd think would make any parent proud.

Afterward I approached Janelle while she was alone. "Janelle, is everything all right at home?"

"No," she said. "I'm not a bad kid, and I really try hard at everything I do. But all my father is concerned about is work and reading the paper. He never talks to me or my mom. He never comes to my plays or concerts. He has no interest in my life. He doesn't care."

Janelle is not alone. There are lots of kids whose parents just don't care. Maybe it's a matter of messed-up priorities. Maybe they never wanted to be parents in the first place. Maybe they're so at odds with themselves and their own pasts that they have no time or energy to care for spouses or kids. Parental apathy can take many different forms. But there's one common thread: When parents don't care, there's no way to close the cultural-generational gap and grow as a family. Janelle's dad didn't even have time for a five-minute conversation. How could he find the time to discover what was going on in her world?

Janelle's dad was quickly forfeiting his ability to positively influence his wonderful young daughter. In the end, most of the Janelles fall prey to whatever cultural voices seem most inviting. A few kids, by the grace of God, will find a teacher, neighbor, youth worker, grandparent, or other adult who will guide them through the teenage years and into adulthood. Regardless of how kids of apathy turn out, most of them will carry the burden of animosity toward their parents for the rest of their lives.

Something to remember... Think about your relationships with your kids. Would they say you're "missing it"? We can love our kids and care deeply about them yet still be apathetic about getting to know them by getting to know the world in which they live. We need to take the time and energy to say, "I love you. I care about you. I want to walk with you and guide you as you grow up. And in order to do my best, I'm going to take the time to get to know the culture you're growing up in so that when you need me to, I can help you understand it, respond to it, and get through it in a way that's pleasing to God."

"It Can't Be That Bad"

A few years ago, in an effort to beat my body back into shape, I took up jogging. I quickly learned that among the biggest hazards I had to face on our local roads were the dogs. During one afternoon jog, I found myself overcome by terror (while trying to look cool on the outside) as I rounded a bend just in time to see a very large Rottweiler charging down the hill and right at me. His bared teeth and throaty growls sent my heart to my feet and a shiver up my spine as I realized there was no way I could reason with this beast. With no place to run and not a single tree to climb, I wondered what part of me he'd eat first. I tried to act brave and conceal my fear by yelling something like, "Down, Lucifer!" The dog appeared to be deaf. Just as my life began to pass before my eyes and Cujo was only about five feet away from a big supper, the dog's master appeared around the corner. With a loud and angry yell, the man shouted a command (it sounded to me like "No! I'm making you a steak!") that stopped the dog dead in his tracks. With his head down, the dog ran back up the hill to his master. I felt like running up and kissing the guy.

As I continued my jog, I thought about my surprising confrontation with the dog. At the initial moment of panic, my wisdom and experience had told me in no uncertain terms I was in danger and I needed to react. I could have stood there and denied there was a dog running at me. I could have tried to convince myself that even though there was a dog, he wouldn't hurt me. If I were really stupid, I could have watched the dog take a chunk out of my leg while yelling to the owner, "Don't worry about it! He's not serious. He's just playing."

Now, I'll be the first to say that not all elements of contemporary culture are negative or dangerous. Like everything else in this world, culture is a creation of God that is fallen and polluted by sin. At times it gives honor and glory to God. At other times, it gives honor and glory to the world, the flesh, and the devil. But let's focus on the bad for just a minute. As the bad runs down the hill with its teeth bared, inexperienced and uninformed young teenagers might not realize they're in danger. They might even reach out to pet and embrace it. Fortunately, most parents fulfill their God-given responsibilities by acting on their wisdom and experience. They step in to protect their kids from harm and provide for their well-being. But tragically, there are many parents who leave their kids "to the dogs" because these parents never got to the point where they see the danger. They look at the rapidly changing world and say, "It's not all that bad; it hasn't affected me. And anyway, my kids are smart; it won't affect them. If it does, they'll grow out of it." But parents who deny the power of culture handicap themselves when they could be helping their kids grow into healthy adults.

Something to remember... Contemporary culture is a powerful influence on the values, attitudes, and behaviors of kids. How aware are you of the teenagers' world? Parents and youth workers who get serious about understanding the reality of the influences on teenagers equip themselves to respond mightily in the fight to safely lead kids through "the dogs."

"Times Have Changed—Lighten Up!"

The last reason for the continued growth of the cultural-generational gap is perhaps the most frightening and difficult to deal with. It occurs when parents become so entwined in the prevailing cultural soup that they fail to stand back and look at it critically. The result? They fail to see any need to understand or deal with it. Unlike others whose apathy, busyness, and denial keep them from acknowledging and understanding the powerful influence of culture on kids, these folks know the culture too well because it's too much a part of them and they're too much a part of it. It's as if they were hijacked by the culture so long ago that they're now enjoying the ride.

I was once speaking to a group of church parents on teenage sexuality. My presentation included an overview of teenage sexual behavior, the reasons for an increase in sexual activity, the consequences of premarital sex, and some suggestions for how parents can begin to instill healthy sexual attitudes in their kids that reflect God's design for our sexuality.

During the question time, a woman obviously puzzled and frustrated by what I'd just said raised her hand and asked, "Do you mean to tell me that God wants me to teach my 14-year-old daughter that she has to wait until she's married to have sex? After all, she's reached puberty. That's so outdated. This is the *nineties*."

Tragically, it hasn't been unusual for me to hear parents of teenagers in my own community justify their decision to provide alcohol and a place to drink it for their kids and their kids' teenage friends. I've known most of these people for years. Our kids played together. We coached together. We attended the same back-to-school nights at our local elementary school. At times it doesn't seem possible to me that these parents who were once concerned and involved have now chosen to stay involved in a way that's illegal, immoral, and just plain dangerous.

Sadly, these types of cultural accommodation have infiltrated the church. The Barna Group's continued research has concluded that many Christians are only living a Christian façade that doesn't demonstrate or reflect the spiritual depth, commitment, or integration of faith into all of life that's required of Christ's followers. Instead, they're living "soft Christianity." George Barna says,

Americans are willing to expend some energy in religious activities such as attending church and reading the Bible, and they're willing to throw some money in the offering basket. Because of such activities, they convince them-selves that they're people of genuine faith. But when it comes to truly establishing their priorities and making a tangible commitment to knowing and loving God, and to allowing Him to change their character and lifestyle, most people stop short. We want to be "spiritual" and we want to have God's favor, but we're not sure we want Him taking control of our lives and messing with the im-age and outcomes we've worked so hard to produce.[79]

Some of us have become so much like the world that we don't see it as we should. We create for ourselves a comfortable mix of bits and pieces from the world and from our faith. Then we begin to enjoy the world and its culture.

Author and cultural analyst Tom Sine says this: "Until we rec-ognize our captivity we cannot be free. To the extent that our secu-lar culture's values captivate us, we are unavailable to advance God's Kingdom...We all seem to be trying to live the American Dream with a little Jesus overlay."[80] If we fail to model and teach our kids about true faith, we'll only hurt our kids. And the cultural-generational gap will continue to grow.

Something to remember... When we're honest with ourselves, we know we can't guide our kids through the soup of today's culture until we deal with the inconsistencies in our own lives first. We have two choices. We can take the easy way out (for now) and keep sail-ing along on the same course, preferring not to rock the boat. Or we can row vigorously into the sea of youth culture and strive to un-derstand it. I'm hopeful that the fact that you're reading this book indicates you've chosen the latter option.

But before you read on, let me challenge you to conduct a personal inventory with the help of your family and a few close friends. Do you fall prey to any of the following excuses for con-tinuing the growth of the cultural-generational gap between you and your own kids?

- I'm scared.

- Not now...I'm too busy.

- I didn't know!

- Who cares?

- It can't be that bad.

- Times have changed—lighten up!

Ask for your spouse's opinion. Ask your kids for their opinions. And then really listen to what they have to say. And don't forget—you asked because you want answers that will lead you to make positive changes.

If you find that you need to overcome one or more of the obstacles, develop a plan that is guided by prayer and the advice of family and friends.

Principles That Bridge the Cultural-Generational Gap

Note to youth workers: Most of the following points apply directly to parents and will come in handy as you coach them and minister to them when they're looking for help with their kids.

1. Understanding the World of Kids Is Primarily a Parent's Calling

Youth workers, Sunday school teachers, pastors, and other significant adults all play important roles in the spiritual development of kids, but Scripture is clear: The primary arena for Christian nurture is the home. Parents are called by God to teach the truth of God's Word by precept and example. An understanding of our kids and their culture helps us to function as cross-cultural missionaries—taking the Word of God from our culture into theirs. It helps us to prepare them for the reality of the unique challenges they'll face in today's world. Only then can we effectively teach them to walk through difficult times by integrating Christian faith into all of life.

2. It's Never Too Early

Don't wait until your kids are 11 or 12 years old to develop a working understanding of youth culture. Prevention is still the best medicine. We live in a world where youth culture doesn't just affect teenagers. Second graders talk about having sex; kindergarten boys cry if their hair doesn't look just right; third-grade girls go on diets; four-year-olds watch MTV and other music television networks, while their parents naively sip coffee in the next room; and eight-year-olds carry guns to school. The innocence of childhood has been lost in a world where children begin to swim in the soup of youth culture from the moment they emerge from the womb. Kids face pressures that were once limited to the teenage years. They desperately need well-informed parental guidance as they deal with an increasing set of choices and expectations.

Many parents would echo the thoughts and frustrations of a father who approached me after I finished teaching a seminar on contemporary youth culture: "This was really great. I learned so much," he said. "I only wish I had heard this 10 years ago." *Now* is the time to begin to understand the world of teenagers. An early and ongoing understanding of youth culture will equip you to take conscious and informed steps to counteract the youth culture's negative influences and affirm its positive influences while your kids are still young, minimizing the later effects of the cultural-generational gap in your family.

3. It's Never Too Late
What if your kids have already entered the adolescent years? Every time I speak, I see the war-weary faces of parents who feel as though they've failed. In spite of trying "everything," communication has broken down. Hurt and heartache rule at home, and they're haunted by guilt. Is it too late for you if this is your situation?

A man once came to me with tears streaming down his face. "My son and I used to do everything together. But for more than a year he has shown no interest in church or Christianity. He won't talk to me. And when he is home, he shuts his door and just retreats into the world of his music. He is angry. He has even pulled a knife on his mother. I have spent the last year trying so hard to understand him and figure out what has happened." He looked at me, waiting for a response.

What could I say to him? I wish I could have handed him a 10-step plan guaranteed to correct complex problems in an even more complex world. But there's no such thing. Instead, I told him it's never too late. No situation in life is unredeemable because God is sovereign. In the midst of crisis, conflict, and turmoil, these words can sound like a cliché. Yet, they're true. I know, because I've been there.

Hurting but not hopeless, this man has continued to pray about his relationship with his son. He has not given up. His hope is in almighty God. He continues to work hard to understand his son and his son's world in the hope he might exercise a redeeming influence in the situation. And guess what? God is honoring his work. This father has since told me his newfound understanding of his son has opened the door of communication. The slow process of healing has begun.

Whether your relationship with your teenager is full of heartache or extremely comfortable, it's never too late to increase your understanding of youth culture.

4. It Won't be Easy

When you begin to study youth culture, it won't be long before you realize there is only one thing of which you can be sure: Youth culture is always changing and evolving. This book will serve as a springboard on your quest. You don't need to know everything. None of us does. But listen hard to know what cultural elements are a part of your teenager's world and life. Then, take the time to spend some time there yourself. Here are some suggestions on how to stay in touch with today's emerging youth culture soup:

- *Continue to read literature written about the world of your teenagers.*

- *Watch programs and videos that are popular with your kids, and visit the Internet sites they frequent.* This will give you a window into your child's heart and mind.

- *Observe teenagers at a mall, church gathering, or at your house to help you gain insight into their attitudes, values, cares, and concerns.* Listen, watch, and notice what's going on.

- *Don't be afraid to ask your teenagers questions.* Ask them about their heroes, fears, friends, hopes, dreams, and so on. Good questions can't be answered with a yes or a no.

- *Visit the Center for Parent/Youth Understanding Web site on a regular basis.* Updated daily, www.cpyu.org is loaded with literally thousands of searchable pages. You can read youth culture news, look at statistics, read helpful articles, and get practical advice. In addition, the site serves as a gateway to numerous other helpful resources.

Wise parents and adult leaders work hard to take as many paths as possible to understand the unique world of teenagers.

5. Pain Is a Blessing

I'm a fairly stubborn person. I like to do things myself. That way I know I'm doing it *my* way, which is to my way of thinking (sadly) usually the right way. I've learned that the best prescription for that kind of self-sufficient, know-it-all attitude is a heavy and regular helping of humble pie. I've also learned that God is good at serving it up, just as I need it.

For someone like me who likes to keep everything in order, the "humble pie" of a crisis can be paralyzing, especially when that crisis involves your kids. My kids, like yours, have minds of their own, and sometimes they use those minds to make some pretty dangerous decisions. I've had enough experience to know these situations come at me in two ways. First, it's extremely upsetting. None of us wants to see our kids fall into danger, especially when they bring that danger on themselves. Second, I usually discover the reality that's been there all along—I'm not in control of the situation. Taken together, the heartache and realization that I'm not in control combine in some pretty heavy emotional and spiritual pain.

But I've also learned that pain is the classroom where my heavenly Father does his best work in my life. There is something wonderful about falling into the arms of my heavenly Father and admitting "I'm at a loss" and "I don't have a clue what to do." At these times, I find myself echoing the Psalms of lament. But in the end, when I'm able to look at the situation in the rearview mirror, I'm always amazed at what God has done in me. Not only is he about the work of redeeming and restoring my kids, but he's also about the business of doing the same work in me.

6. Understanding Youth Culture Equips Parents to Pass on the Torch of Faith

Maybe you've heard your teenagers moan and groan about how boring and irrelevant church is. Sometimes kids have a legitimate gripe. Granted, the message of God's Word is as relevant and necessary as ever. But the problem lies in the communication of that Word: We haven't always taken into account the cultural context in which our kids live.

Maybe it's time we take a clue from the ministry of Jesus. His starting point with people was always an understanding of them and what made them tick. He wasn't a dispenser of pat religious answers and formulas. Rather, he spoke to the deep needs and hurts of the people he understood intimately. The God-man took the time to know people and the world in which they lived. His communication was effective and relevant because he knew how to bring the light of God's truth to shine on the darkness of people's needs.

We need to see that it's difficult to pass on the faith apart from knowing and understanding the cultural context of our kids. There is value in knowing what our kids watch and listen to. There is value in knowing how they think, what they believe, what they value, and how they communicate. Our culture is challenging our kids to get in step with the times and do whatever they think is right to do at any given moment. But armed with a well-informed understanding of youth culture, we can begin to present the never-changing truth about God in ways that our kids—who're living in and influenced by an ever-changing world—can understand. You're a cross-cultural missionary.[81]

7. Understanding Youth Culture Fosters Relational Closeness

When teenagers were asked to describe their relationships with their fathers, the majority of daughters described them as distant, uncomfortable, and withdrawn. Sons most frequently reported that their fathers were judgmental, withdrawn, insensitive, careful about what they said, serious, uncomfortable, critical, and distant.

Rarely were sons or daughters likely to be playful, relaxed, or open, or to feel loved and accepted when around their fathers. The study concluded that, in comparison with other important persons in their lives, teenagers feel most distant from their fathers.[82]

Statements such as, "We just don't talk anymore," "I don't think they understand me," "We haven't spent time together for who knows how long," and "We've grown apart" are being spoken with increasing frequency by both parents and teenagers. In his classic book *The Five Cries of Youth*, Merton Strommen identified one of the five cries as the "Cry of Psychological Orphans" who "need to be a part of a family where we love and accept and care about each other."[83] In his later book *The Five Cries of Parents*, Strommen's research identified the parents' "Cry for a Close Family."[84] The crying hasn't stopped. It's gotten louder, and it continues to echo through our culture today.

Over the years I've led numerous parent-teenager weekends. In preparation for my time with families, I ask a group of parents and teenagers to gather and discuss what they feel their needs are as families. And every time they do, parents and teenagers unanimously agree on three major needs. First, they want to relearn (or in many cases learn for the first time) how to communicate with each other. Second, they want to relearn how to play together so they might enjoy laughter as a family again. And third, they sense they're not functioning as a healthy family and they want to discover what God is calling their family to be. Combine these three needs into one and what do you get? A desire among parents and teenagers to come back together, eliminate the gap, and be the family they were created to be.

Getting Personal

A recent television talk show on parent-teenager relationships confirmed the need for closeness in families. Teenager after teenager shared stories of heartache about life at home with parents who were out of touch with their kids. As the show came to its conclusion, the host asked the audience for their comments. A 14-year-old boy stood up, with his mother standing beside him, and shared these words with a national TV audience: "This is my mom. She's the best! She knows me."

Closeness *can be* restored through loving and caring. Be a parent who closes the gap by taking a loving interest in your child and your child's world; be a youth worker who closes the gap by going the extra mile to understand youth culture.

3

Media:
The New Face of Nurture

Although the purpose of "entertaining" is usually seen as mere amusement or moneymaking, its real purpose is education. The teenager goes to the school of adolescence with entertainment as the friend and teacher.

—QUENTIN J. SCHULTZE, *DANCING IN THE DARK* [85]

Every culture is reflected by its artists.

—MARILYN MANSON[86]

Take a look around. It's everywhere. It fills their eyes and ears through screens, speakers, headphones, and more. It's media, the means or instrumentality for storing, communicating, and widely disseminating information to the public—including teenagers. And as quickly as media's ever-expanding technologies, outlets, and content continue to grow, our kids gobble it up with a passion. Do teenagers love their media? You'd better believe it! Just try taking it away from them sometime. You're bound to have a fight on your hands.

The rapid rise in new communication and media technologies is changing the face of adolescence and childhood in ways yet to be realized and understood. A growing array of options and outlets keeps teenagers in touch with media and media in touch with them 24/7, no matter where they are or what they're doing. It bombards their senses at home, school, work, sporting events, malls, and in the car. Most carry portable media devices with them wherever they go. Everything is not only changing, but the pace of change is accelerating on a daily basis.

Sure, teenagers are still using the traditional "old" media forms of television, radio, movies, and magazines, but they're using them in new ways. Radio can still be heard on the AM and FM dials, but more young people are accessing the medium through satellite and Internet hookups. Movies can be viewed anywhere and anytime through computers, iPods, and even cell phones. What used to be an entire record collection (which I still have, by the way) can be digitally downloaded into a portable listening device the size of a credit card, lipstick, or pen. And although magazines are still printed on paper and show up in the mailbox, most can also be accessed on the Internet, where visitors are able to interact with even more content that can be read, heard, and watched.

New media technologies have changed where and how kids are listening and watching. Family room floor plans are designed around elaborate media centers and state-of-the-art televisions costing thousands of dollars. But even the shared family room media experience is going the way of the dinosaur, as kids are piling up more media outlets in their bedrooms.

All of this old and new media technology has changed the face of the world and how teenagers live in it. They're now able to interact globally in real time, thanks to instant messaging, cell phones, and other new technologies. They use media to shop, communicate, be entertained, and learn. Media is not only at their fingertips; it's woven in and through the fabric of who they are.

The most recent research conducted by the Kaiser Family Foundation has resulted in a new label—"Generation M" (for "media")—for eight- to 18-year-old kids. The study found that "young people today live media-saturated lives, spending an average of nearly six and one-half hours a day (6:21) with media."[87] During that period of 44 1/2 hours each week, young people are spending 26 percent of the time using more than one medium. In other words, they might be listening to music, instant-messaging friends, and reading a book for school simultaneously. Almost one-third of young people (30 percent) say they either talk on the phone, instant message, watch TV, listen to music, or surf the Web "most of the time" while they're doing homework. Another third (31 percent) say they do so "some" of the time.[88] Teenagers between the ages of 12 and 17 multitask more than any other age group, with teenage girls multitasking more often than teenage boys.[89] As new media forms and outlets develop, it's reasonable to assume that this tendency to multitask will continue to rise.

All in all, average children are actually exposed to eight hours and 33 minutes of media content per day, and they're packing that into less than six and one-half hours of time.[90] These numbers are staggering when you consider the same study found they only spend two hours and 17 minutes "hanging out with parents," one hour and 25 minutes in physical activity, and one hour pursuing hobbies or other activities.[91]

Any serious attempt to understand our teenagers requires an ongoing effort to comprehend media and the role it plays in their lives. It's no easy task. Take music, for example. A quick trip to the local record store can be overwhelming. Racks of CDs are loaded with thousands of different albums featuring as many singers and groups. Genres vary from pop to rock to R&B to country to rap—all appealing to the varying tastes and preferences of teenagers. And the growing prevalence of online music options makes it even more complex.

To make matters worse, the definition of what's hot and what's not changes every week. An artist at the top of the charts today might struggle for an audience in just a matter of months. Just the mention of the name can bring groans of disapproval from kids who may have been the artist's greatest fans at the height of his popularity. More and more, the fast-changing face of popular music makes "X is so yesterday" an accurate description of music's growing list of has-beens.

While groups and performers come and go and while kids' tastes change rapidly, certain aspects of the relationship between kids and media remain static. In this chapter, I'll attempt to begin to navigate the confusing labyrinth of media. We'll examine the major media outlets and some of the unique features of each. We'll look at several aspects of the relationship between kids and media, along with some general facts about the different media they use.

Keep in mind that my focus will lean heavily toward the world of popular music. The reason? Popular music has been a primary ingredient of youth culture for a long time. It's also woven in and through all the other media outlets in a variety of ways, shapes, and forms.

(Because the world of popular music and media is changing at breakneck speed, I keep references to specific musicians, shows, films, and so on at a minimum because they can become dated rather quickly. Instead, the focus is on enduring trends and aspects of music and media. For that reason, I encourage you to discover the specific music and media interests of the kids you know and love, and then take steps to gather information that will help you understand their particular music and media so you can help them make wise and godly music and media choices. For a list of these resources, consult the Center for Parent/Youth Understanding's Web site [www.cpyu.org] to find updated lists of popular artists, films, shows, and so on, along with helpful links and other resources you can use to quickly gain awareness.)

Media's Life-Shaping Power

In recent years a number of incidents regarding the supposed power of media have received a large amount of press. While the names and details differ, the story is always somewhat the same: A teenager or group of teenagers is driven to some bizarre behavior—perhaps even killing himself or someone else as a result of listening to popular music, playing violent video games, or watching violence in film. While the stories are tragic and the accusations may have some merit, they can distract those who're truly interested in understanding the power of media from the real issues.

First, these accusations tend to equate media power with only those media outlets or expressions that are violent in nature. In reality, all media has power and influence, not just violent stuff. The danger with this approach can lead us to assume that as long as it's not violent, there's really no influence. But the fact is that all media has power and influence that can affect the sum total of the values, attitudes, and behaviors of teenagers. Even the most seemingly innocent and unoffensive media can influence.

Second, focusing on these isolated incidents of sensational behavior can sidetrack parents and youth workers from understanding the role that media plays in cooperation with all the other socialization factors in a teenager's life. In other words, media can become an easy scapegoat to blame for rebellious teenage behavior. But media doesn't act alone; it's merely one of many cultural forces that shapes adolescents. Media influences the life of all sorts of teenagers, not just delinquents or deranged killers.

Media sways the lives of our teenagers in two powerful ways: It helps them define their perception of life and reality, and it shapes their behaviors.

Media Maps Out Life and Reality for Kids

To fully understand how media exercises power in the lives of our kids, we must remember that teenagers are adults waiting to happen. They're in a tumultuous period of tremendous physical, mental, emotional, and spiritual change. They want to know what life is all about and how to approach it. Adolescence, like all periods of change, is a time of uncertainty. Most of us have experienced the process of evaluating and making decisions regarding a major life event. When we consider marriage, a job offer, a move, or having kids, we look outside ourselves for guidance and direction. As kids go through adolescence, they're no different from the rest of us. Their uncertainty leads them to seek and process new information from a variety of sources in the hope of solving their dilemmas and easing the difficulties of growing up.

Musical artists speak for many teenagers. They meet teenagers right where they are and answer their questions in exciting, convincing, and attractive ways. Media influences their evolving worldview and life view, shapes their values and attitudes, and plays a significant role in determining who they'll become as adults, for better or for worse. Therefore media guides teenagers—a group that desperately wants and needs understanding and direction. It's not unusual to hear a kid say about their favorite artist, "I relate to him because he knows exactly how I feel."

The power of music and media to define reality is far greater than it once was. A synthesis of 18 studies completed in the early 1980s that compared the influence of various institutions on the values and behaviors of 13- to 19-year-olds (and how this influence has shifted over time) showed that in 1960 the family exercised the greatest influence on teenage values and behavior. Other institutions of influence were—in order—school, friends and peers, and the church. It can be assumed, for the most part, these four institutions were in agreement on basic values and matters of right and wrong, thereby providing a relatively unified voice in terms of their influence on teenagers.

By 1980, just 20 years later, friends and peers had jumped to number one as the greatest influencer of teenage values and behavior. The family dropped to number two, and media jumped onto the list at number three. School dropped two notches to number four, and the church dropped out of the top-four list altogether.[92] In addition to the change in order and relative strength of the influences, teenagers were hearing mixed messages, as these institutions couldn't agree on basic values.

What would this list look like if the data was gathered and evaluated during the first few years of the twenty-first century? Media would be at the top of the list. Friends and peers, immersed in and influenced by the same media voices, would drop to number two; while the family would fall to number three. School would stay at number four.

One group of six college professors conducted an 11-month study of this growing, changing, and powerful influence of music and media on youth. Their goal was to understand and evaluate the relationship between media and teenagers. Without any axes to grind or agendas to advance, their research culminated in what I believe is the most informed and balanced discussion of teenagers and popular music available today. The thesis of their book, *Dancing in the Dark*, is "youth and the electronic media today are dependent upon each other. The media needs the youth market, as it's called, for their own economic survival. *Youth, in turn, need the media for guidance and nurture in a society where other social institutions, such as the family and the school, do not shape the youth culture as powerfully as they once did* (italics mine).[93] In other words, media is raising the kids.

The authors of *Dancing in the Dark* suggest that the entertainment industry has developed the masterful ability to provide teenagers with "maps of reality" that serve to guide them through the maze of adolescence and into adulthood. Media interprets and defines life for teenagers. It suggests legitimate and proper responses to the different situations, problems, and opportunities teenagers will face each day. It serves to define the meaning of life, values, attitudes, behavioral norms, and social and gender roles.[94] Media has become a powerful socialization authority for teenagers. It's as if music holds out its attractive and inviting hand while saying, "Teenager, I know you're confused and full of questions. Come with me and I'll show you the way." Today's media is "extremely well-suited to provide information relevant to many of the questions adolescents face."[95] Neil Postman has said, "Whether we are experiencing the world through the lens of speech or the printed word or the television camera, our media-metaphors classify the world for us, sequence it, frame it, enlarge it, reduce it, color it, argue a case for what the world is like."[96]

Media Shapes Adolescent Worldviews

What's a worldview? Scholars and critics have defined it in a variety of ways. According to Christian scholar James Sire, "A worldview is a commitment, a fundamental orientation of the heart, that can be expressed as a story or in a set of presuppositions (assumptions which may be true, partially true or entirely false) which we hold (consciously or subconsciously, consistently or inconsistently) about the basic constitution of reality, and that provides the foundation on which we live and move and have our being."[97] Another definition is that it "is simply the sum total of our beliefs about the world, the 'big picture' that directs our daily decisions and actions."[98] And, a "worldview is variously described as a lens, a model, a picture, or a framework consisting of fundamental beliefs through which we view the world and our calling and future in it."[99]

"Picture for a minute the face of a young person you know. Now, put a set of glasses on that face. Those glasses represent his or her worldview—the lenses through which he or she views and interprets all of life. Those glasses shape his or her presuppositions, principles and convictions. They color every thought, decision, value, attitude, and behavior in their world."[100] Each teenager lives his or her worldview every day. It's the basis for how they think and act. Some of us consciously choose our worldviews; but more often than not, teenagers assimilate their worldviews as unconscious and subconscious collections of information they've picked up along the way. Much of that information comes from media.

A quick glance at today's youth culture shows that our teenagers have embraced media's directive power, allowing it to shape their thoughts, beliefs, values, decisions, and behaviors. Granted, few teenagers consciously decide to be socialized and nurtured by music and media. No study has ever shown that kids turn on the television, go to a movie, or listen to a downloaded song for the purpose of learning. This doesn't mean, however, that media doesn't teach or communicate information. Learning takes place even when learning isn't the reason for listening or watching. Although I've never turned on my television to watch the commercials, I still see them, and they influence me.

The changing values of young people globally on issues related to sexuality, politics, authority, God, body image, violence, alcohol and tobacco use, and personal and corporate morality, stem greatly from the cranked-up volume and growing pervasiveness of media and its principal players.

Media Shapes Kids' Behaviors

Sometime during the mid-1960s, three little boys got in big trouble. Their behavior around the house was increasingly out of control. While they claimed it was all being done in fun, there were times when their make-believe eye pokes, kicks, slaps, and pratfalls led to anger, tears, and real fights. It wasn't long before their mother and father discovered the boys were only imitating antics they'd seen during their daily dose of *The Three Stooges*. My brothers and I still maintain our innocence, but that didn't stop our parents from removing Moe, Larry, and Curly from our TV diet for a few weeks.

It's been said that art imitates life, but there is a very real sense in which life imitates art. The experience of my parents' three impressionable young boys is representative of all teenagers and adults. The fact is that whether we realize it or not, what we see, hear, and experience in and through the media influences our behaviors.

Imagine for a moment you're going to separately visit three middle-school-aged boys who live in three very different communities. One lives in the inner city of Detroit. Another lives in a wealthy, upper-middle-class suburb of Philadelphia. The last lives on a remote farm situated on the plains of Nebraska. At each stop you arrive unannounced and knock on the door. While the three settings couldn't be more diverse, something amazing happens each time a 13-year-old boy answers the door. In every case the boys look, dress, talk, and act very much alike. Why? They've all grown up spending several hours a day immersed in the same media offerings.

Welcome to the ever-growing and changing world of today's media and its ability to shape the behaviors of vulnerable teenagers. The dynamic language of our kids provides more evidence of media's power to shape a generation. Parents are often baffled by the strange slang terms heard in the course of teenage conversation. Those who long to understand the ever-expanding nuances of urban street slang can consult *The Hip Hoptionary* by Alonzo Westbrook, an English to hip-hop and hip-hop to English dictionary. The rise in instant and text messaging fostered the growth of a whole new lexicon of abbreviations and emoticons largely unknown or understood by older folks. Have you heard your kids say something new, confusing, and unusual lately? It might have something to do with the influential world of their music and media.

Hair and clothing styles are also heavily influenced by teenage media heroes, most of whom have been hired and commissioned to deliberately market new styles so manufacturers can tap into the growing disposable income of teenagers. Some of these media icons have tapped into the market themselves by launching lines of clothing, hair care products, cosmetics, footwear, and a host of other consumer goods. While the tendency to follow the fashions of the stars is nothing new, the visual bombardment of music videos and product placements in films, television shows, and on the Internet allows more—and younger—kids to keep up with the latest fashion, language, and behavioral trends like never before. Media has fueled and fed youth culture's obsession with style, clothing, and being on the front end of the latest trends.

Because of where they're at developmentally, teenagers are especially vulnerable to media's messages that model and portray behaviors as right, wrong, normal, and so on. Most of these messages are embedded in stories and pictures, so media's power to guide kids' behavior is on the rise. When media offers depictions of sex without boundaries or consequences, teenagers are prone to initiate sexual activity earlier, more often, and in a variety of ways. Teenagers who view depictions of characters who smoke and drink are more prone to engage in those behaviors themselves. More research shows that violent media can lead kids to see violence as a legitimate and normative conflict resolution strategy.

Media has become one of the most effective teachers, preachers, and evangelists of our time. Its following is an entire youth culture. Its power lies in its ability to define reality and shape world- and life views. And its messages are providing guidance to a generation that is being molded in the image of media itself.

Media's Multiple Outlets

If media is limitless in its ability to send life-shaping messages to teenagers, the ongoing development of new media technologies will only strengthen that ability as kids spend more time engaging with a growing number of media options as they pass through adolescence on the way to adulthood. It seems as though the sky's the limit when it comes to the new and different ways teenagers are accessing and using media.

The rise in portable media devices makes media content more accessible. In days gone by, kids had to sit with media in their homes, rooms, and cars in order to listen or watch. The development of the portable transistor radio allowed music to "follow" the kids wherever they went. Most recently, portable multiplatform devices allow kids on the move to always be in touch with music, video, television, the Internet, and their friends (through text messaging, e-mail, cell phone conversations, and so on). Consequently, media has become more pervasive, personal, and influential in the lives of teenagers.

While the rate of media device and technology development has accelerated to the point where what's new today might be outdated tomorrow, there are still some media forms and outlets that kids will be accessing and using for a long time. What follows is a summary of several of these forms and outlets, with an emphasis on popular music.

Popular Music

There's no question popular music, through numerous outlets, is impacting and educating our teenagers. Even when parents are present and the school and church are doing their jobs, music remains a powerful influence that must be recognized, understood, and addressed. Bruce Springsteen recognized the power of music to define reality when he wrote "No Surrender" for his landmark album *Born in the USA:* "We busted out of class/ had to get away from those fools/ We learned more from a three-minute record/ than we ever learned in school." Two decades later, murdered Pantera guitarist "Dimebag" Darrell Abbott was memorialized in *Rolling Stone* magazine. The obituary quoted Abbott's feelings about his personal connection with music, a connection I've heard verbalized by numerous teenagers: "It's our f____ religion. It's what drives me from the moment I wake up to the moment I sleep."[101]

Kids are listening. In some ways, our kids are no different than we were growing up. We loved our music and we spent lots of time listening to it. Of course, our access was limited to a transistor radio, a car radio, a record player, a stereo, and perhaps an eight-track or cassette tape player. (Remember those?) Today's kids no longer have to tune into the radio or drive to the record store to get their music fix—even though many still do. They're able to use the Internet to access and download the music of their choice to a variety of portable listening devices based on their ever-changing personal preferences and moods.

The average teenager in America listens to lots of music every day. Early studies based on radio-only listening estimated the amount at two hours a day. More recent studies put the estimate at more than five hours a day.[102] Hard-and-fast data is difficult to come by since teenagers often report being engaged in other activities while music is playing in the background. For example, the most recent and exhaustive survey of eight- to 18-year-olds conducted by the Kaiser Family Foundation reports that the average eight- to 18-year-old listens to one hour and 44 minutes of music (radio, CDs, tapes, mp3s) a day, with older teenagers (15- to 18-year-olds) listening two hours and 24 minutes a day.[103] And it's reasonable to assume they're listening to much more music than they're reporting. When surveyed about how they use their time, teenagers' second most frequent activity is "listening to CDs, tapes, records, mp3s" (ranked right after "watching TV"), and their fourth most frequent activity is "listening to the radio" (ranked right after "hanging out with friends").[104] During the six years from grades seven to 12, the average teenager will have listened to 10,500 hours of music, just slightly less than the 11 thousand hours spent in the classroom from kindergarten through high school.[105] Most adolescent listening takes place alone in one's room, through headphones, or while riding in the car.

In a typical day, 74 percent of eight- to 18-year-olds report listening to the radio, and 68 percent report listening to a CD, tape, or mp3.[106] Most eight- to 18-year-olds are able to easily access music in their homes, as 99 percent of their homes have a CD/tape player and 98 percent have a radio. Slightly fewer have a CD/tape player (86 percent) and a radio (84 percent) in their rooms. In addition, kids with computers and Internet access have a 24-hour gateway to limitless artist/band Web sites, music and video downloads, Internet radio stations, and more. While the percentage of kids with this access is snowballing, recent studies show computers in 86 percent of the homes of eight- to 18-year-olds, and 20 percent of all eight- to 18-year-olds already had Internet access in their bedrooms.[107] With the use of computers and portable players to download and listen to music on the rise, sales of CDs continue to drop, while legal downloads of single tracks have more than doubled.[108]

Several studies and surveys point to the fact that teenagers who do homework without music are the exception. In one study, more than 58 percent of the students surveyed said they "often" or "always" listen to music while doing homework.[109] "Most adolescents report studying with music a good part of the time."[110]

While music serves to fill the time and minds of kids, teenagers' interests fill the pockets of those involved in the business. Stars are offered multimillion-dollar recording contracts. Kids spend big money to purchase or download the music (although about one-third of all CDs worldwide are copied illegally), attend the concerts (generating millions in ticket receipts), and buy large amounts of music-related merchandise (T-shirts, posters, and other items).

One thing is clear: Statistics on how kids spend their money and their time prove that the childhood and adolescent love affair with popular music shows no signs of slowing down. Kids like to listen to music, and the lyrics serve as a powerful shaper of their values, attitudes, worldviews, and behaviors.

Kids are watching—from MTV to MTV.com. My first exposure to popular music allowed my imagination to run wild. While I could hear the music through my trusty transistor radio, it was my mind's eye fueled by my imagination that allowed me to "see" the performers and create visual images to accompany my favorite songs. While I could visually identify each of the Beatles by name, the endless line of other popular recording artists was nothing more than songs and voices. I rarely saw them. Then, that all changed.

August 1, 1981 might be the most significant date in entertainment history. It was 12:01 AM when MTV came on the air with the Buggles' video, "Video Killed the Radio Star." Suddenly, the world was able to "watch music." It was the dawn of the video age and the beginning of a phenomenon that was to change the face of global popular culture. No understanding of the power of popular music and media is complete without a short look at the MTV story.

The popular music industry hit rock bottom as record sales plummeted during the late seventies (blame it on disco). Virgin Records chief Jeff Aygin recalls, "We (the record industry) were looking for a savior and it came in the form of MTV."[112] Record sales skyrocketed, and popular music found new life as exposure on MTV almost guaranteed a group's success.

In those early days, MTV reached only 1.5 million homes and it was the only all-music cable channel available. Its reach was limited, as cable operators didn't want to take a chance on a channel that was programmed with round-the-clock music videos. In response, MTV launched a direct-marketing campaign using leaflets, television commercials, and other forms of advertising. Using the slogan "I want my MTV," the network had found its way into 10.7 million homes by 1982 and 18.9 million homes by 1983. MTV is now a fixture on virtually all cable systems across the United States. Currently reaching almost 500 million households worldwide, MTV has become a major commercial and educational force. In fact, it's now the world's largest network. The authors of *Dancing in the Dark* call it "one of the most powerful forms of contemporary propaganda."[113]

MTV founder and chairman Robert Pittman was the heart and soul behind MTV. His quotes from the early days speak volumes about the concept behind MTV, the reasons for its success, its development over the years, and its enormous impact on shaping not only individual kids, but also global youth culture:

- "We're dealing with a culture of TV babies. They can watch, do their homework, and listen to music all at the same time."

- "The strongest appeal you can make...is emotionally. If you can get their emotions going, [make them] forget their logic, you've got 'em."

- "At MTV we don't shoot for the 14-year-olds, we own them."

- "The only people who can understand the new way to use that television set are the people who grew up with it... They...will accept almost anything over that screen."[114]

Originally and for a good portion of its history, MTV's programming was anchored around the music video. Almost all the videos played on MTV are furnished free of charge by record companies. In effect, the network has functioned as a 24-hour commercial. In his book *Pop Culture Wars*, Bill Romanowski writes, "MTV is aimed at passive consumers. Its primary if not exclusive purpose, as executives see it, is to maximize its profits as a promotional tool for the entertainment industry."[115]

Growing yearly profits have allowed the network to expand way above and beyond the music-video format. In fact, video programming fills very little of the network's daily schedule. The network features a variety of shows focusing on political and social issues, music news, fashion, sports, and sexuality. In addition, they've launched numerous original reality shows featuring music icons, entertainment stars, everyday people, and extreme sports players. MTV has created movies, animated series, and ongoing dramas. Other shows run the gamut from concerts to car make-overs to group living to risk-taking and stunts to over-the-top birthday parties for spoiled rich kids.

In August 1996, MTV launched M2 (now MTV2), a sister network featuring round-the-clock-all-video programming. Since 1981, they've added numerous other networks including mtvU, VH1, Music First, Logo, Nickelodeon, Comedy Central, Spike TV, and many more. One of the most successful ventures in TV history, MTV has become a cultural institution. In fact, it was the first media outlet (prior to the Internet) to shrink the globe by erasing geographic cultural boundaries and replacing them with a worldwide youth culture. MTV now estimates at least one of their networks is available in one-third of the world's homes. Part of the Viacom family of entertainment companies, MTV Networks—the world's largest television network—reaches almost 500 million households in more than 165 territories and more than 25 languages via more than 120 locally operated TV channels. It reaches millions more households and kids through its more than 100 Web sites. MTV estimates about 80 percent of its viewership now lives outside the United States. Today's kids, teenagers, and young adults haven't known a world without MTV.

The impact of MTV's innovative approach to programming and production led to wholesale changes throughout the entertainment industry. Record companies began to sign, develop, and market stars whose visual appearance sometimes eclipsed their musical ability.

Prime-time broadcast television immediately felt the ripple of MTV. In 1983 then NBC programming chief Brandon Tartikoff wrote the words "MTV cops" on a piece of paper and handed it to TV producer Anthony Yerkovich. From that came the hit series *Miami Vice*, a slightly surrealistic police show with a sound track featuring some of the most popular rock singers and bands of the time. In many ways, it was a one-hour video. Yerkovich acknowledges MTV "reeducated and expanded people's capacities and brought a new style of storytelling to the small screen."[116] Today, MTV's mark on television programming can be seen not only in production techniques, but in the fact most shows targeting a teenage and preteenage audience include soundtracks featuring carefully placed artists and songs—both new and old alike—in an effort to not only connect with kids, but to sell music.

The movie industry also followed MTV's lead back in the '80s with films like *Flashdance, Footloose, Pump Up the Volume,* and a rash of other productions with popular music soundtracks. Some of the films were actually extended music videos with the plot unfolding between the songs. Today, film soundtracks featuring popular music are often released prior to the film in the hope that excitement will be generated not just about the film, but about the featured musical artists.

Advertising has also been influenced and changed by MTV. Phillip Dusenberry, chairman of the ad agency for Pepsi and Apple Computers, says, "MTV's impact, first and foremost, is as a teacher. It has educated people, particularly young people, to accept lots of information in a short period of time."[117] Commercials aimed at young consumers are like rock videos. Visual, aural, and technical trickery all reflect the influence of MTV. At times, it's difficult to distinguish between music videos and commercials. Since the advent of MTV, commercials have increasingly featured music taken from well-known popular songs, most of it sung by the original artists themselves. Have you paid attention to television ads lately? Listen for popular music—both present and past—and you'll see how music from the different decades is being used to target and sell to each particular generation.

In the more than 25 years since MTV burst onto the scene, numerous other all-music television networks have been created (BET, CMT, VH1) and built around a variety of genres and programming to satisfy our culture's growing love affair with both watching and listening to music. In addition, a growing number of Internet sites allow visitors to view and download music videos on demand at no charge. MTV and other networks like it are effective teachers that keep kids' attention. And it's these networks, record companies, and advertisers whose pockets overflow with the bounty of an attentive teenage and preteenage market segment. Gone are the days of listening only. MTV, other music networks, and the Internet have changed all that by adding the visual dimension to the world of popular music.

Shortly after celebrating their 10th anniversary, the folks at MTV ran a one-page ad in an advertising journal in an effort to entice marketers to advertise on their network. The ad featured the back of a young man's head with the MTV logo cut into his hair. Underneath were these words: "Ever hear anyone refer to the NBC generation? MTV is not a TV channel. It's a cultural force. People don't watch it. They live it. MTV has affected the way an entire generation thinks, talks and buys. No other network can say that." Sound boastful? Yes. But it's also true.

How Does Music Mold and Shape Kids?

When I was in elementary school, I often fell asleep listening to the Philadelphia Phillies lose baseball games via my trusty nine-volt transistor radio. And that little radio also introduced me to the exciting world of popular music. It wasn't long before I was spending more time with the Beatles, the Monkees, and the Mamas and Papas than with the Phillies. But in the sixties, our windows into the life-shaping world of music were limited to a transistor radio, a few scratched-up 45s, and an occasional hour of *American Bandstand*.

Today, CDs, mp3s, expensive car "systems," elaborate home theater setups, hundreds of broadcast and satellite radio stations, 24-hour music television, fan magazines, concert tours, the Internet, and a host of other media outlets have made music a powerful teacher. How does music shape and teach our teenagers? Let's look at four avenues: lyrics, visual images, highly publicized lifestyles, and concerts.

Learning from the lyrics. While many kids say they don't listen to the words of songs, experience and observation prove otherwise. If you've driven in the car with a teenager while the radio is on, you know they usually sing along to their favorite tunes. After hearing the song only a few times, most kids know the words. Like childhood nursery rhymes, the ABCs, and the books of the Bible, words and concepts are much easier to learn and recall when put to music. When was the last time you tuned into an "oldies" station and heard a song from your own adolescent past? Perhaps months and years have passed since you last heard that song. But most likely, you were able to sing or at least hum along.

Teenagers approach popular music with dozens of adolescent questions, open minds, and a limited and undeveloped sense of discernment. They're like sponges, soaking up anything that fits into their pores without questioning its composition or the effect it might have on them. Researchers have discovered that some kids are more vulnerable to lyrical messages than others. Those who place more importance on the role of music in their lives place greater importance on the lyrics. Especially vulnerable are kids who've experienced chaos, loss, or relational breakdown. They tend to be drawn to music that expresses their own experiences and feelings.

Fans of more aggressive music styles, such as hard rock, heavy metal, and hip-hop—i.e., music that's typically oppositional, defiant, alienating, threatening, or controversial with regard to mainstream culture—also tend to pay greater attention to the lyrics.[118] "In hip-hop we've got a couple of generations of fatherless kids who haven't been given any direction," said veteran rapper Chuck D of the group Public Enemy, "and there's a certain type of face that's put out there because of what sells, and that's gonna have an effect. A nine-year-old is gonna be influenced by what a 20-year-old says."[119]

Singers and songwriters believe in what they write and what they sing; their songs express different aspects of their worldview. By packaging their messages in music that's appealing to young ears, they become powerful and effective teachers.

I've often heard both parents and teenagers protest and argue that the singers "don't really believe or mean what they're singing. It's just a song." This isn't true for a number of reasons. First, Jesus made it clear that our words reflect who we really are and what we believe (Matthew 12:34; 15:18). Second, our experiences as people who communicate affirm Jesus' point. While we may say some things we "don't really mean," it's the conviction of our hearts that it's all right to say them—otherwise, we'd just be quiet. And third, the singers and songwriters admit their desire to express themselves through their songs.

Madonna, one of the most enduring pop stars of the last two decades, says, "With everything I do, I ask two questions: Am I being true to myself, and does it say what I want to say? It's not about pushing limits, it's about expression."[120] She's not alone. Most musicians readily admit their songs reflect who they are, the issues they've faced in life, their hopes, their beliefs, their failures, and their dreams.

The tendency to think that many popular song lyrics, particularly those that are sexually or violently explicit, are intended as a joke and shouldn't be taken seriously is dangerous and naive. While this may be true in a very limited number of cases, by what criteria does one decide the song in question is being sung in jest? If we're never told, we don't know. How can kids and young teenagers, without the benefit of well-developed critical faculties, discern between the satirical and the serious? And even if the song is a joke, there's still a good chance the lyrics will lead listeners to laugh at something that isn't the least bit funny.

The classic case of this lyrics-as-a-joke line of reasoning proves just how much this mind-set has permeated our way of thinking and clouded our good sense. Way back in 1990, the rap band 2 Live Crew stretched bad taste with the song "Me So Horny." The lyrics described the singer's insatiable appetite for sex along with violent descriptions of sexual acts including oral sex, anal sex, and "busting" a girl's vagina. They were acquitted of obscenity charges in a Fort Lauderdale courtroom by six jurors who explained they regarded the lyrics as "comedy," but certainly not obscene. One juror even said, "In this day and age, this is the vernacular of youth."[121]

Assume for a minute these lyrics *are* just a joke and intended to be funny. If teenagers grow up on this type of lyrical diet without realizing it's a joke (which I don't for one minute believe it really is), they'll assume this type of sexual behavior is normal, acceptable, and laughable. Unfortunately, repeated exposure might lead to these kinds of songs representing the way kids talk and act.

It's been almost two decades since 2 Live Crew's 15 minutes of fame, but the bounds of decency have continued to stretch since that time, perhaps proving that ideas and beliefs expressed through lyrics do, over time, take root and grow. In a postmodern world where right and wrong are negotiable, music can and does introduce kids to values, attitudes, and behaviors that although now seen as neutral and normal, used to be viewed as wrong. Our culture's continued bent on objectifying and using women is just one example of how this plays out.

Whether positive or negative, the lyrics of today's music speak loud and clear to a generation that is looking and listening for someone to give them answers.

Learning from the images. The visual dimension of music has not only smothered the use of the imagination and created a generation of passive viewers and listeners, but it's also increased the ability of popular music to shape our kids for better or for worse. Educators know that the most effective teaching strategies are multipronged, engaging students by appealing to more than one of their senses. Lessons that are heard *and* seen are far more likely to "stick" than those that are only heard. Researchers have found that "the marriage between television and music is powerful... Multi-sensory input reinforces any message, specifically by enhancing learning and recall."[122] That powerful influence increases for those who spend the most time watching music. With 73 percent of boys and 78 percent of girls ages 12 to 19 watching, there's a good chance your teenagers are in the mix.[123]

The visual component of today's music videos serves many purposes. In some cases the video clarifies the meaning of a song. In others, the surrealistic and dreamlike nature of many videos, enhanced with numerous special effects, can serve to confuse a song's meaning and do more to facilitate sensory overload than enhance the song's message. This is especially true in a postmodern world where a pastiche of random and confusing images combine with the lyrics to leave viewers sometimes scratching their heads. In other cases, video "stories" add meanings that are not obvious in the lyrics.

A summary of the experimental research done on the results of exposure to music videos shows that videos do affect "how teenagers and college undergraduates perceive, interpret, evaluate, and respond to a variety of social stimuli."[124] In their book, *It's Not Only Rock & Roll*, Peter Christenson and Donald Roberts offer this summary of several key studies:

- Videos laced with many violent images made viewers more antagonistic in their orientation toward women and more likely to condone violence against themselves and others.

- Antisocial videos increased acceptance of subsequently observed antisocial behavior.

- Highly gender-stereotyped videos increased acceptance of gender-stereotyped behavior.

- Sexually charged videos led viewers to perceive subsequently observed ambiguous behavior as sexier and to be more accepting of premarital sex.

- Rap videos in general reduced academic aspirations among African American teenagers.

- Politically radical rap videos caused white teenagers to become more racially tolerant and less likely to sympathize with reactionary racial political positions.[125]

Popular music's ability to teach kids visually extends beyond the music videos to the world of album covers and musician-related artwork. The drawings, paintings, and photos that appear on the inside and outside of CD packaging are art forms that serve to describe the contents inside the package while communicating a message. Once they're opened, they contain lots of additional artwork and photography and textual content, offering additional input and lessons to kids who choose to read what's written. In addition, virtually all bands and artists have extensive Web sites featuring additional visual content, including band pictures, screensavers, and desktop themes. Whether good or bad, these images communicate messages to our kids.

The already powerful ability of music to educate and shape reality for our teenagers is greatly enhanced when it engages the mind through more than just the ears.

Learning from lifestyles. Madonna's story is the classic example of how a performer's lifestyle can mold young hearts and minds. When she began singing and dancing her way to stardom way back in 1985, Madonna was an immediate hit, especially with the pre-teen and young teenage audience. She was radically new and different from anyone or anything ever seen in the music industry. Her songs and image were a strange mixture of schoolgirl innocence, sexual suggestiveness, and religious imagery. But her first hit song, "Like a Virgin," was not about Mary the mother of Jesus.

Shortly after she arrived on the scene, thousands of elementary schoolgirls joined the legion of Madonna wannabes. Their moms and dads were shocked to learn about the unwritten wannabe dress code that included everything from wearing innocently teased hair piled high in a scarf to wearing black lacy undergarments as outerwear. One of her early concert performances was described as follows: "A sweaty pin-up girl come to life. She wiggled her tummy and shook her a--. She smiled lasciviously and stuck out her tongue. She rolled around on stage and got down on her knees in front of a guitarist. And when she raised her arms, her scanty see-through blouse also rose, revealing her purple brassiere...What Madonna is really about is sex, and there was plenty of that."[126]

In the years since 1985, Madonna has endured by continuing to change her image, maintaining her popularity while other singers have long since been forgotten. Her self-proclaimed one-woman crusade to change America has extended beyond the world of lyrics and video to include books, kids' books, movies, television appearances, and a pervasive Internet presence. She has allowed young people an ongoing voyeuristic look into her own personal worldview and lifestyle. Now older than 40, she's teaching lessons on how to be a mother. She's also living and promoting Kabbalah, a hybrid of Judaism and mysticism that plays well in our postmodern world. Kids thinking consciously about their spirituality and what to believe are also embracing Kabbalah.

With Madonna, nobody knows what's next. As a pop culture icon, she's become a woman whose offstage lifestyle may have become more influentially powerful than the sum total of her music. In effect, Madonna became a brand, adopted by and assimilated into millions of lives; she'll most likely continue to play a powerful role in shaping and educating anyone who's willing to listen to her.

An interviewer once asked Madonna if she saw herself as a "kind of sexual missionary." This was her response: "I suppose that's one way to look at it...Sex is the metaphor that I use, but for me really, it's about love. It's about tolerance, acceptance and saying, 'Look, everybody has different needs and wants and preferences and desires and fantasies. And we should not damn or judge somebody because it's different than yours.'"[127]

Madonna knows people are listening and watching. With so many glimpses allowed into her life, more than two decades' worth of fans and followers can't help but know what she stands for. Over the years, she's been a part of stretching the moral and ethical bounds of our culture on everything from sexuality to spirituality.

Madonna is just one example of how the public and private lifestyles of the stars shape young lives. Kids know more than the lyrics and videos of music's movers and shakers. Television tabloids, reality shows, MTV specials, fan magazines, Web sites, along with Internet chat rooms and forums, allow kids unprecedented access into the lifestyles of today's music and media heroes. When the stars change hairstyles, clothes, language, values, and behaviors, the kids are sure to follow. When the stars engage in substance abuse, violent behavior, cohabitation, gambling, marital infidelity and breakdown, and all sorts of sexual activity, the modeling of how to live one's life in this world is taking place.

And lest we assume this type of imitation is all negative and dangerous, we should remember it can also have a positive impact. When stars such as U2's Bono become involved in charitable social causes and relief efforts, our kids benefit from imitating his lead.

Today's teenagers have been given more than a peek into the private and public lives of popular music heroes. Sadly, the messages these stars communicate, which help define reality for our kids, are all too often opposed to those things God says are good, true, right, and honorable, rather than being positive and godly.

Learning from concerts. Another educational avenue of popular music is the live concert. Not just an opportunity for kids to see their heroes in person and to hear their favorite songs performed live, concerts include so much more, such as elaborate staging and sets, choreographed stage shows, and between-song chatter. Any adult who decides to attend a concert may come out saying, "Boy, did I ever get an education."

In today's world, a growing number of concerts feature on-stage antics including simulated sex, profanity, pornography, and cultural criticism related to a wide variety of social issues. It's not unusual for certain artists to be under the influence of alcohol or drugs while performing, encouraging the audience to do the same (and many of them have probably heeded these instructions well).

While not all concerts are celebrations of hedonism and debauchery, it's a good idea to be aware of what's going on at concerts. A quick Internet search using an artist's name along with the words *concert review* will yield critical reviews of past concerts. Visiting an artist's official Web site can also be informative, as it often includes links to descriptive reviews. Many artists have faithful and loyal fans who create unofficial fan sites where detailed reports of concerts, song set lists, and discussion forums can be found. Spending some time clicking around on these sites can be a valuable avenue for learning more about an artist's onstage behavior and banter.

What Music Do Your Kids Listen To?

Rolling Stone magazine once asked its readers to vote for their favorite songs of all time and to defend their votes in a brief essay. Reader after reader responded with eye-opening comments, some of them baring their souls to show how important music is in their lives. One comment not only stuck out, but it continues to offer insight into popular music's powerful ability to connect with kids.

Cathy, a 16-year-old from California, wrote: "I had been an abused child all my life, and something about the music moved me. Feelings of hurt and anger that had been bottled up all those years took over. I started shaking and crying, and that night I made the decision that what they were doing to me was wrong and I wasn't going to let anyone use me as a punching bag ever again." Cathy goes on to describe how she wound up in court and eventually moved in with her grandparents for a year and that the song kept her from committing suicide.[128]

Cathy's comments give us insight into the incredible role popular music plays during the years of adolescent development and confusion. Many are experiencing deep relational problems and breakdown. One of the reasons kids are drawn to certain types of music and bands is that the music speaks to them, addressing their specific problems and circumstances.

Media as "mirror." Earlier, we looked at the fact that media is a map that defines reality, shapes worldviews, and guides kids through adolescence and into adulthood, teaching them how to live in the world. But there's another side to media that parents and youth workers must understand. It also serves as a mirror. For those of us who care about and want to understand kids, one of the best ways to get to know them, their cares, concerns, and problems is to stand over their shoulders and look at the "mirror" of their media interests and preferences, allowing their media to speak for them and show us what's going on in their minds, hearts, and lives.

Dean Borgman has spent years studying the power of media in the lives of young people. He recognizes that media's function is multifaceted. For kids who wander through adolescence without a place to belong, media often serves as an escape from the pile of cares, concerns, and pain in their lives. And when we look into the mirror of their media, those cares, concerns, and pain will jump out at us. For some kids, media gives them a voice that frees them from social neglect; for others it's a form of lament, much like the biblical psalms. At times, media serves as a form of protest against being victimized and oppressed. It can be a way to express and work out anger. It can even go so far as to serve as religion, especially where the church has not spoken into a young person's life.[129]

Perhaps music—because there's so much of it and kids can choose that which speaks best to them and for them—is the biggest and brightest media "mirror" at our disposal. While we might feel frightened and threatened by what we see when we look over their shoulders, it will open our eyes to their realities and help us to communicate with teenagers and lead them to spiritual health. Knowing their music helps us know and communicate with them.

Hans Rookmaaker spent his life critiquing art and music from the perspective of his deep Christian faith. He discovered that art and music are never neutral. They always reflect the worldview and "religion" of the artist, even if the artist denies the God of the Bible. In this sense, popular music is always "true" since it expresses the artist's reality. At the same time, we know it's a lie if God is denied or left out of the account. So should we ignore popular music that lies? Rookmaaker shouts an emphatic "NO!" He says, "This art (music) is the work of your neighbors, your contemporaries, human beings (your kids!) who are crying out in despair for the loss of their humanity, their values, their lost absolutes, groping in the dark for answers. It is already late, if not too late, but if we want to help our generation (our kids) we must hear their cry. We must listen to them as they cry out from their prison, the prison of a universe which is aimless, meaningless, absurd."[130]

Take away their music, and the questions, struggles, problems, and pain remain. Stand behind them and look into the mirror of their music, and your eyes will open to the issues you need to lovingly discuss and address. I realized a long time ago that if I want to intimately know teenagers, I need to stop and listen long and hard to them *and* their music.

The American Medical Association has said, "Physicians should be aware of the role of music in the lives of adolescents and use music preferences as clues to the emotional and mental health of adolescents."[131] But it's not enough for parents and youth workers to understand the power of media and music to mold and shape adolescent reality. It's not enough to understand the many teaching strategies and outlets media employs. And it's not enough to have a working knowledge of the prominent themes in popular music. Parents and youth workers must go a step further and understand the different types of popular music, the unique features of each genre, and the reasons why kids are drawn to certain bands and types of music. As Dean Borgman says, "Behind music that shocks are often neglected social and personal issues needing to be explored."[132]

Make use of the Internet. A simple Web search of a band's or artist's name will yield countless Web sites that will take you into the world (lyrics, histories, biographies, photos, genre information, and so on) of that band or artist. Also make a point of regularly visiting the home page of the Center for Parent/Youth Understanding (www.cpyu.org), where information on youth culture, media, and music is updated daily. In addition, you'll find loads of helpful music and media links.

For a more detailed explanation of musical genres and subgenres, visit the Ultimate Band List (www.ubl.com) and Wikipedia (http://en.wikipedia.org), where you can search for information by genre. (And you can visit the CPYU Web site for supplemental information in relation to this book, including a detailed summary of music genres and how they function in the lives of children and teenagers.)

The world of music changes continually by design. Record companies are constantly signing and releasing new bands and artists. While the task may seem overwhelming, parents and youth workers can and must take the time to know what is happening on the popular music scene. While your kids may or may not spend as much time watching music videos or listening to music as others kids do, they're living in a world where most teenagers *are* listening. Our kids are part of an emerging youth culture defined and directed by the music and musicians they listen to. As a result of his research, George Barna has concluded that "for teenagers, music is much more than mere entertainment or a diversion from the stress of homework, household chores and worries about the future. For millions of young people, music produces a life philosophy for them to consider and follow; cultural heroes and role models to look up to and imitate; values and lifestyles to embrace; a common language to employ that sets them apart and provides a distinctive identity; and the opportunity to develop community related to a shared sense of common sound, ideas or artists."[133] By knowing the world of your teenager's music, you'll be better equipped to know your teenager, understand the world of teenagers, and lead yours into a healthy adulthood.

In short, kids know music. The music industry knows your kids. Get to know your kids by getting to know their music.

Television

There's a house in my neighborhood that stands as a late-night monument to the place of television in American culture. Night after night, the eerie blue glow of the television provides the only visible illumination in the house. For many men, women, and kids,

TV has taken its place as an illuminator, clarifying and explaining life.

Television first captured the imagination of Americans at the 1939 World's Fair. Network service began in the late forties, and by the 1950s the medium was growing by leaps and bounds.

In his book *Redeeming Television*, Quentin Schultze calls television "one of the major educators of modern society."[134] As television communicates its lessons to a passive and usually uncritical audience, it becomes, as communications theorist George Comstock has said, "an unavoidable and unremitting factor in shaping what we are and what we will become."[135] We're all vulnerable to the messages of television. Among other things, television teaches us how to resolve problems, how to relate to others, how families function, what to wear, how to talk, how to walk, and how to love.

Because of where they're at developmentally, teenagers are especially vulnerable to television's influence. Like popular music, television's ability to define reality and guide teenagers through life has increased over time in proportion to the decreasing influence of the family, school, and church. Parental influences deteriorate when parents are absent from the home or oblivious to what their teenagers are watching. These kids learn about life and the outside world from someone other than Mom or Dad. All too often, that someone is the electronic babysitter. As long as they have the ability to turn on the TV and operate the remote, kids of all ages have unlimited access to television's good and bad, including information and programming that is often unsuitable for adults.

Television facts and figures. Children's book author E. B. White once predicted that television "is going to be the test of the modern world...We shall stand or fall by television."[136] If White was right, then television's pervasiveness in our culture and world should cause us to evaluate ourselves to see if we're standing tall or teetering dangerously.

- In 1946 there were 10,000 television sets in America; by 1950, 10.5 million sets; by 1960, 54 million sets.[137]

- The Nielsen Media Research organization reported that by 1995, 99 percent of American households owned televisions. In fact, more owned televisions than phones.[138]

- By the end of the twentieth century, 99 percent of kids ages two to 18 lived in homes with a TV set. Sixty percent lived with three or more TVs, and more than half had a television in their bedrooms.[139]

- Today, almost three-quarters (73 percent) of all eight- to 18-year-olds live in a home with three or more televisions. Fourteen percent of homes contain five or more.[140]

- Almost seven out of 10 teenagers (68 percent) have a television in their bedrooms, with 37 percent having cable or satellite hookups to those televisions, and 20 percent receiving premium channels.[141]

- Believe it or not, 43 percent of all four- to six-year-olds and 30 percent of all zero- to three-year-olds have a television in their bedrooms.[142]

Not only are Americans faced with choosing which of their TVs to watch, but they're also given a smorgasbord of channel choices. In 1996, the average American could choose from 27 different channels.[143] That's a long way from the four VHF and four UHF stations my family could access when I was a teenager—and that happened only when the rabbit ear antenna chose to cooperate. But we've come even further today. The advent and growth of cable and satellite television has jacked the numbers much higher. These days the average American household receives 96.4 television channels, an increase of more than 50 percent since 2000.[144] Local cable networks provide subscribers with a full spectrum of "basic" and "premium" packages offering dozens of different stations and networks. While industry experts once predicted it wouldn't be long until the average home had a choice of 500 channels, that prediction has yet to come true.

However, the prediction regarding emerging technologies has already come true. Broadcast and satellite television are increasingly being viewed on expensive high-definition and plasma television screens. In addition, advances in Internet technology mean that more computer users are able to watch seemingly endless video and television options via the World Wide Web.

Living rooms, family rooms, dens, and bedrooms across America have become television's temples. Typically, the furniture is arranged so every seat in the house affords an unobstructed view of the tube. And every day parents, kids, and teenagers across America gather in their family and individual temples, together and alone, to watch the electronic god. Studies have shown "program content is not the principal factor in assembling an audience for television." We just go and turn it on "when no other activity is preferable, obligatory, or necessary."[145]

How much TV do we watch? The average household in America has the television turned on for eight hours and 11 minutes a day.[146] The average amount of television watched daily by eight- to 18-year-olds is three hours and four minutes. If you add watching video and recorded TV (DVR or TiVo), they're watching just under four hours a day (three hours and 51 minutes). It's interesting to note that the younger the child, the more television they watch. Kids ages 8 to 10 watch three hours and 17 minutes of television a day (four hours and 10 minutes when including video and recorded TV); kids ages 11 to 14 watch three hours and 16 minutes of television a day (four hours and two minutes when counting video and recorded TV); and kids ages 15 to 18 watch two hours and 36 minutes a day (three hours and 20 minutes when counting video and recorded TV).[147] It's estimated American children ages six and under watch about two hours of television a day. And 43 percent of kids under the age of two also watch television daily; 26 percent of kids that age even have a television in their bedrooms.[148] This means young children who are unable to distinguish fact from fantasy will have spent thousands of hours watching television before they begin their formal schooling. Over the course of a year, the average child will spend 900 hours in school, and almost 1,023 hours in front of the television.[149]

It's not just teenagers who are spending countless hours in the temple. Eighty-four percent of all college students have a television in their dorm rooms, typically with at least a hundred channels of cable to choose from.[150] The average college student watches 24.3 hours of television a week.[151] The move into the adult years brings an increase in television viewing, with the average American adult female watching four hours and 40 minutes a day, and the average American adult male watching four hours and two minutes a day.[152]

Other viewing habits serve as indicators of how important television has become in today's culture. Among eight- to 18-year-olds, 63 percent live in a home where the TV is usually on during meals, 53 percent say their parents have no rules about watching TV, and 51 percent report the TV is on "most of the time."[153]

We have become, as Quentin Schultze has suggested, a nation of "grazing videots."[154] Like cattle eating grass in a pasture, we sit comfortably in our chairs flicking the remote and satisfying our tele-visual hunger with hour upon hour of TV's often unhealthy fare.

There are those in our culture who've had it with television. Believing the medium is inherently evil, they call us to lock our sets in the attic or throw them out. But we need to recognize that televi-sion can and does teach us and our kids positive messages about life. TV can raise our awareness of problems in the world; it gives us insight into the pressing issues of our time; it opens us up to the wonders of the world by taking us to places we've never been; it makes us laugh. And it can stimulate spontaneous discussion on important issues when families or youth groups view together.

But too often, we give television and all of its characters, mes-sages, morals, and values—whether good or bad—unlimited and unchallenged access into our homes and lives. Columnist Richard Reeves makes a good point when he writes, "If TV is producing trash, guess what it considers its waste dumps. That's right: your living room, your brain and your soul."[155]

While television can and does educate viewers in positive and constructive ways, there are some alarming trends. Teenagers are especially susceptible to television's negative and destructive themes and messages. In the last paragraph of the book *Watching America*, the authors speak of the incredible power of television in our culture: "In the brief span of little more than a single genera-tion, television has become the great American dream machine, the source of an alternate reality whose profound impact is widely assumed but little understood."[156] As parents and youth workers, we must understand the medium and messages of this educator of our kids. The next chapter contains an overview of several thematic emphases of all media—including television—that merit continued parental and youth worker awareness and attention.

Movies

Is the world of movies real? As you ponder this question, consider this sampling from a humorous list of "Things Hollywood Has Taught Us" that I found on the Internet:

- It does not matter if you're heavily outnumbered in a fight involving martial arts. Your enemies will patiently wait to attack you one by one, by dancing around in a threatening manner until you have knocked out their predecessors.

- When you turn out a light to go to bed, everything in your bedroom will still be clearly visible, just slightly bluish.

- If you are blonde and pretty, it's possible to become a world expert on nuclear fission, or anything else, at the age of 22.

- It's easy to land a plane, providing there is someone in the control tower to talk you down.

- Once applied, makeup never rubs off even while scuba diving or after fighting alien monsters. But only if you are beautiful. If you are overweight, your mascara will run and your lipstick will smear.

- A man will show no pain while taking the most ferocious beating, but will wince when a woman tries to clean his wounds.

- If you decide to start dancing in the street, everyone around you will automatically be able to mirror all the steps you come up with and hear the music in your head.

When we stand back and look at the multibillion-dollar movie industry, we chuckle at how unrealistic Hollywood's depictions of life can be. But don't underestimate the power of film as a shaper of values, attitudes, and behaviors of teenagers, and, yes, even adults. For that reason, we need to be careful not only about what we watch, but also about what we allow our movie-watching kids to see.

If you've been to a movie lately, you understand why. On the one hand, the technical brilliance and special effects are usually amazing. But on the other hand, movie content sometimes leaves much to be desired. If our kids have not been taught how to think critically and biblically about the movies they watch, they're more prone to accept, believe, and perhaps even assimilate the moral and spiritual values of films that can harm their developing characters. Movie producers know that films that address a teenager's search for identity, desire for intimacy, interest in developing sexuality, and quest for social acceptance will sell because they speak to the deep questions kids face today. As a result, the movie industry often forfeits its potentially positive power to become a factory that cranks out more negative values, attitudes, and behaviors that our deeply impressionable kids so readily absorb.

Movie-viewing facts and figures. Do kids go to the movies? Absolutely. Movies are an important part of the adolescent experience. Teenagers love stories, and movies tell stories.

- In 2005, 535 new films were released.[157]

- Moviegoers between the ages of 12 and 29 represent more than half of all theatrical admissions (57 percent), with 12 percent of all admissions sold to young people ages 12 to 15, and 16 percent of all admissions sold to young people ages 16 to 20.[158]

- A higher portion of teenage moviegoers (47 percent) go to the movies more frequently than adult moviegoers (21 percent).[159]

- In addition, families with teenagers tend to go to the movies more frequently than families with kids under the age of 12.[160]

A survey conducted by Teenage Research Unlimited asked teenagers where they spend their free time. On weekends, the highest-ranking place where teenagers say they spend their time is a friend's house. A movie theater was ranked second. The mall was ranked third. When on a date, the movie theater was the over-whelming number one answer.[161]

Teenagers are an attractive and profitable market segment in a moviemaking industry that grosses about $9 billion annually.[162] Surprised? As you already know, movies aren't just for theaters anymore. With 88.7 percent of households owning at least one VCR, and 76.2 percent having at least one DVD player, everyone's able to watch movies in the comfort of their own home, and even in their own bedroom.[163] The growing number of homes with cable TV access, satellite TV provision, and movies-on-demand allows viewers to watch movies whenever they please, 24 hours a day.

Most teenage movie viewing is done without adult supervision. It's no surprise R-rated films are among the favorites among teenagers. Filmmaker Brian Godawa says not all accounts of sex and violence are "intrinsically immoral. It is the context through which these misbehaviors are communicated that dictates their destructive or redemptive nature...In fact, the acknowledgement of evil is treated (in the Bible) as the necessary prerequisite to redemption."[164] But much of the R-rated fare marketed to and viewed by teenagers contains gratuitous, graphic sex and violence that is sometimes packaged in a humorous format. According to researchers at the National Study of Youth and Religion, 17 percent of the teenagers ages 13 to 17 who say their faith is "extremely important," 26 percent who say their faith is "very important," and 32 percent who say their faith is "somewhat important" report that all or most of the movies they watch are R-rated.[165] Not only do these films play a powerful role in shaping the values and attitudes of teenagers, but they also shape behavior. One study found that teenagers who watch R-rated movies are nearly seven times likelier to smoke cigarettes, more than five times likelier to drink alcohol, and more than six times likelier to try marijuana.[166]

Parents also should be aware that even though a film may garner a more kid-friendly rating due to the absence of violence, sex, and profanity, a film's overall message and worldview could still be cause for concern.

Movie themes fall into the same categories (see next chapter) that are portrayed in television. But there is one difference: Movies, by nature of the fact that they're never "censored," are able to carry out those themes in a more explicit and graphic manner. If our teenagers are seeing sex, violence, and rebellion on TV, then they're seeing a more intense version of those themes on the big screen—whether they go to the big screen or they bring the big screen home. For that reason, it's important to know what films your kids are viewing and how those films portray life in God's world. Then you can make informed decisions about what films are appropriate and inappropriate, and have the necessary knowledge to discuss those films with your child.

The movie industry is a powerful element in the media package that influences the values, attitudes, and behaviors of our kids. It fills the eyes and ears of our teenagers with the invitation to "come, follow, and experience life." Will you raise your awareness of the world of film and prepare yourself to guard the hearts and minds of your kids in age-appropriate ways? Will you teach and equip them to evaluate films biblically and make good film choices on their own?

Radio

The radio is a media outlet used heavily by teenagers. Popular music and all of its messages are transmitted over the airwaves around the clock. In addition, disc jockeys and other radio personalities fill the time between songs with comments, skits, gags, humor, and banter. While radio, like other media outlets, has the tremendous potential to be a positive and uplifting force in the life of a teen, a casual survey of the most-listened-to stations and program formats indicates that the radio increasingly reflects the changing moral landscape of America.

In his study on teenagers and radio, Paul Gullifor says, "Radio introduces themes that are ignored or downplayed by the dominant institutions such as the family. For example, many of the topics addressed on commercial radio are topics that are often omitted from family discussions."[167]

Radio speaks the language of kids. It has the powerful potential and ability to serve as a surrogate parent, providing teenagers with information and advice on life that they aren't receiving at home. At times, the information is helpful, good, true, and right. At others, that information is offensive, explicit, and inappropriate.

Radio facts and figures. Radio is cheap. For the initial cost of a set, some electricity, or maybe a few batteries a month, radio provides up-to-the minute access to the world and popular culture. You can turn it on while in the car, in your room, or—through the technology of earbuds and headsets—anywhere you might be. Numerous studies and surveys indicate that kids begin to listen to the radio at a young age. The Walt Disney Company recognizes this fact and has therefore created a child-oriented program format that's broadcast through Radio Disney.

As children grow, listening time increases due to the growing importance of popular music in their lives:

- In a typical day, 76 percent of eight- to 18-year-olds report listening to the radio, second only to watching television. Overall, they spend an average of 55 minutes a day tuned in to the radio airwaves.[168]

- Of course, the older they get, the more they listen. Average daily time spent listening to the radio:
  – 29 minutes for eight- to 10-year-olds
  – 57 minutes for 11- to 14-year-olds
  – one hour and 15 minutes for 15- to 18-year-olds[169]

- Over the course of a week, 93 percent of all 12- to 17-year-olds listen to the radio.[170]

- According to one study, teenagers listen to the radio for an average of one hour and 42 minutes a day on weekdays, and four hours and 30 minutes a day on weekends.[171]

- Teenagers can be found listening to the radio—
  – at home (44.6 percent of the time on weekdays and 48.3 percent of the time on weekends)
  – in the car (40.3 percent of the time on weekdays and 41.2 percent of the time on weekends)
  – at work or other places (15.1 percent of the time on weekdays and 10.5 percent of the time on weekends).[172]

- Of kids ages eight to 18, 97 percent live in homes with a radio, and 84 percent have a radio in their bedrooms.[173]

Nearly all adolescents listen to stations that feature popular music formats. Currently, the top three radio formats among teenagers are Contemporary Hit Radio, Urban, and Alternative.[174] But when they tune in, they hear more than music and advertisements.

Kids who get ready for school with the radio on are typically tuned in to one of the many morning shows featured during the AM drive time. In fact, more than 63 percent of teenage boys and 76 percent of teenage girls tune in Monday through Friday from 6 to 10 AM. The time slot typically features one or more personalities who solicit adolescent listeners and laughter through popular music, humor, and sexual innuendo. Methods include song parodies, spontaneous phone calls to unsuspecting persons, practical jokes, impersonations, and other gimmicks. Other morning shows feature "shock jocks," radio personalities who take indecency so far that one has to wonder why they don't get thrown off the air.

After school and evening hours are also popular listening times for teenagers. From 3 until 7 PM on weekdays, 69 percent of boys and 81 percent of girls are tuned in. From 7 PM until midnight, 55 percent of teenage boys and 69 percent of teenage girls will tune in.[175] The programming during these hours is typically hosted by a single on-air personality with formats similar to early morning programming.

While many predicted radio would go the way of the dinosaur, it continues to go strong, due in large part to the fact that it has adapted to new technologies and developments. For instance, more and more teenagers are using satellite radio in their cars and at home. They're drawn to satellite's alternative programming formats and tendency to play more new talent than traditional broadcast radio. In addition, teenagers who spend time online have access to an almost limitless amount of radio options, as more broadcast radio stations stream programming onto the Internet, as well as the growing number of Internet-only radio stations. These technologies have allowed radio stations to go global. Radio's accessibility and ease of use mean any child, no matter what age, can listen in if she knows how to flick a switch, move a mouse, or tune a dial.

While it may be easy to miss radio's message because your kids are listening in private, responsible parents will take the time to discover and address what their kids are hearing. Take time to talk with your teen, praising the good content and challenging the bad. Always discuss the "why" behind your concerns.

Magazines and Books

Contrary to what many might think, teenagers still spend time reading. Even though visual and sound media have become more pervasive, teenagers still read print media, particularly magazines and books.

A trip to the magazine rack at the local bookstore offers proof that teenagers are buying, reading, and sharing a growing number of attractive and glossy publications published just for them. These magazines are "delivery vehicles," delivering advertisements and articles that powerfully shape teenagers' values, attitudes, and behaviors. They tell them what's most important in life and what to aspire to as they enter their adult years. They reach out to the teenage population with suggestions, information, and answers to life's questions. Because teenagers aspire in the "now" to feel, be seen, and be treated as older than they really are, they tend to "read up." For that reason, magazines that appear to be targeting high school girls are actually being read by much younger girls. High school girls are drawn to women's magazines like *Cosmopolitan* and *Elle*. In fact, 12- to 17-year-olds comprise almost one-quarter of the readership of women's magazines.[176]

Teenage girls typically read magazines filled with advertisements (usually about half of a magazine's content) and articles that deal with fashion, hair and makeup tips, fitness, and romantic relationships. In recent years, more magazines have added spirituality sections with a focus on astrology and horoscopes. Covers feature current celebrities whose looks and personalities function as role models for impressionable young readers. In addition, weekly celebrity magazines (think *People* and *Us Weekly*) are growing in popularity among teenage girls. These magazines focus on music, entertainment news, and celebrity gossip.

Peter Zollo of Teenage Research Unlimited explains why magazines are more popular among girls than boys:

More gregarious and social than most guys, girls actively seek out precisely the mix of information and entertainment that teenage lifestyle magazines provide—from style and fun to dating and relating, with many focusing on the traditional big-three topics of fashion, beauty, and boys... No wonder many girls consider their favorite magazines more than just a media option—they're fashion tools and guides that help ease teenagers through some of the most confusing, exciting, and challenging years of their lives.[177]

Teenage boys are drawn to magazines that speak to a specific hobby or interest (snowboarding, skateboarding, motorcycles, sports, cars, music, electronic gaming, and so on) and to the growing number of young men's magazines that feature scantily clad females on the cover (such as *Maxim* and *FHM*). The editorial content of these lusty men's magazines is typically a hedonistic combination of fashion, sports, gadgets, sexuality (although not nudity), and other "manly" pursuits.

Books are also popular among teenagers, with publishers releasing new fiction titles and fictional series targeting teenagers on a regular basis. While many teenagers might complain about the amount of reading required in school, the good news is many are opting to read books of their own choosing when they're not in school. Teenagers are attracted to books that speak to their interests and needs. Many girls enjoy books about romance and relationships. Boys like books about adventure, sports, and science fiction.

Magazine and book facts and figures. In a typical day, almost three out of four (73 percent) of young people ages eight to 18 report reading for pleasure, spending an average of 43 minutes a day reading.[178] "Interestingly enough, those young people who spend the most time watching TV (the 20 percent who watch more than five hours a day) don't report spending any less time reading than other young people do; and those who spend the most time playing console video games (the 13 percent who play for more than one hour a day) spend *more* time reading than those who play fewer video games."[179] But kids do read less when they have a TV in their bedroom, live in homes where the TV is left on all the time, or have parents who haven't established rules about TV watching.[180]

When it comes to time spent reading—

- Eight- to 10-year-olds spend an average of 12 minutes a day reading magazines, four minutes a day reading newspapers, and 27 minutes a day reading books for pleasure.

- Eleven- to 14-year-olds spend an average of 15 minutes with magazines, five minutes with the newspaper, and 21 minutes with books.

- Fifteen- to 18-year-olds spend 13 minutes with magazines, seven minutes with newspapers, and 24 minutes with books.[181]

With more magazines building homes on the Web, teenagers are also able to access digital versions that feature additional multimedia and interactive content.

Teenage magazines are using Web sites to solicit feedback from readers and to secure e-mail addresses and other demographic information used for marketing purposes. In addition, magazine Web sites offer another avenue into the world of teenagers, where teenagers find information on emerging trends, and they help marketers develop and promote new products. Teenagers also create and access their own online-only "web-zines" that feature content written by teenagers for teenagers. These sites are also highly interactive and can serve the purpose of providing kids with a sense of community.

Magazines set standards for teenagers in relation to body image, relationships, fashion, and spirituality. Covers, ads, and content dictate to our teenagers the image and character they think will make them valuable, normal, lovable, and worthwhile. "In-depth interviews with girls ages 12 and 13 who were regular readers of teenage magazines found that girls used the magazines to formulate their concepts of femininity and relied heavily on articles that featured boys' opinions about how to gain male approval and act in relationships with males."[182] Magazines have the power to promote and normalize standards among the teenage population.

Reading is healthy if the material is positive. If a teenager gets "lost" in books or magazines, work to discover if it's because of her love for reading or if it's an escape route that needs to be addressed. It's important to encourage teenagers to read—and to read widely and critically. As with all other media, teach teenagers to discern between right and wrong by evaluating all they see and read on the pages in light of the standards and truth of God's Word.

Video Games

It all started in 1972 with a groundbreaking game that sent a little white dot careening back and forth across a monochrome television screen. In the 35 years following the advent of *Pong*, the video game revolution has swept the world to become a $25 billion-a-year global industry, with sales of $10.5 billion in the United States alone.[183] One study found that video and computer game enthusiasts are spending an average of $700 a year on console games, PC games, and gaming accessories, with the breakdown as follows: $341 on console game titles (those played on video game consoles), $233 on PC games (those played on a personal computer), and $140 on gaming accessories.[184] Those numbers are fueling the industry's drive to churn out new gaming platforms and titles, along with the development of more sophisticated gaming technologies.

More than eight out of 10 (83 percent) eight- to 18-year-olds have a video game console at home. A majority (56 percent) have two or more. Almost half have one in their bedrooms (49 percent), and 55 percent have their own handheld video game player.[185] Not surprisingly, eight- to 14-year-olds are the ones who have the most access to video technologies in their homes and bedrooms. Among eight to-14-year olds, 84 percent have video game players in their homes and 52 percent have them in their rooms, as compared with 15- to 18-year-olds (81 percent and 41 percent).[186]

During the course of a day, the average amount of time spent playing computer games is 20 minutes for eight- to 10-year-olds, 17 minutes for 11- to 14-year-olds, and 19 minutes for 15- to 18-year-olds.[187] The average time spent playing video games on a video game platform or handheld game player is 65 minutes for eight- to 10-year-olds, 52 minutes for 11- to 14-year-olds, and 33 minutes for 15- to 18-year-olds.[188] Kids aren't the only ones tapping into the growing video game phenomenon. Forty percent of American adults play video games on a computer or game console.[189]

One new and growing gaming platform is the cell phone. Recently the number of households engaged in cell phone gaming almost doubled, jumping from 16.3 million to 27.9 million.[190] As cell phone technology continues to advance and more people use the gadgets, these numbers will continue to skyrocket.

A growing number of interactive online games are available to kids who visit the games' Web sites. In an effort to more effectively market their products to teenagers, marketers are developing and placing interactive games on product Web sites selling everything from cereal to tennis shoes to deodorant. Other sites feature games developed by aspiring game designers. Players can visit the sites to play the games and are often advertised to by site sponsors.

One relatively newer gaming trend is the placement of advertisements into the game itself. It's predicted that by 2010, the in-game advertising market will reach $732 million.[191]

A walk through the video game section of any toy or video store can be overwhelming. Hundreds of titles adorn slick packaging filled with several types of games. The games' covers feature a rating from the Entertainment Software Rating Board (ESRB), running the gamut from "EC" (Early Childhood) to "AO" (Adults Only). One ongoing survey of video game violence and youth found M-rated games are very popular among preteen and teenage boys. The M-rating indicates the game may contain intense violence, blood and gore, sexual content, or strong language. The study found 87 percent of boys play M-rated games, and 78 percent say an M-rated game is among their favorites.[192] The National Institute for Media and the Family found "half of the time, young kids are able to walk out of their stores with M-rated games in hand."[193] Another study found that among T-rated games (may contain violence, suggestive themes, crude humor, minimal blood, or infrequent use of strong language), 98 percent included violence, 42 percent depicted blood, 77 percent included death by violence, and there was an average rate of 122 deaths an hour.[194] The ongoing development of new game titles, new hardware technologies (cell phone gaming, portable game players, new generations of game consoles, and so on), and new gaming technologies (such as interactive multiplayer online gaming) ensures our teenagers will continue to be targets of marketing efforts to keep them buying and playing for a long, long time.

Should parents be concerned about video games? Research shows video games shape the values, attitudes, and behaviors of teenagers. Links have been made to violence, childhood obesity, sexual violence, and other social problems (see the next chapter for more information on the effects of video games on teenagers). Sadly, there's a widening gap between what kids are playing and what their parents know about those games. The MediaWise survey found "half of the parents who participated in our survey said they do not allow their kids to play M-rated games, but nearly two-thirds of surveyed students said they *owned* their own M-rated game. What explains this gap? Maybe this statistic: Only half of the parents say they were with their kids the last time they purchased a game."[195]

One trend that bears vigilant parental oversight is the growing prevalence of kids who become addicted to and escape into games. Some players, so distraught about the difficulties of living their life in the real world, escape into the games, assuming the identities of the game's characters as a way to avoid dealing with what's happening in their real lives. This type of escapism is especially prominent in Massively Multiplayer Online Games (or "MMOGs") and Massively Multiplayer Online Role-Playing Games (or MMORPGs). Played on the Internet, these games are accessed and played in a giant virtual world by hundreds or thousands of players at a time. Players compete with and against each other, developing identities and friendships as they spend lengthy amounts of time in these virtual worlds. And advances in game-playing hardware technology are making it increasingly possible for gamers to engage in these online games by using the portability of their cell phones.

The gaming industry is also tapping into and feeding our culture's increasing fascination with pornography. The sex game industry is still relatively young, but it's working not only to insert mature themes and sexual content into a growing number of games, but also to develop sex-themed games. Sadly, "most parents don't have rules about which games their kids can play."[196] Among all eight- to 18-year-olds who have video games, only 21 percent say their parents have any rules at all. They range from 32 percent of eight to-10-year-olds to only five percent of 15- to 18-year-olds.[197]

Are your kids playing video games? If so, how much do they play, where are they playing, what games are they playing, and what lessons are they learning as they play?

The Digital Revolution

Carly's not a real person, but two minutes after signing on with a major online computer service, she got lots of unsolicited attention. You see, to find out what can happen to a teenage girl when she spends time in the growing virtual online world, I invented "Carly."

While it was way back in 1995 that Carly came into being, what happened to her then provided an eye-opening yet small glimpse into where computers were taking kids and youth culture. Within minutes after going online for the first time, Carly went into a chat room, a place where computer users can communicate in real time by typing messages that appear in script form on each other's screen—a kind of telephone conversation that's typed rather than spoken. (Of course, most of you reading this have been there yourselves. However, for the few who are still unfamiliar with personal computers, the Internet, and how they operate, I've chosen to be very descriptive.)

Before Carly had a chance to say anything, a personal message from "Steve" appeared at the top of Carly's computer monitor: *Hey, Carly, wanna chat?*

Carly innocently replied, "Okay."

Steve's subsequent questions and comments indicated he'd checked Carly's personal profile just seconds after I created it. He was interested in talking with this average, naive, 15-year-old high school sophomore whose hobbies included swimming, dancing, and cheerleading.

Unbeknownst to Steve, "Carly" quickly checked his personal profile and discovered he was a 30-something married man living in the Midwest. His motto said, "Do something even if it is wrong." And Steve lived up to his creed. Without hesitation, he asked for Carly's measurements, bra size, panty size, and whether or not she had a boyfriend. Carly didn't answer his questions, and she abruptly ended the encounter when Steve solicited Carly's picture and offered a graphic description of his penis. Believe it or not, all this took place within five minutes after Carly went online. Welcome to the big, exciting, overwhelming, fast-growing, and sometimes dark world of computers and the digital revolution.

In 1983 computers could be found in only 7 percent of American households. By 1997, 60 percent of households with kids had computers.[198] By 2005, 86 percent of all eight- to 18-year-olds lived in a home that had at least one computer. Seventy-four percent of those homes had Internet access, and 31 percent had high-speed Internet access. More than 31 percent of all eight- to 18-year-olds had a computer in their bedrooms, and 20 percent of all kids had Internet access in their rooms.[199] The Kaiser Family Foundation reports "nearly all young people have used a computer (98 percent) and gone online (96 percent)."[200] During the course of a typical day, 48 percent of young people go online from home, 20 percent do so from school, and 16 percent go online from someplace else. More than one in 10 kids (13 percent) say they have a handheld device that allows them to connect to the Internet.[201]

The rapid development and growth of the Internet has combined with a growing number of kids with computer access to increase the amount of time kids spend with their computers. According to a Pew Foundation study, 87 percent of all U.S. teenagers ages 12 to 17 use the Internet. By contrast, 66 percent of adults use the Internet.[202] Among all eight- to 18-year-olds, that amount of time has increased from an average of 27 minutes a day in 1999 to an average of one hour and two minutes a day five years later.[203] The older the child, the more time they spend using their computers: Eight- to 10-year-olds spend an average of 37 minutes a day, 11- to 14-year-olds spend one hour and two minutes a day, and 15- to 18-year-olds spend one hour and 22 minutes a day.[204]

What do they do while they're online? They play games, instant message (IM) their friends, visit Web sites, send and receive e-mail, shop, and study or do research for school projects and papers. Even though they're spending a growing amount of time on the Internet, only 28 percent of eight- to 18-year-olds report that their parents have rules about how much time they spend on their computers, 32 percent have rules about what they can do on the computer, 30 percent report that their parents know which Web sites they're going to, and 25 percent have parental filters on their computer.[205] Among students in grades seven to 12, less than one-quarter say their parents have set rules about how long they can use the computer (23 percent) and what they can do on the computer (23 percent). Only 22 percent report that their parents know which Web sites they're visiting.[206]

With kids growing up computer-savvy, it's important that parents take the time to investigate the ever-expanding world of computers and the Internet. In an effort to help you steer your kids toward the wealth of positive Internet resources and away from the kind of garbage Carly encountered, take the time to familiarize yourself with this new technology and how your kids are using it every day.

The Internet is an amazing and fast-growing technology. It's a place where *anyone* can put *anything*, and *anyone* who has access to a computer with an Internet connection can get to almost *anything* that's out there in a split second. Because I'm a baby boomer born in the 1950s, I grew up in a world where computers were the stuff of science fiction movies and futuristic dreams. For us, an electric typewriter was advanced technology. None of us could have imagined having multiple computers in our homes and never having to leave home to access university libraries and government agencies, find information on any possible topic, book an airline ticket, conduct business, go shopping, and communicate with somebody who lives on the other side of the globe in real time. The list goes on and on. But our kids have never known anything but this type of a world.

Consider how fast the Internet has developed. Established in 1968 by the Defense Department as a communication network in case of a nuclear war, the Internet has grown to become a network of networks, connecting millions of computers and covering the entire globe. You don't even need a wire to connect. Personal home use of the Internet was virtually nonexistent until the last few years. Since that time, it has snowballed like nothing before. Consider that in 1992 the *Reader's Guide to Periodical Literature* listed only two articles on the Internet. In 1993 there were only 20. Today, there are too many to read, with dozens and dozens of magazines devoted entirely to the online world.

The Pew Internet and American Life Project discovered—and it's no surprise—that our curious and vulnerable teenagers are going places and doing things on the Internet that are dangerous and immoral. The survey found "62 percent of parents of online teenagers and 62 percent of online teenagers say that they believe most teenagers do things online that they'd rather their parents not see."[207]

But the digital revolution isn't limited to the computer and the world that's opened up to the kids who sit in front of the monitor. The emerging generation has been called "the technology everywhere generation" for good reason. Phone technology continues to change with "landlines" becoming old-fashioned as wireless advances. Pull up in front of any middle school or high school at the end of the day, and you'll see scores of kids flooding out the doors with cell phones in hand, looking down at their screens, text messaging with their thumbs, or pressing them to their ears. In fact, more kids at the elementary grade level are starting to live out this daily scenario as well.

While the statistics on cell phone usage change every day, it's worth noting that at the end of 2005, 69 percent of the U.S. population—or 208 million people—were using cell phones, a 14 percent increase over the previous year. The number of wireless subscribers worldwide was more than two billion, and 6 percent of U.S. households had eliminated landline service and were only using cell phones.[208] By the end of 2005, almost half of all 10- to 18-year-olds had a cell phone, representing a market value of $10.7 billion. On average, a teenager gets her first phone at age 14.[209] Those numbers are sure to skyrocket when virtually all teenagers will either own or be using cell phone technology.

While many adults long for the good old days when people weren't walking, driving, playing, eating, and even sleeping with their cell phones attached to their ears, our media- and tech-savvy kids are using them with increased frequency and expertise. Cell phone technology is developing at breakneck speed with new models loaded with advanced features dropping onto the market every day. Most teenage cell phone users use phones that are able not only to make and receive calls, but also to text message, send instant messages, send and receive e-mails, download music, shoot and send or receive still photos and videos, download and play games, download ringtones, and more. To teenagers, cell phones have become an extension of their personalities and a defining symbol of who they are. And they also keep teenagers connected with their social network and the world 24/7.

Your daily travels and interactions with kids—perhaps even while sitting in the quiet of a weekly worship service—prove that ringtones are one of the cell phone features kids see as a way to define themselves. Scan any teenager-targeted or music magazine and you'll find many pages advertising ringtone downloads. An Internet search yields hundreds of ringtone pages where kids are able to download songs, sounds, voices, and so on to their phones. The technology is so advanced that kids can download a unique ringtone for every different caller. Often they'll choose a song whose title or lyrical message represents the caller in some way. (Have you checked what ringtone they've downloaded to announce your call?) In addition, they're able to download unique ringtones for callers to listen to while they're waiting for the teenager to answer the phone.

Ringtone downloads are aggressively marketed to kids—and they're costly. At anywhere from 99 cents to $3.95 each, ringtone sales totaled $500 million in the United States in 2005, and were expected to increase to $600 million in 2006. Globally, sales of ringtones generated $4.4 billion in 2005.[210] In fact, the practice has become so popular that *Billboard* magazine now charts ringtone downloads in the same way they've been charting music for years.

Other recent cell phone developments include special phones created by companies who are targeting teenagers with their marketing efforts. Some companies market phones to eight to-12-year-old "tweens"; the phones are parent-friendly with parental control features, including the ability to restrict phone use, a locator that allows parents to find their kids with the touch of a button, as well as a load of content from the company, including screen savers, games, ringtones, and wallpaper. Another phone provides access to live news feeds, games, music, video and picture messaging, and the ability to check and post content on the users' personal MySpace profile pages. A third phone lets users access music, sports, entertainment, live events, and scantily clad female models delivering the news.[211]

Cell phone gaming is another trend that is rising in popularity. In 2004, there were 16.3 million U.S. households involved in cell phone gaming. By the end of 2005, that number had risen to 27.9 million families.[212]

Rapid developments in digital technologies have also fostered the equally rapid rise of portability in the lives of our teenagers. "According to the GenWorld Teen Study from ad agency Energy BBDO, portable media have moved from being technology for the elite to the mass market. It is the 'hallmark of mainstream cool,' and is no longer just for geeks and rich kids anymore. Our technologically enabled teenagers have been dubbed 'SuperConnectors,' described as 'a large group of teenagers who wield a host of communication technologies to maintain their always-on social network and constant connection to information and culture.'"[213]

Mp3 players (mp3 stands for "MPEG Audio Layer 3," a compressed, downloadable digital audio file format) are small, portable listening—and in some cases viewing—devices that have quickly overtaken portable CD players as the preferred music platform among today's teenagers. While the most popular and well known of these players is Apple's iPod, numerous other companies have now developed their own versions of the players and are currently marketing them. In the first five years after it was created, more than 42 million iPods were sold. In its first two years of existence, Apple's iTunes music download service sold more than 850 million songs and eight million videos. Among 12- to 24-year-olds, 85 percent say they prefer their iPods to traditional radio. It's projected that by the year 2010, music download revenues will total $10.7 billion.[214]

The appeal of these new technologies is both their portability and their ability to be personalized. Like their cell phones, portable digital players are personal accessories that say something about

YOUTH CULTURE 101

who I am. They come in a variety of colors, shapes, and sizes, with a host of optional accessories (covers, straps, docking stations, and more). With marketers seizing on our teenagers' social and developmental insecurities, it's easy to sell both products and the idea that what you have and what you wear defines who you are and can improve your social standing among your peers.

In addition, iPods and other mp3 players are controlled by the owner, who is able to download and play only those songs they want, giving them the ability to individualize their playlist to their own tastes and preferences. Also, teenagers are able to use simple computer software to record "podcasts" that can be downloaded by others, thereby allowing the creator to become a talk show host or DJ.

Parents and youth workers need to keep their eyes on another emerging trend that comes with the new digital technology territory: convergence—a blending of multiple technologies that our teenagers currently use in a variety of different devices into one piece of equipment. Soon, teenagers will be able to use one device to make phone calls, listen to music, create "podcasts," take pictures, play games, surf the Internet, text and instant message, access satellite and broadcast radio, and use GPS technology in what will be a pocket-sized communication portal.[215]

We can only imagine what the impact of this growing digital revolution will be on our teenagers and their culture. It'll cost them money, they'll be subjected to advertising every minute of every day, they'll spend less time at home and with their families, they'll lack media supervision and accountability, and they'll run the risk of being dependent on and overloaded by media. So here are some trends and phenomena related to these developments that are notable and worthy of your continued attention.

First, the increased use of digital technologies is changing the way kids relate to others. If you go back 30 or more years, the after-school ritual for most kids was this: Rush home from school, change into your play clothes, and get outside for as much face-to-face play time with your peers as you could get. Coming home for dinner was an interruption to that time that wasn't always embraced. But dinnertime was spent around the table, face-to-face with other family members. Then, the evening hours were typically divided between doing homework and doing something with the rest of the family—even if that "something" was circling up in front of the family's only television set. Those days are long gone. And the digital revolution, if allowed, will lead to kids engaging their media alone and in ways that limit interaction with others in their families. Others are shut out by walls when kids engage with digital media in their rooms or outside the home as they go "portable," or through the simple use of ear buds and headphones that can shut kids off to the outside world even when they're in the same room as family members and friends. In addition, after-school activities are increasingly centered on coming home and, rather than going out to play, engaging in instant messaging activities where keyboarded textual messages to online "buddies" are replacing face-to-face play time with friends.

Second, this "alone" time and tendency toward "flying solo" in the digital universe leads to greater autonomy and less accountability. In other words, younger and younger kids who are accessing and using a wider variety of digital media devices are left to make media decisions, interact with media, and evaluate that media without adult guidance, rules, and accountability. In many ways, allowing vulnerable teenagers to wander alone in the digital universe is just as irresponsible as allowing them to come and go as they please from our homes without guidance, direction, boundaries, and rules. Just as we watched them like hawks when they first started to live and play outside, we should also watch them as the outside world enters their lives under the roof of our own home. By building in accountability, we're preparing them to move gradually into a healthy autonomy.

Third, instant and text messaging are huge—and they're about a lot more than words. I often tell my kids the most valuable class I took during my high school years was typing. During that class, I learned a skill that has served me for life. I also tell them that if I had a choice between typing a letter or making a phone call, I'd choose the phone option. Because I have a tendency to be lazy, speaking is much easier than typing. As I've watched my own kids grow through adolescence, it's boggled my mind how much they embrace the "work" of engaging in typed-out conversations, rather than talking with others on the phone. In our house, all four of our kids have online screen names, they all use an Instant Messaging program, and they all spend time IMing their circle of family and friends. Seventy-two percent of American teenagers use IM on a daily basis.[216] Text messaging is also something my cellphone-using older kids engage in regularly. As an old-fashioned dad, I often wonder why they're more willing to "type" on "the world's smallest typewriter" rather than call that person on the phone—especially when text messaging costs 10 cents a pop to both send and receive.

One study found that 50 percent of IM-using teenagers have included a link to a Web site in an instant message, 45 percent have used IM to send photos or documents, and 31 percent have used IM to send video or music files.[217] Interestingly enough, only 29 percent of teenagers who use IM or text messaging have used it to communicate with their parents.[218] One study found if teenagers had to give up something forever, 25 percent said they'd miss instant messaging or e-mailing with friends and family the most.[219] An AOL survey found Instant Messaging is now a part of the fabric of everyday life. The top uses of IM are (in descending order): to chat with family or friends, to share photos, to send celebratory wishes, to set up weekend or evening activities, to gossip, to share files, to flirt, to make and talk to new friends in chat rooms, to keep in touch with family and friends overseas, and to communicate with others at work.[220] The move toward increased text-based communication is bound to grow. Keep an eye on it so you know what your kids are doing when they're communicating with those they know *and* don't know.

Fourth, social networking and blogging are changing the ways kids relate. In times past, diaries were the very personal and private possession of girls who typically used them to write out their innermost secret thoughts. Only in rare cases were they ever shared. More often than not, they'd be locked and hidden away. Girls whose diaries were discovered and read by others were usually devastated. My, how the times have changed. In today's world where kids are hungry for relationships and connections, teenagers of all ages are sharing their thoughts, photos, secrets, and very lives with anybody, anywhere through the fast-growing Internet segment of online journals and diaries. There for all the world to see, these online diaries—or "blogs" (short for "Weblog") have become online "reality shows" by including commentary on everything from politics, to religion, to sports, to love, to the most obscure aspects of one's life. Millions of teenagers and young adults have created personal pages on social networking sites such as MySpace, Facebook, Xanga, and LiveJournal (for a primer on how to access and navigate these sites, along with instructions on how to find your teenager's site online, log onto the tutorial contained on the CPYU site at www.cpyu.org).

When kids create their own sites, they typically post lots of personal information about themselves and their interests. Their personalized and customized sites include photos, background music, artwork, writing, and diaries of their thoughts, hopes, dreams, struggles, and daily lives. They write about problems with teachers, parents, and friends. They might discuss their love interests, sexual activities, and partying escapades—including information and photos about alcohol, tobacco, and drug use. Users create links to sites of people they already know, and those they meet online. What develops is a large and complex social networking community that sometimes functions as a hook-up service.

While these sites can serve as a fun way to meet and interact with new people, experts warn there are numerous safety concerns that are tied to this rapidly growing phenomenon. Kids often reveal way too much information about themselves, including photos, e-mail addresses, cell phone numbers, where they go to school, screen names, and even their home address. The Polly Klaas Foundation found that 42 percent of teenagers who go online say they post enough personal information to allow others to contact them, 30 percent have talked about meeting someone they have met online, and 27 percent have talked about sex online with someone they have never met.[221] Not surprisingly, pedophiles and online predators love these sites. Online relationships can quickly evolve into inappropriate relationships and cybersex. The fact that many kids are posting sexually provocative and suggestive pictures of themselves on their sites fuels this reality. One law enforcement officer says, "This is like a pedophile's fishing hole."[222]

These sites can also be used to bully someone else online. Recently a concerned mother called to ask if I'd look at the site of her daughter's ex-boyfriend. The young teenager had broken up with him a few weeks earlier, and her mom was concerned about personal threats the young man had posted on his site. His threats were so serious that I instructed her to call the police immediately. The police got involved and helped to squelch a situation that was rapidly getting out of control. Parents and school administrators are increasingly accessing these sites and responding to what they're finding. In numerous cases, students at both the secondary school and college levels have been expelled from school or dismissed from extracurricular activities because of the incriminating nature of the content on their sites. In other cases, police officers have used the sites to find evidence of criminal behavior. Even some job recruiters have denied employment to people due to information they've found on an applicant's site.

Because these sites are so much a part of our kids' lives, parents and youth workers must realize that most teenagers don't have the wisdom and experience necessary to create and maintain their sites without falling into potential danger. CPYU offers the following suggestions to keep in mind as the world of online teenage social networking continues to expand:

- While they're writing their thoughts and feelings in a very open and accessible forum, they still view their "journal" as private. They write for themselves and their friends. While some won't mind the inquiring eyes of adults, many believe their sites should be off-limits to the adults in their life. Be sensitive as you read, and even more sensitive if you choose to discuss their writings with them.

- We need to realize that what we are reading is usually very real. Most of what the kids write is truth as they see it. If they talk about smoking marijuana, odds are they have actually done it. While some writing may be embellished, most is an accurate depiction of what is going on in their lives. You'll learn about what they think and feel, about issues as diverse as family life, spirituality, sexuality, relationships, school, and more. Let kids know you're reading these sites. Talk to them about what you read. Help them understand you're not there to squeal on them unless you discover stuff serious enough to warrant that. And even in those more extreme cases, only go to the parents after you've spoken to the kid and feel you've exhausted all other avenues of recourse. If you see something that bothers you, lovingly confront them. Make the teenager understand why something might be inappropriate, but this is only after building bridges and creating an environment of trust and respect. Having said that, we should also realize that some of the "drama" in their lives may be manufactured. Kids who are generally happy and come from good homes sometimes use their online world to "create" drama. *Drama* is a big word in today's youth culture. In order to fit in, some kids may exaggerate the problems in their life in order to get attention. We need to be able to discern when this drama is real, perceived, or merely manufactured.

- We need to be very realistic and prepared for anything. Walking through the online diaries of your kids may be very eye opening and perhaps discouraging. Our kids may actually be leading very different lives than the ones they show us at home or in church. We need to be prepared for disappointment. Look particularly for clues about their spirituality.

- We must realize that these sites often serve a good purpose. Kids who don't feel they can talk to their parents or youth pastors may use their Web page as a catharsis, allowing them to get their feelings out in a very real and positive manner. These sites can also be outlets for creativity. When an area 15-year-old girl took her own life, many of her friends used their sites to work through their feelings, while others created new sites to pay tribute to their friend.

- We need to know how we are going to use the information we find as we minister to our kids. A two-pronged approach can be very effective. This allows us to minister to our kids on a one-to-one basis, discussing with them what we have read, while also using this information to minister to our teenagers as a group, giving us ideas for issues that need to be discussed from a biblical perspective.[223]

Fifth, kids have pornography at their fingertips. With the amount of time kids spend online increasing, parents and youth workers should be aware of the prevalence and easy accessibility of pornography. I was 12 years old, naive, and very curious when I was first exposed to pornography. I was also huddled behind a neighbor's stone wall with four of my childhood friends. We knew we were doing something wrong, and we feared getting caught. Today, even the youngest of our kids—if they have access to a computer and know how to conduct an Internet search—have access to a world of online pornography that's getting bigger every day. In cases where kids have computers in their rooms or surf the Net without parental rules or supervision, the chances of them deliberately or accidentally accessing pornography are greater.

Consider these recent stats on Internet pornography from ProtectKids.com:

- Two out of five Internet users visited an adult site in a single month.

- In another month 63.4 million unique visitors logged on to adult Web sites, reaching 37.2 percent of the Internet audience.

- There are at least 420 million pages of pornographic material on the Internet.

- The Internet pornography industry in the United States generates $12 billion in annual revenue ($57 billion worldwide)—larger than the combined annual revenues of ABC, CBS, and NBC.

- And perhaps most shocking, the age group that views Internet porn most frequently is between 12 and 17.[224]

Teenagers are curious about their developing bodies and sexuality, so it's not too surprising they'd be drawn to Internet pornography, especially since it's so easily found. Not only is involvement in pornography wrong and a distortion of God's wonderful gift of sexuality, but it also has dangerous short- and long-term effects.

1) We can expect a growing number of kids to be exposed to pornography at younger and younger ages—while they're *alone*.

With so many kids accessing the Internet on home computers *in their bedrooms,* they'll find or be found by pornography in an environment void of adult supervision and interaction. Most parents won't respond because they just won't know. No one will be there to tell them it's dangerous and wrong. In many cases, it will shape their values and attitudes long before they experience the sexual feelings and urges that come with physical maturation.

2) The envelope will continue to be stretched. When I was a kid, the envelope was not using the word "pregnant" around my grandmother. To her, it was a dirty word. Not so anymore. While I don't think a convincing case could be made to support my grandmother's bias, it does serve as an example of how much things have changed. Sadly, in today's world yesterday's hidden smut can be an everyday reality for young eyes, minds, and hearts. Based on this pattern, tomorrow's smut will be unimaginably more extreme than today's.

3) The more they see, the more desensitized they'll become. In other words, sinful behavior no longer shocks. It's become an everyday reality that is not at all surprising to them. In fact, what is surprising to our kids is that this stuff is alarming and surprising to us. In other words, expect your astonishment to be met by those words we hear all too often from our kids, "Mom, Dad, I've seen worse. You're so old-fashioned."

4) Pornography use will increasingly become a matter of personal preference, and decreasingly be viewed as sin. Our postmodern environment has combined with the pervasiveness of pornography to create a world where if you want to look at it, that's perfectly okay for you. Do whatever you feel like and whatever works for you.

5) The sinful values and practices promoted in pornography will become normalized. I recently heard about a group of 10-year-old boys in the Southeast who were discovered by one of their mothers as they took turns performing oral sex on one of their male classmates. The parents of the boys were stunned. Some of these kids were from Christian families. Where did they learn to do such a thing? When all the facts were known, one of the boys had discovered pornography on the Internet. Over time, he went deeper and deeper into some of the more extreme sites, all the

while inviting his naturally curious peers to look over his shoulder. Before long, they were doing what they'd seen on the screen. After getting caught, they were bewildered as to why what they were doing was wrong. As time goes on, Internet pornography will shape and normalize youthful behavior, impacting how young people view and treat each other, both now and for the rest of their lives.

Sixth, the digital revolution will fuel cheating. Many of today's teenagers are under intense pressure to reach a high level of academic achievement. Others are so burdened by the brokenness in their lives that they're struggling just to advance to the next grade level. For both these groups—and everyone in between—cheating is often employed as a strategy to get better grades. Digital technologies are now routinely employed by students who choose to cheat to get ahead. Cell phones with camera capabilities are being used to photograph exams, which are then given or sold to others who want to get an advance look at the test. Text messaging during tests is becoming more common, as those taking the exams text their friends with the questions, who in turn fire back the right answers. Internet plagiarism is on the rise as students access sites to purchase papers, or as they cut and paste someone else's research into their own work, passing it off as their own. Among high school students, more than 70 percent have admitted to cheating on a test, and more than 60 percent have admitted to some form of cheating.[225] These figures are expected to rise.

Finally, Internet addiction is a growing concern among those who track the health and welfare of teenagers. Like similar addictions to alcohol, drugs, and tobacco, symptoms include increasing tolerance, withdrawal, mood changes, and interruption of social relationships. "Kids and adolescents who have become addicted to the Internet will require increasing amounts of time online in order to feel satisfied. When they do not have access to the Internet they may have symptoms of withdrawal, which include anxiety, depression, irritability, trembling hands, restlessness, and obsessive thinking or fantasizing about the Internet."[226] Overall, a person's virtual world becomes more important and real than his actual world. Researchers have identified five types of Internet addiction: To online gaming, online relationships, information, computer games, and pornography. As parents and youth workers, we must realize our kids could easily fall into the trap of Internet addiction. Remember, they're part of "Generation M." While the Internet can be positive, fun, and educational, it can also be an extremely dangerous place.

It's no secret our kids are growing up in a high-tech world. The information age and its accompanying technologies are shaping kids and youth culture deeply. We must be aware of where and how they're spending their time so we can teach them how to responsibly control the high-tech world so it doesn't wind up controlling them.

Getting Personal

The media is everywhere around us, shaping our culture and guiding our teenagers. While it can serve as a productive force in society, far too often media serves a destructive purpose. Our teenagers, because of their ages and stages in development, are easily fooled into believing what they hear and see.

As youth workers and parents, we can begin to help our teenagers through the sometimes muddled maze of media's messages. Although watching and listening requires work, it pays off big dividends when we give our kids the opportunity to learn how to tell the difference between the media's truth and lies.

The Media:
How It's Shaping Kids

4

I feel like I'm here to change people's hearts and minds, to say something that's right for a change.

—KANYE WEST[227]

When I was in my early 20s, I started filming and editing commercials. I learned the power of film—creating a message that reaches a lot of people.

—JERRY BRUCKHEIMER[228]

During the summer between sixth and seventh grades, my best friend Glen told me his family was moving. He squelched my initial shock when he said his family's new house was only a mile from where they currently lived, so I'd still see him every day when school started back up in the fall. For as long as I'd known him, Glen's family had lived in a small three-bedroom ranch house with a small yard. Glen excitedly told me their new house was big, old, had three floors, and a large yard surrounded by woods. They wouldn't be moving in, however, until his parents had the old "fixer-upper," which had been uninhabited for several years, in better shape.

Later that week, my mom dropped me off at Glen's for an afternoon of sixth-grade play. About halfway through the day, Glen asked me if I'd like to see his new house. To get there, we'd have to ride our bikes over some fairly dangerous roads; and because his mother didn't want us over at the new house alone, we'd have to sneak off without her knowing about it. We set out on our adventure.

When we rode our bikes into the driveway of Glen's new place, he stopped so I could take in the panoramic view of the house and its property. While I didn't say anything to Glen right away, the house and surrounding woods gave me an eerie feeling that I still remember. It was a large, old Victorian without drapes or blinds in the windows. It looked deserted, overgrown, and in need of some new paint. And the afternoon's overcast skies turned the eerie factor up a notch. Or two.

I followed Glen up the driveway and we parked our bikes behind the house. We walked around to the front door, and as we did, I noticed a big old cemetery across the street. Glen reached up over the electric meter to grab the key, but it wasn't there. Without saying anything, he glanced over at me with a funny look on his face. My feeling of relief that we didn't have to go inside after all quickly disappeared when Glen grabbed the doorknob and twisted it—the house was unlocked.

The big wooden door creaked open to reveal a large foyer with a huge staircase leading up to the second floor. While I'm sure both of us were somewhat scared as we started through the house, neither of us would cave to our fear and admit it to the other one. That is, until we walked up to the second floor. At the top of the winding staircase, Glen found a man's leather belt draped over the railing. He picked it up and looked at it, then wondered aloud about where it had come from and to whom it might belong. He was sure he hadn't seen it there before. My heart was almost beating out of my chest by now. He took me past the belt and into one of the bedrooms. In the corner sat a large pair of men's shoes. Glen didn't remember them being there before, either.

I'm not sure what happened next, but I do know the two of us high-tailed it down those steps, out of that house, and onto our bikes. We rode furiously back to Glen's house. Out of breath, we confessed to his mom that we'd left without her permission and found evidence of someone having been in the unlocked house. As it turned out, Glen's dad had been there all day painting. He'd changed his shoes and taken off his belt to save them from paint splatters. And the house was unlocked because he was at the hardware store buying more paint.

I laugh when I think back to that day and the absolute horror and fear we felt as we visited the house. In hindsight, I think our minds were working overtime and processing everything about that house through the framework of things we'd seen and heard on television, in our comic books, and at the movies. The house looked like something out of *The Munsters* or *The Addams Family*, two very popular sitcoms featuring ghoulish clans. Glen and I had also watched the film *Night of the Living Dead*, along with numerous other scary movies. Our television fare had included *The Outer Limits* and *The Twilight Zone*, two series you never watched without first pulling the shades and locking the doors.

I'm sure our memories of those films and TV shows were with us that day. Because of what we'd seen and where we were developmentally, our minds developed a sense of what we thought was really happening, and our hearts were filled with fear. What Glen's parents saw as a great place to raise a family, we saw as a setting for a great horror flick.

Media has life-shaping power. In the last chapter, we discussed media's many outlets, along with a short description of two interrelated facts: Media has a tremendous power and ability to map out life and reality for kids, and media shapes kids' behaviors. Just as it was for Glen and me, media tends to influence kids gradually as they're repeatedly and cumulatively exposed to similar media portrayals and messages. Confused and curious as they grow through childhood, adolescence, and then on into adulthood, kids are very vulnerable to media's life-shaping power. And, with the emerging generations of teenagers spending greater amounts of time with a growing number of media outlets, media's power has increased immensely since "the olden days" when Glen and I were getting ready to head off to junior high.

In this chapter we'll look at the consequences and effects of media use. It's never a neutral force in a young (or old) person's life. It can be positive or negative. Take, for example, the rapidly expanding media outlet of video games. The National Institute on Media and the Family reports there are many positive effects of playing video games. Video game playing introduces kids to computer technology. Games can help them learn and practice how to follow directions. Some games help them to develop logic and problem-solving skills. Games can also provide practice in the use of fine motor and spatial skills. Video games can foster family closeness when parents and kids play together. Kids are introduced to new information technologies. Games are entertaining.

And finally, some games have therapeutic applications for patients dealing with a variety of ailments and handicaps.[229]

But the very same organization also warns us of numerous dangers related to video games, including fostering aggressive behaviors, confusing reality and fantasy, teaching kids to solve conflict with violence, using profanity, and stifling individual thought and creativity.[230] It's important for parents and youth workers to remember that media has the power to be both a positive and negative force in the life of vulnerable teenagers.

In addition, we must avoid falling into the trap of believing that *all* media and *all* media expressions and messages affect *all* kids in the same way. That's just not true. Imagine for a minute that a mix of 500 preschool, elementary, middle, and high school students are assembled in an auditorium. As the lights dim, their eyes are drawn to a large screen on the stage. The screen lights up and music blares from the speakers. Over the course of the next four minutes, everyone in the room watches the video for the current number one song in the country. When the music fades and the lights go back up, will each one of those 500 kids have processed and been affected by what they've just seen and heard in the same way? Will they all be influenced and convinced to think about and live life in an identical fashion? Absolutely not. The ways kids process, adopt, and react to media use and messages depend on a variety of factors, two of which are important for us to consider.

First, kids process and are affected by media depending on *where they are in the developmental process*. To state it simply— those who are younger tend to be more easily influenced because they're at the point of believing anything anyone says. This is why we warn our young kids, "Don't take candy from strangers," "Don't get in the car with strangers," and "If someone approaches you that you don't know, run home right away." Young kids have difficulty telling the difference between fiction and reality. They're easily swayed because of their trusting natures. As a result, young kids are very vulnerable to the life-shaping messages in media.

Teenagers, because of where they're at developmentally, are vulnerable as well, albeit in a different way. Their vulnerability doesn't come so much from believing *anything*, as much as it comes from wanting to believe and know *something*. They're going through a period of both tremendous change *and* deep questioning. Their search takes them down many avenues as they look for answers. They'll consider the opinions and ideas of parents, peers, teachers, the media, and so on. Media that speaks directly to their developmental issues and questions is especially good at drawing and keeping their attention as they decide who and what they're going to believe about life in this world. Because different kids struggle with different developmental issues to different degrees at different developmental stages, our room full of 500 kids will produce 500 different responses.

The second variable in how kids process, adopt, and react to media use and messages is their *life context*. Young people have their own stories that are made up of a unique mix of life circumstances. Their stories include numerous subplots related to parents, peers, faith, and the interaction between these and a variety of other factors. The most influential of these subplots is the story of their family lives. While media has power to affect all teenagers, media's messages (both positive and negative) are more prone to take root and grow where the soil of a child's life hasn't been nurtured by the flood-rains of parental love, time, listening ears, and attention. I see it all the time. Media steps in by default and fills the void left by parents who have opted out of their child's life by choice or circumstance. If Mom and Dad aren't guiding and nurturing their vulnerable kids who are prone to believing anything and everything, then media will.

Where teenagers' stories are filled with hurts, they'll turn to media to make sense of those hurts and look for guidance in how to respond. If their stories are filled with questions, they'll turn to media to find answers for those questions. If they're looking for a map to get them from the dependence of childhood to the independence of adulthood (which all teenagers are), then media will become the map that shapes them both now and for the rest of their lives.

I've found it helpful to understand the potential life-shaping power of media on the teenagers I know by asking these questions about their life context:

• Are they being guided and nurtured in the home?

- How are they being guided and nurtured in the home?

- Is their family intact?

- Do their parents love them and love each other?

- Are Dad and Mom active and involved in their lives?

- Do they spend a lot of time alone? With the Internet? TV? Radio? Music?

- Are there guidelines for media consumption in the family?

- Have they experienced some trauma or crisis in their lives?

- What place does Christianity (or some other spirituality) hold in their lives?

- What are their interests?

- Who are their peers and what is the life context of those peers?

- How are they treated in school?

- What is their personality, social status, socioeconomic status, age, gender, race, temperament, and so on?

Think again about the 500 young people sitting in the auditorium. Each one will process and respond to the music video uniquely, based on what is or isn't happening in their lives. Where traditional institutions of nurture are failing or weak, media steps in and takes the reins of a kid's life, shaping his values, attitudes, and behaviors for better or for worse. Media fills the socialization and nurturing voids. If I'm a kid and I have questions about the opposite sex that nobody is answering, I'll go to my media. If I have questions about calling, vocation, the purpose of life, authority, right and wrong, how to treat others, spirituality, God, how to resolve conflict, what to value in life, what makes a person valuable, and so on—media is there to give me guidance and answers.

Remember: Over time, the more media that is watched and consumed, the more power it has to subtly persuade, like the slow and steady influence and erosive power of a stream to shape a rock. This fact has coupled with media's growth in outlets, options, and influence to create a situation where even health care professionals have had to get involved by developing prevention and response strategies to counter media's power. As one researcher tells pediatricians,

> [T]he powerful messages in mass media (advertising, movies, music lyrics and videos, radio, television, video games, and the Internet) influence the way kids perceive their environment, their relationships, their bodies, and various risk behaviors. Media-consumption habits in kids and adolescents predict risk behaviors and adverse health outcomes as diverse as overweight and obesity, violence and aggressive behavior, tobacco and alcohol use, and early sexual debut.[231]

The article goes on to tell pediatricians to spend time discussing media-consumption habits with patients and their parents.

The Media's Influence on Teenagers

If you watch TV, turn on the radio, log onto the Internet, rent a movie, subscribe to a magazine, play video games, or read books, then you've opened up yourself and your family to the direct influence of today's media. And even if you haven't done any of the former, in today's world it's impossible to remain untouched by the powerful influence of media—unless you're a hermit.

The remainder of this chapter provides a brief overview of some of the more powerful effects media has on our kids, along with an overview of some of the more powerful life-shaping messages that are coming through with increasing frequency and depth.

Please keep two facts in mind as you continue to read. First, I've chosen to focus on messages and effects that tend to be more negative in nature. This doesn't mean all media messages and effects are negative or dangerous. That's simply not the case. As you learn to watch and listen with your kids, you'll have opportunities to discover, point out, and celebrate the positive. However, since most people are largely unaware of media's powerful and negative influences and effects, I've chosen to focus on those in order to raise your awareness. This will be especially helpful to you as you work to keep your teenagers from harm and provide for their well-being, as well as when you move on to read the next chapter on helping teenagers evaluate their media.

Second, remember that what follows is simply an overview. It's not exhaustive, nor have I provided a large number of examples. Rather, I want to help you understand general themes and effects without presenting material that would become cumbersome or quickly outdated. A good approach is to read through the material in the rest of this chapter, familiarizing yourself with general effects and themes. Then take that knowledge and use it as you monitor your kids, their media consumption, and what they're encountering while engaged with media. Look for these themes and effects. As you learn to recognize both the good and the harmful messages, you'll have the opportunity to evaluate ways in which media has affected your family or the students in your ministry. In the next chapter we'll develop guidelines for taking positive action to encourage healthy media consumption and to protect teenagers—both now and in the future.

What's offered here is only a starting point. It's crucial that you take the time to discover what's happening in the world of media (both the good and the bad) by listening, watching, and exploring for yourself. The more aware we are of the media scene as a whole, the more easily we can guide our teenagers through these influences on behavior and lifestyle choices. As a recent public service announcement says about surfing the Internet, it's just like surfing in a real ocean—you have to be aware of your surroundings at all times, watching out for sharks and other dangers. What are the "sharks" and "other dangers" to our kids as they swim in the great big sea of today's media?

Media Often Presents a False View of Reality

TV's oldest reality show provides a great example of just how easily media can and does distort reality. Launched by MTV in 1992, *The Real World* quickly became the highest rated cable-TV show among the 12- to 34-year-old age demographic. The premise of the show is this: A group of seven diverse, college-aged kids are chosen to live and work together, while MTV's cameras are rolling the entire time, catching film of the "real" lives, drama, and interactions of these "real" people. Since 1992, the show's audience has grown every year as a new cast moves in together in some new exciting location, while sucking in impressionable young viewers who are looking for lessons on life and how to live it. What these young viewers see teaches them loads of lessons on relationships, vocation, love, sex, marriage, God, conflict, body image, self-worth, and whatever other topics the characters might discuss while the cameras are rolling.

Over the years, many topical taboos have disappeared—a reflection of what's happening in our larger culture. *The Real World* has become more "spicy and dicey" with a "plot" that reads more like a soap opera. Of course, the formula works, and then the audience gets hooked on the show and it continues to grow. But what's actually presented on each episode is edited tape gleaned from hours and hours of filming. The reality that viewers see is not really "reality" at all. Rather, it's the reality that producers choose to show—nothing more than an artificial or contrived reality. The viewer is treated to an edited and manipulated version of reality, something made even more suspect by the fact that the cast plays to the camera.

Consider the flow of one episode from *The Real World's* 14th season. Frankie (who met her fiancé in a porn store) gets drunk and makes out in a hot tub with cast member Brad (who is also in a "committed" relationship at the time). Frankie gets sick after her excessive drinking and feels remorse for her actions (which, by the way, she can't remember). In later episodes, Brad breaks up with his girlfriend in order to party with his female housemates; Randy and Robin hit it off; and Cameron extols the virtues of her vibrator. By episode five, the females exchange kisses with one another on a dare, and Brad exposes himself to prove his manhood. In episode six, the cast creates fake IDs for their two underage cast members in hopes of getting them into a bar; and Robin gets arrested for public drunkenness. Eventually, they all joke about how going to jail is just a normal part of life. Back in the house, Frankie gets drunk again and "fools around" with Randy. The next morning she claims she "blacked out" and can't remember what happened. The show's Web site even features info on cast hook-ups that viewers can visit for the latest news. Remember, all this is being watched by a devoted group of young viewers who are learning this *is* "the real world," and this *is* how you should live your life.

Media often tells lies. When kids don't have or take the opportunity to view the world through God's Word, they run the risk of living these destructive lies, rather than living the liberating truth. And we'll find it more difficult to reach out to kids when they've been numbed to the truth. When media's messages stand in antithesis to God's truth, our kids' minds and hearts are less receptive to and believing of God's will and way.

For example, consider these media messages and how the message of God's Word stands in sharp contrast to media's "reality":

"MEDIA SAYS—"

- To be worthwhile, you must be beautiful

- Avoid pain and pursue pleasure at all costs

- Sex is a recreational pursuit, there are no consequences, and everybody does it

- Violence is an acceptable way to deal with your problems

- In the real world, it's okay to use anyone for any purpose

- Money brings happiness, and you should grab and hold onto all the stuff you can

"GOD SAYS—"

- I care about who you are, not what you look like

- Expect suffering and exercise perseverance

- I've given you the gift of sexuality for the purpose of procreation, intimacy, and expressing oneness in marriage

- Turn the other cheek and love your enemies

- Treat people with dignity, love your neighbor, and sacrifice your own rights for the rights of others

- Seek first my kingdom and don't worry about the things that moth and rust so easily destroy

As media becomes more powerful and pervasive, more kids will run the risk of buying into media's lies and false realities. If they're to hear and embrace the truth, we must proclaim that truth in a manner that addresses the specific lies of media head-on and exposes those lies for what they are by both teaching and living God's will and God's way.

Media Provides Many "Heroes" and "Role Models" Who Aren't Worth Emulating

In today's world, it's not unusual to run across a list of current child and teenage heroes. Many of these lists are researched and published by marketing firms who strive to help companies connect the appropriate spokespersons with their child- or teen-targeted products. Many times, the only qualification for being a hero or role model today is not what one stands for, but one's celebrity status. Teenage heroes are often rich and famous. They get to do exciting things in real life and in the movies. And today's stars no longer let their abilities and accomplishments do the talking. Instead they believe their status should be a platform for expressing views on everything from religion to politics. Most of them have Web sites where fans can read these celebrities' blogged thoughts on a variety of topics.

But if you listen closely to what they say, examine their life-styles, watch their movies, and so on, you soon realize many lack direction and a biblical sense of right and wrong. Their *personal* morality is just that—a personal morality that's often ambiguous. And a media obsessed with many of these celebrities' every waking moment combined with teenagers eating up whatever the media serves gives these celebrities the platform to be role models for youth.

Of course, with the popularity of reality TV, a growing number of teenagers are cheering on regular people whose hard work takes them from nowhere to somewhere—enter the ordinary hero. Perfect for youth who're questioning the status of celebrities. And with celebrities' lives opened up like never before, some kids resent our culture's worship of looking good and having money and fame. Instead they love ordinary people, just like themselves, who work hard to achieve fame and fortune.

Of course the media also confuses the villain and the hero. One recent poll found that among video game players, 41 percent like to play the hero while 59 percent prefer to be the bad guy. Researcher Sean Kang says, "Online games have thriving social communities, and it's only natural that they, as gamers, should follow similar trends to followers of other forms of media. Films, videogames, comic books, all borrow from each other and it's often the same audience being entertained. And right now, villains are in."[232]

For better or for worse, media also provides young users with role models for what it means to be a mother, father, man, or woman. One recent study deconstructed 101 top-grossing G-rated films. The study concluded that most of the male characters in these kids' movies are either "Casanovas, criminals, or clowns." The study also concluded that these films are dominated by aggressive, white male characters, with minorities seldom rising above the status of "sidekicks, comic relief, or villains." In addition, non-white males are typically portrayed as "physically aggressive or violent" 63 percent of the time, compared with 37.6 percent for the white male characters.[233] It's important for parents to monitor how family and gender roles are portrayed, celebrating those that affirm biblical truth, while challenging those that stereotype others or affirm sinful values, attitudes, and behaviors.

We need to encourage and help kids examine their heroes according to a biblical standard. Otherwise, they run the risk of accepting the whole package and emulating traits and attitudes that are dangerous and wrong.

Media Often Creates Unrealistic Body-Image Standards

Adolescence is a time when our kids need to be encouraged and built up. But by setting standards for beauty and body image that are largely unattainable, the media can mentally, emotionally, physically, and spiritually rip our kids apart.

Consider television. Let's face it—unattractive and overweight people don't make it on TV unless they're cast as unattractive and overweight people. Unfortunately, our definition of what's unattractive and overweight has been defined, in many ways, by television. TV is overloaded with "beautiful people" who don't look anything like the people we see in the mirror. The women are slim and trim. The men are slim and muscular. And everyone is "good looking." Today's shows are engaging, but they provide our kids with more than just a half hour or hour's worth of entertainment. They're full of spoken and unspoken lessons on life that shape impressionable young hearts and minds.

One of TV's most powerful lessons is that of body image and appearance. Kids learn that teenagers who have fun with their friends also have nice bodies, beautiful hair, and clear complexions. While these messages are no doubt life-shaping for males too, girls pay the highest price. Quentin Schultze summarizes TV's appearance message:

> It's impossible to miss the point: women are what they look like, not what they accomplish or what they value and believe. Their looks are their essence, for their bodies determine their identity as well as their image in the minds of family members and especially peers. Without the proper look, identity and intimacy will never be satisfactorily achieved.[234]

A few years ago a middle school girl came to me in tears over her looks. "I'm too short. I don't like the color of my hair. And my face looks funny." When I asked her why she wasn't happy with the way she looked (she was a beautiful kid), she began to describe each feature she'd like to change and gave me an example of someone who had the particular characteristic she coveted. Sadly, each person she mentioned was one of the "beautiful people" she'd seen on TV, in videos, on the movie screen, or in any number of magazines. She wanted to become them because she hated herself. In reality, she hated herself because she believed these people had become what she saw on paper and film. In later conversations I learned she'd been trying to build herself up by telling her friends she'd just signed a modeling contract. She also told me she was seriously thinking about plastic surgery.

All the images our kids see combine to define a culturally created standard of beauty few people ever reach. You may wonder why your kids are so consumed with spending time in front of the mirror. The answer is simple: They're trying to measure up to the images they've seen plastered on TV, the printed page, the big screen, and billboards. They balance perilously between trying to measure up and the frustration of never measuring up. Guys spend time trying to develop big biceps, ripped abs, and the look of the handsome guys in the ads who seem to be getting all the attention of one or more girls. My two daughters have grown up in a world where you're led to believe you have to look like a supermodel for guys to like you. Sadly, my sons have grown up in a world where they're led to believe this is what any girl worth your time and attention looks like.

As time passes, the standards change, becoming increasingly unrealistic and more difficult to attain. Mary Pipher, author of *Reviving Ophelia*, reports that in 1950, the "White Rock Girl" (the woman portrayed in the ads for this mineral water company) was 5 feet 4 inches tall and weighed 140 pounds. Today, she stands 5 feet 10 inches tall and weighs only 110.[235] These same unrealistic standards pummel our kids through daily media portrayals. A recent study that examined the effect of teen-targeted television on teenage viewers concluded that "as in most of television, these shows tend to cast svelte, attractive females and, to a lesser extent, handsome and 'buff' males. In terms of body type, *no heavier-than-average* main teenage characters appeared on these programs."[236]

These are the standards being adopted by viewers who encounter them in media. One study traced this growing problem by measuring the level of body satisfaction among women. In 1972, 23 percent of women felt "wholesale displeasure" about their bodies. That number had increased to 38 percent by 1985, and to 48 percent by 1997.[237]

A more recent study looked at the problem of female body dissatisfaction on a global scale. The study found that only a minority of women see themselves as being above average in appearance, and only two percent describe themselves as "beautiful." More results from this study:

- 48 percent strongly agreed with the statement "When I feel less beautiful, I feel worse about myself in general."

- Only 11 percent strongly disagreed with that same statement.

- 63 percent strongly agreed with "Women today are expected to be more physically attractive than their mother's generation was."

- 60 percent strongly agreed with "Society expects women to enhance their physical attractiveness."

- 59 percent strongly agreed with "Physically attractive women are more valued by men."

- 57 percent strongly agreed with "The attributes of female beauty have become very narrowly defined in today's world."

- 68 percent strongly agreed with "The media and advertising set an unrealistic standard of beauty most women can't ever achieve."

- 76 percent strongly agreed they wished female beauty were portrayed in the media as being made up of more than just physical attractiveness.

- 75 percent strongly agreed that they wished the media did a better job of portraying women of diverse physical attractiveness, including age, shape, and size.[238]

After reviewing the study's results, and to their credit, the Unilever Company (makers of Dove soap), who commissioned this survey, began a new advertising campaign featuring more "normal" and average-sized female models.

It should come as no surprise that a connection has been made between media body-image standards and the rise in occurrence of eating disorders. One study found media consumption "significantly predicted" symptoms of eating disorders among women and attitudes in favor of thinness and dieting among men.[239]

How has this affected young people? College-aged students who watch TV shows and read magazines that overemphasize sex and the body tend to be more prone to define themselves by how their body appears to others.[240] Another study measured the effects of soap operas and music videos on teenage viewers, concluding "boys who watched music videos were at higher risk of developing the male version of body obsession—a drive toward lean, hyper-muscular physiques," and TV soap operas (daytime and primetime) "may help make adolescent girls desperate for a thinness few can healthily achieve."[241] Other research finds that for boys and girls who identify with television stars—girls who identify with models, and boys who identify with athletes—there is a positive correlation with body dissatisfaction.[242]

Just when you thought it couldn't get any worse, the Internet has become a place where young people who are struggling with their own body image can go to be encouraged—yes, that's right, *encouraged*—to celebrate eating disorders such as anorexia nervosa and bulimia as fashionable. These pro-anorexia Web sites have become online communities and support groups for those who worship the goddess "Ana" (short for "anorexia"). These sites offer tips, tricks, quotes, images, and creeds (which summarize the ideological beliefs of disordered eaters).

On the bright side, there are those in the media who are taking responsibility by spearheading efforts to reverse media's negative influence in regard to body image. For example, then-43-year-old actress Jamie Lee Curtis appeared on the cover of *More* magazine in September 2002. While she'd appeared on the covers of numerous magazines before, this time it was for a different reason. Inside, the article and photos revealed the truth about magazine photo shoots, how they're doctored, and how long it takes to prepare a model for one. In fact, Jamie told readers it took 13 people three hours to get her ready for the *More* shoot.

But that's not all. Jamie wanted readers to see what she *really* looks like. Wearing a black sports bra and briefs, Curtis had the magazine photograph her "as is" and insert the undoctored photograph next to the article. Her honesty was admirable, and the Jamie Lee Curtis in the undoctored photo looked remarkably normal—and different than the cover version. They're photos all teenagers should see.

Another positive step was taken when Christina Kelly took over as editor of *YM* magazine. Aware of the body-image issue, Kelly banned dieting stories and started featuring larger-sized models in the popular teen-girl magazine. When she made the jump to a similar position at *Elle Girl,* she decided to do the same by getting rid of stories on weight loss and dieting.

While these are steps in the right direction, they're only small ripples in a very large mass of media water. Media's unhealthy obsession with body image and the resulting pressure on kids yield two results. First, they sell a slew of products designed to make us more attractive and to slow and stop the inevitable process of aging. And second, they sell an image that 99.9 percent of the people in this world will never attain. As a result, kids and adults waste terrible amounts of time, energy, and money in pursuit of the dream, only to be let down over and over again.

We're raising a generation of kids—both girls and boys—who've been hammered by images of culturally defined beauty and perfect body types since the day they were born. Consequently, they believe they're nothing unless they look and are shaped a certain way. The media never tells them that even if they have nothing in this world but a relationship with God through Christ, they'll still have everything.

Media Often Nurtures the Boring Life Syndrome

Today's teenagers are part of what has been variously labeled "Generation M," "The Wired Generation," and "Prime-Time Teens." Through their constant active and passive immersion in the fast-moving world of media entertainment, they've forgotten how to actively listen, make their own fun, and enjoy silence. When compared with television, music, movies, and video games, real life is dull and boring.

While my informal surveys are not scientific by any means, I've seen a marked difference between teenagers who spend unlimited time immersed in media and those who don't. For example, kids who watch a lot of television get bored when the set is turned off; they don't know what to do with their time, how to entertain themselves, or how to be creative in making their own fun. And the more they watch, the more they want to watch. It's almost like a drug addiction where constant use leads to increased tolerance. More of the drug is needed to get high, and the withdrawal is painful.

Kids whose parents set limits on media consumption are better communicators. They develop the ability to make their own fun. Real life for them is anything but boring. When I asked several of these kids what they think about television, they said they enjoy it. But when it's off, they don't miss it. They realize there are other ways to spend their time.

If the teenagers you know and love find it difficult to have fun alone, as a family, or in a group of peers, take note of how much time they spend immersed in media consumption. Sitting around and doing nothing but consuming media makes it difficult to get up and have fun. And after years of doing this, it's difficult to even remember *how* to do it. Those kids who are being nurtured by media are being nurtured into a life where moments of media absence are to be avoided because they're the moments where life is not only boring and dull, but where the silence is not a welcome respite—it's undesirable and overwhelming.

Media Often Fosters and Teaches Violence

In the early 1980s, television viewers in parts of Pennsylvania were watching a live press conference during which a state official was making an announcement regarding some financial matters. To the horror of everyone watching, he then pulled out a loaded pistol, made a few frantic remarks, inserted the gun into his mouth, and pulled the trigger. The TV audience had just witnessed a suicide. Several stations across the state were later chastised for their decision to run the uncut tape of the incident on newscasts later that day.

On an evening early in 1992, viewers watching the NBC network news were treated to another horrific piece of videotape. The tape showed a fatal meeting at a Florida cemetery where the burial of a teenage suicide victim had just concluded. The dead girl's father, now divorced from her mother, arrived at the cemetery and angrily blamed his ex-wife for their daughter's death. The video showed the man as he pulled out a gun and murdered the woman. The TV audience had witnessed a murder.

The similar airing and re-airing of videotaped violence also served to make Rodney King and Reginald Denny household names during the early nineties.

Sadly, these televised accounts that were once viewed as unusual, pushing-the-envelope fare have become so frequent in today's media environment that they fail to draw the criticism they once generated. Media violence, both staged and real, has become another part of everyday life. The emerging generation of teenagers has never known a world where they couldn't watch, play, and celebrate all types and forms of graphic violence as normal, fun, or entertaining. With real-world youth violence acknowledged as a growing social problem, researchers are diligently monitoring media outlets and expressions to discover the amounts and types of media portrayals of violence, and if those portrayals affect the values, attitudes, and behaviors of teenagers.

Television. Television has become a primary deliverer of violent media fare. Because young kids watch lots of television, they're seeing lots of televised violence. In their annual content analysis of kids' television (entertainment programming for kids ages five to 10 on broadcast television and expanded basic cable), the Parents Television Council found that in the 443.5 hours of kids' programming they analyzed, there were 3,488 instances of violence, or an average of 7.86 violent incidents per hour.[243] PTC's analysis found that kids are actually seeing more televised violence than adults are. "To put this figure in perspective, consider that in 2002 the six broadcast networks—combined—averaged only 4.71 instances of violence during an hour of prime-time programming."[244]

The same organization found (in its content analysis of 171 hours of MTV programming during spring break) MTV averaged six violent instances during an hour of programming, as compared with 5.8 instances of violence an hour during broadcast television's 10 PM time slot.[245] The National Television Violence Study found that nearly two-thirds of all television programming contains violence, that kids' shows contain the most violence, that portrayals of violence are usually glamorized, and that perpetrators of violence usually aren't punished for their acts.[246] Over time, the amount of violence our kids witness on television adds up. By the time they reach the age of 18, they'll have witnessed 40,000 televised murders and more than 200,000 acts of televised violence.[247]

Both formal and informal studies show that TV violence has increased over the years. Baby boomers will recognize the name Sherwood Schwartz, creator of boomer favorites such as *The Brady Bunch* and *Gilligan's Island.* A few years ago Schwartz conducted his own survey of prime-time programming, going back more than 30 years. He found that in 1955—early in the history of television—there were no violent crime shows on the air during prime-time viewing hours. In 1965, there were six hours of violent programs, including one in the 8 PM slot (a time when teenagers are usually watching). In 1975 there were 21 hours of violent shows with two of them broadcast at 8 PM. And in 1985, violent programming had increased to 27 hours with nine such shows airing at 8 PM.[248] By 1998, 61 percent of all television programming contained violence.[249] Today the preponderance of reality television, fighting competitions, and prime-time crime dramas has upped the amount and intensity of violent programming.

Of course, it's always important to investigate the context of TV's violent fare. If the violent act is depicted as horrific, immoral, and punishable, the portrayal may have a positive effect on viewers, teaching them that crime is wrong. The ongoing National Study of Television Violence found that among violent programs, 3 percent have an antiviolence theme, 16 percent show negative consequences to violence, 55 percent show violence in realistic settings, and 45 percent of violent shows have "bad" characters who go unpunished.[250] Here is a summary of the study's key findings:

- Much of TV violence is still glamorized. Good characters are the perpetrators of violence, with nearly 40 percent of the violent incidents on TV initiated by characters whose personal qualities make them attractive role models.

- Most violence on television continues to be sanitized. Roughly half of all violent incidents on TV show no physical harm or pain to the victim. Less than 20 percent of the violent programs portray the effects of violence on the victim's family, friends, and community.

- Much of the serious physical aggression on TV is still trivialized. At least 40 percent of the violent scenes on TV include humor, and more than half of the violent incidents feature physical aggression that would be lethal or incapacitating if it occurred in real life.

- Very few programs emphasize an antiviolence theme. Only 232 programs out of the 5,000 programs with violence conveyed a strong pro-social message about violence.[251]

Movies. In the 1995 film *The Basketball Diaries*, a fantasy sequence shows the character played by Leonardo DiCaprio entering a classroom at his Catholic high school. He then proceeds to gun down his classmates with a rifle. Fast-forward to the beginning of 1998, to a hallway in Heath High School in Paducah, Kentucky, where a 14-year-old student interrupts a before-school prayer meeting and slays three of his classmates with a gun. In an interview with law enforcement officials after his arrest, the boy said he patterned his rampage after *The Basketball Diaries*.[252] While there's always a multiplicity of precipitating factors in incidents like this, there have been a growing number of high-profile juvenile cases in recent years where life seems to bear a troubling resemblance to violent art. Again, these are complex cases with histories that extend far beyond the release date of the movie cited. But in a growing number of cases, film violence has served to spark or confirm the violent ideas of some angry young kids.

One recent study looked to discover how the Motion Picture Association of America (the organization that assigns ratings to films) treats violence in the movies they've rated PG, PG-13, and R. Looking at the top-grossing films in a one-year period, researchers found that a total of 2,143 violent bodily actions occurred. Perhaps not surprisingly, they discovered the total number of violent acts for each rating category increased. PG films averaged 14 acts of violence, PG-13 films averaged 20 acts, and R films averaged 32 acts. However, "the range in number of violent acts revealed a more diluted relationship between violence and rating. For instance, PG films contained anywhere from a single act of violence to 97 acts of violence; R films were remarkably similar, ranging from 1 to 110 acts."[253]

Another study found "violence...increased significantly in movies between 1992 and 2003," with "ratings creep occurring as films now rated PG-13 have content similar to R-rated films of a decade earlier."[254] The implications are clear, violence in film is on the rise, and parents should not trust the ratings when it comes to violent content.

Violent films are popular among teenagers. And it's no wonder—the special effects are amazing. As the audience comes to expect bigger and better violence, the movie industry will answer by making movies more violent and graphic than ever before.

However, all too often, the world of movies portrays violence as a normal part of life, just like sleeping, eating, and drinking. Sadly, the context of that violence (unlike films such as *Saving Private Ryan, Schindler's List, The Passion of the Christ,* and so on) often tends to glorify the violent perpetrator and the violent act.

Music. Violent themes are often expressed in and through popular music as well. Parents and youth workers who are diligent about knowing what their teenagers are listening to, and who then listen to that music themselves, will be able to identify those themes and address them with their kids.

In recent years, critics have cited rap music as a genre that is particularly violent in not only its lyrical and visual content, but in the lifestyles of the artists themselves. With rap music being a relatively young genre in the music world, little research has been done on its effects on listeners. One study, however, looked at the genre's effect on 14- to 18-year-old African American females. The study concluded that "compared with adolescents who had less exposure to rap music videos, adolescents who had greater exposure to rap music videos were 3 times more likely to have hit a teacher" and "more than 2.5 times as likely to have been arrested."[255]

Over the years violent themes have also been more prevalent in a variety of other genres, including country, heavy metal, and thrash. Again, we should be listening with diligence as violent themes can rear their ugly head in any type or genre of popular music. Parents should be aware of and concerned about the rising tide of teenage violence and the types of music that teach vulnerable young listeners and viewers that violence is a legitimate method of dealing with both justified and unjustified anger.

Video games. If you've ever played video games, you know that violence takes center stage in many of them. Numerous top-selling games take players through plots based on violence and aggression. In one study, 50 percent of boys said violent games were their favorites.[256] Players tally up points and "win" by using weapons, killing, kicking, stabbing, and shooting. In some of these games, players must become increasingly violent in order to win.

Games that are "first person" in nature put the player in control as he experiences violent action by controlling and manipulating the game character who is the perpetrator of the violence. Research continues to make a connection between video-game violence and real-life aggression.[257]

Lt. Col. David Grossman, an expert on the psychology of killing and the author of *On Killing* and *Let's Stop Teaching Our Kids to Kill*, offers compelling and convincing insight into how our teenagers are being conditioned to pull the trigger. Grossman is an expert in the field of "killology"—the study of the methods and psychological effects of training army recruits to circumvent their natural inhibitions to killing fellow human beings.

And how exactly do we train kids to kill? Of course there are numerous factors involved. Grossman says it's a skill learned from years of violence and abuse in the home, as well as from the entertaining violence of television, film, and interactive video games. These cultural forces are better understood, says Grossman, by looking at four techniques the military uses to increase the killing rate of soldiers. Media, especially video games, uses the same four techniques on kids.

Military boot camp is all about **brutalization and desensitization**. From the moment the recruits step off that bus, the drill instructors use screaming, yelling, and herding to break down the recruits and instill a new set of values that embrace destruction, violence, and death as a way of life. The same things happen to the hearts and minds of the average kid who sees or commits thousands of murders and other acts of violence while playing video games.

Classical conditioning is a subtle yet powerful mechanism that teaches military personnel to *like* killing. That's what happens when kids eat popcorn and drink soda while sitting in movie theaters or while playing violent video games in family rooms for hours on end. Over time, violence becomes associated with pleasure, which leads to what Grossman calls AVIDS—Acquired Violence Immune Deficiency Syndrome. It destroys your violence immune system and conditions you to derive pleasure from violence. Suddenly, it's much easier to throw a fist or pull a trigger.

The repetition of a constant stimulus-response procedure is a powerful teaching technique known as **operant conditioning.** Pilots are trained this way in flight simulators. When it comes time to react in a real situation, past repetition leads them to respond reflexively to a crisis. Law enforcement officers are trained the same way as they shoot at pop-up human silhouettes on the shooting rage. Grossman says every time a child plays an interactive point-and-shoot video game, he's learning the exact same conditioned reflex and motor skills. *Point and shoot, point and shoot, point and shoot...*

Finally, the military drill sergeant is a **role model** who embodies violence and aggression. Today's media provides our kids with highly influential role models who exemplify how to handle conflict through violent means. Consider the fact that even in the popular world of professional wrestling, kids are now rooting for the bad guy to win. In many violent video games, teenagers control the villain or antihero.[258]

A year after the Paducah school shootings, David Grossman and I corresponded about the interesting facts he discovered:

> Michael Carneal, the 14-year-old shooter in this case, had never fired a pistol in his life, and had fired a .22 rifle at camp a little. He stole a .22 pistol from a neighbor, fired a few practice rounds, and took it to school. FBI data shows that trained law enforcement officers average less than 20% hits in real world situations. Michael Carneal fired 8 shots at a high school prayer group as they were breaking up...firing at a milling, screaming, running group of kids. Michael hit 8 different kids with 8 shots, five of them head shots and the other 3 upper torso. I trained the Texas Rangers and the Texas State Patrol, and when I told them, they were stunned. Nowhere in the annals of military or law enforcement history can I find an equivalent "achievement." Where does a 14-year-old boy who never fired a gun before get this skill? Video games.

Grossman went on to describe the fact that Carneal had several arcade-quality point-and-shoot video games in his home:

A hundred things can convince someone to WANT to take a gun and go kill, but only one thing makes them ABLE to kill: practice, practice, practice. Not practice shooting bull's-eyes or deer, but practice shooting people. All witness statements state that Michael stood, never moving his feet, holding the gun in two hands, never firing far to the left or right, never far up or down, with a blank look on his face. He was playing a video game...simply shooting everything that "popped up" on his "screen." Just like he had done countless THOUSANDS of times before. As an aside, it is interesting to note that it is not natural to fire at each target only once. The norm is to fire until the target drops. But that is what most video games teach you, to shoot only once, since the target will always drop after being hit. And, by the way, many of the games give extra credit for head shots.[259]

Computers and the Internet. Besides the fact that kids are able to now play violent interactive videos online, watch violent video clips and shows, and visit a variety of Web sites that encourage and celebrate violent behavior, there's something else violent going on in the online world. It's a growing phenomenon known as "cyber-bullying."

No longer is bullying limited to the schoolyard. Now, kids are bullying each other through threats sent via e-mail, text messages, and instant messaging. The threats can be sent directly, or through the rumor mill, where threats, gossip, and humiliation spread like wildfire. In some cases, the bully hides anonymously behind a fictitious name or screen profile. In other cases, the bully is known. At times, the bully may circulate embarrassing photos or a private note. All he has to do is hit a key on the keyboard and the photo or message is sent via the Internet to dozens, hundreds, or even thousands of recipients. Sometimes bullies go so far as to create a Web site—in the name of the person they're targeting—on one of the many social networking sites frequented by teenagers. Once it's set up, they fill the site with false information and photos.

The damage can cut deeply as targets are teased and harassed. Girls tend to mock others about their physical appearance. The boys make physical threats to each other, and sexual comments to girls. The sad fact is that cyber-bullying is happening at all levels, from elementary school right on through high school. While nobody knows for sure how many kids are bullying or being bullied online, the problem is becoming more widespread. Some estimates state that about 45 percent of teenagers have been victimized by cyber-bullying.[260]

What are the results of media's violent content? While life can be violent and ugly at times, media paints an unrealistic picture of what real violence is actually like. As a result, our kids can grow up with a false notion of reality. First, violence occurs far more frequently in the media than it does in the real world. The actual real-life, violent-crime rate in America is only a small fraction of the violent-crime rate in the media, especially for those kids who are playing violent video games. And second, crime has long-term consequences for both the victim and the aggressor. Crime hurts and kills people; criminals get caught and go to jail. I've been amazed by some of the stories I've read recounting incidents of violent juvenile crime. Kids don't realize there are consequences. After getting shot, one teenager was shocked to discover it actually hurt and the bullet wound bled.

What price, if any, do our kids pay for being on the receiving end of media's hefty diet of violence? *First, media may lead our teenagers to become desensitized to the horrors of violence.* "So, what?" says the teen, in response to a mother's horrified reaction to a graphic TV scene. "I've seen all this and much worse before. That's nothing!" He's telling the truth. Our kids risk losing a sense of the true value and dignity of people when they become insensitive to personal violence, as well as violent behavior in society. Consider the findings of one study involving Scottish youth: Researchers found that teenagers have become so used to seeing violent images in the media that they find photos depicting cruelty to animals more distressing than pictures of dead humans and severed limbs.[261]

Second, media violence can make kids more aggressive. In 1960, Dr. Leonard Eron studied 875 third-grade boys and girls and discovered there was a direct relationship between the violent TV programs they watched and their aggressiveness at school. He examined the subjects again when they were 30 years old. Those who had watched significant amounts of violent television were more likely to have been convicted of more serious crimes, to be more aggressive when drinking, and to inflict harsher punishment on their kids. Concludes Eron, "What one learns about life from the television screen seems to be transmitted even to the next generation."[262] Another study found that teenagers and young adults who watch more than three hours of TV a day are more than twice as likely to commit an act of violence later in life, compared with those who watch less than one hour of TV a day.[263] But as might be expected, the youngest kids are most affected by media violence. "Violent imagery increases 'the likelihood of aggressive or fearful behavior in younger kids, especially boys,'" say researchers at England's University of Birmingham.[234]

Third, kids may imitate violent behaviors they've encountered in media. In his study on television and violence, Dr. Brandon Centerwall found that following the introduction of television in the United States, the annual white homicide rate increased by 93 percent from 1945 to 1974. While he doesn't blame TV as the sole factor behind the rise in violence, he concludes that "if, hypothetically, television technology had never been developed, there would today (in 1992) be 10,000 fewer homicides each year in the United States, 70,000 fewer rapes, and 700,000 fewer injurious assaults."[265] Studies of population data for various countries show that after the introduction of television into the culture, homicide rates double in 10 to 15 years.[266] The rise in teenage violence, especially on school campuses and among younger and younger kids, is more evidence of the influence of media violence.

Finally, media violence may lead kids to develop an unrealistic view of the world. The world is, in fact, a violent place. But cumulative exposure to media often results in "mean-world syndrome" as kids exhibit a heightened fear for their own personal safety. Media violence causes many kids to have nightmares, while also instilling in them a fear of being harmed.

Our teenagers imitate the world around them. Every week they engage with media and witness murders, rapes, assaults, gunplay, and a host of other violent activities. What kids don't see is the horror and pain of the aftermath. What they don't feel is the physical pain. What they don't understand is the immorality of violent behavior. It shouldn't come as a surprise that America has become the most violent of the industrialized nations, with teenagers doing unto others what they have seen done thousands of times in the media. David Walsh of the National Institute on Media and the Family summarizes this ugly reality: "It is tragically ironic that at the very time we are wringing our hands about violent behavior among young people, we are simultaneously entertaining them with it."[267]

Media Shapes Their Sexual Understanding and Behaviors

Broadcast and cable television are constantly stretching the sexual envelope, particularly in programming targeting young adults and teenagers. Sex has gone from being a dirty word to a regular event. The proof lies in the fact that the overwhelming majority of today's teenagers have been marinating in the soup of sexualized media for so long, they find little or nothing shocking or wrong. And when Dad, Mom, or any other adult in their presence expresses shock, the kids look at them as if they're hopelessly out-of-date and old-fashioned. The edge just keeps moving further away.

Teenagers, struggling to understand and know how to express their developing God-given gift of sexuality, used to rely on Dad and Mom for information about the birds and the bees. But now, if they want, Dad and Mom can stand back and allow media to explain the facts of life to their kids. Exposure to media allows kids to see and hear numerous instances of sexually explicit, perverse programming during the crucial years of moral development. And judging from the rising rate of sexual activity among teenagers (and even younger kids), they're following the lead of their media heroes and role models.

Media aimed at young kids appeals to their very natural sexual curiosity by including innuendo. Some media portrays adolescent sexuality in a manner that assumes all teenagers are doing it—and that sex is a regular, normal, and expected part of the adolescent experience. Still others encourage promiscuous behavior through humorous portrayals of the teenage sexual appetite. After all, if you can get an audience laughing, their defenses break down. Media targeting an older audience not only includes all these elements, but also depicts numerous types of sexual promiscuity, premarital sex, extramarital sex, and perversion as a regular part of adult and teenage life. While the makers of some sexually explicit shows and films sometimes have ready explanations regarding their intent and the socially redeeming qualities of their work, it can be assumed the average media users (especially teenagers) are led by their hormones and not their brains.

*Television.*With almost 100 percent of teenagers living in a home with at least one television, and a growing number watching the television in their own bedrooms while being unsupervised by parents, television has become a prime source for sex education among teenagers.

When researcher Barry Sapolsky analyzed one week of prime-time network television during 1989 to compare its sexual content to a week of programming in 1979, he found that sex was playing a bigger role. Young viewers were provided with frequent lessons on how to look sexy, act sexy, practice sex, and have sex. Every four minutes characters were talking about sex or displaying sexual behavior—and in 1989, only one verbal reference to intercourse out of a total of 91 occurred between a married couple. Sapolsky wrote, "Premarital and extramarital sex is an accepted part of television comedy and drama; marriage is inconsequential. In an era when monogamy in marriage is promoted as an important means to avoid sexually transmitted diseases, sexual titillation abounds among the unmarried."[268] Sapolsky was writing then about the television world that existed *prior to* the birth of all of today's middle and high school students.

In their 1996 survey of prime-time TV fare, the Media Research Center found that 57 percent of the shows "promote as a major theme, sexual permissiveness. It's usually premarital sex, but sometimes adultery or homosexuality thrown in for good measure."[269]

In case you're wondering, sex on TV is still increasing. The most recent data concludes that the number of sexual scenes on television nearly doubled over a seven-year period. The Kaiser Family Foundation study, *Sex on TV 4,* revealed the following data:

- Among the 20 shows teenagers watch most, 70 percent include sexual content and nearly half (45 percent) include sexual behavior.

- During prime-time hours, sex is even more common with nearly eight shows in 10 (77 percent) including sexual content, averaging 5.9 sexual scenes per hour.

- Two-thirds of all shows (68 percent) include talk about sex and 35 percent of all shows include sexual behaviors.

- Among the 20 most highly rated shows for teenage viewers, 10 percent of those with sexual content include a reference to sexual risks or responsibilities at some point in the episode.

- About half of all scenes with intercourse (53 percent) involve characters who have an established relationship with one another. Fifteen percent of scenes present characters having sex when they have just met—up from seven percent.[270]

While many of the kids in the five- to 10-year-old age group are exposed to sexual content via programming created for teenagers and adults, they're also learning lessons about sex via programming created just for them. The Parents Television Council discovered recently that in more than 400 hours of monitored kids' programming were 275 incidents of sexual content—an average of more than one every two hours. "Adult subtext, innuendo and double entendre (128) were the most prevalent form of sexual content followed by nudity and partial nudity."[271] The study concluded that one of the "more disturbing trends" was "the amount of adult-oriented subtext that was laced throughout scripts of both the animated and live-action programs. Perhaps this trend has been spawned by similar approaches in movies where scripts seem to be written on two levels, one for the kids and one for the adults. Perhaps producers think that if they can entertain parents with double entendres and innuendo the parents will encourage the kids to watch. Whatever the reason, sexual content is present in kids's programming."[272]

If any network has succeeded in showering young viewers with "sex education," it's MTV. For years, MTV was criticized for the edgy sexual content contained in its round-the-clock airing of music videos. But in recent years, MTV has demoted music videos to a very small segment of its daily programming menu. In its place, the network has created cutting-edge programming including numerous specials, ongoing reality shows, and dramatic programs. As I've continued to tune in as the network makes changes and evolves, the boundaries regarding sexual content have stretched to the point where they almost seem to no longer exist.

After surveying 171 hours of MTV programming around the clock over a one-week period, researchers recently discovered the following:

- There were 1,548 sexual scenes containing 3,056 depictions of sex or various forms of nudity, and 2,881 sexual references.

- Kids watching MTV are viewing an average of nine sexual scenes per hour with approximately 18 sexual depictions and 17 instances of sexual dialogue or innuendo.

- The network's reality shows had more sexual content than the music videos. Analysts recorded 833 segments containing sexual content in 66 hours of reality programming, or 12.6 scenes per hour. Within those 833 segments, there were 917 verbal references and 905 visual depictions of sexual activity.[273]

Why so much sex on TV? The bottom line is that sex sells – it helps the networks and cable outlets boost ratings and build an audience.[274] Talk shows, reality shows, sitcoms, dramas, and even sports broadcasts know the formula works. They're enlisting it in an effort to draw viewers, no matter what their ages.

Music. Too often, teenagers' openness and curiosity about sexuality is answered by the voice of music, which teaches them that sexual pleasure is an end in and of itself. In other cases, music "ministers" to kids who are lost in loneliness due to relational starvation caused by absent or indifferent parents. The sexual messages (both lyrical and visual) of today's music lead many to pursue relationships and love by walking down the road of sexual intimacy.

My ongoing monitoring and evaluation of popular music over the last two decades has convinced me our culture's changing attitudes on sexual freedom expressed through a promiscuous and boundary-less lifestyle are one of the most overt and prevalent themes in today's music. Research has shown "depending on the music genre, one-fifth to one-half of all music videos portray sexuality or eroticism."[275] The most recent survey of popular music's lyrical content among the 10 top-selling CDs "indicated that of the 159 songs analyzed, 42% contained sexual content, 41% of which were pretty explicit or very explicit."[276]

The music industry, like most other media outlets, insists they aren't educating kids but only reflecting the sexual values and commitments already present in mainstream culture. In reality, they're doing both as they serve as a map *and* a mirror. The media does, however, increasingly express an obligation to educate kids about sexual responsibility. While this may sound noble, understand this usually translates into teaching kids how to avoid messing up their lives by getting pregnant or contracting an STD. The real message coming through loud and clear in far too much of today's music is this: "If it feels good, do it. The only consequences to avoid are pregnancy and disease. Have a good time, but don't catch anything."

Radio. As already mentioned in the last chapter, teenagers spend a lot of time listening to the radio. Sexual messages are broadcast over the airwaves in a variety of ways. First, there's radio advertising that targets teenagers. At times, the ads use sexual innuendo to sell the product. At other times, the product being sold is sexual in nature. For example, Trojan condoms have been advertised on Top 40 formatted radio stations for years. Some of the company's ads feature the product's superhero, Trojan Man, coming to the rescue as various couples find themselves in sexual predicaments without a condom.

Second, the banter between on-air personalities is sometimes sexual in nature, and it's usually done with intention toward humor. And third, a good portion of the music played on stations catering to teenagers features sexual themes.

While few content analyses of radio programming have been conducted, one such study looked at 15 hours of programming on a teen-oriented station. Researchers found that overall, 22 percent of the programming was sexual in nature. Of the segments coded as "including sexual content," 20 percent were "pretty explicit" or "very explicit" in nature. In addition, "very few segments included messages concerning planning or responsibilities (1%), consequences or risks (4%), or fidelity or monogamy (5%). Sexual content on the radio occurred during music segments (45%), during talk segments (30%), and during commercials (9%)."[277]

Magazines. A walk past the magazine racks in any large bookstore or newsstand offers clues to the kind and extent of sexual content that magazines are delivering to young readers. Parents and youth workers should take special note of the covers as they reveal the issue's themes. "Content analysis indicates that magazines aimed at teenage girls provide messages that girls should be beautiful and plan their lives to attract a man, and girls are depicted as objects of male sexual desire in editorial content as well as in advertising material."[278] The same messages are communicated to young male readers, along with the message that they're to aggressively pursue sexual relationships.

Video games. As gaming continues to increase in popularity among teenagers, it's important for those who care about kids to monitor the games teenagers are playing, paying special attention to any sexual content—either overt or hidden—that may exist in those games. More experienced and knowledgeable gamers share secrets that might lead them to find "secret" or buried game content that can only be accessed through the use of "cheats" or codes. These codes take gamers into game levels or areas that are unadvertised, and therefore largely unknown to parents and other adults. Again, know what games your kids are playing and monitor the content.

Movies. Only two studies have targeted the sexual content of movies popular among teenagers. One looked at the content of top video rentals, and the other looked at the content of R-rated movies. "Both studies reported a high amount of sexual content, with the most common sexual activity occurring among unmarried partners...The most common sexual activity among unmarried partners was intercourse, and sexual behavior among married characters was rare and rather mundane compared with those having unmarried sex."[279]

In the movies sex simply is, and it sells. Teenagers can come away from a film thinking that adolescent promiscuity is a normal part of life. And they also risk buying the lie that normal adolescents participate in what most of us know to be immoral or abnormal sexual practices and behaviors.

As with all media depictions of sexuality, we must examine the sexual content in its context. Remember, sex out of God's context is what we want our kids to avoid. But sex within God's design, will, and way is to be encouraged and celebrated. In his outstanding book *At a Theater Near You*, Christian film buff Thomas Patterson encourages readers to consider the context of sexuality in film. He suggests that films with a significant sexual element can fall into at least three categories: (1) those that involve sex for valid reasons and treat it with mature discretion, (2) those that are misguided or unthinking in the treatment of sex, and (3) those that deliberately exploit sex.[280] Patterson writes,

> The best way to make a judgment in this regard is to ask what relationship exists between love (as Christians understand it) and the film's treatment of sex...Christians understand that among other things, love is discipline. The best films that incorporate lovemaking do so with the discipline of restraint and understatement...The mere inclusion of sex in a film is not wrong; lying about the ultimate meaning of sex is.[281]

Christian filmmaker Brian Godawa argues the same point: "Context makes all the difference between moral *exhortation* and immoral *exploitation* of sin."[282] It's the exploitive and gratuitous depictions of sexuality that should cause us alarm. If we allow these depictions to shape our kids' understanding of their sexuality, we run the risk of distorting God's gift of sexuality because of its cheap and immoral portrayals on the big screen.

The Internet. Teenagers can access all kinds of sexually oriented materials on the Internet. "Studies indicate that of the 1,000 most-visited sites, 10% are adult-sex-oriented. In addition, portrayals of violent pornography on the Internet have increased, and access to such material has become easier."[283] There are at least 4.2 million pornographic Web sites, and at least 25 percent of all daily search engine requests (68 million) are pornographic in nature.[284] Photographs and videos abound, and computer-savvy kids who are out there looking for it are learning how to bypass filters and other safety devices so they can access the Internet's dark side.

But their Internet sex education doesn't always come as a result of them seeking to learn. Sometimes it looks for and finds them. One survey found that one out of five teenagers ages 10 to 17 had inadvertently encountered explicit sexual content, and 19 percent had been exposed to an unwanted online solicitation in the previous year.[285] Most of the unwanted exposures that included imagery (pictures or videos) were of naked persons, while 32 percent showed people having sex, and seven percent involved nudity, sex, and violence.[286]

The breakdown of traditional support systems—most notably the family—has also contributed to the number of kids who harness the Internet in search of answers to their legitimate questions about sex and sexuality. Whether it's because they are embarrassed, can't talk to their parents, or their parents are out of the picture for some reason, it appears that half of all teenagers are going online to find health information, with the largest number of those questions being about sex.

We must remember that our kids are naturally curious about this aspect of their lives, and if we aren't there to speak to them about it, they'll be more prone to look for information elsewhere. The Internet increasingly caters to their curiosity, providing answers—both good and bad—to their sexual questions.

Today's teenagers rank media second only to school-based sex education programs as their leading source of information about sex.[287] That said, media is more than happy to contribute to the sex education of our teenagers. Research conclusively shows "adolescents who are exposed to more sexual content in the media, and who perceive greater support from the media for teenage sexual behavior, report greater intentions to engage in sexual intercourse and more sexual activity. Mass media are an important context for adolescents' sexual socialization."[288]

Media Often Shapes Their Attitudes and Behaviors about Tobacco, Alcohol, and Drugs

While the media is a primary conduit used to send messages that warn kids of the dangers, media also serves to provide kids with role models and messages that make tobacco, alcohol, and drug abuse appealing.

Some performers, songs, shows, Web sites, and commercials go to great lengths to encourage kids to avoid drugs. One such organized effort, launched cooperatively by the Musicians' Assistance Program and the Partnership for a Drug-Free America, starred top-name musicians who knew about the ravages of substance abuse from experience. The National Academy of Recording Arts and Sciences also got involved, establishing the MusiCares substance abuse program to help addicted musicians.

While these efforts are noble, they're countered by messages that promote and glorify substance abuse, which has been a lifestyle and thematic element of music for decades—thus the long-used phrase "sex, drugs, and rock and roll." This connection continues, as one-fourth of all MTV videos portray alcohol or tobacco use.[289] Research also concludes there's "a positive correlation between television and music video viewing and alcohol consumption among teens."[290]

Television and film also send out powerful messages about substance use and abuse. As you watch and monitor your kids' big- and small-screen diet, what are they learning from what they see and hear? What about the mixed messages kids receive when drinking is glamorized as a sophisticated adult activity? What about media portrayals where drunkenness is shown to be something funny and without consequences? What about shows that portray teenage characters who are smarter than their parents, yet they're sneaking around and drinking?

Researchers recently found that "the number of youth related movies with smoking released each year has outnumbered R-rated movies with smoking," and, "smoking scenes almost never show tobacco's negative effects, and in fact, leave adolescents with the impression that smoking is glamorous or beneficial."[291] The National Center on Addiction and Substance Abuse found that compared with the 22 percent of teenagers who do not watch any R-rated movies in a month, those 12- to 17-year-olds who watch three or more R-rated movies in a month (43 percent of 12- to 17-year-olds) are nearly seven times more likely to smoke cigarettes, more than five times more likely to drink alcohol, and more than six times likelier to smoke marijuana.[292] Media's educational power can cause viewers to accept such behavior as normal, expected, and appropriate.

Many researchers "have shown advertising to be very effective in increasing youngsters' awareness of and emotional responses to products (recognition of brands, desire to own products advertised). Cigarette advertising seems to increase teenagers' risk of smoking by glamorizing smoking and smokers, and kids who are able to recall ads related to tobacco are more likely to view smoking favorably and to become smokers."[293]

In addition, "alcoholic drinks are the most common beverage portrayed on TV. It has been shown that exposure to alcohol advertising and TV programming is associated with positive beliefs about alcohol consumption."[294] Radio advertising also reaches teenagers almost daily, with many of those ads promoting alcohol. The Center of Alcohol Marketing and Youth found "the alcohol industry routinely overexposed youth to its radio advertising by placing the ads when and where youth were more likely than adults to hear them."[295] The study found the ads were placed on stations with "youth" formats, and they were aired when young people listened most.[296]

The Internet is loaded with sites that promote alcohol and substance use. Cigarette and alcohol manufacturers have online homes for their products, many of which feature the type of interactive elements young people find attractive. Because they have to create and keep new users, these companies are always looking to prepare and welcome young people as customers. In addition, there are scores of sites that promote and educate kids on what illicit substances to use, along with tips and tricks for enhancing the drug experience.

As loving and concerned parents and youth workers, we need to echo those messages that warn kids of the dangers, and challenge those messages that promote substance abuse as a virtue.

Media Often Promotes Sexual Violence

There were about 60 "high-risk" troubled kids in the room. They were there for a weekly after-school gathering that was part of a program established by a guidance counselor who wanted to give them positive guidance and direction. A bunch of guys sat in the front of the room; the girls gravitated toward the back. But the influence of the hip-hop culture was obvious in the way every one of them dressed.

I'd been asked to dialogue with the students about music and media. I began by asking them a question. "Do you think there's any music out there that, in your opinion, is dangerous or wrong?" A hand shot into the air at the back of the room.

"Yeah," a young girl replied. "I don't like that music all these guys are listening to—music that refers to us as bitches and ho's."

Immediately, a 14-year-old boy in the front row—who'd appeared completely uninterested up to this point—scoffed at her comment in a mocking manner: "Most of the girls I know in this school like to be treated like bitches and ho's."

After I asked a few more clarifying questions and worked to get to the source of his conclusion, everything became clear to me. The young man had bought into the messages of the very music that the young girl had said she didn't like. In the end, he was genuinely surprised to learn that girls didn't like being treated that way.

Many in our culture, including those who make media, would dismiss a link between sexual violence in the media and actual teenage behavior as paranoid and ill-informed conjecture. The evidence proves otherwise.

One study showed that 52 men "experienced a number of changes after being exposed to one extremely violent film a day for five days. After this exposure, men found the violence less anxiety-provoking and depressing; they evaluated the injury experienced by female victims of sexual assault as less significant; and they were less able to empathize with real victims."[297] It's frightening to think about the end result of the sex education many of our most vulnerable teenagers are receiving from films, television, magazines, music, and videos. Add to that mix an almost unlimited amount of hardcore and violent Internet pornography that's easily found, and the mix becomes lethal. How will these kids view and practice their sexuality when they become adults?

Our teenagers are learning how to be men and women from the media. This includes education on gender roles and sexual relationships. If media continues to teach males to be aggressive and females to be passive and willing recipients, we'll continue to see a rise in sexually violent behavior. Already, at least one in every three women worldwide has been beaten, coerced into sex, or otherwise abused during her lifetime.[298] In the United States, nearly 25 percent of women "report being raped and/or physically assaulted by a current or former spouse, cohabiting partner, or date at some time in their lifetime."[299]

If media continues to offer up a diet of sexually violent fare that is easily accessed by people of all ages, don't be surprised to see more young teenage boys innocently attempt to justify their sexually violent behavior by saying, "I thought that's the way I'm supposed to treat a lady."

Media Often Teaches Kids to Objectify Females

I often use a rather crude analogy when helping teenagers discover how our culture tends to teach young boys how to treat young girls, and young girls how to expect to be treated by young boys. The image comes from a reality that's emerged due to the ongoing and steady diet of lusty media sights and sounds that have been pummeling kids for years. I tell them this, "Boys have been taught to treat girls no differently than a porcelain urinal that hangs on a men's room wall. Boys are taught to see girls as just something in which they can thoughtlessly relieve themselves." In other words, our kids are being taught to objectify (boys) and to be objectified (girls).

Take some time to watch current music videos, read the advertisements in magazines, think about the commercials seen on TV, and view the latest teen-targeted films. All too often, females are portrayed as "eye candy" and "boy toys," having their value and worth based on what they look like and how they serve the needs of males as sexual things.

Media has done a phenomenal job creating and affirming sexual stereotypes that forsake the dignity of humanity, leading them away from valuing themselves and others in the same way God values them. The Media Education Foundation concludes that "men are primarily portrayed as aggressive, strong, independent and violent...female characters are still mainly valued for their appearance (with extremely narrow definitions of beauty), their sexuality, and their passivity."[300] Females are nothing more than bodies, and those bodies are treated as commodities. Men stare, comment, pursue, and "conquer" as they look to satisfy a hunger portrayed as being natural, normal, and needing satisfaction—with little or no regard for morals. Research into the content of teenage girls' magazines affirms these stereotypes, concluding that girls "should be beautiful and plan their lives to attract a man, and girls are depicted as objects of male sexual desire in editorial content as well as in advertising material."[301]

Parents, youth workers, and those who love kids should help young people not only identify these stereotypes in media, but also consciously and thoughtfully process them in a way that leads them to realize how these images stray from God's design for those who are created in his image.

Media Often Defines and Shapes Kids' Idea of Family

Granted, as was discussed earlier, the family *is* changing. Divorce, cohabitation, out-of-wedlock births, absent fathers, and a host of other negative trends have left many of our teenagers struggling to grow up, find their way through adolescence, and move into a healthy adulthood with knowledge of what a family is and how to properly assume their roles in one. For that reason, negative media depictions may in fact be a somewhat accurate reflection of reality, but they're regularly accessed by impressionable young people looking for guidance.

In those cases, Dad may be portrayed as a weak-kneed, bumbling idiot possessing little wisdom or common sense. Often he's a lazy slob with little or no motivation, like cartoon father Homer Simpson. While TV mothers used to be nurturing and loving, now they're like disengaged men. And kids have become super-brats who lack respect for parents and anyone else in the adult world—and sometimes they wind up parenting their own parents. Other media depictions portray teenagers who function on their own with infrequent mention of or appearances by parents. The message that's often sent says parents are stupid, incompetent idiots who are lucky to have survived for so long, while kids are more than competent enough to survive on their own—even in the midst of life-threatening danger. And marriage is sometimes seen as an impossible or even undesirable burden.

Granted, the idealized family world portrayed by the media 40 to 50 years ago was so sugarcoated it didn't seem real. People in those families rarely had any serious problems. If they did, they were able to happily solve them all in a very short period of time— usually within 30 minutes. But now, the pendulum has swung in the other direction. David Elkind says, "Some family TV shows have gone beyond portraying family life as it really is and are devoted, instead, to ridiculing the values of the nuclear family."[302] The family is sometimes portrayed as an outdated institution that serves to stifle personal growth, creativity, and advancement. In fact, members of traditional families are often portrayed as being doomed to a life full of misery. The home is depicted as being stress producing, rather than stress reducing.

The real-life situation of many media users is that their families are either broken or failing to function properly. Those who grow up in dysfunctional situations know it's not fun at all. Sometimes, the most hopeless, nihilistic, or angry music flows from a heart scarred by years of brokenness, neglect, or even violence in the homes of those making the music. Some of the music reflects the hopeless sense that the cycle of family dysfunction is absolutely unbreakable.

On a positive note, numerous examples of positive themes abound—longing for recovery, reconciliation, and restoration of a relationship with parents that somehow went wrong. When this happens, music serves as a powerful mirror reflecting the ugly reality of the breakdown of the family. But media is also a map, defining family roles and functions for our teenagers. If they choose to follow the role models of media's inaccurate portrayals of family—particularly those of mothers and fathers—our teenagers will grow up to selfishly pursue their own interests, at the expense of family life.

David Popenoe of the Rutgers University National Marriage Project says, "I haven't seen any upturn in television programs featuring typical stable marriages. It's a complete downer."[303] If current trends persist, media will not only reflect, but will contribute to the breakdown of the family.

The next time you engage in some media with your teen, look and listen carefully for the messages. How is marriage depicted? How are parents portrayed? Does the family create problems or solve them?

Media Often Teaches That Meaning Is Found in Materialism

Already believing the lie that "things bring happiness," our kids watch and hear a daily parade of media messages that promote values, attitudes, and behaviors that promise not only to make their lives better, but also to bring them fulfillment and peace.

In an article on the power of images, J. Francis Davis explores several of television's myths (stories or ideas that explain the culture and customs of a people) and how they shape our everyday life. One myth cited is this: "The 'good life' consists of buying possessions that cost lots of money."[304] This is true not only about television, but also about all media as it exists primarily to deliver an audience to advertisers and marketers.

A second myth is "happiness, satisfaction and sex appeal, just to name a few, are imminent—and available with the next consumer purchase."[305] When our kids buy this lie, they build their lives around the pursuit of things they believe will make them happy. They learn that things are more important than people.

Teenagers act on that lesson and grow up into adults who, like most people, are on an endless pursuit of the good life. It's not who I am as a person that gives me value and meaning in life, but rather what I drive, what I wear, what I look like, and where I live. In fact, if I want attention from the opposite sex, material excess is a prerequisite. As media analyst Todd Gitlin says: "With few exceptions, prime time gives us people immersed in personal ambition...Personal ambition and consumerism are the driving forces in their lives. The sumptuous and brightly lit settings of most series amount to advertisements for a consumption-centered version of the good life."[306]

With media simultaneously dropping these values around the globe and through a variety of outlets, global culture is becoming more of a consumer culture. The effect of media's "gotta have it" message, whether from programming or ads, extends well beyond the boundaries of North America. Demographic analyst Chip Walker says, "More than ever, people around the world know about and want the same type of branded goods and services. Rather than a global village, mass exposure to TV (and other media) is creating a global mall."[307] And in this new global economy, "I am what I have" is often an accurate description of media's materialistic message.

Media Often Feeds a Growing Disregard for Self

Teenagers spend a good amount of time and energy trying to answer the question *Who am I?* When the family or church fails to answer this question for teenagers, then by default they forfeit their influence to the media. While media certainly has the power and ability to give teenagers truthful answers to this question, it more often than not leads them astray. When kids are told they haven't been made with a divine purpose, their daily lives and purpose will be shaped by media's guidance.

A University of California study discovered that among preteens and teenagers, there is a link between having a television in your bedroom and engaging in risky behaviors, including smoking cigarettes, using drugs, binge drinking, and casual sex. The study links these risky behaviors to the amount of unsupervised exposure to high-risk behavior in the media.[308]

The increase in media portrayals of dangerous and risky behavior not only reflects this growing sense of disregard and value for self on the rise in our culture, but it offers kids examples to emulate. Kids with a lack of personal value and a low or declining sense of worth are more apt to engage in reckless and dangerous behaviors that involve throwing their physical bodies around. This was a trend glamorized on MTV's hit reality show *Jackass*—which featured dangerous "backyard" stunts that were, at times, hilariously funny—and continued with a variety of reality shows taking the concept to further extremes. Media can guide kids to find their value and purpose through engaging freely in behaviors that are morally wrong, offensive to God, and demeaning to self and to others. These include the indulgence of sexual desires without regard for God's laws or respect for others. In addition, much of the blame for the recent rise in eating disorders and steroid abuse among teenagers can be laid at the feet of media, which has set standards for beauty and status that are not only unattainable, but potentially deadly if pursued.

Media Can Foster a Spirit of Rebellion

As adolescents move from childhood to adulthood, there is always a tendency to rebel. Rebellious media—particularly music—can become an outlet for some of the aggression teenagers feel. Kids who are fatherless or grow up neglected or abused at home, at school, or even in church are naturally drawn to media that challenges anyone in authority because, after all, the authority figures in their lives have either abused or shirked their responsibilities. If you were to read the stories of many of today's songwriters, you'd find their music often serves as an outlet for the anger and frustration they feel as a result of growing up in a terrible situation. They write music to exorcise their "demons."

As you engage with teenagers' media, listen and watch carefully to discover attitudes toward authority and authority figures. Some of the rebellion is directed toward parents. At times, kids are directed to carry out their rebelliousness by doing whatever they want. Rebellion is also directed against the church and organized religion. When teachers and schools are seen as a roadblock to adolescent freedom, they can also become the targets of rebellion. Distrust of and dissatisfaction with the government is also reflected in media, whether through direct confrontation or through the more subtle means of media bias. In our current postmodern situation where teenagers are encouraged to become their own final authority on all matters related to life, we can expect to see a growing sentiment against the authority of law enforcement.

A child's obsession with blatantly rebellious music and media should serve to tip off parents to their teenager's pain and hurt. Usually teenagers obsessed with this type of music and media identify with it and, in doing so, find its unhealthy messages to be a therapeutic outlet for pent-up aggression. Observant parents and youth workers can initiate relationships and begin to offer healing to teenagers who use the music and media to react against deep hurt. But there is always the danger that this same type of media can come between well-adjusted and authority-honoring "normal kids" and their parents by convincing them it's normal and right to dishonor and disobey those whom God has placed in authority over them.

Media Often Shapes Teenagers' Spirituality and Beliefs

There's an emerging trend in today's media that's both follow-ing and fostering a parallel trend among young people—speaking openly about spiritual themes, spiritual questions, spiritual beliefs, and concepts of God. For those who view the world as it should be viewed—through the framework of a Christian worldview and life view—we realize this conscious search grows out of the fact that all human beings have been created to worship God. Media themes both reflect and answer this reality. Popular music is addressing spiritual themes and employing religious imagery more than ever. Books about heaven, angels, and near-death experiences top the best-seller lists. Television and film producers have created a va-riety of programs and movies addressing and employing spiritual themes. Although these expressions are rarely biblical if and when they offer answers, they do reflect our culture's hunger and thirst for the one true God, and a longing for redemption.

But the media's interest in spirituality doesn't necessarily translate into a distinctively *Christian* spirituality and view of the world. Media encourages teenagers to step up to the "spiritual buf-fet line" where they can fill their own plates according to their appetites. Media role models who have done the same before them offer suggestions, such as Scientology, Kaballah, the occult, neopaganism, Near Eastern religions, pop psychology, and mysti-cism.

At a time when teenagers are forming their spiritual values and beliefs, media (in true postmodern fashion) encourages kids to forget organized religion and the God of the Bible and to pursue whatever combination of religious beliefs makes sense to them, based on their own personal preferences. While there's cause for concern regarding the spiritual path much of today's media is taking and promoting, we should be encouraged by the fact that media is asking significant questions, thereby providing followers of Christ with an opportunity to give answers.

When media becomes a type of theology class for teenagers, we need to be conscious of the messages this education is providing about who God is and what he's like. Look and listen for references to God and spirituality. Filter what you've seen and heard through God's revelation of himself, and then point out truth and challenge errors.

Media Often Causes "Christianity Confusion"

Christian kids are sometimes encouraged by the fact that their musical heroes mention God or Jesus. "Did you hear _____ (insert name of music icon here) thank Jesus after he got his award last night? I didn't know he was a Christian." Maybe, maybe not. Religious images, symbols, and chatter, whether in concerts or on CD liners, are becoming a more common part of the music scene. But many of the artists who invoke the name of God or use religious symbols preach some of the most anti-Christian and ungodly messages ever heard in popular music. Chances are your kids could be confused by these messages that re-create God in the images of the musicians and lie about the true nature of the Christian faith.

In a magazine interview for *Blender*, Mary J. Blige was asked, "Mary, you're a devout Christian. How do you reconcile bling with God?"

She answered, "My God is a God who wants me to have things. He wants me to bling! He wants me to be the hottest thing on the block. I don't know what kind of God the rest of y'all are serving, but the God I serve says, 'Mary, you need to be the hottest thing this year, and I'm gonna make sure you're doing that.' My God's the bomb!"[309]

When popular music addresses religious themes, it becomes a type of Sunday school or catechism class for our teenagers, teaching them what to believe and how to live. We need to be conscious of the theological education music is giving our kids, and we must help them develop an ability to discern what is good, true, and right from theology that is anything but biblical.

Media Often Reaches Teenagers with Political Commentary and Messages about Social Issues

In today's world, it's becoming more unusual for a band, singer, actor, or media icon to *not* comment on some pressing political or social issue.

Rock the Vote has been active in presidential campaigns by enlisting music and media stars, radio stations, MTV, record companies, and record outlets to register 18- to 24-year-old voters. It's credited with enlisting millions of voters and contributing to the election of President Clinton. Recently artists hoping for a change in administrations began Vote for Change, putting on concerts in crucial "swing" states.

Numerous music festivals have been staged over the last few decades to raise money and awareness for different charity and relief efforts. Live Aid raised money for the hungry and hurting. Other festivals raised money for Amnesty International's efforts to free political prisoners and correct human-rights violations. The Concert for Life raised money to fight AIDS. Other tours and concerts have been staged for a variety of relief efforts, including local shelters for abused woman and other nonprofit groups. U2's Bono has been campaigning for third-world debt relief and to end genocide. Examples of media's involvement in a variety of issues and causes abound.

Parents and youth workers should be aware of the fact that concerts, songs, albums, interviews, music videos, films, TV shows, and so on are often outlets for media icons and artists to preach social and political agendas. Many of these efforts are admirable and worthy, as they raise our kids' awareness and offer them concrete ways to get involved in helping those in need. Other efforts tend to be partisan, extreme, or even immoral in nature. Regardless, all of these messages shape our kids' world and life views, and it's important for adults to know what the messages are so they can help kids consider their content.

Media Often Teaches Violence as a Conflict-Resolution Strategy

One of the results of our media's current fascination with violence is the growing acceptance of violence as a way to solve problems. In today's world, playground and backyard conflicts are increasingly being settled in ways that would make Dirty Harry proud. Youth-violence expert Deborah Prothrow-Stith says television teaches us "good guys use violence as a first resort. Any amount of killing is all right, so long as one's cause is just. Violence is a hero's way to solve problems."[310] Dr. Aletha Huston of the University of Kansas says, "We keep pumping kids with the messages that violence is the way to solve their problems—and some of it takes hold."[311]

Huston's own research shows "kids who watch the violent shows, even 'just funny' cartoons, were more likely to hit out at their playmates, argue, disobey class rules, leave tasks unfinished, and were less willing to wait for things than those who watched the nonviolent programs."[312] As a result, thousands of kids walk the halls of America's high schools and middle schools fearing for their safety each day. Why? Because when kids enter into disagreements and conflict, they're faced with the decision of whether or not to employ the conflict-resolution "strategies" they've been taught by media. Numerous schools across the nation have instituted programs to teach kids that when they're settling disputes, there are more options than just fists, knives, and guns.

What conflict-resolution strategies are the teenagers you know and love learning from the media on a daily basis?

Media Often Promotes Relativism and Amorality

Media encourages our kids to create truth for themselves. It can be seen and heard in the massive quantity of media that encourages sexual expression without boundaries, sexual violence, rebellion, anarchy, violence, materialism, selfishness, and a "me"-centered spirit of entitlement. The only rule is that there are no rules. In true postmodern fashion, popular media tells teenagers that truth can only be found "inside." To look elsewhere, even to God, is to be untrue to yourself. There is no universal right and wrong. Rather, you must find what is true for *you*. On matters of sexuality and lifestyle, etc., the ultimate authority is self. The end result, if taken to its logical conclusion, is that "every individual becomes a moral nomad, wandering through life without any commonly held standard by which to measure ideas, opinions, and choices. Without an underlying moral compass, everything becomes random and fragmented, with no connecting points. Instead of choosing to obey, one simply chooses."[313]

While themes of moral relativism and amorality are becoming more common in today's media, they often slip through the cracks of our discernment unless we watch and listen carefully. Look for them and discuss them with your teenagers, pointing out the contrasts between God's never-changing truth and the fluid personal "truths" of moral relativism.

Media Can Lead Kids to Hopelessness

Kids who have forgotten, denied, or never even recognized the existence of the living God feel lost and without hope. They describe themselves by using words such as *lonely*, *alone*, *disconnected*, and *hurting*. Kids who swim in the sea of hopelessness identify with music and other media that express these feelings. Today's music and media also reflect nihilism, a byproduct of hopelessness that's a total rejection of tradition, morality, authority, and social order. Nihilism breeds and feeds on hopelessness; hopelessness breeds anger; anger leads to anarchy.

Youth workers Mike Yaconelli and Jim Burns wrote the following words more than 20 years ago that, prophetic at the time, are playing themselves out in the world of music and media today:

> There may be a very disturbing trend emerging that will affect future generations of adolescents. So far, it's only a hunch. And we hope we're wrong. But the signs all point to an emerging generation of adolescents who could erupt in anger...Our fear is that the emerging generation of young people will be angry but have no specific targets, no agenda; it will simply be anger directed at anything and everything. It will be anarchy.[314]

Media Use Can Lead to Relational and Communication Breakdowns

While I was growing up, our family watched its share of television—*together*. We had one television set that was located in our family room, and that set received only a handful of television stations. We had no remote control, except for us kids ("Hey, Walt, get up and turn to channel 6."). Our house had a stereo we'd use to listen to our record collections. In my room I had a clock radio that could only tune in to stations on the AM dial.

As mentioned earlier, the household media environment of today's teenagers has changed significantly. Multiple media outlets are kept in multiple locations in the home, with kids having the freedom to watch, listen, and interact with media *alone* in the unsupervised and uninterrupted privacy of their own rooms. As media time increases, time spent together as a family decreases. As kids spend more time interacting privately with their media, less time is spent with family members in meaningful conversation or interaction. And, when interacting with friends via cell phones and computers, the communication is increasingly nonverbal, as keypads and keyboards are enlisted to text message and instant message.

Media Use Affects Our Kids' Health

At my daughter Bethany's high school graduation, one of the commencement speeches indirectly addressed the negative health effects of today's media on teenagers. While recounting a list of news events and cultural developments that took place during the outgoing seniors' four years in high school, the speaker mentioned how their class was the first to graduate knowing their body mass index, and the first to be prohibited from eating white bread in the school cafeteria. (In an effort to address the growing epidemic of childhood obesity, our school district had instituted mandatory body mass index testing and the removal of unhealthy foods from the cafeteria menu, including white bread.)

Obesity is one of many new health concerns related to the emerging generation's increased engagement with media. "Two-thirds of Americans are overweight or obese. Each year in the United States, 400,000 deaths and $117 billion in health-care costs are attributable to obesity."[315] In addition, the prevalence of obesity in adolescents has tripled over the past 20 years. What's the cause? Experts say our kids are eating more and doing less. Their sedentary lifestyles are a result of spending less time in physical activity and play, and more time sitting around.

Much of that sitting around time is being spent watching television, using the computer, and playing video games. At times, the only body parts that are moving and getting exercise are their fingers and thumbs as they operate remotes, game controllers, keypads, and keyboards. One study found that kids who watch more than three hours of television a day are 50 percent more likely to become obese, as compared with kids who watch less than two hours a day.[316] And the long-term consequences of childhood obesity are severe, including a higher risk of developing diabetes, stroke, heart attack, joint decomposition, and high blood pressure.

Kids who use portable listening devices can suffer from hearing loss if they use their players too much or with the volume turned up too high. With kids sometimes plugging in and tuning out the world for several hours a day, we're certain to see a rise in hearing loss and deafness as this generation of teenagers gets older.

Finally, studies have also linked sleep disorders to excessive television viewing. "Adolescents who watch three or more hours of television per day are more likely to have sleep problems and these problems persist when they become young adults. By limiting television viewing to one hour or less, many of the sleep problems disappear."[317]

What about the Future?

When I was about 10 years old, I remember having a conversation with my dad about his own childhood. I seriously wondered how he could have made it through his early years without a television to watch. In my mind I developed an idea that his childhood had been underprivileged and very old-fashioned. Mediawise, I felt blessed to be born when I was.

With the pace of media development picking up every day, my kids are living in a very different media world from the one I knew. When I showed my son Josh an old 45 rpm record, he looked confused and said, "That's the weirdest CD I've ever seen." When he has kids, their media technology is sure to prompt them to look at their father and ask, "What's a CD?"

While we don't know exactly what their media-future holds, we do know that their future will hold media. As a result, now is the time for parents and youth workers to learn more about their kids' media; to know how it's shaping their lives; and to teach teenagers how to control the media, rather than allowing the media to control them.

Getting Personal

Media has power. Our brief look at media's lessons and effects has only scratched the surface of media's ability to mold and shape the values, attitudes, and behaviors of teenagers.

The world of media changes constantly, as new shows, films, and music come and go. While the task may seem overwhelming, parents and youth workers can and must take the time to know what is happening in the media their kids know and use. While your kids may not be accessing media as much as the average teenager, they're still living in a world where many of their friends are heavy media users. Our kids are part of a youth culture defined and directed by media. By knowing the world of media, you'll be better equipped to know your teenagers, understand their world, and lead them into a healthy adulthood.

In short, your kids know media. Media knows your kids. Get to know your kids by getting to know their media.

5

Through the Maze: Teaching Kids Media Discernment

We need to look as Christians at the stories that contemporary culture is telling us by learning how to discern and evaluate perspectives in these representations of life in God's world.

—WILLIAM ROMANOWSKI[318]

So whether you eat or drink or whatever you do, do it all for the glory of God.

—1 CORINTHIANS 10:31

I believe that while media just might be the most criticized cultural force in today's youth culture, it's also the most misunderstood. We have failed to understand media and how it functions. We have also failed to teach our teenagers the necessary media-discernment skills to help them process music and media biblically, skills I believe are essential for living a God-honoring life in today's media-saturated world.

Guidelines for Dealing with Media

What positive and productive steps can parents and youth workers take to address the issues of music and media? I strongly suggest we address the media challenge in the same way we're to face all difficult issues life sends our way. The place to start is with God, the Creator of individuals, parents, kids, and families. His Word, the Bible, provides direction, truth, hope, and strength in the midst of our confusion and questioning. In it we'll find useful guidelines on how to help ourselves and our kids through the maze of music and media.

Here are some practical and time-tested strategies based on the truths of God's Word.

Guideline #1: Focus on the Message, Not the Delivery System

Some of us grew up in homes and churches where there were some pretty direct and strict media rules. I've run into many people who believe it's wrong to listen to rock 'n' roll because, they say, it's "of the devil." Others make the blanket statement that Christians shouldn't watch movies. But I know of no scriptural argument that supports these rules; I can only conclude that they're myths that have somehow evolved into "reality."

While it might be initially easy for us to handle the maze of music and media by enacting and enforcing these rules with our teenagers, in the long run our kids—if they accept these rules—will only be embracing myths. In addition, they'll miss out on enjoying some wonderful music and media options.

As you address the issue of music and media with your teenagers, realize it's important to differentiate between the media's vehicle and content. The vehicle is the delivery system, be it music (a variety of genres), instruments used, radio, film, television, mp3 player, etc. All too often we focus on condemning the vehicle, which is neutral. Instead, parents and youth workers should focus on helping teenagers evaluate the message in the media.

Theologian Al Wolters offers helpful advice by differentiating between the elements of *structure* and *direction* inherent in the entire scope of the world, including media and music. *Structure* is what makes the media vehicle the thing that it is. For example, film is a structure. The medium of film is neutral. To say all film is evil and Christians shouldn't go to the movies is a false notion. *Direction* is where a particular media piece points—either toward or away from God.[319]

Our concern, then, should be teaching teenagers how to discern the direction of media content, as our desire is to teach our kids to engage with and use media that points them *to* God, rather than *away from* God.

Guideline #2: Teach Teenagers How to Evaluate Everything They See and Hear—Biblically

As Christians, we should use the Bible as the measuring stick for evaluating everything we see and hear. The difficulty lies in the fact that God never gives direct instructions regarding various types of media, styles of music, or particular TV shows, films, or bands. You can read the Bible from cover to cover, but you'll never find the words "Thou shalt not listen to _____ (insert name of musical artist or band)" or "In all your ways acknowledge him, and don't forget to shut off the television and destroy your mp3 collection." But informed and regular study of God's Word yields specific and helpful guidance on what to celebrate and enjoy in the media world, and what to avoid. Using God's Word as the measuring stick, we're able to evaluate the good from the bad and the truth from the lies.

If you could reduce God's message about music and media to its simplest terms, it might go like this:

> Because I love you, I tell you this: Imitate and think about me! Avoid imitating and believing those themes, messages, and behaviors that I say are wrong. They'll slowly steal your heart, harm you, and destroy you. But go ahead and indulge yourself in and celebrate those themes, messages, and behaviors that I say are pure, true, lovely, and admirable. Let me ask you this—does your media lead you closer to me and my ways? Or does your media pull you away from me and my ways? Prayerfully and deliberately look at the world of all media through the "eyes" of my Word. Use your head to think through all your choices, so you'll guard your heart.

We should avoid the extreme of accepting everything out there as being "good," "true," or "okay" without using our God-given minds to carefully think through and assess media. And, as stated before, we should avoid the extreme trap of labeling all popular media as "bad," "false," or "evil." Instead, we should teach our kids to responsibly engage all media so they can learn how to celebrate the good, improve the weak, and grieve over the bad. By following God's commands as they relate to media, we choose to protect ourselves from harm and open ourselves up to all the good things he has in store for us.

In order to effectively evaluate everything you see and hear, you must know where God stands on the issues. This means you must continue to study his Word and learn his will on a daily basis. This will provide you with a strong knowledge of right and wrong. Then, and only then, can you move on to evaluate the music and media you and your kids are exposed to every day.

Most people take the "consume it" approach—they listen to anything and everything without ever thinking consciously or critically about the worldview being expressed in the media piece, whether it be a show, song, film, and so on. This approach could also be called "mindless consumption," as it assumes media is nothing more than neutral and harmless entertainment. But remember what we discussed earlier—media is a powerful teacher. When we "consume it" without consciously thinking about it, the worldview and messages expressed in the media piece powerfully shape our worldview (how we think and live) without us even realizing it's happening.

Instead, we should take a "mindful critique" approach by making a conscious decision to go deeper, listening and watching both carefully and critically. Instead of mindlessly allowing the media to shape our worldview, we mindfully engage the media and its worldview by viewing and listening through the eyes, ears, and mind of a Christian worldview. In this way, we can discern both the positive and negative aspects of the media and make ourselves less vulnerable to its adverse effects on who we are and how we live. With this approach, we learn how to control the media, rather than allowing the media to control us.

Let me suggest a simple three-step plan for evaluating what you see and hear in media. Learn it. Practice it by yourself and with teenagers. And most importantly, pass it on to your teenagers.

Step #1: Discover. Discovery is the process of thoughtfully and carefully listening (watching) to hear (see) the underlying worldview of the media piece. In other words, you're digging deep to discover the message communicated through the media's content. Sometimes it'll be easy to find because the message is very clear. Sometimes it'll be more difficult because the true message isn't found at the surface. But it's important to take your time in the discovery process, as there's always a message in the media.

Doing a simple Internet search on the media piece (artist, band, film title, and so on) will often yield helpful background and explanatory information. Then as you watch and listen, filter what you see and hear through these questions:

- What's the main topic and theme?

- What's the mood of the piece?

- How is it intended to make viewers/listeners feel? How does it make me feel? Does it manipulate viewers'/listeners' emotions in any way?

- Does it make any overt or covert suggestions to viewers/listeners regarding how to think, speak, act, or live?

- What does it say about the way the world is? What does it say about the way the world ought to be?

- Is there right and wrong? What's portrayed as right and what's portrayed as wrong? How are right and wrong determined?

- Is there a hero? Is there a villain? What do they stand for?

- What values and beliefs are presented as virtuous? What values and beliefs are portrayed negatively?

- Who or what is the source of authority? What's the attitude toward authority?

- How is God portrayed? What does it say about God? Who or what is God (god)?

- Is the one true God replaced by some other "deity" (self, money, sex, and so on)?

- How are human beings portrayed?

- Where is human value and worth found?

- How is beauty established, portrayed, and defined?

- What does it say about how to treat others? Are people "used" or portrayed as a means to an end?

- What is the source of happiness and satisfaction in life?

- Does it send any messages about what makes a person "successful" in life?

- What does it say about what's wrong with the world?

- Does it suggest any solution(s) to life's problems? If so, what are those solutions?

- Who or what is glorified?

- What does it say about peace and hope? Are suggestions made about where they can be found?

- Is it hopeful or hopeless?

- What character traits are portrayed as positive? Negative?

Step #2: Discern. Discernment is the practice of looking more closely at what you've discovered and distinguishing those things God says are good, true, healthy, and right from those things God says are evil, false, dangerous, and wrong. Evaluate the worldview you discovered in the media piece against the measuring stick of God's Word in order to ascertain if there's agreement or disagreement with God's never-changing truth and the Christian worldview.

How do you do it? Take another look at all the questions and your answers from the "Discover" step. Now compare the media piece's answers to those questions to *God's* answers to those questions. Go a step further and establish whether or not the media piece has moved you toward or away from a deeper understanding of and love for God.

Francis Schaeffer, a wise and godly man, suggested that every work of art (including all songs, films, shows, and so on) should be subjected to four standards of judgment. These standards are worth considering as you embark on the process of discernment:

1. Technical Excellence—This includes things such as the creativity, sound, unity, and production quality. A media piece can have superior technical excellence, even when you disagree with the writer's worldview. After all, every gifted and creative media maker has received their talent

and ability from God, even if they're not using that talent to his glory.

2. Validity—Is the artist true and honest to himself and to his worldview? Or did he create the piece only for the money or for the notoriety?

3. Content—The content is the stuff that reflects the worldview of the artist. Content is to be judged in light of God's Word. Don't forget, artists who are Christians can create lousy content—and an artist who is not a Christian can create a media piece that reflects a Christian worldview even though he's not a Christian.

4. The Integration of Content and Vehicle—Sounds pretty heady, huh? But it's rather simple: the greatest art is characterized by a sound or style that fits the content or worldview presented.[320]

Practicing discernment may seem a bit difficult at first. But the more you do it, the more it becomes second nature to you. This type of critical, biblical thinking will help your kids determine whether the underlying philosophy, worldview, and message of a media piece point them to or away from God.

Step #3: Decide. Now it's time to make a decision about the media you're evaluating. The decision needs to be made on two levels. First, you need to decide if the media has value for your personal entertainment and enjoyment. If what is being taught is in agreement with biblical truth, reflects a Christian worldview, and draws you closer to the image of Christ, then celebrate and enjoy. But if it seems to contradict what God has said is right and leads you away from Christ, then you need to ask yourself if you should listen or watch. Second, you need to decide if the media has ministry value. In other words, does viewing and knowing this media help you connect with your teenagers and their peers? As you make a decision at this level, you should ask yourself these questions:

• How does this media piece help me to see and understand the worldview and needs of my kids and their culture?

• How would Jesus share his story and message with people who think and live this worldview?

- What biblical examples of Jesus and God's people can shape my response to these needs?

Don't forget, there's a big difference between approaching and processing a media piece as a tool for understanding the pain, hurt, and needs in the world, and approaching and using a media piece as entertainment. Most of us have never taken the time to watch and listen carefully. Or perhaps the extent of our critique has been only to register disgust with the excessive violence, sex, and profanity we see and hear. If this is true for you, you need to go a step further. You must realize that sometimes depictions of violence, sex, and profanity in media are done in the context of that which honors God by being good, true, and right.

Film writer Brian Godawa says,

> We must face the fact that the Scriptures depict sinful acts that are revolting to our sensibilities. The portrayal of good and the portrayal of evil are two sides of God's revelation of his one good and holy truth...God has chosen to include depictions of both evil and good in his revelation of truth to us. So pointing out wrong is part of dwelling on what is right, exposing lies is part of dwelling on the truth, revealing cowardice is part of dwelling on the honorable, and uncovering corruption is part of dwelling on the pure.[321]

Godawa goes on to stress the importance of evaluating the context in which these depictions are put forth, challenging us to realize the difference between depictions that challenge us to honor and please God, and depictions that exploit sin and glorify the behavior.[322]

By taking the time to know God's Word and apply it through critical viewing and listening, you'll learn how to be a healthy media consumer, a skill we desperately need to model and pass on to our teenagers.

Guideline #3: Avoid Extremes

Given the power of media to manipulate, influence, and shape our teenagers, many of us make the mistake of responding by going to extremes. While this may be the easiest, most time-efficient response, it doesn't help kids learn for themselves how to watch and listen with discernment. The following are two counterproductive extremes that you should avoid at all costs:

Extreme #1: "Run for your life!" Once many parents and youth workers discover what's out there in media, they grab their teenagers while screaming "Run for your life!" Is this approach healthy? I don't think so.

First, it equates the world of media to a ticking bomb. Not all media is bad. As Quentin Schultze has said, "Too many parents try to take the easy way toward holiness by naively and ignorantly rejecting the culture."[323]

Second, it's totally unrealistic. There's no way we can successfully separate our teenagers from the media's influence. All they have to do is walk out the door to play with a friend, pick up the phone, or go to school, and they'll interact with a peer group that's been living in a media-saturated world.

Third, teenagers miss the chance to learn how to make good judgments for themselves if parents and youth workers make media choices for them. Sometimes we forget that adolescence is a bridge from childhood to adulthood. We need to honor our teens' developing abilities to think for themselves by walking them through the decision-making process. It's important for them to understand the whys behind our nos. If we want them to develop the ability to discover, discern, and decide on their own, we need to give them reasons, not just restrictions. In effect, we are teaching them to "defuse the bombs" the media throws our way, thereby eliminating the need to run in fear.

Fourth, this approach can destroy family unity and lead kids into rebellion. This is usually the case when parents whose teenagers have already established media tastes and collections come on like gangbusters as a result of their newfound awareness of media's dangers. Older teens are insulted and angered. It shows lack of respect for their teenagers' abilities to work through the issues with parental help, and they risk losing their kids' respect. There are better ways.

Fifth, *"run for your life" is theologically wrong.* It denies the biblical truth that the talents of every musician, artist, and media creator come from the God who created them all. It denies that media might from time to time contain a reflection of what is good, true, honorable, and right. We often forget that the Bible teaches that God reveals himself in a limited way to all people through creation, history, and conscience.

Extreme #2: "I didn't hear anything; did you?" One of the worst possible responses is to yawn, deny you've heard anything unusual, and go right back to sleep. When it comes to media, just let nature take its course and let kids continue to listen to and watch anything and everything. Obviously not a healthy approach—and here's why:

First, *teenagers see that parents and youth workers don't really care about what they listen to or watch.* This silence sends a loud message anything and everything from media's diverse menu is fine because it "really doesn't matter."

Second, *the door is opened even further for other voices to enter and answer teenagers' questions and concerns.* Music and media are happy to take on the job of socializing our kids and molding their worldviews. Without any counterguidance from parents, the media voice becomes even more effective.

Third, *kids run the risk of being rightly in the world and wrongly of the world.* They're left unprotected from the evil one (see John 17:15). It's as if we send them to the front line of a battle without weapons, armor, tactical knowledge, or camouflage. In fact, they stand there wearing a bright orange hunter's vest, giving an unspoken invitation to "go ahead and shoot me!"

Fourth, *failing to offer guidance and direction is an unrealistic, uncaring, and unloving approach to parenting.* While Paul warns parents against exasperating their kids, the second half of that instruction is to "instead, bring them up in the training and instruction of the Lord" (Ephesians 6:4). If we love our kids, we will teach them how to protect themselves as they move through adolescence and into adulthood.

Guideline #4: Examine Yourself

A positive approach to helping your teenagers face the world of music and media begins with you. *What are you doing personally to guide them through the maze of media and music?* Following are a number of tasks crucial to your success in addressing these issues.

Pray. When our kids are immersed in a hostile media world and resistant to our efforts to guide them through it, we can pray.

- Pray for yourself—Ask God to challenge and change your media consumption habits if they're not pleasing to him. Tell God you need wisdom, courage, insight, and strength for the task of steering your teenagers to make good media choices. As you begin to evaluate the world of music and media—and teach your kids to do the same—pray for protection from the negative images and themes you see and hear. Ask God to keep his truth in the front of your mind. Ask him to make it clear to you when you cross the fine line between critique and entertainment, so you'll know when to turn off the media and use your time more wisely.

- Pray for your teenagers—Ask God to help them avoid confusion; develop wisdom to distinguish good from bad, fact from error, truth from lies; and make appropriate decisions.

- Pray for the people who control the media—Producers, directors, writers, singers, actors, and executives all need our constant prayers. Think about it for a moment. What would happen if God changed the hearts of those writing and producing media pieces? What would happen if he changed the hearts of those who create, produce, and perform some of the most godless stuff? It can sometimes seem ridiculous and impossible, but think about the apostle Paul and his experience on the Damascus road (see Acts 9). Stranger things have happened. If God is big enough to change the heart of a persecutor of the church from being a hater of God to a committed servant of God, he could do the same for anyone else. Pray for them with passion and Christlike compassion.

Know where God stands and plant yourself in the same place. Build a foundation from which you can begin to discern right from wrong and truth from lies. Develop a growing knowledge of God's perspective. Take the time to study the Bible on a daily basis. Put your preconceived notions aside and ask him to make his Word live in your life. If you skip this step, all of your other efforts will falter.

Watch your step. Let me ask you a few difficult questions. (By the way, these are questions I often have to ask myself.)

- How much time do you spend in front of the TV?

- What shows do you watch?

- Are there shows you watch only if your kids are out of the room or in bed? And if so, why?

- Do you laugh at sitcom humor that is racist, sexual, or devalues people?

- Do you watch soap operas?

- Would it be difficult for you to turn off the TV and read a book or spend time with your family?

- What kind of music do you listen to?

- Do you avoid and criticize that "nasty" music your kids love so much, only to listen to adult contemporary music that features the same messages and themes?

We must be sure we have evaluated and adjusted our own habits before we begin to deal with our kids'. By consistently modeling responsible media behavior, we can become signposts to point teenagers in the right direction. Otherwise, we're phonies. Teenagers can sniff out and see right through phonies very quickly.

Don't catch egg-on-face disease. It's reached epidemic proportions in some segments of the church, and the symptoms are easy to spot. A group of Christians or an individual criticizes a film, television show, band, singer, or other media form as contributing to the moral decline of society and kids. They levy strong accusations against the "offender" and recruit others to get on the bandwagon with them. All too often, people who take this course act as though they know what they're talking about, when in reality—they're clueless. Why? Because they react based on information they heard secondhand or thirdhand. It isn't long before someone challenges their accusations, and then they look like idiots because they've never seen, heard, or investigated the very thing they're criticizing. They judge without knowing the facts.

If we're going to be responsible in our efforts to help teenagers make good media choices, we'd better prepare ourselves so we know what we're talking about. We can't attack an album, show, or movie on the basis of what we've heard in an extended game of whisper-down-the-lane. We need to get the facts so we can intelligently discuss those shows, films, songs, games, and other outlets that concern us.

This approach has biblical precedent. When the apostle Paul approached the idolatrous and immoral people of Athens, he did so in an informed manner. The book of Acts recounts his methodology and experience.

> Paul then stood up in the meeting of the Areopagus and said: "Men of Athens! I see that in every way you are very religious. For as I walked around and looked carefully at your objects of worship, I even found an altar with this inscription: TO AN UNKNOWN GOD. Now what you worship as something unknown I am going to proclaim to you." (Acts 17:22-23)

Paul didn't open his mouth until he knew what he was talking about; he'd walked through the city with his eyes and ears open. He didn't rely on some book or seminar tape for his information; he went out and carefully did his own research. This approach allowed him to be better informed, credible in the eyes of his audience, more convinced of his own message, and far more effective as a communicator of what was right and true.

People are more apt to listen to us when we've done our research. If we're misinformed loudmouths, they'll laugh us off and never hear what we have to say. The account in Acts goes on to say that even though some of Paul's listeners sneered in disagreement, many wanted to hear more. In fact, a few even believed and became followers (Acts 17:32-34).[324]

Do you want to be credible in the eyes of teenagers? Don't rely solely on the information in this book. It's only scratched the surface. Continue to examine the world of teenage music and media for yourself. Here are some suggestions to help you stay informed:

- Visit the Center for Parent/Youth Understanding Web page (www.cpyu.org) for a few minutes every week. The site is updated daily with loads of information on teenagers' rapidly changing culture, with a special emphasis on the world of media and music.

- Watch the shows and films your kids watch, and evaluate content, messages, and themes.

- Listen to your teenager's music collection. If they have CDs, read the lyrics found on the liner sleeve.

- Do an Internet search for information and lyrics from their favorite artists. Listen to and evaluate the music using the steps outlined earlier in this chapter.

- Watch an hour of music television on one of your teenager's favorite stations each week. Visit the station's Web site, where you can get more information and even view the latest videos.

- Subscribe to or browse through magazines like *Rolling Stone*, *Blender*, and *Entertainment Weekly*. These magazines offer a peek into the latest developments in the world of music, films, gaming, and more.

- Subscribe to *Engage*, the quarterly journal of the Center for Parent/Youth Understanding. (You can do so online at www.cpyu.org.)

Find out why your teenagers like particular films, TV shows, or music. Remember, media serves as a mirror, reflecting the cares, concerns, and needs of our teenagers. Responsible parents and youth workers will work to understand teenagers—their lives and their questions—through understanding their music and media.

Love your kids. Studies show that today's kids are receiving smaller amounts of intimacy and attention from their parents. When intimacy and attention are absent from the home, kids will be more vulnerable to outside influences.

Media has an incredible ability to connect with kids and replace the family. When kids don't communicate with parents, they'll sit down and listen to the TV, radio, and mp3 player. When kids don't feel respected by their parents, the media will accept them for who they are. When parents don't spend time with their kids, the TV is always there to keep them company. And when kids don't feel as though we're committed to them, the TV, in search of advertising dollars and ratings points, is there to let them know they're important and needed.

Yes, media has incredible power. It has the power to fill the void left by absent, detached parents and unloving homes. But this void can easily be filled by parents who express their love to their kids by giving them input, respect, time, and the sense that they're indeed valuable and important.

Guideline #5: Be Proactive

When we begin to realize the powerful ability of music and media to shape our kids, our inclination is to do something fast to counter that influence. If you prefer quick fixes like I do, you've probably been wondering when I'm going to mention some hands-on approaches to use with your kids. Well, here they are. But don't make the mistake of skipping the guidelines I've already mentioned. If you don't follow those first four guidelines, you'll be undermining and jeopardizing the effectiveness of the following strategies. (Most of what follows applies to parents, so if you're a youth worker, you can use this information to help your students' parents.)

Listen and watch with them. Sadly, many of us believe we're protecting our kids by making all the choices for them—telling them what media they should and shouldn't consume. But what will happen to them when they grow up and fly solo without ever having had the opportunity to hold the controls on their own? Kids need flying lessons.

Find out what movies, TV shows, Internet sites, and music your kids enjoy—and then go watch and listen with them from time to time. Afterward, sit down and talk about what you all saw or heard. Take the time to walk them through the evaluation process of discovering, discerning, and deciding. Initially, keep your hands on the controls to show your kids how to evaluate everything they see and hear. Then gradually hand over the controls, and let your kids put into practice what you've been teaching them. Their abilities may be somewhat shaky initially, but don't grab the controls too soon. Most kids don't have the benefit of adults who care enough to take the time to watch and listen with them. You'll be surprised at how much they'll appreciate your involvement. And you'll be surprised at how well equipped they'll be to take off, cruise, and land by themselves as they leave you standing confidently on the ground.

Don't argue and act as though you have all the answers. I'm not going to pretend the "flying lessons" will always be smooth sailing. There will undoubtedly be times when you listen and watch together, only to disagree. In light of the fact that growing teenagers have the ability to think on an adult level (as crude and undeveloped as that ability may be) and need to be treated as having that ability, here are some suggestions on how to handle the turbulence:

- *Be sure you listen hard.* You might have to curb that inclination to assume you know what your kids are going to say. After all, you know you're always right, so why waste everyone's time? But interrupting what your kids are saying tells them you don't value their opinions, you don't respect their ability to think, and you don't want to hear what they have to say. If we use this approach too often, our kids won't ever want to talk to us, and we close the door to good communication.

Many kids cite this as the biggest problem with their parents. They tell me their parents are always interrupting them and are never willing to listen to what they have to say. At the same time, these kids tell me they'd be more than happy to open up to their parents if they were sure they'd be respected and heard. Teenagers have taught me that there are times when I, as a parent, had better be ready to close my mouth and open my ears.

- *Don't get angry.* Our kids will use bad judgment from time to time. We must be patient when they make bad music and media choices. By remaining calm, we open the door to effective communication even wider and compliment them by allowing them the opportunity to communicate with us on more of an adult level.

Families should eat together. A few years ago I asked a large group of high school and junior high students about the amount of time they spent with their parents. One student remarked that the only time he spent with his parents was at the dinner table. When I asked him how many nights a week they ate together, he said, "One or two." I then asked the entire group to tell me by a show of hands how often they ate with their families. The majority said their families ate only two or three meals together in an entire week.

Why do I mention table time as a suggestion for dealing with the world of media? Because chances are if you don't spend time together here, then you don't spend much time together as a family, period. And if you aren't together, you can't communicate. We live in a busy day and age. But if we want to fulfill our God-given role as the primary molders and shapers of our kids, we'd better spend time communicating at the table.

Everyone in your family has to eat. If your kids are still young, make it a priority to be together at the dinner table. Set a precedent early on so the table is a place where the family gathers by habit to communicate. And if you find you're already in the bad habit of not eating together, take whatever steps are necessary to break the habit. If you have a difficult time talking to your kids, ask them about the most important things in their lives. In case you haven't already figured it out, media is one of them. Ask for their opinions and just sit back and listen. The door to communication will be opened.

As my kids are now exiting their teenage years, college, jobs, and sports often keep them out of the house during dinner time. They miss our family dinner so much that when we do have a chance to eat together, they'll often protest when the first person gets up to leave the table. Everyone in our family knows it's a good thing to be able to eat together.

Play with your kids. One of the best lessons I learned from my parents is that there's more to life than sitting around and doing nothing. My parents were available to us on those quiet evenings when it would have been easy to just plop down in front of the tube. But they always thought of something fun to do. We'd play board games or cards, wrestle or box with my dad, build models, work in the basement woodshop, and so on. Sure, we also watched TV, listened to the radio, and played records, but those voices were tempered by the involvement of our parents in our lives. We even learned to enjoy listening to our parents; there was good communication taking place. Because I had such fun-loving parents, most of the neighborhood kids wanted to spend time at my house.

The key to successfully implementing this approach is to start when your kids are young. They'll grow up looking forward to those fun family evenings. And when they're fully grown, they'll realize, as I did, how special and important those times really were. I don't think I can recount the plot of more than a handful of the TV shows I watched as a kid. What I do remember are the fun times I spent with fun-loving parents.

When the going gets rough, offer alternatives. One of my favorite TV commercials of all time is set in the family living room sometime during the 1950s. Two young adolescent girls are sitting on the floor in front of the TV watching *The Ed Sullivan Show*. Their parents are sitting in overstuffed chairs behind them. Ed Sullivan appears on the screen as the two girls anxiously and eagerly await the arrival of his next guest. As Sullivan says, "And now, ladies and gentlemen, here's Elvis!" the girls begin to scream. Just then the TV goes dead. As the girls sigh in disappointment, their father, who unbeknownst to them has unplugged the set, comes around the corner and says, "Must be a power failure. Let's go to McDonald's." In a flash, the girls are happy again as they forget about the disappointment of missing Elvis.

While life may not be that simple (and kids certainly aren't fooled that easily), there is a positive lesson to be learned from that commercial: If we're going to take something away from our kids, we can soften the blow by offering an attractive alternative. Be prepared with some good alternatives. A quick trip to do something special or some positive media and music can all serve to fill the void left when parents exercise their right and responsibility to set media parameters and remove potentially harmful media. Don't just take it away. Replace it with something better.

Have family devotions. Our teenagers need to know that our music and media guidelines are not based on our own personal preferences and opinions. Rather, a higher authority—God—guides us through the confusing mix of choices teenagers and parents face today. When a family sets aside time each day to focus their thoughts on God, amazing things begin to happen. By reading and studying the Bible together, parents and their kids will know which steps are right and which are wrong. The Bible is the anchor and compass of unchanging truth that offers guidance and stability not only in a rocky media world, but also for all of life.

Develop media guidelines and learn to say no. One of the biggest problems facing teenagers today is that many of them are growing up in families where their parents never say *no*. Our teenagers need us to help them learn how to function responsibly in the world. By providing them with clear-cut boundaries, we offer them the opportunity to make their own choices within the safety of limits, while protecting them from the dangers of unrestricted freedom.

Good parents will exercise their God-given responsibility to protect their kids from harm and provide for their well-being by establishing guidelines for their media consumption. If you have younger kids, let me encourage you to discuss media and music standards with your spouse. If your kids are older, you might want to include them in the standard-setting process.

How can you develop media guidelines for your family? Try the following suggestions:

- *Limit the number of media outlets in their bedrooms.* Don't allow your kids to have a television and online access in their bedrooms. Too much media opportunity typically leads to too much media time, unsupervised media time, and less time together as a family.

- *Decide how long the TV will be on in your house each day.* A good start is to allow no more than one hour of television viewing a day by your kids. Parents would benefit from setting and following similar standards themselves.

- *Be sure to spend viewing time together.* This will give you the opportunity to talk with your child about what they've just watched.

- *Develop standards regarding the specific shows, themes, and program content that will and will not be a part of the media menu in your house.* I suggest you require your kids to get your approval for each show or movie they watch, and each album or song they purchase or download. Granted, this rule is best instituted and enforced when your kids are young and just beginning to interact with popular media. Be sure you offer detailed and age-appropriate explanations for your decisions and standards. And be sure to practice what you preach. Don't adopt a double standard that allows you to turn on the garbage after the kids are in bed.

- *Put the TV in a cabinet that closes or set it in a less-than-prominent place in your house.* Don't arrange your furniture so the family room becomes a temple to the electronic god. You might want to put the TV in the basement. I know one family who keeps their TV in a cold, unfinished cellar. When they choose to watch a program, they sit on a pair of old vinyl bench seats they ripped out of a junked van. Extreme? Perhaps. But the principle remains the same—don't give the television set the seat of honor in your home.

- *Limit game-playing time and monitor the games they're playing.* Always know what games your kids are playing. Go online to check out game reviews before deciding on game purchases. Spend time playing games with your kids, and be sure to limit the amount of time they spend playing games each day.

- *Don't be afraid to say no.* Sometimes the parent-teenager clashes on the road to adulthood can result in a logjam. Use your God-given gift of parental intuition to say no when you have to.

Guideline #6: Have Patience

How easy it would be if adolescence were an overnight phenomenon, here today and gone tomorrow. But the process of moving from childhood to adulthood takes time. Not only is the transition painful for teenagers, but it can also be grueling and frustrating for those parents who desperately want to see their kids make healthy choices on the road to adulthood. Some of our teenagers will resist our efforts to help them discover, discern, and decide on music and media. But don't give up. Your efforts will pay off even though there may be no immediate return. Your adolescents are in the process of testing the waters of your values. Your first job is to close the wide-open access that media has to your home. And second, serve as a wise and discerning gatekeeper who lets in all that is good while keeping out all that is bad.

Some Specific Guidelines Related to the Digital Revolution

Because of the rapid development and uniqueness of today's emerging digital technology, here are some specific guidelines to help you equip your teenagers to make responsible and good digital choices.

The Internet Is a Great Resource—Get Online

Living without an online Internet connection is rapidly becoming like living without a telephone, car, or windows. The benefits are many—education, communication, ministry, research, and so much more—and they overwhelmingly outweigh the dangers. With a little investment of time and supervision, parents can train their kids to get in the habit of fastening their seatbelts for a defensive and safe ride through the online world. The positive possibilities are endless and growing.

Talk Openly with Your Kids about Internet Dangers

Kids have lots of questions. Without positive parental input and supervision, many will find the "answers" on the Internet. These "answers" can be good or bad. Like its broadcast counterpart, online advertising targets the teenage market by creating needs and teaching kids that *things* bring happiness and meaning to life.

Kids looking for answers to spiritual questions can plug into one of the many spiritual resources targeting teenagers. While they can visit sites promoting Christianity, they can also visit sites promoting cults, mysticism, and a variety of syncretistic religions. Kids wondering about their sexuality can be easily led astray. Pornography is a multibillion-dollar Internet industry. Every imaginable (and unimaginable) sexual perversion is just a click or two away. We must warn our kids of dangers that lurk in the online world, just as we warn them about predators who may visit our neighborhoods.

Keep Looking over Their Shoulders

A healthy dose of parental supervision can go a long way in keeping kids on the right track. To limit the amount of negative content traffic while offering positive supervision, set up your computer in a high-traffic area, like the family room or kitchen. This way you build in an automatic system of accountability for you and your kids. The principle is simple: "If there's a chance someone might look over your shoulder, you'll be more prone to do what's right." Of course, parental supervision should yield guidelines that teach kids to be responsible for their own behavior.

Establish Time Limits

Too much time at the computer can be dangerous. An "addiction" to the Internet can consume enough time to destroy family relationships and schoolwork can suffer. By delving into the impersonal world of online relationships, many kids withdraw from healthy face-to-face friendships, homework, sports, and church activities. Limit their time!

Establish "NEVER" Rules

When you were young, your parents taught you never to talk to strangers. The same holds true when it come to online time—kids are easy prey. We've all seen news reports and exposés on online predators. Remind your kids: NEVER give out your real name, address, phone number, or other personal information. NEVER arrange for a face-to-face meeting with someone you met online until you've checked with your parents first. NEVER give out a credit card number. And instruct your kids that if they receive an offensive or suspicious message, they're to ALWAYS tell you immediately.

Use a Software Blocker

When your kids sit down at the computer, the Internet literally brings the world to their fingertips. But don't forget—as they navigate and explore this global community with no community standards, teenagers need you to grab them by the hand and lead them safely through this exciting and growing place. Look online or in your local computer store for one of the many programs that control and limit access to certain areas of the Internet. While they aren't all foolproof, these programs can equip your computer to screen and filter out sites containing objectionable material.

Getting Personal

How has the world of media affected your attitudes, values, and behaviors? How have your kids been influenced in positive and negative ways by media's confusing mix of messages? Who are the heroes whom teenagers strive to emulate? Has the media chipped away at your kids' concept of who they are as people created by God with value, dignity, and worth? Is life around your house boring when the TV is turned off? Do you feel comfortable sitting together and just talking? Have the messages of popular music numbed your kids to the truth about God as it's contained in his Word?

Never underestimate the power of media to mold and shape your kids. Take the time to understand the themes and messages offered. Be alert to the influence of media and music in your home. Be diligent in your efforts to guide and direct your kids. And, above all, heed the words of the apostle Paul: "Base your happiness on your hope in Christ. When trials come endure them patiently, steadfastly maintain the habit of prayer" (Romans 12:12, *Phillips*).

6

It All Ads Up: Marketing's Powerful Influence on Teenagers

Kids and teenagers are now the epicenter of American consumer culture, They command the attention, creativity, and dollars of advertisers.

—JULIET B. SCHOR IN *BORN TO BUY* [325]

Advertising has a very influential yet deceptive voice. Because media come in so many forms, the voice is everywhere, suggesting lifestyles, promising belonging, and disorienting its listeners. Somehow in the middle of this din, we are supposed to discern how to be faithful Christians.

—SAM VAN EMAN IN *ON EARTH AS IT IS IN ADVERTISING* [326]

I was a fly on the wall, but it was getting hard to hide. After years spent monitoring and analyzing marketers' advertising efforts to teenagers, I finally decided to step right into the eye of the youth marketing hurricane. It was difficult to hide because I was one of only 300 people who had traveled to the Disney Yacht Club in Orlando for the annual Kid Power marketing conference. [327] As I scanned the list of attendees, I quickly discovered this was a who's who of marketing, with representatives from a variety of companies that market their products to kids. All of them were looking to—according to the conference brochure—"increase revenue by forecasting and capitalizing on kid trends." The marketing material for the conference itself even promised to help us all become more effective at selling to kids between the ages of two and 12. Not surprisingly, much of what I heard during my three eye-opening days at the conference was focused on selling to kids from the minute they emerge from the womb. I determined to return home and inform youth workers and parents of the deliberate, powerful, and life-shaping role that marketing plays in today's youth culture.

During my lifetime, there has always been marketing aimed at teenagers. And, it's always worked. But something is markedly different about advertising today. A host of cultural factors has contributed to the growth in both the size and effectiveness of these marketing efforts, creating a situation where marketing has become a powerful molder of the values, attitudes, and behaviors of kids from the moment they're born.

For years I've been convinced media has become the most powerful, life-shaping institution in the world of teenagers. I've also believed music has served as the most powerful of all life-shaping media outlets. But after observing changes in the music and advertising industries over the course of the past few years, I'm increasingly convinced the balance of power has now shifted and advertising has eclipsed music as the most powerful media force in today's youth culture.

I'm also convinced that at its root, advertising is worth our intentional and diligent attention because, when you get right down to it, it's a spiritual issue. How? Because of our sinful and fallen human nature, we've been cut off from our created purpose to be in relationship with our Creator. We'll remain empty until the holes in our souls are filled by a relationship with God through his Son Jesus Christ, and we're living under God's rule and reign. Marketing plays into and exploits that emptiness and yearning by promising redemption, fulfillment, wholeness, and satisfaction through the purchase and use of products. In effect, marketing substitutes a false gospel for the true gospel. If we believe marketing's promises to deliver—promises that it, in fact, never *can* deliver—we run the risk of falling into the endless cycle of believing the lies and buying product after product in the hope that somehow, this time, we'll be fulfilled.

In this chapter we'll take a revealing look at the world of marketing and advertising, its power, its techniques, how it shapes our teenagers, and strategies for helping the kids you know and love take control of advertising so advertising has less control over them.

Some Indisputable Facts about Advertising

In order to set the context for our look at advertising and the role it plays in today's youth culture, there are some basic facts about marketing and advertising all of us must know and understand.

Advertising Works

While there are those who say they ignore commercials and that advertising is really just an exercise in futility, a look at our culture proves otherwise. For example, if advertising wasn't effective, why is the annual marketing budget in the United States close to exceeding $3 billion annually. Marketers in the United States spend a whopping $278 billion on advertising.[328] To look at those numbers another way, if advertising didn't work, why would marketers spend roughly $2,200 a year per household in an effort to sell products? Or why does it cost marketers $2.5 million to purchase a 30-second segment of TV advertising time during the Super Bowl? And, why are there now almost 50,000 shopping centers in the United States, a 66 percent increase since 1986?[329]

How many products or brands can you identify just by seeing their logos and hearing jingles and tunes and *without* any help from written text or product mention? Take for example the now-famous Nike "swoosh." All people have to do is see the swoosh, and they know whose product is being peddled. How many men can identify the *Monday Night Football* brand just by hearing the first four notes of the theme song? Marketing is so effective that research now shows "kids can recognize logos by eighteen months, and before reaching their second birthday, they're asking for products by brand name."[330] No doubt—advertising works.

Advertising Creates a Need for Products by Exploiting One's Anxieties and Aspirations

The teenage years are characterized by insecurity that makes them easily influenced, especially if what's dangled in front of them promises roads to their hopes and dreams. In other words, teenagers are perfect targets for the marketing machine.

This reality hit home a few years ago when I was a guest on a televised talk show. As I sat offstage and waited for my turn, I watched and listened as the host interviewed a female guest. She was now a writer and motivational speaker, but before pursuing this career path she had been a marketing executive who headed up the advertising campaigns for a well-known fast-food chain.

While going over her bio, the curious host asked her, "I see you once worked in marketing. Tell me, how does one go about starting a marketing campaign to sell hamburgers to kids?"

Without hesitation the guest answered, "We've taken a page from Satan's book. Find a point of weakness and lust in every man, woman, and child, and target that weakness to make them want to buy a product."

Advertising Is Pervasive

During the next 24 hours, take the time to be intentional about noting every single advertising and marketing message you see and hear. You'll be amazed. Advertising meets us wherever we go and through whatever we're doing.

Last year I attended a baseball game in a newly built minor league stadium near my home. When I finally settled into my seat, I took note of the dozens of signs and print ads that covered not only the outfield walls, but every other conceivable spot where an ad could be placed in the ballpark. Because I work to be deliberate about noticing ad placement, I was struck by two particular ads that crossed my senses several times during the game. The first was placed, of all places, on the foul pole screens. The vertical ads on the screens featured the name and Web address of a local university, all in the school's colors. The second noticeable advertisement was audio, and it was played through the stadium speakers each time a player hit a foul ball into or near the windows of the park's luxury boxes. The ad began with the sound of breaking glass, followed by the mention of a local glass repair company.

You can be sure further creativity will yield a host of new placement points, upping the current estimated number of ads (3,500 to 5,000) the average American sees over the course of a day. And with teenagers engaging with media at a growing rate, more ads will be coming their way.

Marketers' Methods Are Increasingly More Sophisticated

Marketers spend billions of dollars in research money in an effort to find out what makes kids tick and to get them to spend their billions of dollars on a growing number of goods and services. But as teenagers become more complex and market savvy, marketers must try to stay a step or two ahead of them.

Just how sophisticated are marketers becoming? Consider a few of the seminar titles from a recent Kid Power Winter conference. There was "How to Use Innovative Research Techniques to Get Under the Skin of Gen X and Gen Y"—reflecting marketing's growing ability to differentiate unique trends and advertising strategies based on the differences among generations. Another was titled "Understanding Kids 24/7: How Wild Planet Builds Brands Through Kid Involvement." This seminar offered a case study on how one manufacturer developed toys by using kids to develop toys. Then there was "Real Kids, Tough Challenges: Breaking Through the Ultimate in Uncool to Change Kid's Lives"—on how to understand and market specifically to kids who've been diagnosed with learning disabilities.

Thus, marketing has become a well-developed and growing science. And it will continue to become more complex, along with our kids and their culture.

Those Who Market to Kids Strategize, Talk, and Implement with Evangelical Fervor

It's been interesting to meet the movers and shakers in the youth marketing industry. They're almost exclusively very young, driven, and energetic. Barely out of their teenage years, these people are incredibly committed to and aggressive in their efforts to earn their share of the youth dollar. Part of my function, as that fly on the wall at the Orlando conference, included doing a lot of listening. As I eavesdropped on conversations and listened in on seminar content, there were numerous words that kept popping up to describe the methods and postures needed to successfully market to kids. Strangely enough, many of them are words I hear used in the church. Marketers talked about kids in terms of "reaching," "building relationships with," "empowering," "converting," "preaching to," and even "evangelizing."

Marketers Understand Kids Better Than Youth Workers and Parents Do

The basic premise of this book is that parents and youth workers are cross-cultural missionaries who are given the responsibility to lead teenagers to spiritual maturity. We do this by closing the cultural-generational gap—a task that requires us to know teenagers and their culture. The reality is that marketers are doing this job themselves; however, the end they have in mind is not teenage spiritual maturity, but their own economic gain.

Still, those of us who desire to know teenagers and their rapidly changing culture can benefit from the efforts of marketers to do the same. We can get to know our kids and their world by tapping into marketer's research (visit www.cpyu.org for links to market research on teenagers) and by deconstructing and analyzing the advertisements that are the fruit of that research. We should pay attention to marketers and the ads they've directed at kids so we can learn from marketers what they've learned about our kids.

Marketers Have Embraced Kids

Earlier we discussed Chap Clark's contention in his book *Hurt* that today's teenagers have been systemically abandoned by the institutions that should be embracing them, including the family and the church. This cultural reality paves the way for marketers to embrace kids. Kids sense that the resulting attention, even though it's highly impersonal, is something they're not getting elsewhere. They're then prone to embrace marketers and their marketing messages in return, thereby opening the door for the marketing messages to take root and grow.

Advertisements' Greatest Power Is Selling Worldviews

Sure, all ads are ultimately about peddling products. But the fact that ads tell stories, depict people in real-life situations, and embed products in messages that promise relief from anxiety and fulfillment of aspirations means much more is being communicated through the ads we see. By selling both a product *and* a message, ads influence the way young people look at, understand, and live in the world. Ads serve as a map for curious young hearts and minds looking for guidance that will drive their behavior. Kids see thousands of marketing messages each day and only purchase a small fraction of the products advertised. But the ads' messages still come through loud and clear.

The Power of Marketing Increases with Spiritual Bankruptcy and Materialism

We've already mentioned how marketing taps into our spiritual emptiness, promising redemptive fulfillment (yet never fulfilling), and continually trying to persuade us that the answer's out there if we just keep grabbing and spending. It's a vicious cycle. Add to that the fact that our culture is increasingly materialistic, and suddenly we're more prone to buy into advertising's empty promises of salvation. (See chapter 9 for a full explanation of how materialism works itself out in teenagers.) Over the course of time, these cultural realities have served to feed and increase marketing's power, and they'll most likely continue to do so.

We've Been Swimming in the Advertising Soup for So Long We Don't Even Know We're in It

Because advertising has been such a pervasive part of the landscape of our lives since day one, it's become like our other surroundings that go largely unnoticed because of their familiarity. Like the houses, trees, and people you pass as you drive up and down your street every day, you know they're there, but you typically don't pay close attention to any of them for the simple reason that they're always there.

The fact that we're immersed in advertising and its messages creates a great situation for marketers. If advertising is a form of propaganda, then immersion increases its power. Joseph Goebbels, Hitler's famed propagandist said, "This is the secret of propaganda: Those who are to be persuaded by it should be completely immersed in the ideas of the propaganda, without even noticing that they are being immersed in it."[331]

By the Time They Hit Adolescence, Kids Have Been Targeted by Marketers

As market research becomes more highly specialized, a growing number of researchers are focusing specifically on the preteen market. They have segmented kids down to preschool, early elementary, late elementary, and tweens, looking to unlock the likes, dislikes, nuances, and spending triggers for each of these age groups. Recently, "total advertising and marketing expenditures directed at kids reached $15 billion, a stunning rise from the mere $100 million in television advertising spent in 1983."[332] In their book *The Great Tween Buying Machine: Capturing Your Share of the Multibillion Dollar Tween Market* (notice the telltale title), marketing experts David Siegel, Timothy Coffey, and Gregory Livingston note how the times have changed:

> Not only have kids become even more influential and powerful as a consumer base, but many of today's marketers, retailers, and services are now zeroing in on this segment. A reporter in *The Wall Street Journal* wrote in October 1998, "The rise in children's disposable income, as well as a corresponding rise in children's decision making power, has prompted a fundamental shift in children's buying patterns over the last several years. Ten years ago, the majority of marketers didn't see kids as able to absorb complicated messages...Now children are looked upon as more mature. That's opening up whole new categories."[333]

We Never Learned How to Interact with Advertising

Most of us approach advertising as we do all other media—with a posture of *mindless consumption*. Instead, we should assume a posture of *mindful critique* that paves the way for us as advertising recipients to control the advertising, rather than allowing the advertising to control us. Later on in this chapter we'll look at how we can begin to practice and teach our kids how to interact biblically with the world of marketing. It's one of the most valuable skills we can pass on to our teenagers.

Why Kids Are Targeted

Teenagers are the most targeted market segment in the world. It's almost as if they're walking around with bull's-eyes on their backs. While marketers have been pursuing the young population for a long time, the intensity and frequency of their advertising efforts have increased greatly, especially in recent years. There are several reasons why.

There Are Lots of Them

There are more than 33 million teenagers in the United States, and all of them are growing up in a materialistic society where living to consume is the unspoken (and often spoken) motto by which they live their lives. (See chapter 9 for more information on how materialism manifests itself in the lives of our teenagers.) More teenagers equals more marketing targets.

They Have Spending Power

Marketers know today's teenagers have money. Unlike their parents and other adults, most kids have no budgeted responsibilities, and they're recession-proof. Their spending is purely discretionary. Without any parental boundaries or restraints, kids are able to "buy what I want to buy when I want to buy it." These days, four- to 12-year-olds spend at least $52 billion annually.[334] In an effort to get them to spend their money, marketers spend $15 billion a year promoting goods and services aimed at kids.[335] Discretionary spending by 12- to 17-year-olds now stands at more than $190 billion a year.[336] (For more facts and figures on child and teenage spending, see chapter 10.) Amazingly, these figures don't include the additional money parents spend on their kids.

They Have Spending Influence

Not only do teenagers have their own money to spend, but they're also experts at influencing the spending of others. This influence is exercised on two distinct groups. First, they influence their parents' spending. A conservative estimate puts the spending influence of children on their parents at more than $600 billion a year, [337] and teenagers on their parents at more than $300 billion a year with an estimated growth of about 20 percent a year.[338]

How? Kids will put whatever they want into their parents' shopping carts. The influence continues even when they aren't shopping with their parents: When parents buy what their kids ask for, what they've observed their kids wishing for or wanting, and when they ask their kids for purchasing advice, especially regarding electronics. Then there's the "guilt money" that gets spent quite often in today's hectic society, as busy parents assuage their guilt over not being with their kids by buying things for them.

The reality of spending influence hit home for me several years ago after giving our then 12-year-old son, Josh, *Sports Illustrated for Kids* as a Christmas gift. When the first issue arrived in our mailbox, I sat down to leaf through its pages. The backside of the magazine's front cover folded out as a three-page ad. (Keep in mind that the magazine's stated target demographic at the time was 8- to 12-year-old boys.) The three-page ad was for a mini-van. Why was an automobile ad placed in a magazine for boys who were at least four years away from driving? Because the automaker knows that "67 percent of car purchases by parents are influenced by kids."[339]

A second group whose spending is influenced by teenagers are their peers. How do kids influence the spending of their friends? By setting trends, telling them about products, and using those products themselves. Remember, peer influence is especially powerful in the lives of our kids as they grow through this vulnerable period of social development, and marketers take advantage of that fact. In a recent Harris Interactive survey of eight- to 18-year-olds, 44 percent said, "I like to buy things my friends have," 29 percent said, "To make sure I buy the right products, I often look to see what my friends use and buy," and 31 percent said, "If I do not have much experience with a product, I often ask my friends to tell me what to buy."[340] Because our kids have tremendous spending influence, marketers are in pursuit.

Marketers Want to Develop Brand Loyalty

Advertisers know that today's young consumers are tomorrow's adult spenders. They know if you reach them now, there's a better chance you'll have them for the rest of their lives. Marketing psychologist James McNeal believes that pursuing brand loyalty and developing a lifetime customer "could be worth $100,000 to an individual retailer."[341] In the marketing industry, this is known as "developing the future market."

The battles waged by Pepsi and Coke to secure "pouring rights" on school campuses are all about developing brand loyalty. In exchange for a school district's signature on a contract that promises to exclusively feature their brand's logo and product on school property, the soft drink giants may offer tens of thousands of dollars worth of equipment (scoreboards, signage, and so on) free of charge to the school. While it might take years of students feeding coins and bills into the machines for the companies to break even, it's long-term brand loyalty and financial return the companies are after. They know that long after the students graduate, they'll remain exclusive to the particular soft drink brand they adopted when they were young.

Kids Are Spending More Time Away from Parents

Marketers know that less parental input leads to less influence, thereby creating greater marketing opportunities among vulnerable "believe anything an adult says" kids and impressionable adolescents looking for direction.

Kids Are Spending More Time with Media

This reality has fostered the advent of new, more creative forms of marketing that reach kids through various media. And the fact that kids usually spend time engaging media without adult input, processing, or guidance means that the marketing message has increased power and influence.

Kids Are Easily Influenced Because of Where They're at Developmentally

Our teens are not yet fully adults, even though they may think they are. They lack the wisdom and experience that come with age. Their impulsivity and desire to feel good makes them especially susceptible to advertising's emotional appeals, a reality that marketers regularly exploit. Marketing critic Susan Linn says that kids' "brains are the least developed, they have the least experience and therefore they are in a perfect position to be taken."[342]

"We'll Get You": Marketing Strategies and Terms

Because marketing is so pervasive and powerful in today's culture, those who love and minister to kids need to be aware of the many advertising strategies marketers employ in an effort to influence teenagers' spending decisions...or "be taken." By knowing how advertisers and advertising works, we're better equipped to help kids understand marketing and it's often manipulative influence, and then we can equip teenagers to think biblically about marketing rather than allowing marketing to think for them.

Remember, every advertisement we see is carefully calculated regarding message, method, and placement. Everything is deliberate. Behind every minute of advertising lie hundreds of hours of market research and strategizing. (The following is a very small sampling of marketing strategies and terms. For a more complete list and explanation, visit the supplemental resource page for this chapter at www.cpyu.org.)

Age Aspiration

"Stop treating me like a child!" How many times have you heard teenagers speak (or yell) those words? Marketers are well aware of the fact that teenagers want to feel, look, be perceived, and be treated as older than they are. One market researcher says that "the gap between how old teens are and how old they would like to be narrows steadily as they age."[343] Research shows that 12- and 13-year-olds aspire to be 17; 14- and 15-year-olds aspire to be 18; 16-year-olds aspire to be 19, and 17- to 19-year-olds aspire to be 20.[344] Therefore marketers create ads to reach the targeted age by catering to the *aspired age*. In effect, marketers exploit a kid's desire to grow up.[345]

Cigarrette and alcohol companies have employed this strategy for years. By depicting young adults smoking, drinking, and having fun in ads, teenagers are led to believe that smoking and drinking are signs of being grown-up. Marketing critic Susan Linn says that "many of the models I've seen in beer commercials look young enough to be under twenty-one. The themes or stories portrayed in some alcohol commercials seem more relevant to underage drinkers than anyone else."[346]

Magazines, particularly those targeting teenage girls, employ the strategy as well. *Seventeen* magazine might be read by some 17-year-olds, but you can be sure that younger teens are drawn to the magazine because of age aspiration, just as 17-year-olds are drawn to magazines such as *Cosmopolitan*.

Branding

Next time you find yourself in a room full of teenagers, take a look around the room. Notice what they're wearing. Chances are you'll see a variety of brand logos touting everything from clothing companies, to television shows, to musical groups, to sports teams, to schools. We live in a "logo-fied" culture where we not only pay companies for their clothes, but also we become mobile billboards for their brands.

Branding is a process in which a brand catches the individual's interest, is adopted by the individual as his own identity, and then becomes an integral part of his life and culture. In a peer-oriented culture where social status and acceptance is of the greatest importance, brands compete against each other for allegiance, knowing full well if they come out on top and make a broad connection, they've accomplished something economically profitable. When marketers brand well, the brand isn't only adopted by kids; it's also immediately recognizable. The Nike swoosh, the McDonald's golden arches, and Adidas stripes are all examples.

The brand's "ethos" is marketed, too. An early example of successful branding is a series of late '60s and early '70s commercials depicting teenage females leaving their boyfriends to pursue "that neat guy in Levis slacks." Adopting the brand and its ethos, in effect, made the male consumer "a neat guy" bound to get attention from females. More recently, the Chrysler Corporation, a car brand long identified with the elderly, began a campaign to rebrand themselves to capture younger customers by featuring former Chrysler ad icon Lee Iacocca playing golf with hip-hop icon Snoop Doggy Dogg.

Research shows that branding starts young, with kids able to recognize logos at 18 months of age. In addition, before they reach their second birthday, kids are "asking for products by brand name. By three and a half, experts say, kids start to believe that brands communicate their personal qualities, for example, that they're cool, or strong, or smart."[346] One expert notes that "once kids bought an article of branded clothing at a department store; now they buy an entire identity, a whole set of clothes by one manufacturer at that brand's ersatz boutique. Kids become Prada girls or Old Navy chicks or Pacific Sun, a.k.a. PacSun boys—and even volunteer their services to these beloved brands to show the extent of their identification and devotion."[347]

In our consumer-driven, materialistic culture, brands will come and go as companies posture and fight for brand supremacy. Keep an eye on the kids you know and the ads targeting them to gain a sense of what brands stand for.

Employ the Cool Factor

The ploy plays into peer pressure, the realities of adolescent social development, and a teen's desire to fit in and not be left out. *Cool* is what's most desirable at any given moment in time. It's doing what everyone else is doing, but doing it first and doing it the best. It's worked best when the advertiser's brand or product finds its place in youth culture as the key to social success.

In his brilliant one-hour expose of teenage marketing, *The Merchants of Cool*, Douglass Rushkoff notes that marketers use *cool hunters*—very young, hip adults who go on shop-alongs and act like kids themselves—who work to uncover and identify the next cool thing so that it can be coopted, manufactured, and mass marketed to teenagers.[348]

Youth marketing expert Peter Zollo lays out the results of his research on how *cool* works in his book *Getting Wiser to Teens*.[349] His research is eye-opening for parents and youth workers. Zollo calls it the "Teen/Types Trend-Adoption Flow." His work segments kids down into four types or groups who function in a hierarchical relationship with each other.

The first group is known as *edge* teenagers—fiercely independent, often outcasts, edgy in dress, attitude, and behavior. They read *Rolling Stone* and *Spin* magazines to stay up on their music interests. Their parents don't care, so they raise themselves. When *cool hunters* embark on their fact-finding missions, they go to *edge* teenagers, as trends usually start with them. Once marketers find an "edge" trend to market, they mass produce it and inject it into the mainstream youth population. The edge teenagers then abandon the now-popular trend and find something else that keeps them on the edge—and the whole cycle starts again. A marketer's dream!

Then there are *influencers*. Membership in this group is highly sought after but very exclusive. This is the most directly influential group on the student population—the kids who the "wannabes" want to be like. They're cool but not edgy. They're big shoppers concerned with their appearance, and they love fashion. They're outgoing, social, and confident. Marketers often refer to them as "alpha kids" or "product evangelists." This is the group that marketers target with the products and styles they've stolen from the *edge* kids. A press release announcing the launch of Blown Away Marketing describes the firm's ability to mobilize *influencers*, saying it can get "trend-setting products to tastemakers across the country. With affiliate youth media groups in 66 major cities and college campuses in all 50 states, it is possible for them to put together a coordinated effort across the country."[350]

The third group is the *conformers*, the largest of the four groups—your typical teenagers who adopt fashions discovered by *edge* teenagers and popularized by *influencers*. They seek out the latest styles and fads in order to make themselves feel more confident. Marketers love the *conformers* since they desire (and have the money) to emulate *edge* and *influencer* peers.

The final group is the *passives*. These are typically academic achievers who struggle socially. They want to be popular and well liked but are too shy to pursue these ends. Males outnumber females in this group 2 to 1. While they do respond to marketing efforts, it takes them a little longer. (They respond best to ads that offer relief from social stress.)

Cool has sold and continues to sell product—and marketers are working to get the manufacturing and marketing of *cool* down to a science.

Exploit—and Even Create—Adolescent Yearning

Rather than allowing God to shape them into the people he wants them to be, most kids lean toward who or what their culture is telling them to be. They yearn for "completeness" they believe will come when they look the part, own the right stuff, wear the right clothes, and hang out with the right friends. Until then, they feel incomplete. Marketers reinforce these yearnings with products that promise to make kids complete.

Marketers are especially successful if they can continually create new yearnings and products to satisfy them. For example, the advent of the cell phone led marketers to convince kids that the ringtones on the phones aren't good enough; instead kids needed to download ringtones that fit their personalities and moods. (Of course, the products never truly deliver because real completeness never comes....a fact marketers are well aware of...which ensures there will always be a market related to unfulfilled adolescent yearnings.)

Exploit—and Even Create—Adolescent Anxieties

Our kids are facing lots of pain. Many are suffering with brokenness, heartache, and hopelessness. All of these anxieties combine to create fertile ground for marketers as they identify a point of anxiety and then offer a "cure"—in effect, a savior. This is why marketers go out of their ways to research teenage problems and fears. A recent ad for Ban deodorant tells teenagers "you've got more important things to worry about than odor." Above these words sit nine photos of teenagers locked in nine anxiety-causing situations common to adolescents, along with the charge to "ban" loneliness, insecurity, stereotypes, drama, peer pressure, angst, self-doubt, fear, and nerves. A classic example of exploiting anxieties is the old McDonald's commercials that told viewers, "You deserve a break today." The hamburger chain's research didn't reveal that people were looking for hamburgers; it said furiously busy and overstressed people were looking for rest. So McDonald's positioned itself as the reprieve.

How Advertising Is Shaping Youth Culture

As a media force pervasive in today's cultural landscape, advertising functions in our kids' lives just like all other media outlets. It's a map that sits unfolded in the laps of vulnerable teenagers who are looking to find their way from childhood, through adolescence, and into adulthood. Like all other media outlets, advertising's 24/7 presence has combined with the breakdown of the family and other life-shaping institutions to turn up the volume on marketing's power and ability to shape our kids' worldviews. It's telling them what to think, what to value, what to believe, and how to live their lives. As marketers form and re-form youth culture, it's also forming and re-forming the values, attitudes, and behaviors of the emerging generations.

It's important for parents and youth workers not only to know the strategies and techniques marketers employ, but also to know *how* advertising's nonstop barrage is specifically shaping our youth. What follows is a look at some of the short- and long-term effects and results of advertising. (They're in no particular order, but each is significant in terms of teenagers' spiritual health.) As you read through them, think about how these effects and results square up to a biblical worldview and life view. In addition, think about the implications for parenting and ministry. Consider ways you can become more proactive in addressing each of them with the kids you know and love.

Materialism Is Becoming More Deeply Embedded

Because they're being marketed to with increased frequency and depth, vulnerable kids will find it easier to believe advertising's messages and promises. As a result, they'll increasingly define themselves by their possessions, seeking happiness, satisfaction, meaning, and redemption in the accumulation of things. More kids will buy into a *live-to-consume* rather than a *consume-to-live* mentality. As this materialism becomes more deeply embedded in the fabric of youth culture, envy and jealousy will become more rampant.

A Rise in Impulse Buying

As materialism takes root and grows, kids will become more impulsive and buy without evaluating or thinking about the difference between *wants* and *needs*. Kids will want to acquire products they really don't need, but they'll want them for the perceived emotional and "quality-of-life" benefits.

Kids Will Work More in Order to Consume More

Over the course of the last two decades, more teenagers are taking on jobs. Those who have jobs are working longer hours, making it difficult for them to stay involved in other areas, including youth groups, school activities, service projects, and family time. While some kids work to save money for future educational needs, a growing number are working long hours in order to fund and sustain large luxury items, including cars, audio systems, cell phones, and so on. They get themselves locked into the "work-to-spend" cycle.

Vocation and Calling Are Understood Primarily in Economic Terms

Every one of us—including our kids—has been created by God, for God, and to be in a relationship with God while living his will and his way under his reign. It's not about us. But advertising consistently sends us a message that says, "It's all about you." Consequently, advertising leads our kids to get it all wrong regarding who should reside at the center of their worldview and who should be in control of their lives. When advertising combines with other cultural forces to convince them to ascend to the place of supremacy in their own lives, they begin to live out a distorted, disordered, and selfish set of priorities. Listening for God's voice to call them to a vocation won't be an option. Their vocation won't be about using their gifts and abilities in service to Christ and his kingdom. Rather, work will be chosen based on economic concerns. Kids will become increasingly committed to making as much as they can, building a big "kingdom" for themselves, and seeking satisfaction in the glorification of self.

Shopping Is a Spiritual Worship Experience

In a culture where selfishness and materialism have replaced God as the driving force in life, the mall becomes the temple people go to for the worship experience of shopping. Researchers are now beginning to study how shopping has become an addiction. It's reasonable to assume it's the experience of shopping that young people will embrace, as that experience gives them a temporary "high" that leaves them feeling good.

The Virtue of Compassion Is Being Replaced by Competition

When Jesus told his followers the parable of the Good Samaritan, he wanted his listeners to know that if they embraced their purpose in life and followed him, they'd view anyone in need as a neighbor. Thus, in the footsteps of the Samaritan who gave everything in response to the wounded man's need, they'd "go and do the same."

The message of today's market-driven world is the exact opposite. Instead of looking out for others, we're to look out for number one. In this kind of world, there is a decrease in generosity and an increase in selfishness. In this kind of world, there is a decline in civility. In this kind of world, we do anything and everything possible—including using people as a means to our ends—to get ahead of anyone and everyone else (who are seen as our competitors).

Growing Disregard for Authority

The current postmodern mindset is one that devalues authority. Everyone becomes a law unto themselves. Marketing efforts that serve to pit marketers with kids against their parents not only play well in this kind of world, but they also facilitate the growing disregard for parental authority that already exists among kids. When marketers exploit the adolescent drive for independence, they undermine authority and foster rebellion. As marketers continue to "empower kids" (translation: make kids independent of and master over their parents), we'll see a related undercurrent of disregard for all types of authority, including other adults, the law, teachers, and even God.

Increased Anxiety and Despair

Marketers promise relief and deliverance via products. When the feelings don't go away, teenagers continue seeking relief from other products. Despair, anxiety, depression, and its aftermath will continue growing in a youth culture that looks to products as the messiah. Kids with limited economic resources will grow frustrated because they believe what they can't afford is what will fulfill;

those with enough money will grow frustrated because what they have doesn't fulfill.

A Culture of Discontent and Dissatisfaction

The emptier kids feel, the more they'll be prone to turn to advertisers' products and the promises they make. The more they turn to advertisers' products, the emptier they'll feel. In reality, this is just what marketers want to happen. Why? Because dissatisfied kids will always be seeking and willing to purchase the next product that promises to "save" them. The cycle of materialism (which we'll address in chapter 10) leaves those who have more wanting more, but it also leaves them less satisfied. However, the emptier you feel, the more likely you are to buy marketing's lies—making you the perfect consumer.

A Generation of Shallow and Plastic People

As they grow older, kids who haven't stepped out of materialism won't know how to embrace the deeper things of life. Because they've never truly gone deep, they'll be unable to go deep. This reality is already working itself out in the lives of many Christian kids. They view their faith and their "feel good" church experience as another consumer commodity. They want everything packaged attractively and done for them. They want to avoid the struggles Jesus promised when he issued his invitation to "come and follow me." Their faith, just like the rest of their lives, doesn't go deep.

A Culture of Kids Locked into Consumer Debt

Not a day goes by that my kids don't receive one or more direct mail advertisements for preapproved credit cards. One credit card company is constantly telling them, "It's your life." The message they get from these and other ads is that life is about consumption. Whether it's their money or money they're borrowing from a credit card company, they're entitled to spend whenever the urge hits them. Sadly, many of today's teenagers will be buried deep in consumer debt long before they marry and start their families.

A Growing Culture of "Adult" Kids

Because age aspiration and age compression are a deliberate part of today's marketing landscape, our kids are pummeled by ads that encourage them to look and act older than they really are. For those of us who are raising or working with kids, the visual and behavioral age acceleration we witness could be quite convincing if we allowed it to be. In other words, we could be manipulated into forgetting that our kids are just that—kids. We cannot and must not be tempted to forfeit the parental involvement and influence our teenagers so desperately need, just because they're looking and acting like adults.

A Growing Culture of "Adolescent" Adults

Just as our youth are encouraged to embrace adulthood, adults are being manipulated to seek and embrace youthfulness. We're told we should not and cannot grow old. Advertising tells us to look and act younger. This mindset could very well begin to feed the view that those who are old are worthless and dispensable.

Increased Adoption of Advertised Values and Emulation of Advertised Behaviors

Because advertising is so pervasive in today's world and the list of things we can buy is seemingly endless, kids will view hundreds of thousands—if not millions—of ads for products they'll never buy. But just seeing the ads means they've been influenced by the values, attitudes, and behaviors those ads sell. Consequently, we can expect tobacco, alcohol, and drug use will continue to be serious social problems. Ads that promote skinny, perfect physical standards will sell kids into disordered eating and appearance alteration (plastic surgery, steroid abuse). Even though food marketers are concerned about preventing childhood obesity, there will still be a rise in obesity. Skinny kids will continue to appear in the food commercials eating fattening foods (without any consequences) and having fun while they're doing it. And ads that undermine authority will combine with increased materialism to contribute to a rise in violence, theft, cheating, and gambling among teenagers. Remember: Advertising doesn't sell just products, it sells a worldview.

Increased Sexual Confusion and a Loss of a Biblical Sexual Ethic

Sex will be commodified, and sexual partners will be objectified in every way, shape, and form. We'll therefore see a rise in sexual abuse, date rape, pedophilia, and other sex crimes. Our culture will continue to lose a biblical understanding of the created purpose, wonder, and joy of sex. Fornication and adultery will increase and abound. And for our Christian kids, the battle between God's order and design for sexuality and the culture's order and design for sexuality will be a difficult one to fight.

Personal Value Is Skin-Deep

Advertising encourages our kids to focus on the external rather than on character. Simply stated, to be beautiful is to be valuable.

Long-Term Relational Problems/Fallout

Advertising's focus on the external, especially sexuality, will combine with other cultural forces to contribute to and reinforce prevailing attitudes manifested in the breakdown of marriages, the rise in cohabitation, out-of-wedlock births, and a low view of marriage.

Dis-Integrated Faith and Disintegrating Faith

Very few of us have ever taken the time to think seriously about advertising, how it shapes us, how we succumb to it, and so on. As a result, we tend to uncritically welcome and assimilate advertising's values, attitudes, and behaviors into our lives, allowing these things to coexist with our faith and failing to see the contradictions. Consequently, we say we believe the gospel, but we wind up living another gospel that is anything but true. Our Christian faith becomes part of our life, rather than the driving force integrated into every area of our lives. This dis-integrated faith leads to the disappearance (or disintegration) of true Christian faith in our lives and culture.

Spiritual Emptiness Will Continue to Rise

Advertising and the materialism it fosters steer us away from the one true God and toward idols. They steer us away from Jesus Christ, the one and only source of redemption, to false promises of other "messiahs" and redeemers. Today's marketing blitz encourages our teenagers to create, pursue, and worship false idols, all the while leaving our kids emptier than before.

A Ripe—Yet Challenging—Environment for the Gospel

When the emptiness grows, the hunger longs to be fed that much more. While today's world might make it more difficult for us to lead young people to faith (because there's so much out there offering empty promises of fulfillment and so many other voices summoning them to "come and follow"), this is a good time for those who labor and long to point kids to Christ. The emptiness will only continue and the cry for redemption will grow louder. We must pray teenagers will see and embrace the only One who can fill their emptiness.

Leading and Loving Kids in a Marketing World—What Now?

After taking this brief tour through the world of marketing to teenagers, youth workers and parents could easily be tempted to respond by viewing marketing as an evil institution whose effects on kids are only negative. As a result, we might assume our best response is to work to remove all exposure to marketing from our kids' lives. However, taking this extreme, knee-jerk approach fails to take into consideration that marketing—in and of itself—is not inherently evil. Marketing serves a valuable function by making us aware of various options regarding the goods and services that are available for our use.

Marketing can be practiced and employed in a manner that glorifies God when strategies, techniques, and advertisements themselves point to the elements of the kingdom of God that Scripture defines as good, true, right, and honorable. As with all media, we must equip our kids to interact with marketing in a way that brings honor and glory to God.

What follows are some suggestions you can use to address your marketing concerns with the teenagers you know and love. There are no easy answers here, and the list is far from exhaustive. But by following up on and using these suggestions, you can begin the process of helping teenagers grow up to consciously and constantly deal with the systemic, deeply rooted, and enduring influence of advertising.

Constantly Proclaim the Creator God as the Only One Who Can Fill the Hole in Their Souls

As already stated, all humans are especially vulnerable to the influence of advertising because of the God-shaped vacuum that exists because of our separation from God. Longing for something to make us whole, we eagerly embrace anything that promises to fix our problems, meet our needs, and make our lives more fulfilling. If advertising's power is increased because of our spiritual yearning, shouldn't we be going out of our way to help kids understand what (or more accurately *who*) they're yearning for? We must help them recognize their hole in the soul, help them see that it's God-shaped, and then introduce them to the Redeemer by sharing the biblical story of creation, the fall, and redemption.

Then we must help teenagers see how advertising seeks to exploit this yearning, how it tells redemptive lies, and how it's ultimately preaching a false gospel that's so easily believed. Doing this requires that we faithfully view, process, and discuss advertisements with them—proactively and from a Christian perspective. In effect, we're laying out for them both the truth and the lies.

Affirm Their Value in God's Eyes

So much of our vulnerability to advertising lies in the fact that we go through life fearing we don't measure up and that others will reject us for this reason. This fear plays on who we are on both the inside and the outside. Consequently, we're easy prey for marketers who promise to make us look better, feel better, and relate better. How different it would be if we'd approach all advertisements and marketing efforts with the sense of personal value, worth, dignity, and security that comes with seeing ourselves as God sees us.

We must go out of our way to walk our kids through the Scriptures, showing them how valuable they are to God. Then, we must live with them in relationships that are characterized by our unconditional love that is based simply on who they are as God's creatures, rather than on what they look like, how they're shaped, how they smell, and other physical traits. And we must be involved with them in the context of a church community that does the same. Turning up the volume on their inherent, God-ordained dignity and worth will go a long way in turning down the volume on advertising's pervasive voice.

Read, Watch, and Listen to Their Media

Take the time to find out what they're reading, listening to, and watching. Then, engage those media yourself, all the while paying careful attention to the marketing messages our kids face while immersed in their media world. By taking the time to monitor their advertising, you'll reap the benefits of knowing specifically what messages are shaping their young lives. You must know about the marketing that's targeting them before you're able to shape your response to it.

Know the Advertising "Map"

As you monitor the ads, ask yourself this question: "How is this ad shaping the values, attitudes, and behaviors of today's teenagers?" In other words, you want to gain as much information as possible about where the advertising map is telling them to go. Then, by knowing what is being taught, you can both affirm any truth contained in the ads, and challenge any lies. If you're a parent, discuss both the truth and the lies with your child, using the Scriptures as the standard of discernment and showing how the Scriptures speak to the specific truths and lies you discover. In effect, you're modeling and teaching critical Christian thinking and the application of biblical truth to all of life.

Look in the Advertising "Mirror"

Marketers are spending millions to conduct market research that unlocks the secrets of teenagers' hearts—and all for the express purpose of getting our teenagers to spend and influence the spending of billions of dollars, both now and for the rest of their lives. If we learn how to "read" and understand the fruit of this market research as it's evidenced in the ads themselves, we'll be tapping into what marketers have learned about their "mission field" of teenagers. This information will be especially helpful to us as we work to communicate the life-changing gospel to that same mission field known as today's youth culture.

Teach Them to Recognize When, Where, and How They're Being Marketed To

Because teenagers have been swimming in the soup of market saturation for so long, many have a difficult time understanding when, where, and how they're being marketed to. A recent Harris Interactive Poll reveals that 91 percent of youth marketers agree or strongly agree with the statement, "Young people are being marketed to in ways they don't even notice."[351] We must lead them to understand that all of their media is designed to deliver them to marketers. In addition, we must help them identify ads by pointing them out when we see them and discussing them in light of God's Word. With my youngest son, this has become somewhat of a game. When we watch television or a movie together, he loves trying to beat me by being the first to point out ads placed in sets, plotlines, and stories.

Take Kids on a Marketing Field Trip

Whether you do this with your own kids or you're a youth worker or educator who does this with your students, a marketing field trip is a great way to teach kids how to notice the placement and pervasiveness of advertising. Whether you go to a place kids frequent (the mall, a high school athletic event, a local hangout), or you map out a drive through a familiar part of town with the radio playing, the goal is to get kids to consciously and deliberately open their senses to discover all the ads they encounter during the course of the trip. Keep a running list of the ads you encounter. When you're done, choose a handful of ads to "deconstruct" and evaluate through the use of ad-filtering questions (see below).

Help Them Process Ads by Constantly Asking the Ad-Filtering Questions

Teaching students to consciously and continually think biblically and critically about advertising is a valuable skill that fosters spiritual formation. By asking good questions, students will learn how to compare advertising's messages and worldviews with the biblical worldview and life view. Not only will they learn more about advertising's methods and power, but they'll also see how the Scriptures speak to all of life.

A good place to start is by using what I call "The Simple Seven" questions as a filter through which to process ads:

- What product is this ad selling?

- What, besides the product, does this ad sell? (ideas, lifestyle, worldview, behaviors)

- What's the bait, hook, and promise?

- Complete this sentence: "This ad tells me, use _____ (the name of the product) and _____ (the result the ad promises)."

- Does the ad tell the truth? What truth? How?

- Does the ad lie? What lie(s) does it tell? How?

- How does this ad and its messages agree or disagree with God's truth? What does that mean for me?

If you want to go deeper, here's a list of additional questions you can use as you teach your teenagers marketing discernment skills:

- Who made this ad?

- Why was this ad made?

- Whom is this ad targeting?

- What do the makers of this ad know about teenagers?

- What do the makers of this ad want me to do?

- What's the ad's plot?

- What are the ad's themes and assumptions?

- What techniques are being used to sell the product?

- What does the camera say is most important? How are the lighting, angles, focus, close-ups, and so on used?

- How is the camera used to manipulate my emotions and create moods?

- How is music used to manipulate my emotions and create moods?

- How are the camera and music used to manipulate and distort reality?

- What longing or need does this product promise to fulfill?

- How are people treated and portrayed? (Men? Women? Kids? Parents? Authority figures?)

- If you use this product, what does the ad explicitly or implicitly say your life will be like?

- If you don't use this product, what does the ad explicitly or implicitly say your life will be like?

- What inadequacies, anxieties, and aspirations does the ad exploit?

- Who or what is the redeemer or messiah in this ad?

- Is this ad exploitive or manipulative? How?

- What role do you think this ad plays in shaping the lives of your peers?

- Is this product necessary? Why? Why not?

- How does this ad try to make you "need" the product?

Getting Personal

A couple of years ago, I was leafing through a magazine in the weeks leading up to Christmas. I came across a one-page ad for Botox that really got me thinking about the role advertising plays in our lives. Laid over a photo of festive ribbons and a trumpet-shaped noisemaker ran the text, "Don't wait until the holidays have come and gone."

The ad reminded me of how effective advertising is not only in the lives of our marketing-targeted teenagers, but in our adult lives as well. Dissatisfied with who we are, how we feel, and what we look like, we yearn for the sin-caused curse of aging to be reversed. As we look in the mirror and see the results grow deeper and wider in the lines on our faces, we just want to be whole.

Isn't it ironic that because of an ad—placed at the time of year and in the context of our celebration of the coming of the one true Messiah—so many of us would be willing to invite a product into our lives, believing that when it comes, we'll be made whole? Advertising doesn't just play well to kids. We're easily targeted and manipulated marks as well. What role are you allowing advertising and its messages to play in your life?

7

Fitting In: The Push and Pull of Peer Pressure

Peer pressure is...having to be what other kids want you to be.

—HIGH SCHOOL FRESHMAN

I am very easily influenced.

—HIGH SCHOOL SENIOR

No peer pressure.

—The response of a 102-year-old woman, who was asked, "What do you think is the best thing about being 102?"

When I was a boy, our family traveled from Pennsylvania to Florida each summer for a month of vacation. When we weren't fishing, swimming, or visiting tourist attractions, my brothers and I would venture out on a "lizard safari." Although we knew chameleons were hiding in every bush and tree, at first we had a hard time spotting them. But it wasn't long before we learned that when the chameleons hide on the green leaves of a palmetto plant, one should look for a green chameleon. Those same chameleons could sit on the trunk of a palm, turn brown, and be almost invisible. At other times, they'd turn almost gray, camouflaging themselves on the stucco walls of the house. As we know, chameleons change color to blend in with their environments and protect themselves from predators.

Teenagers are tempted, to one degree or another, to become like chameleons. Caught in the midst of change, confusion, challenge, media bombardment, family dysfunction, and a host of other stresses, they yearn for stability and normalcy. They'll look for a safe place to belong, to protect themselves from feeling alone—and change colors to blend in with the surrounding environment.

At times, peer pressure and influence can be positive. It can spur kids on to try harder, avoid mistakes, and make good choices; it can even keep them from doing wrong. But negative peer pressure and influence is another story. It's the type of peer pressure that strikes fear into the hearts of caring parents. We want our kids to be spared from harm, we want them to make good and godly choices, and we don't want them to suffer the consequences of the many bad teenage choices we read about so often in the daily newspaper. We know peer pressure has the potential to make life difficult for our kids. One 11-year-old boy says, "Peer pressure feels like having a spotlight shined on you in a big crowd. You need to make a decision quickly, and you don't know what to do."[352]

Without the accumulated wisdom, experience, and fully formed intellectual capacities of adults, kids and teenagers are especially susceptible to negative peer pressure just because of where they're at in the process of developmental growth. Because they're still kids, they'll often allow peer influence to eclipse rational judgment in the decision-making process. Negative peer pressure is also frightening to us because we remember facing it when we were teenagers. We don't want our kids to make the same mistakes and bad choices we did. We want to protect them from the painful pull between doing what is popular and easy and doing what is right. But peer pressure rears its ugly head when our teenagers begin to test and evaluate the values we've worked hard to instill. And it turns its head and snarls at us when the kids we love compromise their learned commitment to right and wrong by going with the flow. Unfortunately, this reality is much more common and likely in a world where there's no absolute right or wrong—just the right or wrong you determine for yourself.

This chapter examines negative peer pressure specifically, the reason it reaches its apex during adolescent years, and how it influences teenagers. We'll look at some of the negative pressures kids face as well as the results of giving in to those pressures. And finally we'll discuss specific strategies to help you counter the influence of negative peer pressure in the lives of the teenagers you love.

Negative Peer Pressure and Influence: The Big Picture

In this section we'll examine some of the basics about negative peer pressure, including how factors such as changing family dynamics, parenting styles, and self-image affect the influence of negative peer pressure.

Negative Peer Pressure and Influence Is No Respecter of Age

On the day before she started kingdergarten, our daughter Caitlin asked me a startling question: "Daddy, when I go to school tomorrow, will people make fun of me?"

"Why would people make fun of you, Caitlin?" I asked.

"Well, what if they make fun of me because of what I look like or what I'm wearing?" she responded.

I wasn't sure why Caitlin had asked this question at such a young age. Lisa and I hadn't consciously done anything to instill prejudice or an obsession with clothes in Caitlin. That night I probed further in the hope that I might find what was at the root of her fear. As it turned out, she had overheard some kids in her nursery school, several months earlier, making fun of one of the boys for the way he dressed and how his hair was cut. Consequently, she feared that as she arrived in a new environment with unfamiliar faces, she might be singled out as one who didn't conform to the standards of the rest of the group. She was, at five years old, feeling the effects of peer influence, pressure, and expectations.

Peer pressure pays no attention to age. Anyone who has raised a child through elementary school knows that peer pressure exists there. Those kids who don't fit in or conform to the majority's standards might be excluded from playground activities, and included only when they're the butt of a joke or prank. One study found that by six years of age, a large number of girls desire to have a thinner figure. Researchers discovered that peer influence played a role as a significant predictor of body image and dieting awareness. "Specifically, girls' perceptions of their peers' body dissatisfaction predicted their own level of body dissatisfaction and dieting awareness."[353]

Bullying is one way that many young kids are subjected to peer pressure. While research shows that bullying peaks during the middle school years, it's already well established at the elementary-school level as kids are subjected to physical and verbal abuse by their peers. Typically the victims are the kids shoved to the fringe because they fail to conform to the group's standards of dress, looks, economic status, race, or behavior.

Adults are victims and perpetrators in the peer pressure game as well. Our clothing, houses, cars, and hairstyles usually reflect what's perceived as acceptable in society. We obsess over weight, body shape, and wrinkles. For others the fear of being labeled as the parent of an "average" kid leads them to place unreasonable and sometimes unbearable pressure on their kids to achieve and excel.

Peer pressure is a part of life for people of all ages.

Negative Peer Pressure and Influence Peaks During Adolescence

Today, Caitlin is an adult. While peer pressure is still present in her life (as it is in all of our lives), it's nowhere near as intense as it was when she was passing through her teenage years. It's been the same for all four of my kids. Along with the rest of the teenage population, Caitlin experienced the natural adolescent shift in social focus from her family to her peer group. As part of their growth toward self-sufficiency and independence, teenagers no longer see their family as the center of their social universe. They begin to disengage from the family while forming more and more meaningful relationships with same-sex and opposite-sex peers. This is not a bad thing. After all, part of our responsibility as parents is to lead them from the dependence of childhood, into an independent adulthood.

Some developmental experts have likened this transition to an orbiting satellite.[354] During the childhood years, our thinking and behavior revolve around what parents teach us. Adolescence brings a "desatellization" as we spin out of the orbit of parental identity to define ourselves as distinct. Naturally, this quest to discover ourselves leads us to our peer group—and as we all know, it's not unusual for parents and peers to disagree. One survey of families with kids in grades six through 12 found that the overwhelming majority of parents say that it's not okay for their kids to smoke cigarettes (98 percent) or drink alcoholic beverages (96 percent); it also found that the majority of students say their school friends believe it's all right to smoke/chew tobacco (63 percent) and drink beer, wine coolers, or liquor (62 percent).[355]

A walk through the halls of any middle school or high school proves that peer pressure and influence is the strongest during these years. Look at their clothing and read the labels. Notice what they're wearing on their feet. Listen to the way they talk. Look at their hair. Listen to the subjects of their conversations. They look and sound alike because most kids go out of their way to identify with some group of peers in their school and avoid being left out. (And if you're tempted to assume this is a new phenomenon, take a walk through the halls of your own high school yearbook!)

Unfortunately, peer pressure peaks when kids are their most insensitive and cruel. One group of researchers spent three years observing and interviewing more than 1,000 junior high and high school students on Long Island, New York. What did they discover? "Everywhere we went, kids made fun of other kids—this was more usual than unusual. 'People make fun of you,' said one student. 'They make fun of your hair and the way you dress. They're just cruel.'"[356] Of course, insecurity drives so much of this cruelty, as kids build themselves up by tearing others down. Researchers have found that "the threat of negative feelings" (including the threat of isolation, ridicule, and the fear of being seen by peers as inadequate) are a motivational force behind susceptibility to peer pressure, the willingness to conform, and the desire to pressure one's peers.[357]

Another ingredient is adolescent impulsivity, an "act first and *maybe* think later" reality that's a distinct mark of developing teenagers. This impulsivity often combines with the lack of wisdom and experience to lead kids to decisions that adults see as risky and flat-out wrong. For example, one recent fad among middle schoolers is the "choking game" (a.k.a., "pass out game," "fainting game," and "tingling game"). Kids tighten ropes, hands, belts, and other items around their necks to constrict the flow of blood to their brains. By strangling themselves and then releasing the pressure, they get a tingling sensation in their bodies—a quick "high." Many kids faint and wind up choking themselves to death. And impulsive middle schoolers who try it pressure their peers to try it, too.

As your kids move through post-high school and college years, the influence of the peer group remains but gradually decreases in intensity. They become more secure and a "resatellization" occurs. Amazingly, your kids begin to look more like you in terms of their values, attitudes, behaviors, and lifestyles even though they're well established in the groove of their own "orbits."

Less Family Presence Adds to Peer Pressure

"It's great to be together as a family again!" a father said to his wife and sons at the end of a parent-teen weekend I'd been leading. His words bothered me. Had they *not* been spending time together as a family? Had he been away on some extended business trip? Had the parents separated? It wasn't any of the latter. Rather, each family member while living in the same house had been so involved in his or her own activities that it took a weekend away from home for them to spend time together again! Now that I've experienced years of hustle and bustle that comes with living with teenagers, I know about this struggle.

While it's natural for parents and teenagers to spend less time together as the kids pass through adolescence, it's unwise to assume that it's all right to not spend time as a family. Parents who become overinvolved in work, recreation, and other outside activities are also making the choice to spend less time with the family. As a result they open the door for their teenagers to spend more time "living with" and listening to their peer group. In addition, when parent-teenager time decreases, parents know less about what their kids are facing, and parental influence decreases as well. When asked by the Gallup Institute, "How would you rate your parents on understanding these things about you?" 38 percent of teenagers rated their parents "fair" or "poor" regarding knowledge about peer pressures they face.[358]

So, after years of little or no family time, an entire generation of "baby busters" has moved through their teenage years and into adulthood with a hunger for deep, meaningful relationships.

The "buster" label is accurate, given the fact that many in this age group look back on their personal history and see a series of "busted" relationships.

Developmental expert David Elkind cites the breakdown of the family as one of the main reasons for the crisis among adolescents in today's world. In his classic, still-relevant book *All Grown Up and No Place to Go*, Elkind says that what teenagers need is time to grow through the normal and confusing changes of adolescence. Yet, our society pushes them through adolescence, forcing them into premature adulthood that they're unable to handle. The deteriorating family, including absent and uninvolved parents, is to blame. The result for our teenagers, says Elkind, is stress and its aftermath.[359]

Much of that stress occurs when the powerful influence and expectations of the peer group are not balanced by loving, involved parents who spend time with their kids. Consequently, close friends wind up understanding teenagers more than their own parents do. In addition, the peer group assumes the nurturing role, thereby shaping the values, attitudes, and behaviors that should be shaped by Mom and Dad. Dean Borgman notes that kids whose lives are marked by resiliency to the struggles of adolescence (including negative peer pressure and influence) are marked by a history of "strong family nurture."[360]

The absence of family nurture has changed how teenagers are relating to one another, and have upped the intensity of peer influence and pressure. Chap Clark's research into the lives and world of today's emerging generations offers convincing evidence that kids are relating in new ways. Clark says that because kids have been abandoned by those who should be there for them, they look for a safe place elsewhere. They find "a family with a set of respected and controlled expectations, loyalties, and values" in peer "clusters."[361] These groups of teenagers who identify themselves as a relational unit "develop because midadolescents know they have no choice but to find a safe, supportive family and community, and in a culture of abandonment, the peer group seems to be the only option they have."[362] Clark identifies one of the distinguishing marks of a cluster (ranging in size from roughly four to ten kids) as "rules and norms: While a cluster is being developed, a subtle, almost imperceptible negotiation goes on among the members. The necessary rules, norms, values, and even narratives of the cluster that serve to bind the members together are all worked out prior to the cluster's ultimate formation. After these have been negotiated and established (again, almost never through explicit dialogue or reflection), the members of the cluster tend to subordinate their own personal convictions, loyalties, and norms to the will of the collective whole."[363] Consequently, the influence of the cluster shapes values, attitudes, and behaviors of an adolescent with an intensity and depth not known by previous generations of teenagers who also experienced peer influence and pressure, but at a markedly different level that was tempered and shaped by a stronger family context.

I believe negative peer pressure and influence would be significantly lower if our families weren't marked by so much lack of togetherness. More kids would be better equipped to handle the stresses and strains of negative peer pressure.

Parenting Style Plays a Peer Pressure Role

By the time he was 16, Andrew had become the antithesis of everything his parents demanded; he modeled his appearance and behavior after a peer group that placed a premium on living life on the edge. His tattoos, body piercings, unusual hair color and style, and edgy clothing were revolting to his folks. He did whatever he wanted, whenever he wanted. He confessed to me, "You know why I act and look like I do? My parents have become so demanding that I do just the opposite of what they tell me to do."

Andrew's parents had adopted an authoritarian parenting style, exhibiting little warmth and affection toward their son. They rarely listened to Andrew. Instead, they functioned as dictators, making all of Andrew's decisions for him.

Research has shown that authoritarian parents and permissive parents tend to raise kids who have more difficulty resisting negative peer pressure. While kids of authoritarian parents find refuge and understanding they long for in peer groups, kids of permissive parents find the direction and guidance they don't get from Dad and Mom in their peer groups. The latter kids get no parental input and guidance, the former nothing but.

A more reasonable and biblical approach is a parenting style characterized by age-appropriate demands for behavior and high levels of warmth, affection, understanding, and grace. In these homes, teenagers are more likely to develop the attitudes and skills needed to say no to negative peer pressure.[364] These parents protect their kids from negative peer pressure by monitoring where their kids are, who they're with, and what they're doing.[365]

Poor Self-Image Invites More Negative Peer Pressure

Teenagers want to belong. If they sense they don't, they'll begin seeing themselves as abnormal. Consequently, pursuing and adopting the images of those who are accepted, desirable, and interesting can become a consuming passion, dictating values, appearance, and behavior. It's even more difficult and intense for kids who deal with a weak or absent family support system. Many kids will even compromise their own uniqueness, identities, and values for peer acceptance.

After observing adolescent behavior for years, researcher Marcel Danesi noticed that kids are either "cool" or "losers." He writes, "*Coolness* has become a synonym for social attractiveness, and its opposite, *loserness*, has become a synonym for ugliness and alienation."[366]

Kids see what happens to the peers who don't fit in: They're outcasts who might have to eat alone, never get asked to a dance, or became the butt of jokes—and understandably "anything is better than the pain of living like that," they say. It all boils down to feeling good or bad about themselves, secure or insecure.

Those who don't make it with the larger peer group will sometimes seek acceptance in a small subculture of "losers" held together by the common experience of rejection. Together, they rally around some kind of shared social code marked by common outward appearance and shared involvement in sometimes deviant behaviors. Over the years, metalheads, Goths, brainiacs, and street gangs have all served this purpose in one way or another.

A few years ago I surveyed a group of Christian kids regarding the pressure to drink. Several of the high school students said that even though they believe underage drinking is wrong, they still felt they had to do it. For them, doing what was wrong was more acceptable than being left out. In our emerging postmodern culture, such choices will become easier to make as kids justify their behavior as "right for me."

The Nature of Negative Peer Pressure Has Changed

Negative peer pressure used to take the form of a *verbal invitation* to participate in some behavior that both you and the inviter knew was *wrong*. There was always a "sneaking around" element; an attempt to get away with something you knew would get you into lots of trouble—if you got caught.

But negative peer pressure is markedly different these days: Now it typically takes the form of an *unspoken expectation* to participate in behavior that the great majority of the peer group believes is *normal* and *right*. It follows that if everybody's doing it, and there's nothing wrong with it, the pressure to conform is more intense. So it's much more difficult for kids to go against the flow of their peers' postmodern moral relativism, especially when the behaviors promoted are no longer sneaky, but celebrated.

One 17-year-old explains it this way: "When you hear *peer pressure*, you think of people standing there going, 'C'mon, do it!' But it's not like that. You go to a party, and everyone's standing around drinking. And you feel left out because you're not. So you get a beer or whatever, and you start feeling more relaxed: 'Okay, I'm fitting in.' You start talking to people, and they start talking to you."[367]

According to Teenage Research Unlimited, "the classic adult perception of peer pressure—an overbearing, perhaps even hostile, peer who all but forces an innocent child into a moment (or lifetime) of loose morals and crime—is outdated...The peer pressure teenagers face is an internal phenomenon. A plurality of teen respondents (45%) believes that peer pressure is a personal desire to 'fit in.'"[368] "Peer pressure is based on internal fears and insecurities more than direct pressure from outside parties, but teens still look to the larger teen population when deciding how to best fit in."[369]

Kids Are Aware of Peer Pressure

Some adults believe that our teenagers are oblivious to the negative influence of their peers. But when asked what they dislike most about being a teenager, the answer given more than any other was "peer pressure."[370]

When I asked a number of kids to complete the sentence, "My friends want me to..." the most common answer was "do and be what they want me to do and be." Our kids are aware of peer pressure.

The Media Fuels the Fire of Negative Peer Pressure

The media, through advertising, sets the peer-pressure agenda, telling adolescents what to push on their peers—how to look, what to wear, where to go, who to be, etc. It's the marketing of "cool" by carefully calculated design. The peer group, following advertising's lead, exerts pressure and influence and becomes a powerful, cost-free sales force. Combine that with the attitudes and lifestyles of media heroes saturating youth culture—rewriting values on sexuality, materialism, the importance of people, and authority—and anyone not buying in is seen by their peers as prudish, old-fashioned, and hopelessly outdated.

Christian Kids Aren't Immune to Negative Peer Pressure and Influence

Almost twenty years ago, Dr. Bob Laurent wrote an enlightening book, *Keeping Your Teen in Touch with God*, that examined the role negative peer pressure plays in alienating adolescents from the church. After studying 400 teenagers from Christian homes over a three-year period, he found that the peer group is their real world. Using statements designed to measure the influence of negative peer pressure, he asked Christian teenagers to respond. The following are the results of his survey listed with the average response:

- "I am more likely to act like a Christian when I'm with my Christian friends and to act like a non-Christian when I'm with my non-Christian friends." *Agree*

- "I get upset when my non-Christian friends leave me out of their activities." *Agree*

- "I'd rather be with my friends than with my family." *Agree*

- "I try to keep up with the latest fads." *Strongly Agree*

- "My non-Christian friends' opinions are important to me." *Strongly Agree*

- "If I needed advice, I'd ask my friends before I asked my parents." *Agree*

- "It bothers me when my non-Christian friends think I'm too religious." *Agree*

It became clear from Laurent's research that when their friends cared little or nothing about religion, it was difficult for Christian kids to care about their faith and live it out consistently. Based on my own observations, Christian kids still struggle with these issues. Since postmodern amorality has led to a watering down of faith, it's much easier for teenagers to succumb to negative peer pressures and influences.

In summary: No matter what age we are, we can expect to face negative peer pressure, at no time in the life cycle is negative peer pressure and influence greater than during adolescence. Parents and youth workers who recognize the strong influence of peer pressure will be wise guides and guards of their kids.

Negative Peer Pressure and Influence: The Specifics

For the next few pages, I will walk through some of the major "pressure points" that teenagers face every day. While this isn't an exhaustive list, it'll get you started on your quest to understand the nature and intensity of negative peer pressure. As you read through the list, keep in mind that peer pressure isn't unique to teenagers—it also enters the world of preteens and young kids. And don't stop there. Do a little bit of self-evaluation to see if you, as an adult, are pressured in any of these same ways.

Pressure #1: Having the "Perfect" Body

Let's face it: Ours is a society that's self-conscious and overly concerned with our appearance. Yes, we're vain.

As bodies change and grow, our teenagers hope they'll end up with the great physiques—however the media defines them. Girls want the shape of a supermodel. Guys need a big chest, six-pack abs, muscular arms, etc. The pressure for the perfect body starts before our kids even get into kindergarten and intensifies during the elementary and middle school years. One study concludes that "body dissatisfaction in girls first appears...between ages 5 and 7 years, and appears to be a function of shared peer norms for thinness."[371]

Self-conscious kids measure themselves against the prevailing cultural standards and believe they're growing too fast, too slow, too big, too short, too fat, or too skinny. They're concerned about their hair color and texture, complexion, size of their breasts, nose, posteriors, and muscles. David Elkind quotes George, 14, whose physical awareness and need for peer approval left him facing an intense predicament. In a letter asking for help, he writes: "Help, I don't have any pubic hair that shows. The boys call me 'Baldy' and the girls want to know why, and it's so embarrassing. I'm 14. Shouldn't I have it by now?"[372] Three years' worth of taunts from peers calling her "Fatty" and "Smelly" haunted Kelly Yeomans, 13. After five neighborhood teenagers pelted her house with butter and eggs, the 13-year-old from London, England, ended her life by overdosing on pills.[373]

The pressure to fit the mold has led many kids on a futile pursuit of the perfect body. More and more are taking drastic measures to get there. The prevalence of eating disorders such as anorxia nervosa and bulimia among adolescent girls is due in large part to the cultural pressure to be thin. Many boys, on the other hand, combine lifting weights with steroids. According to the National Institute on Drug Abuse, 2.5 percent of 8th graders, 3.5 percent of 10th graders, and 4 percent of 12th graders have admitted to using steroids.[374] Why do teenagers go to these extremes? Because their peers will see them as more attractive. If our society continues to equate personal value and worth with outward appearance, the pressure to have the perfect body will continue to be felt by all. Parents and youth workers should be sensitive to the fact that this pressure peaks during the teenage years.

Pressure #2: Just the Right Clothes and "Look"

Maybe you've heard, "No way, Mom. I'd rather die than be caught wearing that outside of our house"; or "Come on, Dad. Please give me the money. I need those jeans. Everybody else is wearing them." Many teenagers I know believe that clothes make them. (Clearly advertising works!)

One study of high school students showed that those who wore out-of-style clothes were automatically classified as nerds who wore "ugly sweaters that look like their parents' choice, or hand-me-downs." Another commented, "They're in a different world. Like striped shirts that don't match."[375] Parents and youth workers should pay close attention to style preferences their teenagers value, as these will change.

Dress is one of the strongest types of adolescent peer pressure and influence. One girl says, "Kids make fun of you when you're different, like you're not cool or you don't wear the right kinds of clothes."[376] Rarely will you meet a teenager brave and daring enough to be the first to try something new and different; many of these kids have already been ostracized (or were never a part of) the cool crowd; their radically different clothing style is their way of saying, "I'm different. I don't belong. Leave me alone."

Many parents have expressed frustration with their teenage daughters' immodest clothing. Whether it's form-fitting or skin-revealing, these clothes have become especially prevalent in recent years. Those parents who want their daughters to dress differently are further frustrated by the fact that it's difficult to find more modest clothing in stores. But when you talk to kids about their choice of immodest and "sexy" dress, you quickly learn that their goal isn't immodesty or looking sexy; it's about wanting to appear older than they are, to be in style, and to be accepted by their peer group.

Several years ago this trend took a frightening turn when kids were getting murdered over clothing, athletic shoes, and jewelry. Students who were interviewed after the murder of a 17-year-old Philadelphia girl over her $450 gold earrings complained about the pressure to keep in style and the resulting fear of traveling to school or work. Still, most of them said they'd stay on the cutting edge of fashion and risk danger rather than lose acceptance and popularity.[377]

Responsible parents and youth workers must instill a sense of personal value and worth in teenagers that hinges on something other than their hairstyle or clothing brands. They must help them discern needs from wants—good stewardship and the health of our wallets depends on it. Still we can't write off our kids' concern with clothing and appearance, either. The pressure they feel is very real, and the price of peer rejection is too much for them to pay.

Pressure #3: Being Socially Linked with the Right Kids in the Right Activities.

At times, teenagers see their parents' rules and expectations as the greatest roadblock to social connectedness and popularity: "Aw, come on. Nobody's doing anything wrong. Everybody else is going. I'll be the only one left behind. This isn't fair!" Even if we have the best reasons in the world for saying no, if our kids are the only ones left behind when all the *right* kids are doing all the *right* things, teenagers will say we're unfair.

What makes a teenager cool in the eyes of their peers? Teenage Research Unlimited asked teenagers that question, and four of the top five characteristics cited have something to do with social and relational abilities and factors—being funny, having an outgoing personality, having lots of friends, and popularity with the opposite sex.[378]

Parents will become aware of this pressure in two distinct stages. The first stage occurs at or near the onset of adolescence, when kids begin the journey of dependence on parents to total independence. It's also during this first stage that kids begin to feel the pressure to have a boyfriend or girlfriend. Researchers looking at sexual pressure among teens found that many kids go into boyfriend/girlfriend relationships because others are doing it, and they don't want to feel left out.[379] The second stage begins just about the time your kids and their friends get their driver's licenses. Armed with car keys, some of your child's friends will put almost unbearable pressure on your teenager to "come along" on demand. If you're a parent who wisely exercises your God-given responsibility to set limits and say no, the pressure will become even more pronounced, at least for a while, for your teenager.

Evidence of athletic ability and involvement in sports can also play a significant role in our kids' level of peer acceptance. The middle school boy who's a late bloomer or not athletically inclined might view gym class as the most agonizing part of the school day.

One ninth-grader relates, "If someone isn't good at sports they'll call him a faggot. One time a kid missed the ball or he did something stupid, and they called him a f------ fag."[380] Those who don't excel in athletics become targets for peer sneers and jeers while students blessed with athletic abilities often assume a high profile among their peers. One study of the middle school social ladder found that boys involved in after-school sports and girls involved in cheerleading were the most popular. Their involvement increased the likelihood that others would want to be their friends.[381]

The pressure to do what the rest of the crowd is doing socially and to be connected in the "right" social networks can be intense. Teenagers don't want to be left behind, left out, or forgotten by their peer group. Parents and youth workers should recognize the power of this pressure, and parents must work to strike a balance between too much and too little freedom.

Pressure #4: To drink, smoke, and use drugs

When I surveyed a group of teenagers active in their church youth groups and who professed faith in Christ, they told me drinking and drugs were their greatest pressures.

Are you surprised? I'm not. After all, today's teenagers are immersed in a youth culture saturated with media and advertising messages telling them that alcohol does nothing but improve your life, allow you to have fun, increase your sex appeal, and fill your days with joy. They've grown up watching a generation of adults, sometimes their own parents, model alcohol use as a way to relax and socialize more effectively. And as their drive for independence manifests itself in a desire to appear older than they are, they reason that smoking and drinking are surefire ways to appear older. Add to that a group of peers who approve of and/or engage in substance abuse, and you've got some pretty intense pressure and influence. One middle school girl says, "One night I went to a party. Everyone there was drinking. Some kids were smoking dope, too. My friends coaxed me into having some drinks. I kept wanting to say no, but I was also afraid of getting teased. It's not easy to say no to drugs and alcohol when you're in junior high. Everyone wants to feel included."[382]

A highly publicized *Weekly Reader* survey of upper-elementary students found that kids in fourth through sixth grades are being pressured to abuse drugs. Thirty percent of the kids report they have received "a lot" of pressure to drink beer, 31 percent to use marijuana, and 34 percent to try cigarettes.[383] While the annual numbers on substance rise and fall by small percentages, the numbers remain high enough to indicate that the pressure's on our kids at very young ages.

Researchers continue to see a strong connection between what one's peers are doing, and how that influences one's behavior. A study conducted by the National Institute of Child Health and Human Development found that the main indicator of whether or not teenagers begin smoking or drinking is whether they have friends who do it. The study "found that the single most important factor is the behavior of their five closest friends. These teens are nine times more likely to smoke than early adolescents who had no friends that smoke or drink."[384]

Some of our kids experience substance-abuse pressure with a different twist and intensity. Teenagers who've been picked on, ostracized, or made fun of for an extended period of time will often compensate for being an "outsider" by finding refuge and acceptance as an "insider" in a group of peers who've also been denied entry into the cool club. Together they can become a family—a place to belong. It isn't unusual for the code of acceptance in these groups to include smoking, drinking, and drug use. In a sense, these activities become part of the group's "uniform" or shared behavioral code. Wear it, and you're in; take it off, and you're out.

The pressure to drink intensifies as our kids grow older. Peer pressure to drink is so great among undergraduates that many colleges and universities are establishing "substance free" housing facilities. Students choose to live in a substance-free room, agreeing not to smoke, drink, or use drugs while in their rooms or elsewhere in the dorms. The students who choose to live in these dorms say they have found relief from the intense peer pressure prevalent on so many college campuses today.

While kids drink, smoke, and use drugs for many different reasons, peer pressure is a significant contributor to the alarming number of kids who choose to indulge. Nine out of ten teens experiment with alcohol; three out of five experiment with an illicit drug. But ten out of ten feel the pressure.

Pressure #5: Becoming Sexually Active

Today, premarital sexual activity of all kinds is viewed as appropriate and normal. Teenagers who're virgins might feel at times like they're odd—maybe the last few virgins on earth. While many kids have held to their convictions and virginity, the majority are sexually active. Eight of 10 teenage boys and seven of 10 teenage girls will have sexual intercourse, often with numerous partners. That same majority, by virtue of the fact that they are a majority, pressures the minority to "get real, get normal, and get with the program" by getting sexually active. More and more braggers try to build themselves up in the eyes of their peers by describing real or imagined sexual conquests. The boastings and sex talk don't fall on deaf ears. One study found that a person's perceptions of their peers' attitudes about sex had the strongest impact on their own level of sexual activity. Those who thought that their peers were highly sexually active had a greater involvement in sexual activity themselves.[385]

Changing bodies, exciting new sexual urges, media portrayals of sexual behavior, and changing cultural values all combine to make our teenagers susceptible to sexual pressure. Many kids are doing it for the first time just "to be done with it." The Kaiser Family Foundation polled teens to discover how much pressure they feel when it comes to sex. The following represents those who answered that they felt "a lot" or "some" pressure:

- 89 percent of girls said they felt pressure from boys

- 87 percent of boys said they believe girls felt pressure from boys

- 67 percent of boys said they felt pressure from boys

- 62 percent of girls said they believe boys felt pressure from boys

- 54 percent of both boys and girls felt that girls felt pressure from girls

- 63 percent of girls felt that boys felt pressure from girls

- 49 percent of boys felt that boys felt pressure from girls[386]

Our kids are being lured and invited into sexual activity by many different and attractive voices. All too often the voice of their peers can't be resisted because resistance is a short, one-way street leading to the pain of rejection.

Pressure #6: Getting Good (or Bad) Grades

Research indicates that an adolescent's school achievement is affected by peer behavior, both positively and negatively.[387] The Horatio Alger Association's annual report, *The State of Our Nation's Youth*, reports that among high school students, the "pressure to get good grades" is a major problem for 41 percent of those surveyed, and not a problem for only 20 percent. Indeed, some students are pressured to *not* do well academically as a form of protest or a badge of honor. Still students report that "getting good grades in school" is the number one item of importance to them for fitting in amongst their friends.[388]

Overall, youth culture appears to be moving toward the positive side of doing well in school. After "better looking," teenagers cite being a "better student" as the second most common thing they would change about themselves.[389] While on the surface this trend serves to encourage kids to work hard, there are dangers. Some kids might develop an unhealthy drive to excel that sets them up for failure if their standards of excellence exceed their own God-given abilities.

Negative Peer Pressure: The Results

Result #1: It Can Force Kids into Moral Dilemmas

Several years ago I took 35 high school students on a white-water rafting trip. About halfway down the river, our guide instructed us to pull our rafts to the side for a short break. He climbed out of his raft and went up a path that led to a huge boulder that jutted over the river. He yelled down that anyone who chose to could follow him. He then jumped off the rock and fell 30 feet into the river. I was amazed, wondering how anyone could have the courage to jump off anything so high. I knew that my fear of heights would keep me from doing anything so stupid.

In a flash, three-quarters of our group was up on the rock jumping. They'd hit the water, swim back, and climb up to the rock for more. Then they started jumping in groups. Soon I realized that I was one of only three people still sitting in a raft.

Then it started...*peer pressure*. (Well, not technically from *peers*; but that made it worse!) My fellow rafters began to question their heretofore fearless leader's courage. "No thanks! I'm satisfied to watch!" I nervously yelled. Then one of the kids did the unthinkable. He seized on my fear by questioning my masculinity! Soon all the kids were chanting my name and inviting me to join in. My good sense and experience with heights told me to stay put in the raft. But my insecurity welled up inside me. With my knees knocking like never before, I put on a false air of confidence (believe me, I was terrified!) and climbed out of my raft to their cheers. At that moment, it seemed easier to jump off a 30-foot rock than to paddle down the river listening to remarks about my lack of courage or manliness.

From my vantage point on top of the rock, the water seemed so far down. But I jumped. I had a long time to think on the way down, too. I knew that if I'd been going down that river alone, I'd have paddled right past that rock. But there I was in midair, a well-adjusted, self-confident adult youth group leader.

Who jumped because of peer pressure.

But my experience on the river doesn't even come close to the dilemmas our kids face every day. Parents and youth workers should be aware of the powerful pull of negative peer pressure and influence. In your teenager's mind, moral dilemmas entail more than right or wrong; they're about acceptance or rejection by peers during a life stage when acceptance is more important than it ever was or ever will be again.

Result #2: It Can Lead Our Kids into Buying Lies
The basic premise behind effective brainwashing is this: If a person hears and sees something over and over again, he or she will

eventually believe it, even if it's not true. Brainwashing gets people to buy into lies, viewing them as truth.

Kids, by virtue of the fact that they spend so much of their time immersed in their peer culture, are brainwashed to a certain extent as well—into accepting values, attitudes, and behaviors they hear and see over and over again every day. Their susceptibility to buying lies is augmented by the fact that they're questioning many of the values they've believed prior to adolescence. Part of that process involves swimming in other value systems. This is nothing new or unique to this generation—except that the values, attitudes, and behaviors of youth culture are far more intense.

I've seen strong kids weakened. And when they believe lies, it isn't long before they're dealing with the aftermath of their actions. Some of us will watch our kids live through the guilt of premarital sex and the pain of contracting sexually transmitted diseases. Others of us will walk our unmarried teenage girls through a pregnancy. Some of our kids will use drugs and face legal trouble or addiction. Others will buy the lies of physical beauty and become victims of anorexia, bulimia, and other types of disordered eating.

But there is hope. It's never too late for a child to turn and walk away from the lies. And wise and loving parents and youth workers must be there to help them through it.

Result #3: It Can Destroy Their Self-Image
One of the greatest struggles related to peer pressure and influence is when the victims choose to be untrue to themselves, becoming people they never wanted to be. One girl described it as having to "put on the mask" whenever she's with her friends.

By conforming to peer-manufactured images that are different from who teenagers are, they're commiting self-image suicide. Living lies makes them feel trapped and even more unfulfilled, making it successively harder to accept themselves and see their God-given value and worth. Some get in so deep that they find it almost impossible to get out.

One of the developmental tasks of adolescence is discovering who you are as an individual. When our kids suppress and deny their God-created individuality in an attempt to conform, they can't help but feel worse about themselves. Survival means keeping the mask on while knowing the awful truth that you are living a lie.

Result #4: It Can Strain Parent-Teen Relationships

Did ever hear your parents say, "I don't care what everybody else is doing! If they told you to jump off a bridge, would you?!" (I'm just glad my mother never said, "If they told you to jump off a rock, would you?!) If you ever hear yourself using or thinking that line or one like it, you know that peer pressure has arrived. Although I've never heard a kid answer yes to that question, I have seen them make decisions that are no different than a yes. It defies logic, but, yes, they do "jump off a bridge" from time to time.

There will be moments when our kids—in an effort to make their own decisions, assert their independence, and find acceptance in the peer group—go against our wishes. Sometimes they'll tell us what they've done; sometimes we'll find out from someone else. We'll need to respond with discipline, correction, and grace. No matter how it plays out, you can be sure that there will be tension as you raise, direct, and discipline your kids, especially as they exercise their God-given gift of a developing ability to think and do things for themselves.

Negative Peer Pressure: Response Strategies

Our daughter Caitlin had been in kindergarten for six months when I heard the most amazing words come out of her mouth. As I stood near the fresh flowers cooler in the grocery store, a little voice over my shoulder said, "What the hell is that?"

I spun around in total shock and disbelief. Then calmly, I said, "Caitlin, did you just ask me something?"

"Yes," she said. She pointed at a small potted cactus plant and repeated her question: "What the hell is that?"

Nothing had prepared me for this moment. The only reassurance I had was knowing she couldn't possibly be aware of what she'd just said. I knelt down next to her and said, "Well, Caitlin, first, that is a cactus. And second, where did you ever learn to talk like that?"

Her answers and our ensuing discussion revealed she'd learned her new vocabulary on the school bus. So on the way home, Caitlin and I discussed the inappropriateness of her language. Then my wife and I began talking about how we were going to handle similar situations in the future.

Caitlin had succumbed to a type of passive peer pressure and influence. Just by being with her peers, she'd learned a behavior that was inappropriate. That day we realized that our own kids, even at such young ages, were facing peer pressure and influence. We began taking steps to prepare ourselves for the effects of the negative peer pressure our kids would be facing during their childhood and teenage years. In today's world, taking those steps is necessary.

As I've mentioned before, three of my kids have passed through adolescence and are now young adults, while one is still in high school. Even with all our preparation, discussions, and prayers, every one of our kids has had negative peer pressure battles. At times, God's will and way have won out. At other times, the kids have given in, made mistakes, paid consequences, asked for forgiveness, and struggled with the fallout of their choices.

The remainder of this chapter offers an overview of some effective strategies that have been utilized by parents as they've guided their kids through the reality of negative peer pressure and into a healthy adulthood—but the principles are easily transferable to youth ministry, especially as springboards to discussions and even topical Bible studies on peer pressure. Above all, we must exercise a *preventive* influence early on so that our kids are better equipped to handle pressures when they come. And we must be prepared to exercise a *redemptive* influence so that we may help our kids overcome the results of their bad choices.

Strategy #1: Realize That Negative Peer Pressure Is a Spiritual Battle All of Us Fight Constantly

Peer pressure is always there. It's a fact of life in a sinful and fallen world. We may *know* what is right and try as hard as we can to *do* what is right, but we still find ourselves giving in. Even the apostle Paul admitted his personal struggle with these same sinful inclinations: "My own behaviour baffles me. For I find myself not doing what I really want to do but doing what I really loathe...I often find I have the will to do good, but not the power...It is an agonising situation, and who on earth can set me free from the clutches of my sinful nature?" (Romans 7:15, 18, 24, *Phillips*). No doubt Paul would include in this struggle the moral dilemma between deciding to do what everyone else is doing and deciding to do what God says is right and true.

In Matthew 7:13-14, Jesus describes the spiritual struggle of choosing who or what we'll follow in life. He calls us to make the right choice as we stand at a fork in the road. On one side sits a wide gate that opens onto a broad road. Those who look through the gate will see that the path beyond is wide and well worn from the number of people who have gone down it before them. In fact, many can still be seen walking that way. But this is the path that leads to death.

On the other side is a narrow gate that opens onto a small trail. Maybe we see nobody going down that path, but Jesus commands his listeners to take this second path. Even though very few travel it, he says it's the path that leads to life.

While Jesus' words were intended to communicate truths about eternal life, eternal death, and what it means to follow him, they also say something about the battle with negative peer pressure. In a sense, our kids find themselves standing at a similar fork in the road. Some of them stand there several times a day, in fact, as they face the dilemma of choosing to walk the way of what is right or to travel in the same direction everyone else is going. It's the dilemma between standing alone as a follower of Christ and going with the flow.

While we need to recognize that our kids will make many mistakes and poor choices, we must at the same time point them in the direction of Paul's answer to our tendency to give in to our sinful nature. Paul ends the description of his personal struggle with sin on a victorious note. "I thank God there is a way out through Jesus Christ our Lord" (Romans 7:25, *Phillips*).

Strategy #2: Pray, Pray, Pray

While it's a fact that kids will face negative peer pressure, we cannot forget our source of hope and strength. God invites us to seek his help in the midst of our helplessness by praying regularly for ourselves and for our kids.

Ask God to give you wisdom and courage as you lead your kids. Pray he'll give you the right words to guide your kids into making good decisions. Pray also for patience—the adolescent years can seem to drag on for a long time.

Pray for your kids. Ask God to protect them as they live in the world of their peers. Ask God to guide them into making good decisions. Pray they'll make good friends who'll be a healthy influence. Ask that your kids will become a positive influence on their peers. Similar to praying The Lord's Prayer, ask God to send his kingdom (his will, his way, his order, his reign) into the lives of your teenagers. It might sound a bit strange, but when my kids are resistant to living under God's kingdom reign, I've prayed they'll be miserable until they choose to walk in his will and his way again.

And finally, pray *with* your kids as they face difficult situations. These prayers shouldn't be stored up for times of crisis. Granted, we may need to crawl to God when things spin out of control (I've done some crawling myself). But our prayers with our kids should start when they're young. They should grow up knowing we depend on God and place our lives in his hands. By openly praying with your kids, you'll communicate to them that God does care about their everyday affairs and that they should actively seek his will on all matters. And as they grow older, they'll have the freedom to come and pray with you whenever they feel that need.

Strategy #3: Examine Yourself

The most effective teaching method is example. Our kids are incredibly observant and smart. We're only fooling ourselves if we think we can say one thing and live another. Kids learn from watching how we handle negative peer pressure in our own lives. There have been a few occasions when my son Josh, who can be brutally honest, has noticed that my words do not line up with my actions. While it's incredibly painful, he sometimes reminds me I'm being hypocritical. While my first inclination is to tell him to mind his own business, I know if that's the only response I can muster, then he's probably right. Without intending to, Josh has reminded me over and over again that our kids are watching us, and they're watching closely. He's also reminded me of my need to swallow my pride, confess, repent, and allow God's Spirit to help me change my ways.

Let me ask you some rather pointed questions I've had to ask myself:

- Do you give in to peer pressure?

- Is your self-image healthy or is it dependent on what others think of you?

- Do you give in to the pressure to possess a certain type of body and work hard toward that end?

- Do you often complain about your frustrations with your imperfect body?

- How do you handle the pressure to stay in style?

- Do you emphasize outward appearance over inward condition?

- Do you worry about what people will think of your hair or clothes?

- Does your concern go beyond just looking nice and neat to wanting to make a good impression?

- When you're out socializing, do you have to have a drink in your hand to feel comfortable?

- Are you remaining faithful and obedient to God as you express your sexuality?

These are difficult questions we must answer for ourselves. You're like all other adults in that you face peer pressure. But how are you responding to it? And what type of model are you presenting to the teenagers who are watching *you*? The good news is that even in the midst of powerful and pervasive peer pressure, they're still watching you. George Barna's research has found that when teenagers are asked how much influence comes from various sources, "friends" are near the top of the list at number two. Guess who's number one? "Parents."[390]

Strategy #4: Model the Life of a Christ-Follower

Our kids need to learn that doing what is right is not always the easy choice. In fact, when Jesus called his disciples to "come and follow me," he was inviting them into a life that would be difficult. In the same breath, he told them, "If anyone would come after me, he must deny himself and take up his cross and follow me" (Matthew 16:24). On the surface, Jesus seems to be calling us to a very unattractive and undesirable life. But in reality, it's a call to the most attractive and desirable life a person could ever live.

We need to teach our kids—by our words and example—that following the crowd when the crowd is going in the wrong direction exacts a price. That price, according to Scripture, is the suffering of eternal death.

The flip side is that following in the footsteps of Christ also exacts a price. That price, according to Scripture, may be some suffering and alienation from others in this life. But that temporal suffering is minor when compared with the thrill of entering into the joy of the Lord as a reward for our faithfulness.

Strategy #5: Actively Help Your Kids Build a God-Centered Self-Image

From the time our kids are born, we need to teach them that their personal value and worth is rooted in who they are in God's eyes. God made them the way they are and he loves them for who they are—not what they do, how they're shaped, or what they wear.

But it's not enough to tell them God cares deeply for them in spite of what their friends think. Parents (and youth workers) need to become the hands and feet of Jesus. If we knock our kids down through our ignorance, absence, or cutting remarks, we create in them a deep desire and passion for peer group acceptance and approval, along with an increased vulnerability to negative peer pressure and influence.

Do you communicate to your son or daughter that their value and worth in your eyes do not hinge on their looks, clothes, or performance? Are your teenagers certain of your love and commitment?

When your kids reach the teenage years, your efforts to reaffirm their value in God's eyes may be met with disbelief or resistance. But don't stop telling them. They need to hear it now more than ever (even if they act like your words mean very little to them). In hindsight, they'll thank you for the God-centered self-image you worked so hard to instill in them.

Strategy #6: Help Them to Learn by Asking Them Good Questions

How will you handle it when your teenager gives in to negative peer pressure and makes a bad choice? There's nothing wrong with discipline and communicating your reasons for it. But we shortchange our kids when we handle their mistakes in a way that doesn't allow them to learn and think about the consequences of their actions.

Good questions serve to open the floodgates of communication. They let your kids know you want to listen to what they have to say. Good questions force kids to think through their actions, process the decisions they've made, and consider the resulting consequences. Good questions give kids the opportunity to be treated like an adult, rather than a child. And by being forced to think through their actions, teenagers develop critical thinking skills and form convictions in their hearts.

In my own family experience, I've learned how important it is to ask the simple what, why, and how questions instead of "What happened? Why did it happen? Why was it important for you to get drunk? What should your punishment be for what you did?" and so on.

My father used to ask me good questions and then sit in silence until I answered him. In hindsight, I realize now he did a good job of forcing me to think and verbalize my thoughts. Three things happened as a result of his approach. *First, I learned to think through what I did and why.* It usually became very clear to me how stupid and impulsive I'd been. *Second, we always managed to talk about the real heart issues underlying my behavior.* The door was opened for us to discuss problems rather than symptoms. *And third, the process was more painful than any punishment he could have dished out.* Unfortunately, he didn't think the way I did. Punishment always followed our discussions.

Strategy #7: Give Your Kids the Opportunity to Make Their Own Choices within Clearly Defined Boundaries

Parents who maintain total control over their growing teenagers risk one day having angry and rebellious adolescents on their hands. Many rebellious teenagers have grown up in overly strict Christian homes. On the other hand, parents who release all control all at once may get a positive reaction from their kids. After all, our kids want their freedom. But they usually want that freedom in doses they can't yet handle. This approach is like putting our kids into a boat and pushing them out into the ocean without a rudder, sail, motor, paddle, or compass. They're left to the mercy of the environment and their own inexperience in handling such situations.

We need to protect our teenagers from themselves and from others. They need to learn how to live a disciplined life. They need to learn how to set guidelines and make responsible choices for themselves. It's advisable to allow them to develop these skills by using the "going out to play" model. When our kids are little, we don't allow them to wander around outside by themselves. Mom or Dad takes them by the hand and keeps a watchful eye on them while they play. When we're sure they know not to wander out into the street, we might let them play in the back yard by themselves. Of course, we spend much of our time checking out the window or opening the door to yell, "What are you doing? Are you okay?" As our kids continue to grow up, we begin to trust their judgment more and more. Soon they're able to cross the street without our assistance. They can walk to a neighbor's house or play in a friend's yard. Before long they take long bike rides into other neighborhoods. Even though we might worry about their safety, we trust their judgment because we've watched them make good choices on their own.

We need to implement this "going out to play" model as we set and expand the boundaries of personal choice and responsibility. As our kids begin to earn our trust, we widen the boundaries further. My father used to constantly remind me that in our house, "privileges come with responsibility." As much as those four words used to get on my teenaged nerves, his approach was totally right.

Strategy #8: Be in Their World

Studies consistently show that kids who are being raised by parents who make a deliberate effort to be actively involved in their kids' lives are kids who have an easier time handling negative peer pressure and influence.

A study conducted to assess drug and alcohol use in relation to peer influence found that seventh and eighth graders who abuse drugs and alcohol spend more time with their friends than with their families. In addition, they communicate very little with their parents. On the other hand, nonusing adolescents tend to spend more time with their families and less time with their peers.[391]

I'm not suggesting you become a teenager yourself. Don't try to act and dress the part of a teenager. We've all felt embarrassed for older people who try to act and dress younger than they really are. Rather, you should work to relate with your teenager *without* forsaking your adult responsibilities in caring for him. Discover your teenager's unique interests and abilities. Make time to get involved in those activities with your child. Some fathers purchase an old car to work on with their sons. Other parents make a point of setting aside time each week to ride a bike trail, play basketball, or attend sporting and cultural events with their kids. Several years ago, I purchased a used boat for the purpose of stealing away with my kids (and sometimes their friends) for some uninterrupted time together on a local lake. Smaller than any room in our house, it affords us concentrated blocks of time together. While you might not enjoy your teenager's activities and interests as much as they do, just being with them opens the door for communication and a stronger parent-child relationship built on respect and trust.

Here's one final suggestion on how to become a peer to your child: As your kids grow older, begin to treat them in an age-appropriate manner. Don't talk down to them or treat them like little kids. This is one of the biggest communication door slammers teenagers despise. Make a conscious effort to talk to them in the same way you'd talk to any other adult. This will communicate to your child that you respect their emerging adulthood, thereby strengthening their trust and respect for you.

Strategy #9: Get Them Involved in a Positive Peer Group

This entire chapter has been devoted to an explanation of the power of negative peer pressure. The flip side is that positive peer pressure and influence can be just as powerful in encouraging our kids to make good, healthy, moral, and godly choices.

The best positive peer groups I've ever seen are healthy church or parachurch youth groups with strong adult leaders who are respected and loved by the students. Kids in those groups learn to support each other as they work to live out their faith in school. Here are three steps you and the other parents in your church and community can take in order to ensure that the youth group will become a positive place.

First, encourage your kids' involvement in church activities and youth group, beginning when they're young. Be sure they're actively building relationships with church peers. This will require you to be actively involved yourself.

Second, be sure your church is committed to building a strong youth ministry. Your church budget should reflect that commitment, and your church building should be worn out in an effort to live out that commitment. Your church should be committed to hiring a gifted and mature leader who is committed to building a group of adult leaders, rather than starring in a one-person show or personality cult. And you should invest your time and money in that ministry. If good youth ministry is important to you, you'll support that ministry with your financial, time, and prayer commitments.

Finally, pray and work with other parents and the youth ministry team to make the youth group a place where all teenagers, not just the popular and athletic ones, will be accepted and loved for who they are. Our kids need a place to go where they can interact with their peers without the pressure to be or do something they aren't or shouldn't be. It must also be a place that influences them to be the person God wants them to be.

Strategy #10: Open Up Your Home to Your Kids' Friends

No matter what they look like or how they act, all teenagers are yearning for adult love and acceptance. It's much easier for kids to give in to negative peer pressure and go the wrong way when they lack the input, love, and acceptance of a significant adult in their lives. By opening up your home and making it a warm and inviting place for kids, you'll ensure greater input into the life of your own teenager, while opening the door to other kids who desperately need your input as well.

How can you make your home warm and inviting? Convert your basement into a game room where kids can hang out. Turn a corner of the basement into a weight room where your son and his friends can work out or socialize. Build a lighted basketball court in your driveway or back yard. Have your teenager's friends over for dinner from time to time. If your child has a friend who comes from a bad family situation, take her along on the next family trip or outing. Be creative. Just be sure to make friends with your kids' friends by opening up your home to them.

Strategy #11: Work with Other Parents to Establish "Parental Agreements"

Make an effort to get to know other parents in your neighborhood, church, school, and community. Go out of your way to establish relationships with the parents of your kids' friends. Get to know them so you'll have the freedom to ask them about their standards and expectations for their kids. You might even want to start a parent network in your community, just for the purpose of setting agreed-upon standards for behavior, curfews, transportation, supervision of parties, and so on.

Also, get over your hesitancy or awkwardness about picking up the phone and asking questions. If you're going to give your teenager permission to attend a party or other event at someone's home, you have a right and a responsibility to ask questions about the supervision, planned activities, and so on. And don't assume that just because the parents are "nice people" a call is not in order. I was saddened to learn that in our own community, kids who were attending an after-prom party supervised by a number of parents in a local home were allowed to consume alcohol provided by the parents. The parents present included a pastor, a teacher, and a policeman, among others.

Strategy #12: For Better or for Worse—Friends Influence Friends

Proverbs 13:20 says, "He who walks with the wise grows wise, but a companion of fools suffers harm." Teach your kids about the power of influences. Look for and discuss examples of this principle in the media and everyday life. Be vulnerable: Openly share stories of how you saw this truth acted out as you were growing up. Encourage them to spend time with Christian friends. Discourage their involvement with those who will drag them away from being true to God's will and God's way.

Strategy #13: Don't Be Afraid to Draw the Line and Say *No*

I've met many parents who are just plain scared of their kids. The fact that they're afraid to exercise their God-given authority over their own children allows their kids to intimidate them even further. I also know parents who stand up and say *no* when they have to. Sure, their kids gripe and moan at the time. They may even get angry. Mine have done the same things to me. But even when these kids disagree with parental decisions, they respect their parents. Why? Because these parents are actively involved in their kids' lives. They love their kids, and their kids know it. For these teenagers, rebellion isn't an option they consider for long, if they consider it at all. Love your kids and express that love by saying *no* when they can't or won't say it for themselves.

Strategy #14: Give Them an Out

After Josh graduated from high school, we attended parties for several of his friends. One night we'd just arrived home from one of the parties, when Josh gave us a call. He was still over at his friend's house, and his classmates were making plans for the night. He wanted to know if he could stay over. Based on some past battles with peer pressure, I think Josh knew the night would be a difficult one and compromise might come easy. Even though he was 18 years old, I was impressed with the fact that he called home to ask permission to stay. The hesitancy in his voice betrayed his fear. After learning it was going to be a co-ed sleepover party, I told Josh how uncomfortable we were with that, and I asked him what he thought he should do. He told me he was going to come home. The next week I learned that, among other things, the parents at that party had served alcohol to the kids. In hindsight, Josh was calling me not so much for permission to stay, but for permission to come home.

Let your kids know that when they find themselves in a difficult situation and it looks like saying *no* might be hard to do, they can pick up the phone and call you anytime, anyplace. And you'll come and get them—no matter what.

Getting Personal

Today's teenagers respond to relationships. How's your relationship with your teenagers? Do they feel the freedom to talk to you? Do you spend time with them? Do they know you love them? Do you listen to them? If they don't get these things at home, they'll look for them elsewhere. That "elsewhere" is more often than not their peer group. Think carefully through the time, love, and energy you spend with your kids. What can you do to interact more positively with the teenagers in your home or world?

08

Hooking Up: Understanding Our Sexualized Youth Culture

Fundamentally, it's your body and it's up to you what you do with it.

— FROM *IT'S YOUR (SEX) LIFE: YOUR GUIDE TO SAFE & RESPONSIBLE SEX* [392]

If the pain of all sexual sins were heaped in one place, its enormity would be incomprehensible.

—DEAN BORGMAN[393]

Just when I thought I'd heard it all, a friend called me to pass on an overheard conversation from the corridor of a large medical practice. A physician, his young teenage patient, and the patient's mother were standing outside the opened door of an examination room, where my friend sat waiting to see the doctor. It seems the young patient's mother was so flabbergasted by the impracticality of the physician's diagnosis and plan of treatment that she was protesting all the way into the hallway, without any regard for who heard what.

"So my daughter is not allowed to insert anything into her vagina for one month because of the infection?" she asked. "What is she going to do about her prom? It's in two weeks, and her boyfriend has already reserved a hotel room for the night." Upon hearing the mother's protests, my friend was just as flabbergasted, only his shock came from the mother's casual acceptance of her daughter's prom night plans.

I can't say I've ever met parents who aren't concerned about the sexual well-being and behavior of their children. While parents may disagree among themselves about what constitutes appropriate and inappropriate teenage sexual activity, they all acknowledge there are dangers involved. And our kids are facing these dangers at younger ages all the time. But while that concern used to be channeled into discouraging premarital sexual activity, it's now increasingly being channeled into preventing only the *consequences* of premarital sex—pregnancy and disease. In fact, more parents are accepting all types of sexual activity as a normal and expected part of growing up in today's world. Judging from changing attitudes and the resulting trends, we might be behind the times if we talk about the *teenage* sexuality crisis. A more fitting label might be the *childhood* sexuality crisis.

Today's teenagers are facing a complex set of sexual messages and choices long before their bodies are even equipped to reproduce themselves. It's been going on for some time. It was on a warm spring day more than 15 years ago that our daughter Caitlin arrived home from second grade and announced that her friend was "having S-E-X." (Yes, Caitlin tried to spare her parents some of the shock by spelling the three-letter word.) I was so taken back by her matter-of-fact announcement that I didn't know whether to laugh or cry. My wife's jaw dropped to the floor. Since Lisa was shocked into silence, I was elected by default to do all the talking. In my wildest imagination, I never thought my daughter would initiate the "big talk," let alone do so when she was only in second grade.

"What do you mean she's having S-E-X?" I asked.

"She told us on the playground, Dad. When she goes home from school, she goes next door to the neighbor's house. His parents are still at work. He's in third grade. They go up to his room, take off their clothes, get under the covers, and kiss and stuff."

Realizing my daughter had a pretty advanced understanding for an eight-year-old, I seized the teachable moment and communicated that sex was a wonderful gift from God to be enjoyed by a man and woman after they get married. Poor Caitlin's face turned red as she looked at me with disbelief and disgust.

Horrified by my comments, she angrily asked, "You mean you and Mommy do that? That's disgusting!" I'm not sure what, if anything, I said after that.

Dealing with the sensitive issue of sexuality is not an easy thing for parents these days. But in the midst of all the sex education our kids are getting from their friends, the media, and their schools, parents cannot remain oblivious and silent. Loosened and lowered sexual standards leave adolescents experiencing greater pressure to adopt and live out these standards more than ever before. Today's teenagers need straightforward answers and direction. There is a message about sex and sexuality that needs to be communicated to kids. And I believe our kids are ready and willing to listen.

Over two decades ago, American teenagers were more concerned about sex than their peers around the world were. A magazine poll of teenagers in 59 countries found that 99 percent of the American teenagers surveyed cited sex as the most important issue facing today's youth.[394] As sexual values have changed and all types of sexual activity have become more commonplace and normative among teenagers, it's no longer at the top of the list. The only sexual issues making today's teenagers' lists of social concerns are the possible negative results of teenage sexual activity, with sexual activity not making the list at all. The list of concerns includes abortion (#5), AIDS (#8), sexual assault (#11), and unplanned pregnancy (#20).[395]

Another survey on high school students and pressure lists "pressure to engage in sexual activity before you are ready" as the least felt pressure on the list of eight. Both the pressure's ranking and the way it's stated ("before you are *ready*") indicate that attitudes toward premarital sexual activity have changed.[396]

This chapter offers an overview of the extent and scope of the sexuality crisis, the causes of our kids' current sexual attitudes and behaviors, and some practical strategies for reversing the tide of premarital sexual activity among our teenagers.

The Facts about Teenagers and Sex

Imagine 10 chairs lined up side by side in your living room. Your teenage child sits in one chair, while the rest are filled with nine of her high school-aged peers. Assuming they'll answer honestly, you ask everyone who's had sexual intercourse to stand up. How many do you think will stand?

According to the latest research from the U.S. Centers for Disease Control, half of the 10 high school students will stand. Among high school students in the United States, 47 percent have had sexual intercourse in their lifetime.[397] The good news is this figure has declined steadily since 1991, when 54 percent of students in that age group reported having engaged in sexual intercourse.[398] The bad news is that far too many of our teenagers are engaging in sexual intercourse. Among high schoolers in the United States—

- 34 percent of ninth graders,

- 43 percent of tenth graders,

- 51 percent of eleventh graders, and

- 63 percent of twelfth graders have had sexual intercourse.[399]

- 70 percent of young women and 62 percent of young men today have had sexual intercourse by age 18,[400] compared with 35 percent of young women and 55 percent of young men in the early 1970s.[401]

- When they get to college, 80 percent of students ages 18 to 24 (83 percent of males and 78 percent of females) will have had sexual intercourse.[402]

Adding to these discouraging numbers is the age at which kids become sexually active. Nationwide, 6.2 percent of high school students have had sexual intercourse for the first time before they reach the age of 13.[403] Currently, 20 percent of kids aged 12, 13, and 14 have had sex.[404] One doctor told me he'd treated girls as young as eight and nine years old for severe vaginal injuries resulting from self-initiated sexual experimentation. Parents should be aware that most early attempts at having intercourse are preceded by other sexual activity, including fondling, petting, and oral sex.

Have you ever wondered *where* all this teenage sexual activity is taking place? One survey of sexually active teenagers ages 16 to 18 found that 22 percent had their first sexual encounter in their own homes, and 34 percent had the encounter in their partner's homes.[405] Another study of high school students reported that 43 percent of males and 28 percent of females last had sexual intercourse in their own homes. In addition 30 percent of males and 59 percent of females last had sexual intercourse in their partner's homes. Finally, 17 percent of males and six percent of females last had sexual intercourse in a friend's home.[406]

In regard to *when*, 56 percent of high school teenagers last had sex on a weekday: 18 percent before 3 PM, 17 percent between 3 and 6 PM, and 21 percent after 6 PM.[407] Most surprising is the fact that the act of intercourse often takes place while at least one parent is physically present in the home.[408]

Researchers concerned about the spread of sexually transmitted diseases (STDs) are focusing on the trend toward multiple sexual partners among teenagers. Just over 14 percent of all high school students report having had sexual intercourse with four or more partners during their lifetime. By the time they reach their senior year of high school, 21.4 percent of all students will have had sexual intercourse with four or more partners.[409] One can reasonably assume the numbers are even higher for those having just two or three partners. For example, among sexually active 15- to 17-year-olds, 39 percent reported two to five partners, seven percent reported six to nine partners, and four percent reported having engaged in sexual intercourse with 10 or more partners.[410]

Let's go back to those 10 chairs sitting in your living room. Assume those chairs are filled with Christian kids who've been taught that premarital sexual activity is wrong. How many do you think will stand and indicate they've had sexual intercourse? Unfortunately, there are no recent studies that have isolated Christian teenagers and their sexual behavior. Still, most experts and culture-watchers indicate there is little attitudinal and behavioral difference between Christian teenagers and their non-Christian peers. Those who are evaluating the success of abstinence education and a variety of programs where teenagers pledge to delay sexual activity until marriage are finding that the effects of these programs tend to delay sexual activity for many kids, but not necessarily until marriage. One study found that those who had made and broken their abstinence or purity pledge had delayed their first sexual experience for a year longer than nonpledging teenagers.[411]

It's important to realize that virginity is not necessarily a sign that kids are not sexually involved. There is a growing tendency, especially among those who have made a conscious decision to wait until marriage to engage in sexual intercourse, to go as far as they can sexually without crossing the line. Many view anything less than vaginal penetration as not "sex." Kids who want to remain "pure," whether they've made a purity pledge or not, may be turning to oral sex as a way to remain sexually pure. One study showed that among students who said they'd made and kept an abstinence pledge, 55 percent had participated in oral sex.[412]

A growing body of anecdotal and research evidence points to the fact that more kids are participating in oral sex experiences, while fewer equate the act with "having sex." In her article "Oral Sex Among Adolescents: Is It Sex or Is It Abstinence?" Lisa Remez notes that hints of this new trend did not appear in the popular press until 1997. An article in *The New York Times* reported that "high school students who had come of age with AIDS education considered oral sex to be a far less dangerous alternative, in both physical and emotional terms, than vaginal intercourse."[413]

How prevalent is oral sex among today's teenagers? Researchers are just now beginning to look more seriously at teenagers and oral sex, a practice that has become so prevalent in the teenage population that it's considered to be almost a recreational activity that takes place casually and without any sort of dating relationship, either with one other person or in groups. The most recent data indicates that among 15- to 19-year-olds, 55.1 percent of the boys and 54.3 percent of the girls report giving or getting oral sex.[414] By the time they reach the age of 19, three-quarters of all teenagers will have engaged in oral sex.[415] These numbers will continue to be on the upswing as the practice becomes more prevalent, particularly among younger kids. Oral sex is now more common than sexual intercourse among teenagers.

Evidence that this trend is growing among middle school students was the recent release of the Paul Ruditis novel for young teenagers, *Rainbow Party*. Shortly after the book was released, I picked up a copy and gave it a read. The book explicitly tells the story of Gin, a young teenager who is planning to throw an after-school rainbow party at her house. What's a rainbow party? One of the novel's male characters explains it this way: "Look, it's simple. Each girl puts on a different color lipstick, and the guys all drop their pants. Then the girls do down the line giving each guy head. When they're done, the guys have a rainbow of colors ringing round their d---s. Sweet."[416]

An overview of sexual activity among today's teenagers would not be complete without mentioning how changing sexual attitudes evidence themselves in a variety of riskier sexual behaviors that are moving from the fringes into the mainstream youth culture. A growing number of 15- to 19-year-old males (11.2 percent) and females (10.9 percent) have engaged in anal sex.[417] More heterosexual young people are experimenting with homosexuality, even when they don't claim to have any of the classic feelings associated with the homosexual or lesbian lifestyles. Rather, they're freely engaging in these activities just out of a curiosity fed by a boundary-less sexual ethic. Researchers say 10.6 percent of girls and 4.5 percent of boys ages 15 to 19 report having had same-sex partners.[418]

Back in the old days, most teenage sexual activity took place within the bounds of some sort of established dating relationship. Granted, there were numerous occasions where sexually aggressive guys took advantage of girls they weren't dating. But in today's world, simply having a casual relationship is reason enough to become sexually involved. Consider some of the terminology kids are using to describe these types of relationships.

First, there's the phenomenon of the *hook-up*. I've heard numerous kids talk about "hooking up" with someone of the opposite sex. Contrary to what we might like to think, "hooking up" isn't about meeting someone at a predetermined location at the mall. Instead, a *hook-up* is a sexual encounter—kissing, outercourse, intercourse—of some sort, usually with a complete stranger. Hooking up is listed by 75 percent of teenagers who were asked what teenagers usually do at their parties.[419]

Then there are *friends with benefits*. This language refers to kids who are familiar with each other and engage in sexual activity without any kind of commitment. It's a new twist on premarital sex that allows and encourages sexual activity outside the bounds of the normal boyfriend/girlfriend relationship. There's no official relationship, just an agreement to engage in sexual activity together.

It's interesting to note what types of sexual behaviors teenagers (ages 15 to 17) say are common in both dating relationships (with a boyfriend or girlfriend) and casual relationships. When asked what activities are part of a relationship *almost always* or *most of the time*, kissing was mentioned by 82 percent as part of a dating relationship, and by 70 percent as part of a casual relationship. Touching was mentioned by 65 percent as part of a dating relationship, and by 58 percent as part of a casual relationship. Oral sex was mentioned by 26 percent as part of a dating relationship, and by 23 percent as part of a casual relationship. Finally, sexual intercourse was mentioned by 27 percent as part of a dating relationship, and by 24 percent as part of a casual relationship.[420]

For far too many kids in today's youth culture, premarital sex of all sorts has become a normal and accepted part of growing up. But it's not without its downside. Our teenagers need to learn that premarital sex is a big deal and there are consequences. Consider some of these very real consequences of premarital sexual behavior sweeping across our population of teenagers in epidemic proportions.

Consequence #1: Teenage Pregnancy

By God's design, sexual intercourse often ends in the miracle of a pregnancy.

- One in three teenage girls will become pregnant before reaching the age of 20.

- Half of all out-of-wedlock births are to teenagers.[421]

- One in five teenage births are repeat births.[422]

- More than one out of eight sexually experienced teenage boys (13 percent) will cause a pregnancy.[423]

While the teenage pregnancy, birth, and abortion rates have been on the decline in recent years, the United States still has the highest rates of teenage pregnancy and births in the Western industrialized world, with teenage pregnancy costing at least $7 billion annually.[424] Currently, there are about 820,000 teenage pregnancies a year, with eight out of 10 of these pregnancies unintended, and 81 percent to unmarried teenagers.[425] The most recent national data indicates that among 15- to- 19-year-old girls, there are 84.5 pregnancies per thousand, and 41.2 births per thousand.[426] (These figures have declined since 1990, from 117 and 60, respectively.[427]) Overall, one-third of all pregnancies among 15- to 19-year-olds end in abortion.[428]

Experts indicate that the decline in pregnancies, births, and abortions are due to a combination of several factors, including abstinence pledges, teenagers waiting longer to initiate sexual activity, and contraceptive use. It's important to note that even though the rate of teenage childbearing has declined rapidly over the last 50 years (from 94.6 per thousand in 1956 to 41.2 per thousand in 2004), the rate of nonmarital teenage births has increased during that time from 13 percent in 1950 to 79 percent in 2000.[429] There are two reasons for this change. First, the average age of first marriage has risen from age 19 to age 25. And, fewer pregnant teenagers marry before their child is born.

What happens after a teenage girl gets pregnant and gives birth? Only one-third of teenage mothers go on to graduate from high school. By age 30, only 1.5 percent get a college degree. The children of teenage mothers are more likely to do poorly in school and to suffer from abuse and neglect. Boys born to teenage mothers are 13 percent more likely to end up in prison, while girls born to teenage mothers are 22 percent more likely to become teenage mothers themselves.[430] Among teenage mothers, only 30 percent who later marry are still in their first marriage by the time they reach the age of 40.[431]

Consequence #2: Sexually Transmitted Diseases

A host of STDs are sweeping through the American population in epidemic proportions. In fact, the United States has the highest rate of STDs in the industrialized world.

- Almost half of all new STD cases occur among young people ages 15 to 24.

- By age 25, one out of every two sexually active young people will contract an STD.

- Teenagers (ages 15 to 19) who've had sex have the highest rates of STDs of any age group in the United States.[432]

"Some researchers believe that as many as 80 percent of teenagers with STDs never seek medical attention because they do not notice or recognize symptoms."[433] When all is said and done, 8,000 teenagers a day are infected with a new STD.[434] It's been estimated that the total cost of treating the new cases that occur among teenagers each year is $6.5 billion.[435]

In the early 1960s, medical doctors were dealing with only two STDs that spread through the teenage population—gonorrhea and syphilis. Today, it's estimated that the actual number of STDs physicians face may be as high as 80 to 100.[436] The rise in the number of unmarried teenagers engaging in vaginal intercourse has fueled this epidemic. In addition, many teenagers believe that because oral sex cannot cause a pregnancy, it's also a safe way to have sex without the risk of contracting an STD. Not so. The truth is many STDs, both viral and bacterial, can be transmitted through oral sex. For example, oral herpes has shifted from causing 25 percent of the cases of genital herpes infections to causing 75 percent of them.[437]

Teenagers are also led to believe that so-called "safe sex" will leave them disease-free. Again, not so. Dr. Meg Meeker says, "There is not enough evidence to determine that [condoms] are effective in reducing the risk of most sexually transmitted diseases."[438] For a list of facts and figures on teenagers and specific STDs, access the supplemental resources for this chapter at www.cpyu.org.

Consequence #3: Guilt and Heartache

Kids who choose to satisfy their sexual urges before marriage are often heard to say things like, "I have given myself away," "I feel empty and dirty inside and out," "I was wrong," "I wish I had never done it," and "I feel guilty." One young student who was serious about his faith came to me a few years ago to talk about the sexual temptations he was feeling. I gave him all the reasons I could for waiting until marriage to experience the wonderful God-given gift of his sexuality in all its pleasure, purpose, and glory. He tried to find all the reasons he could to justify having sex with his girlfriend. When he finally made up his mind, he chose premarital sex. After two or three months of acting as though he were enjoying it, he came to me to admit his real feelings.

"I am miserable. You were right. I feel like my search for physical intimacy has cut me off from the intimacy I had with God."

He sounded like King David after his sin with Bathsheba (see 2 Samuel 11-12). In Psalm 51, David cries out and begs God to restore the joy of salvation he once knew, but was now replaced by the guilt and heartache that resulted from his sexual sin. That same emptiness builds in kids today, whether they know it or not. Many would argue that the guilt kids feel is a false guilt resulting from preachy adults forcing antiquated, repressive, and Victorian ideas about sex on them. I don't believe it. The real source of their guilt and heartache is the chasm of spiritual alienation that grows between them and their Creator every time they abuse their sexuality by expressing natural sexual desires in unnatural and disobedient ways.

In an effort to fill the void that exists because of bad choices, some sexually active teenagers choose to sleep around with numerous partners. With each experience comes a deeper sense of emptiness and heartache and a greater desire to move on to another sexual relationship, all in a never-ending quest to make things right.

Another example of how guilt and long-term heartache can haunt kids who choose to have sex is the spiritual and emotional aftermath that plagues girls who choose abortion to deal with their unwanted pregnancies. Thinking they're solving the problem, they're actually creating more. Girls who have chosen abortion can suffer years of ongoing preoccupation with the aborted child, flashbacks to the abortion experience, nightmares, and even hallucinations related to the abortion.

Sadly, our postmodern times have served to encourage kids to engage in all sorts of premarital sexual behavior because, after all, *you're* the one who makes the rules for yourself. In addition, they've also served to remove teenagers' guilt and shame, since there are no such things as right and wrong—except for the right and wrong we define for ourselves. Still, as parents and youth workers, we can and must believe that even though teenagers may have strayed from their created purpose as sexual beings, somewhere down deep inside there is a seed of knowledge that something is deeply wrong with straying from God's plan for our sexuality.

When God created Adam and Eve, one of the most beautiful gifts he gave them was the gift of sexuality. From that time on, men and women have had the opportunity to experience the God-given joy of sexual intimacy and pleasure within the bonds of marriage. Sadly, many teenagers are abusing that valuable gift in ways that are harmful to themselves and others. How and why is this happening?

Why Are Today's Teenagers More Sexually Active?

Brady and Katie were high school sophomores when they met at Andrew's party. Andrew's parents were out of town for the weekend, and he decided to invite some friends over for a few hours of fun. Although Brady and Katie had never met each other before, it wasn't long before they were dancing, talking, and drinking a few beers. Before the night was over, they "hooked up" by finding an empty bedroom, closing the door, and having sexual intercourse. These two teenagers, who hadn't even known each other four hours before, shared themselves with each other on the most intimate level humanly possible. And if their situation played out like thousands of others would that same night, they might never see each other again.

Brady and Katie, along with the rest of our society's sexually active teenagers, made the decision to give themselves to each other for a variety of reasons. What follows are descriptions of several of these reasons that, when combined and considered together, do a good job of convincing kids to "hook up" more easily and with greater frequency and variety than ever before.

Reason #1: Our Hypersexual Culture Says, "The Choice Is Yours!"

Sex has become a god—perhaps *the* god for many people—and it has changed the beliefs of both young and old people alike. George Barna has discovered that among adults—

- 60 percent believe it's morally acceptable to live with someone of the opposite sex outside of marriage.

- 59 percent believe it's morally acceptable to enjoy sexual thoughts or fantasies about someone.

- 42 percent believe it's morally acceptable to have a sexual relationship with someone of the opposite sex to whom you're not married.

- 38 percent believe it's morally acceptable to look at pictures of nudity or explicit sexual behavior.

- 30 percent believe it's morally acceptable to have a sexual relationship with someone of the same sex.

What about our kids? What do they believe? Barna's research found that among 18- to 19-year-olds, they believe the following to be morally acceptable:

- Living with someone of the opposite sex without being married—75 percent

- Enjoying sexual thoughts or fantasies about someone—79 percent

- Having a sexual relationship with someone of the opposite sex to whom you're not married—54 percent

- Looking at pictures of nudity or sexually explicit behavior—50 percent

- Having a sexual relationship with someone of the same sex—40 percent

Chances are these numbers will continue to increase as the attitudes that have already taken root in the soil of our culture grow and bear fruit. Society is saying to its members of all ages, "Go ahead and do *whatever* you want, with *whomever* you want, *wherever* you want, *however* you want, *whenever* you want."

This "the choice is yours" message is being shouted at our kids by a variety of different voices that are loud, consistent, and convincing. Researchers Barbara Dafoe Whitehead and Marline Pearson recognize that there is a "cultural challenge." They write,

"Teenagers today grow up in a world that bears little resemblance to the world their parents grew up in. Almost from the cradle, today's young people are bombarded with sexual come-ons and appeals. By the time they reach their teens, they have absorbed messages about sex from the streets, the Internet and the entertainment media. They are inundated with stories of steamy relationships in soap operas, reality shows, tabloid celebrity news, chatrooms and teen magazines full of 'hottie' fashion tips. They're exposed to pornography via the Internet and soon may be able to view it (or simply listen to moan tones) on their cell phones. But it's not only exposure to explicit pornographic images that is becoming a mainstream part of teen culture today. Even though some media outlets portray the issues of sex, love, relationships, and marriage responsibly, it's also the case that a pornographic aesthetic pervades much of the music, fashion, video games and cable television shows that teens now enjoy. Because of the early exposure to a hypersexualized culture, teens are likely to get their first lessons about sex from the streets, the Internet and their peers long before they get information about sex and related topics from their teachers or even their parents."[439]

In recent years, there's been a battle raging over *when, what,* and *how* to teach sex education to students in schools. At its most basic level, the battle has been over teaching so-called safe-sex messages or teaching abstinence. Some schools are teaching abstinence as an option but then muddying the waters by also teaching contraception. Sex is rarely linked to marital commitment or taught from a biblical perspective. Rather, teenagers are encouraged to wait to have sex until they are "older, more mature, feel like they're ready, and responsible." *Intimacy, personal choice,* and/ or *emotion,* rather than *commitment,* become the bottom line for making sexual choices.

The *Talk About Sex* downloadable guide book for teenagers tells kids they have "sexual rights" that are a part of their basic human rights. One of those rights is, "You have the right to decide how to express your sexuality." The right's clarifying information reads,

> Sexuality is a part of who you are as an individual. People express their sexuality in many ways, like through the clothes they wear, the music they listen to, the way they

dance, what they say and how they say it, and what they do with other people. At every point in your life, you can choose if and how to express your sexuality.

Readers are also told, "You have the right to make decisions about sexuality." How does this work? The teenager establishes a personal set of standards that works for him. In true postmodern fashion, ultimate authority on all sexual matters rests with the individual. [440]

Comprehensive sex education is one of the most popular approaches in our schools today. It's based on several foundational presuppositions about teenagers and sexuality. First, the assumption is that teenagers will have sex. While some may make a personal choice not to have sex, most will. Second, since teenagers are going to have sex, schools and educators need to teach them about it. Third, when teachers discuss sexuality, they should take a neutral stand on morality. And finally, since kids are going to be sexually active, comprehensive sex education should teach kids about contraception so they won't suffer the consequences of disease or pregnancy.

When our teenagers sit through comprehensive sex education courses, they learn the facts about reproduction, sexual development, obtaining and using birth control, sexual abuse, masturbation, homosexual behavior, and abortion. Some of these courses include a component that presents abstinence as an option, but kids are encouraged to make personal choices based on what they feel is right for them.

More than two of every three public school districts in the United States make it policy to teach sex ed. The other 33 percent leave the decisions to individual schools and teachers. Of the school districts with sex ed policies, 86 percent require abstinence education as well. Only 35 percent require abstinence be taught as the only option for unmarried people, and either prohibit discussions about contraception altogether, or limit contraception discussions to its ineffectiveness.[441] Cultural attitudes are reflected in the fact that, according to the Kaiser Family Foundation, 95 percent of parents of junior high school students and 93 percent of parents of high school students "believe that birth control and other methods of preventing pregnancy are appropriate topics for sexuality education programs in schools."[442]

The collective voice of our culture is educating and calling our kids to participate in sexual behavior of all types. Maybe I shouldn't have been surprised when, while discussing sex with my then third-grade daughter, she turned to me and said, "Dad, I know a lot more about sex than you think I know."

Reason #2: Kids Are Craving Intimacy and Love

I've never conducted any research studies on teenagers who are promiscuous, but I've made an effort to spend a little extra time with them in order to figure out why they choose to become sexually active. While I've learned there are multiple reasons for their behavior, one thing I hear repeated over and over again, particularly from the girls, is the phrase, "I just want to be loved."

What does parental love and attention have to do with teenagers' sexual choices and activities? Research has shown that teenagers will often use sex as a means to express and satisfy emotional and interpersonal needs that have little or nothing to do with sex. Sexual intercourse becomes a coping mechanism to deal with the absence of love and affection at home.[443] One recent study of ninth graders sought to discover why young teenagers want or would want to engage in male-female sexual intercourse. Intimacy was the number one reason given, with respondents understanding intimacy as something that would make them "feel close" or "feel loved."[444] Chap Clark discovered in his conversations with teenagers that sexual activity often serves as "a temporary salve for the pain and loneliness resulting from abandonment."[445]

The weakening of the family unit over the last few decades has contributed to the sexuality crisis among teenagers. Studies show "kids with a stable family background had lower levels of premarital sexual intercourse and older age at first intercourse."[446] Teenagers from single-parent families, particularly girls, are more likely to become involved in premarital sex at a young age.[447]

This growing obsession with sexual intimacy and longing for love can be seen in the changing content of girls' diaries. Social historian Joan Jacobs Brumberg has extensively studied teenage girls' diaries written over the last 150 years. She found that girls used to write about their rich spiritual and intellectual lives. But in recent years the pages have been overtaken by the quest for boys' attention and beauty and grooming. She says adolescent girls today are "overwhelmed with insidious feelings of unworthiness and low self-esteem as they obsess about boys and body."[448] In today's world of online "diaries" that are open for the world to see, these issues and feelings sit front and center on many girls' sites. I believe it's a longing for parental love and a weakened family that's led many of our kids to feel bad about themselves, hop into bed at young ages in search of intimacy, and keep on hopping into bed as the years go by. An alarming trend directly related to this adolescent hunger for love is the growing number of adolescent girls expressing the desire to get pregnant and have kids, some as young as 12. In addition, many teenage boys are deliberately trying to father kids out of wedlock. One explanation for this trend is that these kids see a baby as someone who will give them the unconditional love they have been longing for.

Reason #3: Permissive Parents

It doesn't take a parent long to realize that in a "do anything" environment, kids will choose to do anything. The most sexually active teenagers tend to be those who come from homes where parental rules and discipline are lacking or absent. In addition, these teenagers are considered to be at the greatest risk for pregnancy.[449]

Parents who allow their daughters to date at a young age are contributing to the sexuality crisis.[450] As the age of first dating experience increases, the percentage of kids having sex decreases. In addition, girls who had an early dating experience are more likely to go through their teenage years with older sexual partners, a greater number of sexual partners, and sexual intercourse on a more regular basis.[451] A child who comes home to an empty house and is left unsupervised is more likely to participate in premarital sexual behavior as well.

All the evidence points to the fact that when parents exercise good judgment by providing clearly defined boundaries, supervision, and consistent discipline, their teenagers will be less likely to participate in irresponsible and inappropriate sexual behavior.[452]

Sadly, there is also an increasing number of parents who believe their kids are going to have sex no matter what they do or say, so in an effort to protect their kids from "harmful" or "dirty" sex, they encourage and allow them to have sex at home where it's "safe," "clean," and where the necessary birth control is provided.

Permissive parents do harm to their kids. Because teenagers are not yet independent and fully developed adults, a good portion of our parenting time must be spent providing boundaries that, in effect, protect kids from themselves.

Reason #4: Peer Influence

The vast majority of teenagers say peer influence is the reason why they give in and have sex. Eight out of 10 teenagers say they feel pressure to have sex.[453] Who wants to be left out when it seems as though everyone else *is* doing it? While not everyone is doing it, sexual activity among teenagers is so commonplace that it's become "usual" and "normal" in such a way as to leave the impression that most are.

Teenage girls say the pressure mostly comes from their sexual partners.[454] This pressure kids feel to have sex is increased by phrases used during the vulnerable "heat of the moment" when a couple is alone: "Let me show you how much I love you," or "If you loved me you would do this." Teenage boys say they feel the pressure from their friends.[455]

The pressure for both boys and girls is "elevated among youth who believed that they'd gain their friends' respect by having sex."[456] That pressure is also increased by the perceptions teenagers have regarding how many of their friends are sexually active, whether that perception is accurate or not.[457]

Reason #5: Hormones

"See that girl over there?" my youth worker friend asked. "She's only twelve." The girl looked like she was in her early twenties. As I looked around the room, I realized dozens of male adolescent eyes were filled with hormonally active wonder and awe as they stood staring at her. Could I blame them? After all, their emerging sexual identity was being put to the test.

When the beautiful, God-given gift of sexuality begins to blossom, teenagers go through an exciting and confusing time. Many 11-, 12-, and 13-year-olds are physiologically capable of having intercourse. Some 11- and 12-year-old girls can bear kids; and active sperm cells are present in some boys of the same age. Both experience strong sexual urges and desires they're tempted to satisfy. Couple that with a "the choice is yours" culture and you have emotionally immature kids making some very impulsive and unwise choices. Many kids allow themselves to be controlled by their sexual thoughts and desires, instead of responsibly managing their sexuality in a God-honoring manner.

Reason #6: Lack of Information about Sex

Some kids initiate premarital sex because they know all the facts about how to do it, but have had little or no parental guidance on what constitutes appropriate sexual behaviors. Most teenagers want their parents to share sexual knowledge, opinions, beliefs, and attitudes with them. Yet only 15 percent say their parents are a major source of this information.[458] Parents who take the time to teach their kids about sexuality and continue to talk about it guide their kids to make good choices.

But the sad fact remains that most kids go elsewhere for their sexual know-how. Or, in today's world, their pervasive engagement with media means their sexual education comes right to them without ever having to look for it. Who knows how many kids become sexually active because they were never taught right and wrong regarding sexuality? Our silence gives them permission to do it.

Reason #7: Feelings of Invulnerability

There are those teenagers who receive all the correct information and biblical instruction, yet still choose to have sex. They know guilt and heartache may follow. They know God doesn't desire for them to ruin his gift of sex by having it before marriage. They know all about the dangers of STDs and pregnancy. So why do they go ahead and take the risk? Simply put, teenagers have a strong sense of idealistic and unrealistic invulnerability that leads them to reason, "Those bad things only happen to other people. They'll never happen to me."

Reason #8: Feelings of Vulnerability

Seth, age 15, is honest about why he's sexually active. "There isn't a week that goes by that someone in my neighborhood doesn't get shot. I sometimes wonder if I'll live to see my twentieth birthday." With violence and death becoming just "a part of life" for many American teenagers, some of them have become preoccupied with two pursuits: survival and pleasure. They recklessly pursue pleasure during their teenage years so they don't die before they've experienced all the "good things" life has to offer.

Reason #9: I Can't Wait That Long

For some teenagers, it's just too difficult to wait until marriage. Even those who commit to remain chaste until after they say "I do" are finding it increasingly difficult to maintain the commitment required to endure. It's a fact that over the past few decades, the median age for marriage has risen markedly. Back in 1970, the median age for marriage was 20.8 years old for women, and 23.3 years old for men. More than three decades later, the median age had risen to 25.8 years old for women and 27.4 years old for men. "For young people who complete the four-year college degree, first marriage is likely to occur at even older ages. Therefore, those teenagers who are committed to waiting to have sex until marriage now have a much longer wait."[459]

Reason #10: Curiosity

Kids and teenagers are very curious by nature. When they hear about something new and exciting, their curiosity often leads them to experiment so they can experience that new and exciting thing for themselves. In one study, when 15- to 17-year-old teenagers who've had sex were asked to list what factors influenced their decision to have sex, the number one reason cited over and above all others was "curiosity."[460] The pervasiveness of sexual messages and discussions in our hypersexual culture has managed to turn up the intensity level of teenagers' curiosity.

Reason #11: Age Aspiration

As a result of their research, marketers know teenagers want to look and feel older than they really are. The tendency for kids to aspire to be older makes them susceptible to advertising pitches that promise to fulfill this desire. This is why advertisements always utilize models and actors who are actually a few years older than the target audience. This same phenomenon of age aspiration feeds a culture of kids who begin to engage in sexual activity because they perceive this activity as what older people do, and as a result, it will make them look and feel older themselves.

Reason #12: To Strengthen Relationships

Today's teenagers are painfully aware of the fallout from relational and family breakdown. After all, many of them are casualties of it themselves. In an effort to find some way to avoid experiencing any more brokenness, many kids believe the route of sexual intimacy will make their relationship stronger and less prone to falling apart. Some girls go so far as to believe that if they were to become pregnant, their male sexual partners would become more committed to them as a result of becoming fathers. Seventy percent of 15- to 17-year-olds who've had sex say one of their reasons for deciding to become sexually active is they "hoped it would make the relationship closer."[461]

Reason #13: Coercion

Our culture's growing bent toward violence and boundary-free sexual experience has combined with a variety of other factors to create a growing sense of sexual entitlement that encourages sexual aggressors to do whatever is necessary to satisfy their sexual wants and desires. More than 7 percent of all high school students have been physically forced to have sexual intercourse.[462] The prevalence is higher among female teenagers (10.8 percent) than among male teenagers (4.2 percent).[463] Assuming some forced sex goes unreported, it's reasonable to assume these numbers are low. The coercion can be physical or verbal, as kids work hard to convince each other this is the thing to do. This explains why younger teenagers more frequently report that their first experience of sexual intercourse was involuntary or unwanted. It comes as no surprise that teenagers who report their first sexual experience was unwanted "are more likely than others to report that their first partner had been three or more years their senior."[464]

Reason #14: It Feels Good

When God gifted humanity with sexuality, he intended for it to be pleasurable. Our "feel good at all costs" and "avoid pain" culture allows sexual pleasure to be pursued outside of marriage and without any limitations or boundaries. Our kids are just like the rest of us. They desire to engage in experiences that are pleasurable. The reality of the pleasure of sex has combined with our cultural values in a mix that encourages kids to selfishly pursue sexual pleasure.

Now combine all of these voices and reasons together, and think about them for a minute. Imagine what it must be like to hear and feel all of these things while growing and developing through adolescence. Now you're getting a picture of why it's so easy for our teenagers to choose to become sexually active.

Leading Teenagers through Our Sexualized Youth Culture

The increasing number of teenagers who choose to be sexually active is symptomatic of many factors that when merged together have chipped away at any sense of sexual right and wrong our kids might possess, leading them to believe premarital sexual activity is as normal as doing homework or getting a driver's license. Unfortunately, too many youth workers and parents feel powerless in helping their kids wait until marriage. They cave in and feel they've been successful if they can convince their kids to hold off a little bit longer. And when their teenagers do decide the time is right to have sex, we encourage them to do it "safely." The tragic end of this approach is that it not only sacrifices right for wrong, but it contributes to the trail of teenage pregnancies, sexually transmitted diseases, shattered dreams, changed lives, and spiritual emptiness. To put it bluntly, it promotes sin and its consequences.

The good news is our kids are capable of making healthy, proper, and godly sexual choices. The key ingredient missing in this battle has been informed adult (especially parental) involvement. We each have a significant and deliberate role to play to ensure the tide turns in this sex-saturated society. Following are a number of steps you can begin taking now to lead your kids into experiencing the beauty and wonder of God's incredible gift of sexuality according to his purpose and plan.

Step #1: Love Your Kids

When we don't take the time to provide kids with love, intimacy, and affection, we drive them to seek some morsel of "love" that might satisfy those desires. Sadly, many teenagers believe a few moments of "making love" between the sheets (or somewhere else) will satisfy their hunger when, in effect, they have settled for a piece of rotting garbage that makes them feel better for only a few moments. Many continue to hunt and eat the garbage, which in the long run is unhealthier than not eating at all.

Kids who come from families where parents are absent or detached are far more likely to engage in premarital sex. One study has shown that adolescents who are susceptible to initiating intercourse "had fewer positive connections with parents...than nonsusceptible respondents."[465] One young girl who struggled for years to win the love and attention of her father entered into a relationship with a boy who immediately became intensely physical. After having intercourse with him on a regular basis, she confessed she felt "cheap" and "used." The irony of the situation can be heard in her words: "But I finally feel like I am being loved." She also realizes saying *no* to her boyfriend would only lead her to experience more of the rejection she hates so much. Her sad story is being lived out by more kids than you and I can imagine.

Loving your spouse and kids does more than meet their basic needs. A stable and loving home fosters a climate of openness and honesty between parent and teen, making it possible to discuss teenage sexual challenges and choices. In addition, it provides your kids with a model for how to do the same when they have a family of their own.

Step #2: Teach and Discuss God's Sexual Standards

A few years ago I led a Bible study on the topic of temptation with a group of high schoolers who didn't know much about the Bible. To bring the lesson to life, I asked them to think about a time when they'd been tempted sexually. Then I told them God's Word has something to say about sexual temptation.

"You mean the Bible actually talks about sex?" one high schooler blurted out in amazement.

"It sure does," I said. "There's an entire book in the Old Testament that is a graphic celebration of the beauty of physical love between a man and woman."

They couldn't believe it. "Where?" they asked.

I directed them to the Song of Solomon and watched them flip excitedly through their Bibles to find it. Needless to say, I don't think anyone heard anything else I said that entire evening.

On the way out the door, one girl said, "This was great tonight. I learned God doesn't think sex is dirty."

For too long, our teenagers have been subjected to sex education that is anything but correct. The messages of our culture teach them to express their sexuality freely. On the other extreme are churches and many parents who treat sex as a taboo subject, leading kids to believe *sex* is a dirty word. Sadly, many kids (like those in the Bible study group) are left not knowing the truth about sex.

The sex education our kids so desperately need will lead them to understand that God created sex to be wonderful and fulfilling when experienced within the bounds of his plan. Research has shown that teenagers want to learn about sexuality from their parents, yet how many of us take the time to talk to our kids about sex on a deep and meaningful, interactive level? Here are some suggestions on how and what to teach your kids about sexuality.

First, give your kids truthful answers to their questions in an age-appropriate manner. Discuss reproduction using accurate and correct terminology. Even though you might feel uncomfortable with the types of questions young kids are asking these days, you must give them answers. If you remain silent, you risk being the last to be heard. Studies show that the more parents talk to their kids about sexuality, the less sexually active their kids are.

Second, take time to understand and discuss God's design for sexuality. Spend time reading and studying God's Word, making note of passages dealing with sexuality that you can discuss with your kids. Be sure they know that the Bible affirms sex as a beautiful gift from God for a man and woman to experience within the context of marriage. Sex is not dirty. God created sex and he gives it to married couples as a way to pleasurably enjoy themselves, show their love for one another, and have children.

Third, teach your kids that God's sexual guidelines don't result from some divine desire to take all the fun out of life. Rather, they're given to make our sexual lives as fulfilling, safe, and enjoyable as possible. God has reasons for condemning fornication, adultery, and homosexuality, and those reasons flow from his perfect love. Teach them that living a pure life is pleasing to God.

Finally, remember that the most effective teaching tool of all is modeling. Provide your kids with an example of living out God's sexual will and way. If you're married, remain faithful to your spouse and work at building a strong marriage. If you're a single parent, don't give in to sexual temptation. Avoid engaging with media that promotes sexual values and practices beyond the bounds of God's plan for sex and sexuality. Kids need to see it's possible to live a life faithful to God's sexual plan.

God's Word is full of passages that will help you in your efforts to teach your kids:

Genesis 1:27-28

Genesis 2:18-25

2 Samuel 13:1-20

Proverbs 5

1 Corinthians 6:9–7:9

1 Thessalonians 4:1-8

Use this small sampling, along with any others you can find on your own, to start talking about sexuality with your teenagers.

Step #3: Teach Your Kids about the Many Good Reasons for Waiting

Paul's words in 1 Corinthians 6:18, "Flee from sexual immorality," conjure mental images of a person running away from a burning building. These are timely words for today's teenagers. Too many are staying in the inferno as the building burns to the ground. But we must do more than tell them to *run*. We must tell them *why*. Kids should avoid premarital sexual activity not because we said so but because there are several good reasons to do so.

There are physical reasons for waiting. Teenagers who choose to have sex risk doing great harm to their physical bodies. There are millions of teenagers in America who, thinking they were invulnerable and somehow immune, wound up with one or more sexually transmitted diseases. Millions of others have become pregnant. Still others have had abortions. Kids need to know that "safe sex" is a lie. Using a condom isn't the answer to all of their fears: They have a 20 percent failure rate against diseases when used by teenagers, and they don't prevent pregnancy. And considering the fact that a single sperm is five hundred times larger than the AIDS virus, condoms aren't anywhere near reliable at preventing AIDS.

There are emotional reasons for waiting. God created intercourse to serve as a total expression of the lifelong commitment of marital love between a man and a woman. Take away the lifelong part, the commitment, or the love, and sex becomes empty, cheap, and purely mechanical.

There are relational reasons for waiting. For six months Mandy told me about her new boyfriend.

"Austin's wonderful. We do so many fun things together. I really do love him. But he keeps pressuring me to have sex. I told him I want to wait until I'm married."

I told Mandy she should walk away from that relationship immediately. Rather than take my advice, she continued on and eventually had sex with Austin. As is the case in most adolescent relationships where kids have sex, intercourse quickly became "the main course" whenever they spent time together. No longer were they doing those fun things Mandy had enjoyed so much.

"We don't communicate anymore," said Mandy. "All he ever wants to do is get physical." When premarital sexual activity starts—no matter what that activity is—the foundation of the relationship quickly changes, even though the teenagers continue to spend time together.

Premarital sex also affects all of a person's future relationships, including marriage. Every sexual partner who follows will be compared with previous partners. This comparison game can continue to haunt and follow a person right into the marriage bed.

There are future reasons for waiting. Kids who have sex are putting their hopes, dreams, and plans for the future in jeopardy. No one plans an STD or unwanted pregnancy. These aren't things kids experience and magically forget. These things are life changers.

Premarital sex impacts the future in many ways. Girls who are sexually active prior to marriage face a higher risk of divorce and marital disruption than girls who are virgin brides.[466] Those who become teenage parents are more likely to drop out of school, live in poverty, and forfeit all their plans.

And most importantly, there are spiritual reasons for waiting. Premarital sex is sinful. Our kids need to learn that while God is pro-sex, he is anti-sin. Making the choice to enter into a premarital physical union with another person is also a choice to drive a wedge into the spiritual union one has with God.

Step #4: Help Them Grow Spiritually

It makes sense that kids who are truly committed to Christ will be committed to living out a biblical approach to sexuality that reflects God's will and way. Get your kids involved in a church youth group where they'll be encouraged by leaders who teach practical ways to face sexual pressure. They'll benefit from being surrounded by friends who share the same standards for sexuality, relationships, and marriage.

The most effective way for you to instill a desire for spiritual growth and church involvement in your kids is to model those things yourself. Make spiritual growth a personal priority, and you'll pass it on to your kids.

Step #5: Help Them Establish Relational Do's and Don'ts.

Teenage relationships (including friendships, dating, "going out," and so on) can be either safe or risky. Relationships remain safe when there are predetermined rules to follow and obey. But if a couple or group heads out and makes up the rules as they go along, chances are their time spent together might head in whatever direction their hormones take it.

Wise parents will openly discuss and establish relationship and dating standards with their teenagers that will lead to practices that honor God by ensuring sexual purity, and youth workers will do the same. Establishing these guidelines ahead of time will help teenagers know and understand clearly defined boundaries for what is and is not appropriate—before the hormones kick in. By having standards, kids can be prepared to make quick decisions when needed.

Here are some suggested relationship and dating do's and don'ts for you to discuss with your teenager:

- Since marriage is the ultimate result of dating, only enter into dating relationships with other committed Christians.

- Allow your parents to meet and get to know your date before going out for the first time.

- Plan your dates ahead of time. Decide when you'll leave, where you'll go, what you'll do, and when you'll be home. Share those plans with your parents before you leave.

- Pray together before and after your date.

- Don't get stuck alone someplace with nothing better to do.

- Agree to be home by a predetermined time.

- Establish an agreement to call home and ask to be picked up if you find yourself in a situation where you're being pressured or tempted to compromise sexually.

- Decide when it is and it is not appropriate to touch, kiss, and so on.

- The bedroom is off-limits for teenagers and their opposite-sex friends, no matter what the relationship is.

Although controlling our God-given sexual drive is not easy, this difficulty is no reason *not* to set standards. In fact, this difficulty is one of the best reasons for taking the time and making the effort to discuss and establish these do's and don'ts with teenagers.

Step #6: Help Your School Develop or Choose a Good Sex-Education Curriculum

In communities everywhere battles are raging regarding the type of sex education teenagers are receiving and should receive in school. The best way to have a say in what your kids are being taught is to study and evaluate the curriculum being used and make recommendations based on what you discover.

The Family Research Council suggests using these six criteria in evaluating sex-education courses:

1. Role of parents. Does the program encourage parental participation? Is the program open to parental input and review?

2. Abstinence. Does the program clearly and unequivocally encourage teenagers to abstain from sexual activity outside of marriage?

3. Contraception. Does the program send mixed messages to teenagers by including encouragement and instruction on contraceptive use?

4. Abortion. Does the program present abortion as a solution to teenage sexual activity and pregnancy?

5. Linking sex to marriage. Does the program follow God's design and encourage kids to wait until marriage? Or does the program encourage them to wait until they're "older" or "more mature?"

6. Homosexuality. Does the program correctly identify homosexuality as sinful behavior rather than an alternate lifestyle?[467]

A sex-education program that promotes abstinence can work. One example is Elayne Bennett's *Best Friends* program, instituted in Washington, DC. In schools that introduced the program, the rate of sexual activity among teenagers declined from 71 percent to 3.4 percent. In addition, pregnancy rates dropped in one year from 20 percent to 1.1 percent.[468]

Abstinence programs aren't designed to give kids the impression that sex is dirty. Rather, they're designed to encourage teenagers to enjoy sex within the bounds of marriage. Thanks to parents, schools, churches, and communities that are promoting godly standards of sexual right and wrong, more teenagers are choosing to remain sexually pure until marriage. "In fact, according to the CDC, the percentage of teenagers who report they have had sex has decreased from 54 percent in the early 1990s, to 46 percent today."[469] Still, there is much work to be done.

Getting Personal

Our teenagers need youth workers and parents who'll help them understand God's wonderful plan for their sexual fulfillment. What are you doing to accomplish that goal? Don't give up. Helping teenagers to maintain their sexual purity is very possible. More kids are openly discussing the emptiness of promiscuity, the benefits of virginity, and their decision to wait until marriage. This is what they were created for. In order to get there, they need us to fulfill our created purpose to parent them to that end.

9

Living in a Material World

He who dies with the most toys wins.

—BUMPER STICKER

What good is it for a man to gain the whole world, yet forfeit his soul?

—MARK 8:36

Shortly after graduating from high school, a young man by the name of LeBron James signed an NBA contract and inked numerous endorsement deals. Before he even set foot on an NBA basketball court, James was already a multimillionaire. If his basketball abilities hadn't already made him the envy of his teenaged peers, his newfound riches had. In the eyes of most teenagers, LeBron James had become the personification of the American Dream. The collective youth culture longingly sighed, "Oh, to be walking in LeBron's shoes." To most kids, LeBron had it all.

Listening to kids talk about LeBron James took me back in time to a conversation I had in 1991 with a group of high school guys about something we'd just read in the *USA Today* sports page.

"This isn't fair!" Doug said in disbelief as he read the article on sports salaries. Doug read the astounding figures to us. Quarterback Joe Montana made $12,461 for each pass he completed. Boxer Buster Douglas fought two bouts, making $1.3 million for beating Mike Tyson and $24.1 million for losing to Evander Holyfield. Gerry Cooney lasted five minutes in the boxing ring with George Foreman—and made $2.5 million. Basketball star Ralph Sampson made $18,349 for each point he scored during the NBA season.[470] The list went on and on.

I sat back and listened as the guys talked about how unfair and unjust it all was. I had to agree. It didn't seem fair that someone could demand and receive so much for playing a game.

Then the discussion took an unsurprising turn when the guys confessed that the salaries would be just and fair if *they* were one of those sports stars. They'd trash all of their other career hopes and dreams if they could cash in on fame, celebrity, and the big money. Each one said they'd give it all up in a minute to be "successful."

In the years since then, I've spent a lot of time thinking about that conversation. Each of those guys would tell you his most important goal in life was to follow in the footsteps of Jesus Christ. But that day they shared a tempting dream that revealed a different set of priorities and desires.

To be honest, I've had to question my own priorities on a regular basis. I'd like to think if big money ever fell into my lap, I'd spend it in ways pleasing to God. But I know deep down inside that there are some "things" that would be awfully tempting if my wallet were ever that thick.

The world of sports and sports salaries mirrors a commitment that runs deep and wide through the American spirit. Judging by skyrocketing salary increases since my discussion with the guys back in 1991, the commitment is growing. Consider this: Barely out of his teenage years, LeBron James made $229.19 for each second played and $1,865.13 for each point scored during the 2006 NBA season. In addition to his salary, he signed a $90 million endorsement contract with Nike. He's not alone. He represents only the tip of the iceberg.

Success, winning, purpose, and getting ahead have all been defined in material terms. This way of thinking has a profound effect on the way we choose to live our lives each and every day. It determines how we make and spend our money. It dictates how we spend our time, where we go to college, and the type of vocational track we pursue. And to a large degree, it determines how we approach parenting and the few short years we have with our kids. Despite the fact that materialism leads down a dead-end road, and the fact that Jesus warned his followers about the dangers of money and wealth, materialism continues to reign supreme in collective and individual hearts.

Some have suggested that following the materialistic and excessive "me decade" of the 1980s, young people were becoming less materialistic than previous generations. When *speaking* about their own attitudes, many teenagers criticize the materialism of their parents and other adults. However, judging by their teenage *lifestyles*, a different message comes through. They're spending more money in pursuit of success and satisfaction. Marketers know this to be the case and they're tapping into the desires of our teenagers in order to get them to spend money.

The title of one marketing text refers to eight- to 10-year-olds as *The Great Tween Buying Machine*.[471] Another recognizes the effects of this marketing blitz: *Consuming Kids: The Hostile Takeover of Childhood*.[472] Marketing critic Juliet Schor, in her book *Born to Buy: The Commercialized Child and the New Consumer Culture*, says, "The United States is the most consumer-oriented society in the world...Kids and teens are now the epicenter of American consumer culture. They command the attention, creativity, and dollars of advertisers."[473] In her book, *Branded: The Buying and Selling of Teenagers*, Alissa Quart recognizes "some have described teens as a new proletariat, kids who work primarily to consume more goods."[474]

Evidence of this materialistic reality arrives in my mailbox almost every day of the week. Every member of my family receives multiple offers for preapproved credit cards with lines of credit sometimes running into the thousands of dollars. The contrast between this and my own struggle to get my first credit card couldn't be more marked. Upon graduating from college in 1978, I thought it might be a good idea to get a gas card for emergency use on trips. At the time, unsolicited preapproved credit card offers were unheard of. It took me weeks to fill out my credit card application, send it in, and wait patiently for a response. When the response came, the credit card company saw my young age as a risk and only offered me a line of credit worth just a few hundred dollars. Not so today. The only things credit card companies know about my kids are 1) their names, 2) their addresses, and 3) the fact that they're part of a generation whose materialism has them spending money far above their means. It's not surprising that a recent print ad for the American Express card tells readers, "If you can imagine it, we can get you there."

Webster's defines *materialism* as "the doctrine that the only or the highest values or objectives lie in material well-being" and "a preoccupation with or stress upon material rather than intellectual or spiritual things."[475] In this chapter we'll examine the powerful pull of materialism in American culture (and, if we're honest, our own lives) and the specific ways this worldview and life view affects the values, attitudes, and behaviors of our teenagers. We'll also discuss parental pressure and how it tends to be linked with material pressure on our kids. Much of our unhealthy pushing and encouragement is rooted in our desire to see our kids succeed materially in the world.

This may be the most difficult chapter for you to read. Personally, it's the most convicting for me to write. Not all of us have had to deal personally with suicide, depression, substance abuse, and many of the other problems addressed in this book. But if you're a living and breathing human being in America, you've had to deal with materialism. As you read, keep an open mind. Look for ways that materialism has affected you, your kids, and your family. Be honest with yourself as you look to discover the ways you might be pressuring your kids. Then ask God to lead you to reconsider and change any attitudes or lifestyle choices that are unhealthy or wrong.

What Teenagers Believe about "Stuff"

When it comes to materialism, our kids have learned their lessons well. They carry on a legacy handed down to them from generation to generation. How have these lessons influenced their thinking and behavior? This section examines five core attitudes teenagers have about money and things. While kids don't articulate them in so many words, their actions speak for them. As you read through each of these attitudes, don't just focus on how they manifest themselves in your kids. Think about your personal world as well. Are you like me—guilty of living out these same attitudes yourself from time to time, or maybe most of the time?

Attitude #1: Things Bring Happiness
Teenagers believe their self-worth and satisfaction in life are rooted in what they have, how they look, what they wear, where they go

to school, what they drive, and other outward traits. Self-definition and worth hinges on possessions. It's not who they are as unique individuals who were created in the image of God that makes kids feel good about themselves. Rather, *I am what I have* becomes the life motto of many teenagers. This attitude, already learned from an adult culture that lives the same way, becomes entrenched in their worldview and life view as it's reinforced by a materialistic peer group.

I once heard a group of teenage girls describe this way of thinking about life. It was 5 AM, and we were heading out in a car caravan for a day of skiing in the mountains. My station wagon was loaded with kids, including five sophomore girls who sat in the two rear seats. It was a Friday, the first day of their four-day holiday weekend. As we pulled out of the church parking lot, one of the girls asked if I'd turn on the rear dome light and leave it on. I told her having the light on would make it difficult for me to see in the predawn darkness.

"Please leave it on," she begged. "We *have* to study." I was curious. Why would a group of girls have to ruin a great start to a four-day weekend by hitting the books?

"Do you have a test on Tuesday morning?" I asked.

"No," they responded.

"Are you behind in your work?"

"No, we just want to get ahead."

When we arrived at the slopes, all of us took off for the lifts so we could get in a full day of skiing—or so I thought. These five girls stayed in the lodge studying. By the end of the day, they'd only gone down the slopes a handful of times.

On the way home, I asked them about their strange behavior. What followed was a discussion about their life goals. My conversation with them, and with several other teenagers since then, has yielded insight into how these kids were thinking: "I have to study hard so I get good grades so I can be in the honors and AP classes and keep up my grade point average and class rank. Colleges look at those, you know. If I can get into the *right* college (not just any college), then I'll be able to get into the *right* graduate school. This will lead to the *right* job where I'll be able to make lots of money. Then I'll be able to get all the things I want, retire early, and enjoy life."

The underlying motive for this approach to high school academics was their desire to achieve so they might find happiness in the material rewards of their efforts. They were living proof of the worldview that underlies the American spirit. Rodney Clapp, in his eye-opening essay, "Why the Devil Takes Visa," describes what I heard from these girls this way: "The affluent, technologically advanced West seems more focused not on consuming to live, but on living to consume."[476]

This is why teenagers are the most targeted market demographic group in the world. They're so materialistic that marketers couldn't be happier. Today's kids equate happiness with the acquisition of more consumer goods, especially luxury items. They're spinning the wheel of fortune and hoping for the big money. For many, this track appears to be the only path to happiness and meaning in life. "Forty-four percent of kids in fourth through eighth grades now report that they daydream 'a lot' about being rich. And nearly two-thirds of parents report that 'my child defines his or her self-worth in terms of the things they own and wear more than I did when I was that age.'"[477]

Attitude #2: Money Buys Things

The emerging generation of teenagers is the wealthiest in history. The business and retail communities are so sure of our teenagers' commitment to spend money in pursuit of happiness, they spend plenty of their own money each year to discover how to get kids to spend theirs. Advertisements, packaging, and displays are all carefully crafted to trigger the desire to buy and facilitate a sale.

Theologian Jon Pahl says the shopping mall has become, in our society, a "Stairway to Heaven, leading nowhere." He writes, "They function, in fact, as sacred places in a religion of the market...People seek happiness in malls and in the acquisition of commodities not so much because they truly imagine that they will find salvation in this way, but because they have been sold such a 'truth' through the advertising, spatial design, and language associated with malls."[478] This reality is certainly true for our teenagers, and the money spent on advertising to them reflects this idea as well.

Is money spent on marketing to teenagers well spent? You'd better believe it. The spending power of America's teenagers is incredible. As the years pass and materialism takes root in their lives, spending power increases as well. Kids ages 4 to 12 spent $2.2 billion in 1968, $4.2 billion in 1984, $17.1 billion in 1994, more than $40 billion in 2002, and $52 billion in 2006.[479] In addition to spending their own money, kids influence what their parents buy. In the 1960s, they influenced about $5 billion a year in parent purchases. By 1984, that figure had jumped to $50 billion. By 1997, it was $188 billion.[480] It is estimated conservatively that kids now influence over $600 billion annually in parental spending.[481]

There has been a significant increase in teenage spending power over the last several years. In 1983 people aged 13 to 19 spent more than $40 billion.[482] Believe it or not, the average teenager actually had about $200 a month discretionary money.[483] That was more money than the average family had left over to spend any way they wanted in two or three months. Since then, teenage spending power has continued to snowball. A rising teenage population has coupled with greater economic opportunity and materialism to put teenage discretionary spending (ages 12 to 17) at more than $190 billion, a higher figure than the gross domestic product of many countries in the world.[484] Without the burden of normal adult financial responsibilities, virtually all teenage income is disposable. Research on how much teenagers spend in a week puts the figure at $118, with older teenagers spending more than younger ones do.[485]

Where do teenagers get all this money?

- 55 percent get money from their parents.

- 45 percent get gift money.

- 29 percent receive money from odd jobs.

- 29 percent make money working part-time jobs.

- 24 percent receive an allowance.

- 5 percent hold down a full-time job.

- 2 percent own their own business.[486]

With a growing number of kids holding down jobs, there is concern over what that means for both their present and future lives. Many teenagers who are working long hours while attending school do so in order to finance large-ticket purchases, including the costs of buying and maintaining a car. The reality is that many are working to finance their ride to and from work. We should also be concerned that their ability to make large purchases now is not only feeding premature affluence, but also setting them up for a lifetime where they'll expect that their greater income potential will allow for more large purchases, putting them in deeper debt.

The true measure of materialism among teenagers is their spending patterns. Do they buy the lies sold to them by marketing experts and spend, spend, spend? Or do they work to save their money for college and other expenses? Interestingly enough, 62 percent of teenagers report having savings accounts, and 19 percent own stocks and bonds.[487] However, no figures are available regarding the average amount of money in either one.

What we do know is "teenagers have come to feel that consumer goods are their friends—and that the companies selling products to them are trusted allies."[488] Peter Zollo says it's helpful to think of teenage spending as falling into three basic categories. They're making small purchases (CDs, snacks and beverages, gasoline, impulse buys), midlevel purchases (clothes, school club dues, expenditures related to hobbies and interests), and big-ticket purchases (cars, consumer electronics). His research has found "teens spend most on what costs least—51 percent of teens' weekly purchases are for items costing less than $25, and 86 percent are for items costing less than $100."[489] However, a large portion of teenagers do own large-ticket items, including home stereo systems (82%), TVs (82%), computers (76%), VCRs (74%), and portable stereos (74%).[490] This interesting new trend to purchase costlier items might explain some of the growth in teenage savings, as they put aside some of their money to save up for these purchases.

As I've examined all the lists of how teenagers spend their money, there is one gaping hole. Nowhere is any mention made of how much teenagers are spending to meet the needs of others. Instead, their money is being spent on a selfish pursuit of happiness.

Little money is spent on charities, missions, or the work of the local church. Should we be surprised? Probably not. The example we've passed on to our kids in this area is weak.

A recent Barna Survey found that the typical individual gives away about 3 percent of their income.[491] Only 6 percent of Americans tithe their money to churches or to a combination of churches and parachurch ministries, with less than 2 percent of adults under the age of 40 tithing their money.[492] Sometimes it's those who have more who give less. Those with household incomes of $40,000 to $100,000 give away the lowest proportion of their income, while those who make less than $20,000 annually contribute a higher portion of their earnings.[493] We can assume that if our kids make as much as they hope to, they'll be willing to give away less.

When money and material possessions become the driving passion of a person's life, that person is prone to go to any length to get what she wants. Our newspapers are filled with stories about individuals who've lied, cheated, and stolen to get what they wanted. Is it possible that our kids, if driven by the same desires, could meet the same end?

When teenagers start to believe "things" bring happiness and money is the pathway to getting more things, don't be surprised if they take some morally bankrupt detours on their way to making and getting money.

Attitude #3: Get the Edge

Several years ago I was playing volleyball with a group of high school students. While waiting for my turn to get into the game, I was talking with a number of kids who were sitting off to the side. One young man who'd been playing ran off the court for a substitution and joined us. As he leaned over to sit down, his sunglasses dropped out of his shirt pocket and onto the grass in front of me. I picked them up and noticed they were a very nice pair of sunglasses. As I handed them back to him, I said I'd been looking to buy a new pair myself, and I asked if I could try on his.

He reached out his hand to take them back and said, "No. You don't want to try these on. I don't think you could afford them."

I was surprised by his comment and allowed my defensive instincts to take over. "What do you mean, I couldn't afford them?" I asked.

"Well," he answered condescendingly, "you're just a youth worker, and these cost over $100 a pair." He was right—I couldn't afford them. He then proceeded to rub salt in my wounds by saying, "I have three more pairs at home." I sensed arrogance on his part as he tucked the glasses back into his pocket.

I came away from that incident feeling like this kid had dragged me into a race—the same materialistic race our kids find themselves in every day. The winner is the one with the biggest, best, and most, while the loser just tries to catch up. Many of today's teenagers are caught in the vicious cycle of trying to outdo each other.

Kids aspire to be "branded" because they know wearing the right brand assures them of the status they so desperately desire. What does it mean to be "branded"? It simply means a brand label and style is adopted as one's personal identity. Kids who don't wear the right clothes can become the object of peer taunting and exclusion at all grade levels, from kindergarten right on through to the last year of high school. Some parents are going so far as to hire professional shopping consultants to do back-to-school shopping with their kids. One of those consultants, Debra Lindquist, says she knows how to convince a mother that paying $160 for a pair of jeans is worth it because "your daughter is going to get so much confidence from them."[494]

Most of today's teenagers know that what you wear on your feet is an important determinant of status. Any parent who's gone on a hunt for athletic shoes knows there are at least three aspects of the hunt that leave your head spinning: the price, the wide variety of ever-changing styles (a strategy marketers use to sell more product), and your child's insistence and demands. While most kids are begging Mom and Dad for a pair in the $75 to $125 price range, kids who really want to get the edge will pressure their parents to spend even more. This reality has been entrenched in our culture for so long that some kids have acted like the value of a pair of sneakers exceeds the value of an individual's life. A few years ago *Sports Illustrated* noted this trend in a cover story about kids who kill for sneakers titled, "Your Sneakers or Your Life."[495]

Keeping up with and getting ahead of the Joneses is nothing new. But when that competition begins to cost more than a few dollars and cents, that indicates the intensity of the race is building. Teenagers are running hard in this race to get the edge. If they keep going the way they are, they'll be sure to rewrite the record book.

Attitude #4: So What's Wrong with Being Self-Centered?

One sunny Labor Day, I had the opportunity to go boating with a group of six high schoolers in the clear blue waters off the coast of Miami. We enjoyed the beautiful weather while swimming and water-skiing off the back end of a pretty impressive boat that belonged to Dave's father. When it was Dave's turn to ski, I went to the back of the boat to slide him the skis while he dove into the water. When Dave resurfaced, he leaned back and let out a comfortable sigh.

"Ahhhh," he said. "I wonder what the poor people are doing today."

Dave had verbalized an attitude common among today's teenagers. They've become so consumed with meeting their own needs that they forget about—or don't even care for—those less fortunate than themselves. Their actions, particularly their unwillingness to help others, reveal the fact that they're satisfied with being self-centered.

When it comes to integrating their Christian faith into the material and financial parts of their lives, even Christian kids—like the rest of us—are having difficulty. I'll never forget something Kenneth Kantzer wrote that hit me right between the eyes: "The most serious problem facing the church today is materialism—materialism not as a philosophical theory, but as a way of life."[496]

More teenagers today (most likely most of them) who profess faith in Christ see nothing wrong with this type of lifestyle, even in spite of the fact that Jesus called his followers to be totally committed to him—as opposed to being preoccupied with their own material needs. As one who speaks from experience, I can tell you that the more I have, the more those things cloud or block my view of Christ and his calling.

In his research on how religion influences one's view of material things, Princeton University sociology professor Robert Wuthnow has found these attitudes are a part of the fabric of adult culture. He writes,

> Much of the American middle class seems to have forgotten even the most basic claims religion used to make on the material world. Asked if their religious beliefs had influenced their choice of a career, most of the people I've interviewed in recent years—Christians and non-Christians alike—said *no.* Asked if they thought of their work as a calling, most said *no.* Asked if they understood the concept of stewardship, most said *no.* Asked how religion did influence their work lives or thoughts about money, most said the two were completely separate.[497]

Perhaps we shouldn't be surprised by the selfish reflection we see of ourselves in the mirror of today's youth culture. Our kids have been exposed to the disease of self-centeredness. And like adults, our kids run the risk of living with the disease for so long they forget they even have it.

Attitude #5: I'll Never Have Enough

The late Mother Teresa said it this way: "Once the longing for money comes, the longing also comes for what money can give—superfluities—nice rooms—luxuries at table—more clothes—fans—and so on. Our needs will increase—for one thing brings another—and the result will be endless dissatisfaction."[498]

Most kids today believe their standard of living will be higher than their parents'. The reality is that this generation might be on a collision course with downward mobility. In reality, that would be a blessing. Our teenagers have been allowed to grow up with such a high standard of living that there's nowhere for them to go but down. The sad result will be that those kids who expect to find meaning and purpose in accumulating more money and things will be faced with meaninglessness and purposelessness.

Their sense of self-worth will be destroyed. The worst possible result of never having enough or trying to hold onto what they have could be an increased number of young adults who suffer from depression or choose to cope with their "failure" through alcoholism, substance abuse, and suicide. They will have allowed their premature affluence to destroy them.

The Hows and Whats of Materialism

Before we look at some practical ideas and responses to materialism, we must ask ourselves two questions. First, do we know *how* kids get pointed to a materialistic lifestyle? And second, do we know *what* the proper God-given attitude is that we should have toward money and material things?

The Hows of Materialism

The fact that we all too often define ourselves by our work and worldly possessions has not been lost on our kids. In today's world, that message is powerfully and consistently reinforced by the pervasive presence of a marketing machine that sells worldly possessions on the false premise that they're ultimately redemptive, offering us satisfaction, purpose, meaning, and personal peace. Not only are our kids swimming and marinating in the soup of that marketing message from birth, but they're also swimming with millions of their peers who have bought into and believed that same message. All of this combines in a potent mix that leaves us wondering if our positive example can even break through to be seen and heard.

When it comes to the economics of lifestyle choices, the fact that your example is still the most powerful teacher could be good news or bad news. And remember, even well-intentioned Christian parents who have been living in an age and culture of excess can pass on materialistic attitudes to their kids.

The Whats of Materialism

The answer to the *what* question is equally clear: *Our job as youth workers and parents is to help teenagers redefine their idea of success by equipping them to understand and live out God's definition of success.* Of course, this requires we understand and live out his definition ourselves.

God cares deeply about our attitudes toward money and wealth. Did you know that more is said in the New Testament about money and wealth than about heaven and hell combined? Five times more is said about money than about prayer. And 16 of Christ's 38 parables deal with money.

Theologian John Stott sums up Jesus' teaching this way: "What Jesus forbids his followers is the *selfish* accumulation of goods; extravagant and luxurious living; the hardheartedness which does not feel the colossal need of the world's under-privileged people; the foolish fantasy that a person's life consists in the abundance of his possessions; and the materialism which tethers our hearts to the earth."[499]

In 1928 a group of the world's most successful financiers met at the Edgewater Beach Hotel in Chicago. It's said that, collectively, these seven tycoons controlled more money than there was in the United States Treasury. For years newspapers and magazines had been printing their success stories and holding them up as role models to young people across the nation. But do you know what happened to each of these successful men within 25 years?

- The president of the largest independent steel company, Charles Schwab, lived on borrowed money the last five years of his life and died broke.

- The greatest wheat speculator, Arthur Cutten, died abroad, bankrupt.

- The president of the New York Stock Exchange, Richard Whitney, served a term in Sing Sing Prison.

- The member of the President's cabinet, Albert Fall, was pardoned from prison so he could die at home.

- The greatest bear on Wall Street, Jesse Livermore, committed suicide.

- The president of the Bank of International Settlements, Leon Fraser, committed suicide.

- The head of the world's greatest monopoly, Ivar Drueger, committed suicide.

Our kids need to know that God's definition of *success* stands in marked contrast to the definition the world would have us believe. Two different definitions of *success*. Two different paths to take in life. Two different outcomes. We must teach our kids that the real measure of their success in life is how much they'd be worth if they had absolutely nothing.

Practical Steps You Can Take to Counter Materialism

What are some practical steps you can take to help the teenagers you know and love develop healthy attitudes toward money and wealth?

Step #1: Lead and Teach by Example

Here are some questions to ponder as you examine yourself. Take the time to answer them seriously. Discuss your answers with your spouse. You might even want to ask your kids for their impression of what you're teaching.

- What do you want to pass on to your kids? Money and material items (sometimes defined as *financial security*) or godly character traits?

- How much does your lifestyle reflect and conform to the values prevalent in our consumer society?

- If you're a goal-oriented person, what are your goals for five, 10, and 15 years from now? Are they primarily economic (material) in nature?

- If your kids were to write out a definition of *success* based on how you define it through your lifestyle, what would they write?

- Are you always looking to get the competitive edge or keep up with the Joneses? Are you jealous when someone you know acquires something you don't have but want?

- Do you wish for things you don't have, believing their acquisition would make your life better?

- Do you refer to your wants as *needs*?

- When will you know you've "made it"?

- Someone once said to me, "You tell me who or what you spend your time daydreaming about, and I'll tell you who or what your god is." Who or what do you daydream about?

- Do you possess your possessions, or do they possess you?

- Do you focus on what you don't have, rather than being joyful about those things you do have?

- Are you a cheerful, generous, and joyful giver?

- Do your faith and security rest in God or in your things?

One of the most important lessons to teach our teenagers is that God owns everything we have and are. There is nothing in this world that is not his. As a result, every spending or lifestyle decision we make is a spiritual decision. Do your spending and lifestyle decisions reflect that commitment? Are you trying to fill the God-shaped void in your soul with idols and objects that can never, ever fill that hole?

My parents weren't poor, but we had quite a bit less than our neighbors. My parents tell me that as a young boy I was puzzled by the fact that we were the only family on the street that didn't have a maid. Sure, there were lots of things I wanted to have while I was growing up, and I was disappointed when I didn't get them. But my parents passed on something far more valuable—their example. They taught us the difference between needs and wants, constantly reminding me that most everything I begged for because "I *needed* it" was at their roots things I *wanted*. I hated hearing that lesson then, but I'm extremely grateful for it now. They taught us that everything is God's and should be used according to God's rules of stewardship and for his glory. They modeled thrifty living and generous giving, without ever becoming boastful about either. And they taught me that living hand-to-mouth isn't such a bad way to live when the hand feeding my mouth belongs to God.

Step #2: Don't Push and Pressure Your Kids

There is absolutely nothing wrong with expecting kids to do *their* best—as long as it's their best and not some *socially defined* best that is pushed on them.

Let's face it: We live in an age of designer kids. Parents are increasingly afraid of having an average kid, especially in academics, athletics, and the arts. We buy into programs that will get our kids ahead of the pack. We enroll preschoolers in classes or purchase educational products that promise to get them reading before they even know how to play and have fun. Then we structure their play and fun to equip them to get an athletic edge over other kids. Whether we expect them to win an athletic scholarship or live vicariously through their on-field achievements, we aren't helping them by pressuring them.

I recently read about a local youth soccer team that had traveled up and down the east coast to participate in a series of tournaments. Their coach was a former professional player who was spending time tutoring them as individuals and a group. I was stunned to learn that the team of boys were under six years old. Perhaps it's not surprising that even though 80 percent of our country's kids between the ages of 6 and 18 play sports, the Institute for the Study of Youth Sports at Michigan State University estimates that 70 percent of these kids drop out by age 13.[500] Most quit due to a combination of parental pressure and the fact that they're no longer having fun.

Unfortunately, the end result of this parental pressure and pushiness is not what was always intended. Kids stress out. Haunted by the sense that they will never measure up, they begin to feel like failures. They start to believe that their parents' love for them depends on their performance (sometimes kids read the signals correctly). As the stress builds, the parent-child relationship weakens and often breaks as a result of rebellion. Forcing kids to bear an unrealistic burden can also lead to the worst possible end: Depression and/or suicide.

Developmental expert Cliff Schimmels offers parents some of the best advice I've ever heard: "The one prayer I pray most frequently as a parent and a teacher is that the Lord will give me the wisdom to know how much to expect of my kids. If I expect too little of them, they may waste their creative gifts. If I expect too much of them, I may destroy them with an unrealistic burden."[501]

Step #3: Give Them Your Time

I recently read about a busy woman who was struggling to balance the demands of working outside the home while being a wife and mother. One night her nine-year-old son approached her as she typed diligently on her computer in the corner of the family room.

"Mommy," the little boy said, "if you had a dog, and you really loved this dog, and you worked real hard to earn the money to buy him the fanciest dog house and the best dog food, don't you think it would be better if once in a while you played with that dog?"[502]

Parents, when you aren't spending time with your kids, three things happen:

1. Someone else raises your kids for you. It could be anyone from a baby-sitter to a day-care worker to a schoolteacher to the television or other media. One of the risks of living in a materialistic society is that these surrogate parents can instill false values in your kids.

2. Your kids will learn from your busy lifestyle. They'll look at your commitments to career, family, and church and learn that it's more important to achieve, work, and expand social circles that it is to be at home. And what they learn gets passed on to the next generation. If you find it difficult to be at home with your family, your kids will find it even harder to spend time with your grandkids. If you place a premium on job and career, they'll likely grow up doing the same.

3. Your kids may suffer in ways you never imagined. When we're not available to help them through the difficult years of adolescence, we open the door for our kids' involvement in a vast array of dangerous behaviors and problems. Kids of absent-due-to-busyness parents are not only left to listen more closely to the life-shaping messages of media and their peers, but they tend to be more

prone to emotional and substance abuse problems. The reason? Mom and Dad are absent, a reality that can hurt so deeply that kids may enlist unhealthy ways to deal with their pain.

When we choose to have kids, we also make another choice—one commonly forgotten in these materialistic days. We choose to become parents. Parenting takes time. Don't allow yourself to fall into the trap of believing "quality time" is more important than "quantity time." Quality time always has a way of fitting a parent's schedule while disregarding the needs of the child. We must learn to say *no* to other demands that aren't as important as our kids. When we don't spend time with our children, they'll begin to interpret our actions as rejection. It isn't long before rejection becomes resentment, and resentment turns into hostility, which in turn leads to rebellion.

Step #4: Give Your Kids the Best Life, Not the Good Life

More and more, the nasty effects of living the good life are being seen in even our youngest kids. Pediatrician Ralph Minear was puzzled by the physical and emotional symptoms of stress that he and his colleagues were seeing in kids as young as preschool age. Included are nausea, headaches, eating disorders, anxiety, depression, and high blood pressure—all because they've been given too much of the good life "whether it's pressure to perform, freedom, money, food, protection, or parental sacrifice."[503] Dr. Minear diagnosed the malady as *Affluenza*, or "Rich Kids Syndrome." These are kids whose parents want them to have all the benefits of the good life. Consequently, they push them to be perfect kids, cramming them with more cultural, educational, athletic, and material opportunities than they can handle. And its victims aren't just those from wealthy homes. The disease is as common in middle-class and poor families as it is in those with lots of money.

What are the options for those of us who realize it's dangerous to give our kids the good life? The good news is there's something better. In fact, it's the "best life." Our lives and actions should communicate to our kids that the best life is found by living in relationship with God by God's will and way, according to his standards of success. The best life consists of directing all we have, do, and are toward loving God in every nook, cranny, and minute of our lives. And then, because of our love for him, we should love those around us rather than treating them as the competition or the means to material ends.

John Wesley had these priorities in mind when he gave this timely and timeless advice: "Work as hard as you can, to make all the money you can, to save as much as you can in order to give away all that you can."

Step #5: Let Your Kids Be Themselves

While there's nothing wrong with taking a healthy interest in our kids' lives, it's dangerous to live vicariously through them. When our own insecurities lead us to push them to become all we weren't or to accumulate all we never had, we force them to become something they are not, nor were they ever intended to be. If you grew up in a situation like that yourself, you know firsthand about the incredible weight this approach puts on a child's shoulders.

Think about each of your kids and ask yourself these questions:

- What are my child's unique, God-given abilities and interests?

- How does my child use spare time?

- How is my child different from the rest of the family?

- What career path does my child wish to pursue?

- Am I pushing my child to be or do something they were never meant to be or do because of my own desires or insecurities?

- Am I encouraging my child's abilities and interests?

God has blessed each of our kids with unique gifts, abilities, and interests that they're to use in service to him. Let's point our kids in God's direction, rather than our own.

Step #6: Instill in Them Missions-Mindedness and Christian Service

As more teenagers discover the empty, dead-end of materialism, they'll become increasingly interested in looking for activities that give meaning and purpose to their lives. One of the marks of this emerging generation of teenagers is a willingness and desire to help others and to get involved in a variety of social causes. This is a good sign and something we can't let slip through the cracks without seizing upon it.

Veteran youth worker and missions expert Paul Borthwick has seen firsthand how missions involvement combats a materialistic outlook on life and can even lead to a change in lifestyle choices. He writes,

> One girl, after seeing a poverty-stricken barrio in Colombia, decided to stop her habit of window shopping because "it led me to think I needed things that I now know I don't need at all." Another began financially supporting a child she met at an orphanage in Costa Rica. Another student who worked hard on a mission team saw how much he could accomplish. On returning home he sold his television set because "I saw how much time I had been wasting in front of the tube."[504]

By modeling selfless involvement in mission and service projects, you can grow a desire in your kids to make a difference through service to others in the name of Christ. As their interest grows, enable them to take opportunities to participate in short-term mission projects on a local, national, and international scale. Experience shows that one of the most effective ways to build and cement the faith of teenagers is to involve them in missions and service.

Getting Personal

Have you ever wondered how they catch all the monkeys we see during our trips to the local zoo? The rather primitive traps they use in Africa are quite unique. A coin, button, or some other shiny, metallic object is placed in a long-necked glass jar that is then attached to a tree. As the monkeys swing through the trees, the reflection of the sun on the shining object catches their eye. Reaching into the jar poses no problem at all for the curious monkeys. But when they try to pull their closed fists out of the narrow openings, they can't do it. To gain freedom, all the monkeys need to do is let go of the worthless object. Instead, the monkeys sit by the jar and hold onto the object until their captors come to take them away.

"Stupid monkeys," you say. I know. But are they that much different from you and me?

My wife and I know that the shiny objects of materialism are awfully attractive. Yet, there are many times when we find ourselves trapped when we hold on and won't let go. We've learned firsthand how easy it is to lose our freedom at the hands of misplaced values and priorities. Our personal experience and study of God's Word led us a long time ago to make some serious decisions regarding what we believed was most important to teach our kids. We haven't always done a good job, but I know this is what we've needed to do. I encourage you to do the same.

Let me share those decisions with you in the form of three questions and their answers:

- *What is success?* True success in life is faithfulness to God and obedience to his commands, whether your net worth is 10 cents or 10 million dollars.

- *What do you and I want our kids to become?* Our desire for our kids should be the same as our heavenly Father's desire for them: that they become like Christ in all things.

- *What must you and I do to make this happen?* We must know the truth as it's contained in God's Word, talk about it, live it, model it, experience it, and prayerfully trust God to change our kids' hearts and minds.

C.S. Lewis once said, "If I find in myself a desire which no experience in this world can satisfy, the most probable explanation is that I was made for another world."[505] Are you pointing kids to that other world?

Under the Influence: Teenagers and Substance Abuse

10

Liquid Fun.

—FROM A PRINT AD FOR MILLER LITE BEER

I just feel better. That's what it does for me.

—16-YEAR-OLD BOY'S EXPLANATION FOR WHY HE LOVES BINGE DRINKING

It was one of those childhood memories that cements itself in your mind forever. I was nine when I attended the annual neighborhood Memorial Day picnic. The peanut scramble for the kids was over, and the adults were gathering to play their games. Dozens of wives and kids watched as several fathers positioned themselves at the starting line for their annual 40-yard dash. The only difference between their race and the sprints at the local high school track meets? These men were to complete their run while chugging 16-ounce cans of beer.

On "Go!" the fathers took off for the finish line with their heads tilted back and beer cans to their lips. It was strange for me to see my friends' fathers "let down their hair" as they dashed across the yard with beer running down their necks and onto their chests. The wives and children laughed and applauded louder than they would the rest of the day, leaving me with the impression that everyone thought this event was the best part of the gathering. To my nine-year-old eyes, drinking looked like a lot of fun.

But as I grew up, my parents' sound advice, along with several other experiences, taught me that substance abuse was anything but fun. When I was in high school, I worked as a volunteer at a psychiatric hospital. On one occasion I helped chaperone several adolescent patients during an educational trip to a local greenhouse. I watched as one of the residents, a 15-year-old named Tom, approached an elderly woman who was busy tending the plants.

He politely asked her, "Excuse me, ma'am. Where do you keep your marijuana plants?" Tom wasn't joking around or being disrespectful. His question came from a brain severely damaged by a self-administered overdose of the drug PCP (also known as angel dust). He'd allowed substance abuse to visit his life, and while he looked and sounded normal, it had taken a devastating toll.

Another time a group of teenage guys I knew were out on one of their regular weekend drinking binges. As they drove from house to house in search of another party, Rick stuck his head out the window to vomit. When the other guys, who were also drunk, pulled Rick back into the car, he was dead. Apparently, his head had struck a telephone pole. Rick had invited substance abuse to visit his life, and it had done damage that could never be undone. But in just a matter of weeks, the shock of his death wore off, and the guys were getting drunk again. I wondered if any of them would follow in Rick's footsteps.

Just a few years ago, our community was rocked when two of my son's high school classmates perished in a car accident caused by their drinking. Our community grieved, and students—many of whom wept at their funerals—pondered the consequences of drunk driving for a few days. But shortly after the funerals were over, the dust settled and life went on with few, if any, lessons learned. Just two weeks after the boys were buried, I attended a Christmas concert at the high school. While using the boys' restroom, I noticed some scribbling on the tile wall. There in large letters was a handwritten memorial to the pair, which included their initials followed by R.I.P. In addition, the tribute's author encouraged others to memorialize the boys' deaths by—believe it or not—drinking in their honor. Sadly, what happened in our community is not a rare occurrence in this country.

If you don't think America has a drug problem, consider a recent spring break issue of *Rolling Stone* magazine. The edition included "A six-site guide to the ultimate in boozing, cruising and other disturbing behavior" for college students looking for an education on the "where to go's" and "what to do's" during spring break. Describing the six most popular destinations from Cancun to Steamboat Springs, the guide listed helpful information about each location, including the best bar, chances of getting served with a fake ID, fine for underage drinking, local drug of choice, and best regional drink.[506]

If you're concerned about substance abuse among teenagers, your concerns are well founded. Since my initial exposure to drug and alcohol problems during my high school years, I've met hundreds of teenagers who've struggled with recreational and addictive substance abuse. Over the years I've known and worked with dozens of kids whose choice to abuse drugs and alcohol has led to death, debilitating injury, pregnancy, addiction, violence, and a host of other dangerous or immoral behaviors. The latest research indicates that by the time they reach their senior year in high school, more than half of all teenagers have used an illicit drug (53.5 percent), 47 percent have used marijuana, three-quarters have used alcohol (75.1 percent), and half have used cigarettes (50 percent).[507]

But substance abuse is not a problem limited to the teenage population. Teenagers have grown up in a world filled with attractive substance abuse messages. Others have experienced the harsh reality and ugliness of the costly toll of substance abuse. When the laughter and fun of our neighborhood picnic ended, a few of my friends went home to houses filled with the pain and nastiness of alcoholism. Some kids today are too scared to turn out the lights or close their eyes at night for fear of what might happen when their father explodes in a drunken rage. Ironically, many kids who are scarred by a parent's or other adult's substance abuse will likely grow up and turn to substance abuse themselves, embracing it as a coping mechanism to deal with their own pain and heartache.

In this chapter we'll examine the problem of teenage substance abuse and these parental questions:

- Are kids really using drugs and alcohol? If so, why?

- What substances are today's teenagers using and abusing?

- How can I tell if a teenager is using drugs or alcohol?

- What can I do to prevent my child from becoming a substance abuser?

- What should I do if I discover my teenager has a problem?

Facts and Figures: What Are Teenagers Using and How Much?

No matter what the reason, substance abuse remains a major problem among teenagers. When asked what they thought was the most important problem facing people their age today, teenagers listed drugs/smoking/alcohol at number one.[508]

In this section we'll examine the current statistics and facts on teenage substance abuse in an effort to come to an understanding of who is abusing substances, what they're abusing, and how much.

Alcohol

Americans love to drink. Over the course of a year, the average American drinks 27 gallons of beer[509], 2.77 gallons of wine[510], and 2 gallons of hard liquor.[511] In one recent year, alcohol beverage sales in the U.S. topped $130 billion.[512] This love affair with alcohol is shared by the teen population. Alcohol is by far the number one drug used and abused by teenagers. Drinking has become a normal adolescent activity and serves as a rite of passage for kids as they move from childhood into adulthood.

Teenage drinking facts and figures. The average student takes her first drink at the age of 11, a fact that shows a trend toward earlier use over the last few years.[513] Among the eighth graders surveyed about their first taste of alcohol,

- 6.3 percent took their first drink in fourth grade or before,

- 5.4 percent in fifth grade,

- 9.2 percent in sixth grade,

- 13.8 percent in seventh grade, and

- 9.2 percent in eighth grade.[514]

And as our teenagers grow older, they drink greater amounts with greater frequency. "Binge" drinking is defined as drinking five or more drinks in a row, and it has become more common among teenagers. Eleven percent of eighth graders, 21 percent of tenth graders, and 28 percent of high school seniors reported they'd binged during the two weeks prior to the survey.[515]

On college campuses, where drinking has become a rite of passage for many, 42 percent of students engaged in binge drinking during the two weeks prior to being surveyed,[516] and 62 percent reported binging in the last month.[517] While boys have typically "out-binged" girls for years, a growing amount of research points to the fact that girls are now binging as frequently as boys.

Joseph Califano, President of the National Center on Addiction and Substance Abuse at Columbia University says, "Kids who begin drinking before age 21 are more than twice as likely to develop alcohol-related problems. Those who begin drinking before age 15 are four times more likely to become alcoholics than those who do not drink before age 21."

What teenagers are drinking. Besides beer, hard liquor, and wine-cooler kinds of drinks, teenagers are finding alternative methods of getting alcohol into their bloodstreams.

The drink of choice is beer, and they're drinking it at younger and younger ages. When asked if they had drunk beer in the last year, 4.3 percent of fourth-grade students, and 5.1 percent of fifth-grade students answered *yes*.[519] Not surprisingly, the numbers increase with age: 15 percent of sixth graders, 21 percent of seventh graders, 31 percent of eighth graders, 40 percent of ninth graders, 48 percent of tenth graders, 51 percent of eleventh graders, and 56 percent of twelfth graders said they had consumed beer during the previous year.[520] Included in beer use are malt liquors, which contain up to twice as much alcohol (8 percent) as beer (between 4 and 4.8 percent). Drinking malt liquor is becoming more and more popular among teenagers because it's cheap, powerful, and fast acting. It's also highly addictive.

Why do kids say they like beer? Teenagers who choose beer as their favorite alcoholic beverage say they do so because it tastes good, is easy to obtain, is cheap, and doesn't get them drunk as fast as other alcoholic beverages. Also, beer is always plentiful at teenage drinking parties. Teenagers are also consuming wine and wine coolers. Among sixth through twelfth graders, one-third have consumed wine coolers during the past year.[521]

And one-third of all sixth through twelfth graders drank liquor during the previous year. Not surprisingly, high school students drink the most liquor, with 38 percent of ninth graders, 48 percent of tenth graders, 52 percent of eleventh graders, and 58 percent of twelfth graders reporting use.[522]

Teenagers arc also finding new ways to abuse alcohol. Some are mixing alcohol into gelatin. The sweet flavor of the gelatin masks the taste of the alcohol, making it easier to hide the alcohol content in these "zippers" from adults, and making them dangerous for unsuspecting kids who normally avoid alcohol.

They're drinking something known in the alcohol industry as "alternative beverages." "Alcopops" were originally introduced in Great Britain and Australia back in the early 1990s. With the same alcohol content as beer—anywhere between five and seven percent of volume—these lemonade and other fruit-flavor-based "malternative" drinks are packaged using lots of bright colors and sold with slick and trendy logos. The taste of the alcohol is also "hidden" using three drink elements kids love—alcopops are sweet, fruit-flavored, and full of carbonated fizz.

Thus, the packaging, marketing, and taste are all very attractive to teenagers, but there are some legitimate concerns that alcopops are being marketed to entry-level drinkers and to those who don't like the taste of beer and other alcoholic beverages. Aggressive marketing through print, broadcast, and Internet outlets has put alcopops on the collective consciousness and into the hands of a growing number of teenagers. And a study by the American Medical Association found that one-third of all girls over age 12 had tried them.

When all is said and done, our teenagers are abusing alcohol at alarming rates. Only 21 percent of high school students say their friends *never* use alcohol.[523] Even more frightening is the fact that 6 percent of middle school students and 7 percent of high school students report having received treatment or counseling for alcohol or drug use.[524]

Other alcohol facts. I here are other aspects related to teen drinking that parents should be aware of. *First, teenagers find it easy to get alcohol.* Teens report getting their alcohol out of the family liquor cabinet, from a friend, from their parents, at a party, or—believe it or not—they purchase it for themselves. If they want it, any teenager in America who looks hard enough can get it. Among fourth to sixth graders, 23 percent say it's easy to get beer, 18 percent say it's easy to get wine coolers, and 14 percent say it's easy to get liquor.[525] Also, 64 percent of eighth graders, 84 percent of tenth graders, and 93 percent of twelfth graders say alcohol is "fairly easy" or "very easy" to get.[526] Perhaps it's not surprising that in one year, underage drinkers consumed $22.5 billion, or 17 percent, of all alcohol sold.[527]

Fisrt, drinking and driving remain a major problem and a killer among adolescents. While most students would say it's wrong to drink and drive, during the 30 days preceding a recent survey, 29 percent of high school "students nationwide had ridden one or more times in a car or other vehicle driven by someone who had been drinking alcohol."[528] In addition, during the 30 days prior to the survey, 10 percent of high school students had driven a car or other vehicle one or more times when they had been drinking alcohol.[529] During one year, 20 percent of 18- to 20-year-olds and 28 percent of 21- to 25-year-olds report driving under the influence at least once.[530] To wit: 31 percent of all drivers between the ages of 15 and 20 who died in traffic accidents had been drinking alcohol.[531]

Second, many parents actually enable their kids' drinking. In fact, some even provide alcohol in their own homes. They assume their kids will drink anyway, so why not give them the alcohol and a place to do it safely? In my own community, I'm constantly hearing about parents who not only open their homes to students, but also provide alcohol for their parties.

Third, alcohol use plays a role in dangerous, promiscuous, and criminal behavior. Alcohol is often a key factor in assaults, manslaughters, murders, attempted murders, robberies, and burglaries. About 40 percent of all violent and nonviolent crimes are committed under the influence of alcohol, and 40 percent of convicted rape and sexual assault offenders said they'd been drinking at the time they committed their crimes.[532] Two-thirds of the victims of "intimate partner violence reported that alcohol was involved in the incident."[533] And alcohol is also a factor in many suicides.

Alcohol's role in dangerous behavior is best understood by the alarming facts related to what happens to teenagers who've started drinking by the time they head to college. Consider these facts from the College Drinking Prevention Web site (www.collegedrinkingprevention.gov):

- 1,700 college students die each year from alcohol-related, unintentional injuries.

- 599,000 college students are unintentionally injured while under the influence of alcohol.

- More than 696,000 students are assaulted by another student who's been drinking.

- More than 97,000 students are victims of alcohol-related sexual assault or date rape.

- 400,000 students had unprotected sex, and more than 100,000 students reported being too intoxicated to know if they even consented to having sex.

- More than 150,000 students develop an alcohol-related health problem.

- Between 1.2 and 1.5 percent of students say they tried to commit suicide within the past 12 months due to drinking or drug use.

- 11 percent of college students report vandalizing or damaging property while drunk.

- 31 percent of college students meet the criteria for a diagnosis of alcohol abuse, and 6 percent for a diagnosis of alcohol dependence in the past 12 months.[534]

Finally, alcohol is the leading "gateway" drug. There is a definite link between alcohol use and the tendency to move on to heavier types of drugs. Sixty-one percent of all drug abusers report alcohol was the first drug they ever used. In addition, kids aged 12 to 17 who use alcohol are 7.5 times more likely to use other drugs than those who never drank.[535]

When all is said and done, underage drinking costs Americans $62 billion a year in costs related to crime, lost work, hospital bills, and long-term damages. Every underage drinker costs society an average of $4,680 a year.[536]

Tobacco

Many elementary-age kids let their curiosity get the best of them, and they enter the grown-up world of adults and older teenagers by trying to smoke. My father was aware of the temptation I'd feel to smoke while growing up because of his own experience as a young boy. Consequently, when I was in elementary school, he told me on several occasions that when I wanted to try smoking, all I had to do was tell him. He also let me know my initial puffs would be on several of the biggest cigars he could buy, all smoked in succession. He knew my curiosity would be satisfied quickly if I had a near-death experience that included coughing, choking, and vomiting. Little did my father know his offer came long after my first attempt to smoke—at age five. Fortunately for me, my young neighborhood friend and I couldn't light the cigarettes we'd stolen from her mother's kitchen cabinet. (We didn't realize you were supposed to inhale instead of exhale.) Needless to say, I never became a smoker.

A recent survey notes that more than 70 million people aged 12 and older used a tobacco product at least once during the month prior to being interviewed.[537] Twenty percent of the adult population smokes cigars,[538] almost 8 million people over the age of 12 use smokeless tobacco regularly.[539] The Centers for Disease Control and Prevention report that tobacco use "remains the leading preventable cause of death in the United States, causing approximately 440,000 premature deaths each year."[540] Over the last 40 years, cigarettes have caused 12 million deaths, including the deaths of 94,000 infants due to mothers smoking during pregnancy.[541] When all is said and done, smoking is responsible for one in five deaths[542] and costs the U.S. more than $167 billion a year in health-care costs, including $92 billion in productivity losses and $75.5 billion in medical expenses.[543]

*Teenage tobacco facts and figures.*Each year the tobacco industry spends $15.5 billion—or $34 million a day—advertising their products.[544] Of that money, $237 million is spent on advertising smokeless tobacco.[545] In addition, almost $18 million is spent on distributing free samples of smokeless tobacco in the hope of generating new users.[546] Billboards, magazines, and even race cars have been used to encourage kids, teenagers, and adults to partake of the "benefits" of smoking and using tobacco products. Everyone knows that when it comes to tobacco addiction, if you can hook 'em young, then you'll have 'em forever.

Thirteen percent of all high school seniors report they initiated cigarette use by the sixth grade.[547] Among today's high school students, more than 54 percent have tried smoking, 13.4 percent have been regular daily smokers, and 23 percent had smoked cigarettes during the 30 days prior to the survey.[548] One-third of all of today's smokers had their first cigarette by the age of 14.[549]

What most parents don't realize is that early tobacco use isn't just limited to cigarettes. Each and every day, 2,200 young people (ages 11 to 19) try smokeless tobacco ("snuff" or "chew") for the first time, and 830 become regular users.[550] Originally thought to be a safe alternative to cigarettes, smokeless tobacco is addictive and dangerous. Keeping a pinch of smokeless tobacco in your mouth for 30 minutes delivers as much nicotine to the body as smoking three to four cigarettes.

In addition to cigarettes and smokeless tobacco, 12.8 percent of high school students and 5.2 percent of middle school students are current cigar smokers. More than 3 percent of high school students and 2.6 percent of middle school students are current pipe smokers. In recent years, teenagers have discovered hand-rolled, flavored, herbal cigarettes known as *bidis* (pronounced "bee-dees"). Imported from India and sold cheaply, they come in a variety of flavors (such as cinnamon, orange, chocolate, vanilla, and grape) and are likened to a dessert and smoking all rolled into one. Kids who don't like regular cigarettes are easily drawn to the trendy and cool bidis. Three percent of high school seniors report having smoked bidis.[551]

Kreteks (pronounced "cree-techs") are clove cigarettes that have recently made their way into the teenage population. More than 7 percent of high school seniors have smoked these Indonesian cigarettes.[552]

No matter what they say, the tobacco industry is targeting your kids. Its economic survival depends on it. The industry knows that 4,500 new smokers must begin smoking each day if it's to maintain sales levels to compensate for those who quit or die.[553] Current tobacco-use trends among teenagers indicate the industry's efforts are successful. If they continue on the same track, 80 percent of American smokers will have become regular smokers before they reach the age of 18.[554]

And finally, studies indicate that if your kids are smokers, then they're many times more likely than teenaged nonsmokers to use a variety of other drugs. Teenagers (ages 12 to 17) who reported having smoked in the last 30 days are three times more likely to use alcohol, eight times more likely to smoke marijuana, and 22 times more likely to use cocaine during those last 30 days than those who had not smoked.[555]

Drugs

America has a drug abuse problem that is touching too many of our teenagers. More than 53 percent of all teenagers will have used an illicit drug at least once by the time they reach their senior year of high school.[556] More than 40 percent of America's high school seniors reported using illicit drugs during a one-year period.[557] Statistics for the entire U.S. population show that 62.5 percent of all American adults have used an illicit drug by the time they reach their late twenties.[558]

It's sad to note that many are in the dark when it comes to teenagers and drugs. Not only are we unaware of the types of drugs kids are using, but we also don't know when our kids are using them. We must be aware of the fact that many teenagers are experimenting with illicit drugs and some become regular users. What types of drugs are today's teenagers using?

Depressants. Teenagers who want to relax or reduce their level of anxiety will often turn to depressants. While these drugs sedate and slow down the activity of the central nervous system, many teenagers will use stronger and more toxic doses in order to enter into a state of euphoria and excitement before the sedating power of the drug takes effect. These drugs initially elevate a person's mood. Kids are using them to reduce anxiety and lower their inhibitions.

Just over 10 percent of America's high school seniors report having used some sort of depressant without a doctor's prescription.[559] Tranquilizers and barbiturates are among the most commonly used and abused depressants. Another popular depressant is Quaalude (also known as "methaqualone"), a commercial drug removed from the market in the early 1980s due to widespread abuse, although it continues to be manufactured and sold illegally. It's still found in the student population, with 1.3 percent of high school seniors reporting use.[560]

Depressants are highly addictive, and long-term users develop physical and psychological dependence on these drugs. In addition, those who abuse depressants on a regular basis build a physical tolerance, requiring greater and greater dosages in order to feel the desired effects of the drug.

The physical side effects of depressant addiction can include convulsions, fatigue, nausea, impaired memory and concentration, fever, depression, slurred speech, drowsiness, confusion, cirrhosis of the liver, sexual impotence, paranoia, irritability, mood swings, violence, coma, and death.

There are several trade and slang names for different types of depressants, most of which are ingested orally in the form of tablets and capsules (although some forms are injected): methaqualone, Phenobarbital, Nembutal, Seconal, Amytal, Luminal, Ativan, Halcion, Xanax, Valium, Librium, Mebaral, Serax, Tranzene, Dalmane, ludes, soaps, quacks, blue devils, yellow jackets, blue heavens, downers, barbs, reds, phennies, tooies, yellows, red devils, purple hearts, rainbows, double trouble, Christmas trees, goofballs, candy downers, sleeping pills, tranks, mandrex, quad, quay, and blockbusters.

One depressant that's made frequent news in recent years is Rohypnol (pronounced *ro-hip-nol*), a sedative that's relatively cheap, odorless, colorless, tasteless, and dissolves quickly. It should come as no surprise that the drug is often used in sexual assaults because it can produce "anterograde amnesia," meaning people who take it may not be able to remember what happened to them while under its influence. It's become known as a "club drug" or "date rape drug," due to the fact that sexually aggressive males will secretly slip it into an unsuspecting female's drink. The victims can't taste it, but then they wake up several hours later often unable to remember anything that happened.

As with all dangerous and illicit drugs, parents should beware and be aware. The white pill can be identified by the imprints "ROCHE" or "RH" and a number 1 or 2. In addition, this is a drug that consistently drug-free kids should be aware of. Because while they may never purchase and use roofies themselves, it may be unsafe for them to assume this drug wasn't placed in a drink of theirs at parties.

Another popular club or date-rape drug is GHB (gamma-hydroxybutyrate), known on the street as G, Georgia homeboy, grievous bodily harm, liquid ecstasy, vita-G, soap, and easy lay. This central nervous system depressant was originally used by body builders to aid in fat reduction and muscle building. Colorless and odorless, it can be slipped into an unsuspecting victim's drink without detection.

Hallucinogens. Almost 9 percent of America's high school seniors report using a hallucinogen sometime in their lives.[561] Hallucinogens act on the central nervous system, producing mood and perceptual changes, including a loss of contact with reality. Teenagers report using hallucinogens because they give "insightful experiences," feelings of exhilaration, and a sense of being powerful.

Chronic users can become psychologically dependent on the drugs, craving the altered mental state they produce. There's no proof that any sort of physical dependence develops, although there are numerous short- and long-term consequences to their use.

There are several types of hallucinogens being used by teenagers today. The first is LSD (lysergic acid diethylamide), a drug that has been used by 3.5 percent of today's high school seniors.[562] In recent years, the drug has found renewed interest among suburban teenagers. LSD is relatively cheap. A hit that lasts from 10 to 12 hours can be purchased for two to five dollars on the street. Kids who use LSD will ingest it, lick it off paper, place it in their eyes with an eyedropper, sniff it, or inject it. In the short term, users can expect to take an exhilarating trip through a hallucinatory fantasy world.

While there are some who claim LSD is relatively harmless, it's extremely dangerous and very unpredictable. One doctor says, "Taking acid is equivalent to playing Russian roulette with chemicals."[563] Users can suffer from panic attacks, nightmares, and psychosis. Another common adverse reaction is the flashback, a reexperiencing of the effects of the drug, sometimes weeks and months after taking it (this has been known to occur among 25 percent of LSD users). "Bad trips" can lead to violence and self-destructive behavior. LSD is also known as acid, sugar cubes, trips, hits, doses, tabs, windowpane, blotter, boomers, cubes, microdot, yellow sunshines, big D, the beast, blue cheer, California sunshine, the hawk, the ghost, and sacrament.

Another of the more popular hallucinogens is PCP (phencyclidine), which has been used by 2.4 percent of today's high school seniors.[564] It was first developed in 1959 as an anesthetic agent to dissociate or detach patients from all bodily sensations so no pain was felt during surgery. Because of its negative side effects, its use on humans was discontinued, and it was used solely in veterinary medicine. It comes in tablets, capsules, and colored powders. PCP users usually smoke the white crystalline powder in tobacco or marijuana cigarettes and may also snort, eat, or inject it. Initially, this dangerous drug produces colorful hallucinations and even out-of-body experiences. While under PCP's influence, users can experience blurred vision, slurred speech, muscle rigidity, seizures, bizarre behavior, violent behavior toward self or others, coma, and even death. The full range of PCP's long-term effects is not known; however, some users experience long-term psychosis. This psychologically addictive drug is also known as angel dust, horse tranquilizers, embalming fluid, killer weed, crystal, superweed, supergrass, rocket fuel, peace pill, boat hog, boat, love boat, Shermans, ozone, wack, and hog.

Although not as popular as LSD and PCP, other hallucinogens teenagers are using include *psilocybin* (a brown mushroom) and *mescaline*, a substance found in the peyote cactus, which has been widely used by Native American tribes as part of their religious rituals.

In recent years, a variety of new hallucinogens have found their way into the teenage population. Many have been popularized through the Internet, where curious teenagers and experienced drug users share ideas and learn new "tricks of the trade." A small number of teenagers have used *jimsonweed*, a hallucinogenic and poisonous plant that's legal, free, and sometimes deadly. Also known as "thornapple," jimsonweed is an annual from the potato family that grows three to five feet high and bears a round, spiny fruit roughly two inches across and full of black seeds. The plant's leaves are rank smelling, lobed, and five to eight inches in length. Known by the botanical name *Datura Stramonium*, the plant's showy light blue or white trumpet-shaped flowers are four inches in length.

The history of jimsonweed use for its hallucinatory and medicinal effects is well documented. The seeds and leaves were used in rituals by eastern Woodland tribes of North America. The smoke is used in India to relieve severe cases of asthma. The active chemicals in jimsonweed (atropine, scopolamine, and hyoscyamine) are sometimes found in drugs used to control heartbeat and spasms during surgery.

Teenagers looking for a high get more than they bargain for when they eat jimsonweed seed or drink a tea brewed with the plant's leaves and regular tea, the two most common forms of ingestion. While the high from the tea is reported to be tamer than eating the seeds, both are extremely intense and dangerous. Jimsonweed abusers experience deliriousness, bizarre hallucinations, and strange behavior. Parents who suspect jimsonweed abuse should look for these signs along with restlessness, irritability, dry mouth, headache, coma, convulsions, decreased sweating, dilated pupils, and heart-rate abnormality. Experienced drug users have described the jimsonweed high as being one of the worst they ever experienced.

Another hallucinogen experiencing new popularity is *Salvia Divinorum*, a substance touted on one Internet site as "the mind bender" that will "jumpstart your senses." A member of the mint family, Salvia Divinorum (a.k.a., divining sage and herb-of-the-virgin) is a perennial herb and powerful natural hallucinogen as powerful as LSD. But unlike LSD, Salvia is entirely legal and unregulated, making it very easy and cheap to obtain. The drug can be bought at some record, health, and spirituality stores, but is more easily obtained on the Internet. You can even bid on it on eBay. The plant is native to Mexico, where it was used by the Mazatec tribe in spiritual and medicinal rituals. The plant grows in clusters to more than three feet in height. It has large green leaves and squared hollow stems. Users typically smoke or chew the leaves. When smoked, the effects are felt within 30 seconds and last about 30 minutes. When chewed, the effects appear within five to ten minutes. Users experience visionary trances (bright lights, vivid colors, pronounced shapes), a loss of control of their body, slurred speech, and a sense of being transported to a different place and time.

Ketamine is another hallucinogen that's become increasingly well known over the last few years. This legal animal tranquilizer has become a popular "club drug" frequently used by teenagers who attend long-running rave parties—its effects are intensified by using it in combination with alcohol, ecstasy, or other drugs. Odorless and tasteless, it's often slipped into drinks and used as another date-rape drug. The drug produces a high that can last up to two hours and includes a loss of sense of time and identity, a feeling of being lifted out of one's body, hallucinations, and a dream-like state. Available in liquid, powder, and pill form, it's ingested through swallowing, snorting, injecting, drinking, or smoking. Ketamine is also known as Cat Valium, K, Special-K, Vitamin K, new Ecstasy, psychedelic heroin, Ketalar, Ketaject, Super-K, and breakfast cereal.

Narcotics. These drugs depress the central nervous system and, at the same time, relieve pain. Narcotic users like the drugs because of the initial euphoric high and the feelings of relief and relaxation. The user feels an almost immediate surge of pleasure that yields to a gratifying high. Users become very docile and dreamy when under the influence. This would explain the reported use by teenagers seeking relief from the anxiety they feel as they pass through adolescence.

There are many short- and long-term negative effects related to narcotic abuse: drowsiness, nausea, vomiting, and death due to central respiratory system depression can all occur during usage.

The symptoms of heavy long-term use are severe psychological and physical dependence, high tolerance and the accompanying need for bigger and bigger doses, constipation, loss of appetite, and death from overdose.

Since many narcotics are taken by injection, users also run the risk of contracting AIDS, hepatitis, and other communicable diseases that might be spread through the use of a dirty needle. Those who try to get off the narcotic habit find it extremely painful and difficult to withdraw. Narcotics are so addictive that even short-term use can result in enough dependence to cause severe withdrawal symptoms.

There are several types of narcotics, many of which are derivatives of *opium*. Opium is made by air drying the juice that has been extracted from the unripened seed pods of the oriental poppy plant. The juice dries into a brownish gum that's formed into cakes or bricks. After being ground into powder, opium is either smoked or eaten. It is also known as O, op, black pills, block, black stuff, tar, gum, and hop. Other opium derivatives include paregoric, Dover's powder, and parepectolin. The chemical substance in opium that causes its effects is morphine, which is injected or sniffed by those who abuse it. Narcotics and opiates other than heroin have been used by almost 13 percent of today's high school seniors.[565]

The most well-known derivative of opium is *heroin*, a highly addictive narcotic gleaned from morphine, and it's extremely deadly. Developed in 1898 by the Bayer Company in Germany, heroin was found to be a more effective pain reliever than morphine. Pure heroin is a white crystalline powder that is sniffed, smoked, or injected. It's usually liquefied from powder, cooked, and injected ("shot up" or "mainlined"). While 1.5 percent of high school seniors report heroin use, the biggest usage increases are occurring at younger ages, where already 1.5 percent of eighth graders have used the drug.[566] The rise could be attributed to new and inexpensive forms of heroin that are high in purity and can be sniffed or smoked rather than injected. Heroin is also know as H, horse, junk, smack, scag, stuff, harley, harry, brown sugar, skunk, white horse, mud, hairy, joy powder, and thing.

A growing number of teenagers are abusing prescription narcotics found in the family medicine cabinet. These include anything containing *codeine, Darvon, Percocet, Demerol, Percodan,* and *Vicodin.* Prescribed as analgesics to treat pain, abusers will swallow or inject them. They're highly addictive. Nearly one in five members (19 percent) of the teenage population have used these prescription medications without a prescription, with one-third of all teenagers believing there's "nothing wrong" with using prescription medicines without a prescription "once in a while."[567]

In recent years, the fastest growing prescription narcotic of choice is *OxyContin.* Originally developed by Germans in 1916, OxyContin was approved by the FDA in 1995 as a 12-hour time-release prescription painkiller for those who suffer from chronic pain. Since then, millions of legitimate users have heralded Oxy-Contin as an oral drug that's allowed them to resume a normal lifestyle while managing debilitating pain from arthritis, backache, or cancer recovery. Reports are that kids are paying upwards of $1 per milligram for the drug, also known as oxy, oc, killers, and oxycotton. The demand on the street has grown so fast that kids are robbing pharmacies, forging prescriptions, committing health care fraud, and "doctor shopping" (faking pain as they go from doctor to doctor in search of a prescription). Between 2002 and 2005 alone, there was a 38 percent rise in abuse of this drug among 18-year-olds.[568]

The drug has recently been labeled "Hillbilly Heroin" not only because of the intense high, but because its abuse among youth first appeared in the rural areas of Appalachia and Maine. The growing rates of abuse in those areas paralleled its legitimate use among residents of those blue-collar regions who found the drug to be helpful in calming the chronic pain they felt as a result of working years of manual labor in steel mills and coal mines.

After crushing or chewing the pills to disable the drug's time-release coating, kids who snort, swallow, or inject OxyContin report experiencing a powerful and immediate high. Along with the high come feelings of intense happiness and euphoria where all the world's troubles seem to disappear. Short-term effects include constipation, nausea, vomiting, dizziness, headache, dry mouth, weakness, and even death. Long term effects include physical dependence, addiction, and tolerance.

Designer drugs. These drugs are manufactured by "street chemists" who alter the molecular structure of illegal drugs, thereby making them "legal." At first, the user experiences feelings of strength, confidence, and euphoria (often accompanied by hallucinations), while the side effects include tremors, impaired speech, paralysis, drooling, and permanent brain damage. Injected, inhaled, or ingested, these drugs mimic the effects of other drugs; however, designer drugs are sometimes several hundred times stronger than the drugs they imitate. As a result, it's not uncommon for users to overdose.

The most popular of all designer drugs is ecstasy, which has been promoted (to teenagers) as a way to achieve warm and loving relaxation. It's been used by 5.4 percent of high school seniors.[569] Using ecstasy also lowers inhibitions while heightening the sensory experience. So it's no surprise the drug has also found widespread acceptance among those who attend rave parties—all-night celebrations where partygoers dance to the accompaniment of music, videos, and light shows.

Ecstasy (a.k.a., Adam, X-TC, MDMA, clarity, essence, roll, hug drug, Eve, lover's speed, hug, beans, peace, STP, X, and E) is a synthetic mind-altering drug with hallucinogenic and amphetamine-like properties. The drug was patented in 1914 by Merck and used as an appetite suppressant by soldiers during World War I. The drug was then tucked away until it was tested on animals as part of a series of CIA mind-control experiments in the 1950s. During the 1970s, therapists rediscovered MDMA and began to use it as a "miracle drug" that would get their patients to open up and release their emotions. Therapists touted MDMA's benefits for patients who were depressed, anxious, suffering from Post-Traumatic Stress Disorder, or who were experiencing rape-related trauma. In June 1985, the DEA banned the drug's manufacture, sale, and possession since it has no medicinal usefulness and a high potential for abuse.

Ecstasy takes effect between 30 and 45 minutes after ingestion and leads to a three- or four-hour high or "rolling." The drug is particularly attractive to ravers since reported effects include an increased sense of happiness, emotional connectedness, and the ability to move and express oneself freely. But side effects can include confusion, depression, sleep problems, anxiety, psychosis, nausea, blurred vision, muscle tension, and rapid heart rate.

Since 1993, individuals seeking the ecstasy high have sidestepped its illegality by using forms of *herbal ecstasy* (a.k.a., Cloud 9, Ultimate Xphoria, X, and Rave Energy), a legal and cheap organic alternative. Sold in health-food stores, specialty shops, and boutiques, herbal ecstasy is an attractively packaged combination of the herb mu huang (a.k.a., ephedra, an amphetamine-like stimulant used in cold remedies, weight-loss pills, and muscle-builders) and other herbs high in caffeine content (Kola nut, green tea, etc.). Advertised to deliver increased energy, sexual sensations, and inner visions, the combination takes effect in an hour. But investigations into herbal ecstasy continue amid reports of heart attacks, nerve damage, strokes, seizures, nervousness, vomiting, insomnia, high blood pressure, and even death associated with its use. Not surprisingly, its sale has been banned in several states, and the federal government banned the sale of dietary supplements containing ephedra in 2004.

Synthetic heroin (Tentanyl) is known on the street as China, White China, white, Persian white, dance fever, friend, goodfella, jackpot, murder 8, Tango and Cash, and TNT. As it's 100 to 200 times more potent than heroin, this powerful designer drug can be fatal even in very small amounts. It has been known to cause Parkinson's disease-like symptoms and irreversible brain damage.

Inhalants. Several years ago I was speaking at a junior high retreat when the camp's kitchen crew discovered that an entire case of canned whipped cream was faulty. Every can was out of gas. After further investigation, my theory proved correct. A group of boys had raided the kitchen and sucked the nitrous oxide propellant out of the cans in an effort to get high.

Inhalants are easy to obtain, inexpensive, and popular, especially among younger teenagers who have difficulty obtaining alcohol and drugs. They're the most widely used class of drug among eighth graders, and many elementary school kids are experimenting with them. Kids will sniff them directly from the source, from a paper bag, or from rags saturated with the substance. The most popular of these "garbage drugs" are Scotchgard, nonstick cooking spray, gasoline, turpentine, nail-polish remover, butane, typewriter correction fluid, room deodorizers, brake fluid, glues, spray paint, hair spray, and aerosol propellants. Some teenagers even get high from bromochlorodifluoromethane (BCF), the propellant used in gas-based fire extinguishers. Others are using butane-lighter refills, squirting the butane right down their throats.

Like other central nervous system depressants, inhalants are used for the initial high and euphoria they give. More than 17 percent of eighth graders surveyed said they'd used inhalants at least once.[570] Inhalant abuse kills brain cells; damages the liver, kidney, lungs, and bone marrow; can result in hearing loss; and can cause cardiac arrest. Death can result from heart attack, choking on vomit, losing consciousness while a plastic bag is over the head, or losing consciousness in a dangerous place (falling or drowning).

While use is difficult to detect, you can discern signs of teenage inhalant abuse by looking for teary, glazed, or red eyes; facial rash; chemicals on their breath; erratic behavior; slurred speech; and a decline in school performance.

Teens refer to these garbage drugs as laughing gas, whippets, poppers, snappers, bullet, locker room, bolt, rush, climax, gunk, and buzz bombs.

Steroids. Four percent of all high school students have taken steroid pills or shots without a prescription at least once during their lifetime.[571] The great majority of steroid users are boys, who say they use them in an effort to improve their speed, strength, athletic performance, physique, and popularity.

Teens who use steroids find that the habit is costly, with the expense extending beyond their wallets. There are 70 known side effects of steroids use. The physical effects of anabolic-steroid use include severe acne, premature balding, jaundice, breast enlargement, shrinking testicles, stunted growth, liver disease, heart disease, cancer, kidney disease, sterility, and blood-pressure problems. Also common are sudden bursts of anger and violent behavior. Sadly, most kids ignore the nasty side effects of steroid use because of their preoccupation with looking better.

In spite of these risks, only 55.7 percent of high school seniors see great harm or risk in taking steroids.[572] A surprising number of students find that steroids are "easy" or "very easy" to obtain, including almost 20 percent of eighth graders, almost 30 percent of tenth graders, and 42.6 percent of twelfth graders.[573] Known on the street as juice, Arnolds, gym candy, pumpers, stackers, weight trainers, and roids, steroids come in both liquid and tablet form and can be taken orally or injected.

Cocaine. As early as their senior year in high school, 8 percent of our teenagers have tried cocaine, the most addictive drug currently known to humankind.[574] For years, cocaine has been popular as a white-collar drug used socially and extensively among middle- and upper-class adults.

Cocaine, a central nervous system stimulant, is a white powder that comes from the leaves of the South American coca plant. Relatively inexpensive at $70 to $100 a gram, cocaine is usually inhaled through the nose or it can be injected. Frequent use can lead to ulcerated and collapsed nostrils. Cocaine is also injected under the skin or into veins, increasing the risk of becoming infected with a communicable disease transmitted through dirty needles. A more dangerous method is known as "freebasing," in which volatile solvents are used to prepare the drug for smoking. Death or severe injury can occur when the mixture explodes.

Used in low doses, cocaine produces a short-lived sensation of euphoria with feelings of increased energy and alertness. Larger doses intensify the high but can lead to bizarre and violent behavior. Coming down from the high can slide the user into a depression. Physical effects include accelerated heartbeat, faster breathing, sweating, rise in body temperature, tremors, nausea, chest pain, convulsions, and impotence. Death from overdose is not unusual. Those who become addicted begin to center their lives on obtaining the drug and getting high. The drug becomes central to their thoughts, emotions, and activities.

Cocaine is also called coke, snow, flake, white, blow, bump, Charlie, nose candy, big D, snowbirds, lady, sneeze, star dust, happy dust, and toot. Taking the drug is often referred to as doing a line.

Crack. Almost one in every 25 high school seniors has tried the highly addictive and inexpensive smokable form of cocaine known as *crack*.[575] For just a few dollars, a teenager can buy a product four to 10 times stronger than cocaine, although the physical and psychological side effects of crack are virtually the same as those of cocaine.

The effects of crack's potent high are felt within 10 seconds and last from five to 20 minutes. Users describe the initial feeling of euphoria as similar to having sex. And the craving for another high can cause psychological addiction in a matter of days. Coming down from the high has been described as a crushing depression.

The process of converting cocaine to crack (by mixing cocaine, water, and baking soda) is so easy and simple to do that it's being done in kitchens all over the United States. The finished product looks like small lumps of soap shavings that have the texture of porcelain, and it's usually packaged in small vials.

Crack is also known as rock, readyrock, French fries, and teeth.

Stimulants. Drugs that stimulate the central nervous system and increase the activity of the brain or spinal cord are known as *stimulants*. The 13.1 percent rate of usage among high school seniors can be explained by the drugs' production of greater energy, increased alertness, and feelings of euphoria.[576] Kids under tremendous pressure to perform (especially academically) and balance a busy and tiring schedule are especially attracted to stimulant abuse. Kids are also attracted to the feelings of self-confidence, competence, and power that come from using the drugs. The downside is that as a stimulant wears off, depression and drowsiness occur.

The class of stimulants known as *amphetamines* produces effects that resemble those of the naturally occurring substance adrenaline. Amphetamines were initially used during World War II when high doses were given to soldiers and pilots in an effort to combat battle fatigue and to increase alertness. Today many truck drivers and students use them in order to stay awake for long periods of time. Amphetamines appear most commonly as capsules and tablets. Slang names include bennies, black beauties, crosses, hearts, LA turnaround, speed, truck drivers, uppers, dexies, pep pills, diet pills, footballs, cranks, splash, copilots, bumble bees, zip, go-fast, and mother's little helpers.

Stimulant users build a tolerance to the euphoric effects of the drugs and eventually need to use more in order to achieve the desired results. Psychological dependence on stimulants leads to long-term addiction and can sometimes end in brain damage or death.

A run is an extended period of stimulant use that lasts from three to five days. During the first day, the user feels euphoric, self-confident, and extremely sociable. The second day brings an inability to concentrate and severe mood swings. Visions, paranoia, and violent aggressive behavior are not unusual. Toward the end of the run, the user finds it increasingly difficult to cope with the world and will sink into an exhausted and lengthy sleep.

Methamphetamine. An amphetamine derivative that deserves special mention and attention is methamphetamine, a highly potent and addictive drug that has been sweeping through youth and young adult culture at increasing levels over the past few years. Nearly 5 percent of high school seniors said they'd used it; and, sadly, methamphetamine use is occurring at younger and younger ages. During that same year, 3.1 percent of eighth graders had also used this dangerous and deadly drug. Users ingest, smoke, inject, or snort the drug. Most users are attracted to the drug for the intense euphoria of the initial rush—or flash—that is quite pleasurable.

Also known as "meth," this potent central nervous system stimulant is usually used in powder or crystal form and is illicitly manufactured in crude countertop meth labs across the country. Its manufacture and abuse has reached such alarming proportions the government is limiting the sale of over-the-counter cold medications that contain pseudoephedrine.

The effects of methamphetamine are devastating. Users can become addicted after only one use. It's not uncommon for users to experience paranoia, violent behavior, confusion, and anxiety. Brain damage, convulsions, strokes, and death can also occur. Another side effect is meth-mouth, characterized by a rapid rotting of the teeth. Regular users appear to age decades after only a handful of months or years of use.

"Ice" is a smokable form of methamphetamine that is high in purity and similar in size and appearance to quartz or rock salt. As addictive as crack and cocaine, ice is so pure that all of its stimulant properties are intensified. Users feel an immediate and powerful euphoria, followed by a long-lasting high of eight to 24 hours. An ice high makes one feel bright, awake, happy, and good about oneself. During initial use, ice facilitates the ability to function so effectively that more can be accomplished in less time. In addition, users report an increase in sexual pleasure and performance.

Ice has been reported to cause nausea, vomiting, rapid respiratory and heart rates, increased body temperature, and coma at high dosage levels. Overdoses are common as it is difficult to control the amount of potent smoke that is inhaled. Long-term side effects include aggressive behavior, hallucinations, paranoia, kidney failure, and addiction.

Finally, a growing number of teenagers are abusing, without prescriptions, *Methylphenidate* (trade name Ritalin), along with other prescription stimulants. While the drug is widely prescribed and used for the treatment of ADD and ADHD, students who've not been diagnosed with these disorders often offer to purchase pills from those who have. Students typically abuse these pills as a way to keep alert while trying to complete academic work. Non-prescription use was reported by 2.4 percent of eighth graders, 3.4 percent of tenth graders, and 4.4 percent of twelfth graders.[577] Street names include Kibbles and Bits, Pineapple, JIF, MPH, R-ball, Skippy, the smart drug, and vitamin R.

Cannabis (marijuana). The cannabis plant, or hemp, is the source of marijuana, hashish, and THC (tetrahydrocannabinol), its biologically active ingredient. Almost 45 percent of today's high school seniors say they've used marijuana.[578] One in 20 smokes the drug on a daily basis.[579] By the time they reach eighth grade, 16.5 percent have used marijuana.[580] Among those one to four years beyond high school, almost 58 percent of those not in college, and just over 49 percent of college students have used marijuana.[581] As one of the "gateway" drugs that leads to further and harder drug use, marijuana is increasingly popular among younger teenagers.

The least potent and most commonly used form of cannabis is the dried leaves, buds, and stems of the plant. Hash, a more potent form of THC, is made from the plant's resin and is pressed into small cakes or bricks. The most potent form of THC is hash-

ish oil, a condensed and distilled liquid resin that is often added to a joint (marijuana cigarette) and smoked. While marijuana's potency varies from climate to climate and ounce to ounce, today's crop is two to 10 times more potent than the marijuana of 15 to 20 years ago.

Sold by the ounce or "lid" (slightly less than an ounce), marijuana is smoked in a joint or pipe. Others remove the tobacco from a Phillies brand Blunt cigar and replace it with marijuana, something known as "smoking a blunt." A bong or rush tube is used to send the smoke to the lungs more efficiently. A small clothespin-like roach clip is used to hold a joint and allows the user to smoke it right down to the end. Some users bake marijuana into brownies, but less THC is absorbed when it's eaten.

Teenagers smoke marijuana for the euphoric high that often leads to fits of laughter and talking more than usual. Other short-term effects include increased heart and respiratory rate, reddening of the eyes, and sleepiness. Used in very high doses, marijuana's effects can be similar to those of hallucinogens.

Continued use can lead to respiratory problems, lung cancer, loss of energy, confused thinking, slow reactions, impaired memory, and apathy. Some frequent users lack initiative and don't seem to care about the future. They find it difficult to stay motivated, thinking things will take care of themselves. This is often referred to as "amotivational syndrome." Regular use builds up tolerance to the drug, requiring increased dosages in order to achieve the desired high. Physical and psychological dependence may also result.

Teenagers often refer to marijuana as pot, grass, weed, reefer, dope, Mary Jane, Thai sticks, Acapulco gold, herb, joint, smoke, buds, boom, chronic, gangster, blunt, dope, ganja, grass, skunk, bag, roach, dime, sinsemilla, and refer to the effects of the drug as getting high, getting wasted, getting stoned, and getting loaded.

Other drugs. By nature, drug-abusing teenagers are a curious bunch, always looking for new ways to get high or dull their senses. As a result, the last few years have seen teenagers embrace some new and different substances to abuse.

The family medicine cabinet and drug store shelf is where kids have found cough and cold medicines containing the cough suppressant DXM (Dextromethorphan) and codeine, substances that both have the potential for abuse. DXM is readily available as the active ingredient in more than 120 different brands of over-the-counter cough and cold medicines, including Robitussin. While safe in prescribed and recommended dosages, kids down larger doses to achieve a high that's likened to PCP or LSD. The cough syrup is rapidly guzzled and sometimes mixed with alcohol or soft drinks to enhance the flavor. Others ingest DXM through pills. Abuse of DXM is often called robodexing, robotripping, or robo-dosing. In some cases, the practice has been deadly.

Finally, some teenagers are abusing Viagra in the hope it will improve their sexual performance and endurance.

Why Are Teenagers Using Drugs and Alcohol?

As someone who has studied youth culture for the last two decades, I've seen the statistics, heard the stories, and come face-to-face with far too many people who've suffered the consequences of substance abuse. As a father of four, I've wrestled with the issue as it has touched my kids' lives in the world of their friends and peers. The situation is bad. To begin to turn the tide of adolescent substance abuse, those of us who are working with or raising teenagers must get beneath the statistics and behaviors to uncover the many "root reasons" why kids get involved with alcohol and drugs.

Reason #1: Curiosity and Experimentation

I've never met a teenager who used drugs and alcohol with the intent of getting hooked. The fact is, most kids, especially those who are younger, have their first experience with drugs and alcohol without understanding there are dangers involved. And those who are aware of the dangers somehow think they're immune—the it-will-never-happen-to-me syndrome.

Reason #2: Peer Pressure

The pressure starts early. One survey of fourth through sixth graders found that 30 percent report getting "a lot" of pressure from their classmates to drink beer.[582] My own conversations with middle and high school students indicate that pressure to drink alcohol is one of the most intense pressures churched kids feel from their peers. With a constant desire to fit in, be accepted, and be loved, teenagers who feel insecure and unloved at home are more susceptible and will give in to the pressure more easily. In some teenagers' minds, possible negative results of smoking, drinking, and using drugs become less of a price to pay than alienation from the crowd.

Reason #3: It's Fun

When asked why she drinks, Mary Ellen speaks for many teenagers: "It's fun, and besides, life is boring. I drink because there's nothing else to do." Today's teenagers are bored. Many of them find drugs and alcohol to be an exciting form of recreation that's cheap, easy, and fun to do with a group of friends.

Reason #4: To Look Grown Up

When teenagers realize they aren't kids anymore, they don't want to *look* like kids anymore either. Because they're growing, they aspire to look, feel, and be perceived as older than they really are. Sometimes they believe doing "adult" things will make them look and feel like adults.

Reason #5: Availability

Teenagers say drugs and alcohol are easy to obtain. More than 50 percent of eighth graders say cigarettes are "fairly easy" or "very easy" to get.[583] More than 81 percent of tenth graders say the same thing. Even though it's illegal to buy cigarettes until the age of 18, many underaged teenagers are still able to purchase tobacco products without being asked for proof of age. And alcohol is even easier for teenagers to acquire, as more than 64 percent of eighth graders and almost 84 percent of tenth graders find it "fairly easy" or "very easy" to get.[584]

Perhaps the most alarming source of alcohol for many teenagers is their parents. Some younger teenagers take their first drinks from the family liquor closet when left unsupervised at home. Kids who come home to an empty house are more likely than those supervised by adults to use cigarettes, marijuana, and alcohol. Other kids report that their parents allowed them to sip alcohol or even drink a full glass during holiday celebrations, as early as elementary school years. And I know of several cases where parents of teenagers supplied the alcohol and the location for parties in the hope that this would prevent their kids from drinking and driving. When Mom and Dad put their stamp of approval on drinking, how can a teenager believe any other voices that might say underage drinking is dangerous and wrong?

The growth of the Internet has contributed to the growth of prescription drug abuse among teenagers. Dr. Joseph Califano of the The National Center on Addiction and Substance Abuse says, "Any child can get, without a prescription, highly addictive controlled substances like OxyContin, Valium and Ritalin from Internet drug pushers. The trend of teen 'pharming parties' will continue to increase as long as these drugs are so easy to obtain."[585]

Finally, and perhaps most surprising, is the fact that the majority of high school seniors report that it is "fairly easy" or "very easy" to get marijuana (85.6 percent) or amphetamines (51.2 percent).[586]

Reason #6: Advertising

Ads are especially effective at recruiting young smokers and drinkers. Research shows that among teenagers, "exposure to advertisements has been shown to create positive opinions about alcohol, stronger intentions to use alcohol, and more alcohol consumption."[587] Because of where they're at developmentally, teenagers are fair game for advertising messages that suggest that drinking and smoking lead to maturity, sophistication, beauty, fun, and acceptance.

Reason #7: Pop-Culture Pressure

As stated earlier, many of today's pop-culture icons and role models send pro-substance abuse messages through their lyrics, videos, and high-profile lifestyles. But it's not just the world of popular music. Movies, television, radio, sports heroes, fashion, magazines, and the Internet are also cited as sources of substance-abuse pressure. The National Center on Addiction and Substance Abuse found that compared with teenagers who don't watch any R-rated movies, those who see three or more in a typical month (43 percent of 12- to 17-year-olds) are seven times more likely to smoke cigarettes, six times more likely to try marijuana, and five times more likely to drink alcohol.[588]

Other research points to the fact that about 75 percent of youth-rated and 90 percent of R-rated films contain tobacco use and imagery. It's estimated smoking in films is responsible for 38 percent of young people beginning to smoke.[589]

Reason #8: Family Problems

Numerous studies have shown a relationship between the family environment and the use of drugs and alcohol among adolescents. But anyone who's ever spent any significant amount of time with kids doesn't need scientific studies to prove the link. Kids who come from homes where there is divorce, separation, an absent parent, discord, marital conflict, unreasonable pressure or expectations, poor communication, abuse, or alcoholism are more likely to abuse alcohol and drugs. Conversely, kids who come from homes characterized by love, nurturing, affection, involvement, and marital harmony are less likely to abuse drugs and alcohol.

Reason #9: Escape

The life of the normal teenager is filled with all kinds of stresses. Drugs and alcohol often become the coping mechanisms for teenagers who have no other way to grow constructively through adolescence. Many teenagers report they drink when they're upset in order to feel better. Teenagers also report smoking helps them calm down when they're feeling a lot of stress.

In spite of the fact that alcohol and drugs deliver only a temporary high and escape—and are often followed by an even deeper depression—most kids believe it's better than suffering all the time.

Reason #10: To Cope

In recent years, experts have isolated a segment of the teenage population that seems to be embracing drugs and alcohol in an effort to cope with their inability to function properly during their adolescent years. This growing group appears to be self-medicating in an effort to feel or perform better. While the research is still in its infancy, it appears there's a link between teenagers who suffer from diagnosed or undiagnosed ADHD and substance abuse. Research is suggesting that the impulsive behavior of teenagers with ADHD keeps them from properly regulating their behavior, thus making them more prone to choose to abuse alcohol and drugs.

Other research suggests many teenagers with ADHD have discovered that the use of certain drugs helps them focus more clearly and accomplish more. Once they make the connection, they tend to self-medicate. While this is a trend certainly worth monitoring, it's important for parents of teenagers who struggle with ADHD to realize their kids may be at a greater risk for drug experimentation, abuse, and addiction.

Reason #11: Addiction

A teenager who abuses drugs and alcohol on a regular basis risks becoming one of the millions of kids who have serious problems with addiction.

In their book *Adolescents, Alcohol and Drugs*, Judith Jaynes and Cheryl Rugg describe the stages of drug and alcohol addiction among teens.

- **Stage 1 is Experimentation,** the time when the teenager's occasional use leads to mood changes that are generally positive, predictable, and enjoyable with few or no side effects. Not all adolescents stay in the experimentation stage. Some, their curiosity satisfied, quit. Others move on to stage 2.

- **Stage 2 is Social Use.** Adolescents remain in control of how much they use, when they use, and the effects of use. The use is moderate and for the purpose of fitting in. Kids in this stage will limit alcohol and drug use to weekend parties and social gatherings.

- **Stage 3 is Misuse.** The focus shifts from socializing to a personal desire to get high. The euphoric effect becomes more important than having a good time with friends. Use becomes more frequent and isn't limited to weekends and parties.

- **Stage 4 is Abuse.** When adolescents enter this stage, there's a preoccupation with being high. It's in this stage that parents, friends, and family members begin to see the obvious and ugly effects of substance abuse in their lives. Many kids in this stage will steal to support their daily habits. The goal is to stay high since a letdown leads to depression and aggressive behavior.

- **Stage 5 is Chemical Dependency.** When teens are depending on drugs and alcohol to feel normal. No longer are they "fun." The sense of euphoria is gone. Getting and taking drugs become a matter of survival. If daily, 24-hour use is interrupted, the adolescent feels powerless to function physically or mentally.[590]

Drug and alcohol addiction is the ugly end to what begins as curious experimentation. At this point, drugs and alcohol become the objects of worship in a life of physical and psychological dependency.

Signs and Symptoms of Teenage Alcohol and Drug Abuse

How do you know if a teenager needs help? Following are several charts listing major signs and symptoms of teenage substance abuse. Whether you're a youth worker or a parent (or both), DO NOT assume your kids are somehow immune to the pressures that lead to experimentation and addiction to drugs and alcohol. Instead, be aware of the signs so you'll know what to look for. Ignorance is your worst enemy.

Behavioral Signs of Teenage Substance Abuse

- An increase in erratic and drastic mood swings for no obvious reason
- Hostility and rebellion toward those in authority (such as parents, teachers, church)
- Stealing and shoplifting

- Unexplained increase in spending
- Little regard for personal safety and an increase in risky behavior (such as driving fast)
- Traffic tickets
- Vandalism
- Signs of depression (see chapter 11)
- Changes in eating habits
- Promiscuous sexual behavior
- Withdrawal from family and a dramatic increase in time spent alone at home
- Disorientation regarding time
- Memory lapses
- Cutting class
- Truancy and tardiness
- Decline in grades
- Involvement in fights
- Inability to concentrate
- Lack of motivation
- Verbal abusiveness
- Lack of communication with family
- Secretive behavior and telling family members to "stay out of my business"
- Panic, paranoia, suspicion
- Hallucinations or loss of touch with reality
- Change in activities
- Dropping out of sports programs
- Inability to hold down an after-school job
- Staying out all night or sneaking out
- An increase in mysterious phone calls
- Preoccupation with music or other media that promotes substance abuse

Social Signs of Teenage Substance Abuse

- Changes in their circle of friends
- Suddenly becoming more popular
- Suddenly becoming a loner and purposely separating from others

Physiological Signs of Teenage Substance Abuse

- Disheveled appearance
- Lack of concern for personal hygiene
- Smell of alcohol on their breath
- Smell of smoke on their clothing
- Constant smell of mints or onion rings on their breath (to cover up alcohol or marijuana use)
- Dilated pupils
- Bloodshot eyes
- Staggered speech
- Lethargy
- Long periods without sleep
- Long periods of sleep
- Sickly appearance
- Dramatic weight loss or weight gain

Obvious Signs of Teenage Substance Abuse

- Discovering drug paraphernalia (pipes, rolling papers, vials, lighters, burners, mirrors, razor blades, scales, matches, small plastic bags, pills)
- Spending time with kids who are known to use drugs and alcohol
- Disappearance of money or alcohol from the house
- Intoxication
- Expressing concerns about their substance abuse problem
- Burn marks on clothing or furniture
- Needle marks
- Arrest(s) for drug- or alcohol-related incidents

What Can You Do to Help Teenagers Make Safe and Godly Choices about Drugs and Alcohol?

Every one of our teenagers will be faced with the pressure, temptation, and opportunity to abuse drugs and alcohol. What choices will they make? As parents and youth workers we have the responsibility to give them the information and assistance they need in order to make the right decisions. If we choose not to give them guidance and support, they'll still have to make a choice. Do we want to let them make these decisions on their own?

The following suggestions for preventing and dealing with teenage substance abuse in your home might sound ridiculous because of their commonsense nature. But by making the effort to implement these strategies in your home, you'll be taking steps to steer your child away from substance abuse and its dangers.

Suggestion #1: Look in the Mirror

When it comes to drugs and alcohol, what kind of lifestyle are you modeling for your kids? Parents who drink often raise kids who drink. Alcoholics often raise alcoholics. Those who rely on prescription and over-the-counter drugs for relief from every little ailment raise kids who learn to do the same.

So ask yourself the following questions:

- Do you ever find yourself needing a drink in order to wind down in the midst of a stressful day?

- Do you feel you must have a drink in your hand in order to socialize at parties and with friends?

- Do you medicate yourself or your kids at the first sign of fever, tension, or the smallest pain?

- Does your family have a history of alcoholism or drug abuse?

- Is your medicine cabinet full of remedies?

Suggestion #2: Establish Standards and Rules

While discipline without love usually leads to rebellion, discipline with love is one of the greatest gifts we can give to our kids. Contrary to what some people may think, alcohol and drug use is relatively low among adolescents whose parents have set strict rules about chemical use. These rules are most effective when parents monitor their child's behavior and enforce those rules with rewards and punishments.

Researchers have found "strongly monitored adolescents are, in essence, doubly protected from substance abuse involvement: They have the protective benefits of effective socialization in the family and because they themselves are less likely to begin using drugs, they are less likely to find themselves in situations in which they will be exposed to drug-using friends."[591]

Take a stand and set some boundaries. Tell your kids what behaviors are and are not acceptable. Tell them why you won't allow them to drink, smoke, or use drugs. Spell out the punishment for breaking the rules. And if the rules are broken, carry through.

There are times when your kids will be out with their friends and forced to make a spur-of-the-moment decision about whether or not to participate in drinking or using drugs. The decision will be a whole lot easier for them to make if they already know your rules and expectations. At these times kids really appreciate the rules you've set for them. To be able to say, "No, I can't drink. If I do, my parents will flip," or "No, if I drink, I'll lose my license for a year," is a perfect escape route for your kids to take out of a pressure-filled situation.

Suggestion #3: Encourage Involvement with a Peer Group That Doesn't Support Drug and Alcohol Use

Substance abuse is strongly related to what a person's friends do. When it's always in your face, the temptation is huge. The Search Institute has concluded "parents can undermine the negative influence of friends both by steering kids away from certain associations and toward other relationships where the influence is known to be positive."[592] This was a strategy my wife and I had to battle through with one of our own kids for two years. It wasn't easy, as it was met with some resistance; but in the end, it paid great dividends.

Positive peer groups should include a church youth group, as well as other extracurricular involvements that will fill teenagers' time and make their potential involvement contingent on remaining substance free (sports teams, school clubs, and so on).

Get to know your teenager's friends. Unite with other parents in your community to ensure that social events for young people are substance free. Don't assume they are—always make a phone call to find out. And take the steps mentioned in previous chapters to build a strong positive peer group at your church. Healthy youth groups exercise a tremendous amount of positive influence on teenagers.

Suggestion #4: Don't Be an Enabler

Don't make it easy for your kids to drink and use drugs. Parents who give their kids lots of money and too much freedom risk letting them step beyond their abilities to make the best choices they can. Kids who are given free use of the car, unlimited gas, and unsupervised use of the house are at greater risk for getting into trouble with alcohol and drugs. Don't give a teenager alcohol or allow parties in your home that provide alcohol.

And finally, don't give them any excuse to drink. Build them up by loving them for who they are. Let them know they're important to you by giving them your time. Build a strong home and make your family life a priority.

Suggestion #5: Teach Your Kids about Drugs and Alcohol

Most teenagers are left to get their information about drugs and alcohol from unreliable sources. Some learn from their friends. Others learn from the media. Still others say they just "picked up" what they know. Only about one in three middle schoolers and high schoolers say parents talk to them "often" or "a lot" about tobacco, drugs, and alcohol.[593]

Seize teachable moments as your teenagers encounter drug and alcohol use and abuse in the media. Teach them to discern the true and false messages on TV shows. Help them pick apart the ridiculous promises and nature of alcohol and cigarette ads.

Finally, teach them it's against the law for minors to buy or drink alcoholic beverages. And if they get caught, be sure they're given the wonderful opportunity to learn from their mistakes by suffering the legal consequences of their actions. Don't work to get any of the legal ramifications "fixed" for them.

Suggestion #6: Teach a Biblical Theology of Substance Abuse

Our bottom-line desire for our Christian teenagers is that they'll bring honor and glory to God by being obedient to his will. We must help them come to an understanding of what it means to live the life of discipleship in regard to their attitudes and behaviors toward alcohol and drugs.

First, we must teach them that God has given them the responsibility to obey the laws of the government. Take the time to read and study Romans 13:1-3, 6-7 with your kids.

Second, study what Scripture has to say about drunkenness in passages such as Proverbs 23:20-21; 1 Corinthians 5:11; Galatians 5:19-21; Ephesians 5:18; and 1 Thessalonians 5:5-8.

Third, discuss the spiritual nature of the problems that lead kids to drink. Study the Bible together to look for God's answers to those problems.

And finally, walk your talk. A code of biblical moral conduct lived out in the house is the most powerful shaper of your child's own spiritual values and behaviors. Research has shown that parents are "more effective as advocates of drug abstinence if they can say, with credibility, that drug use is morally flawed behavior."[594]

Suggestion #7: Protect Them from Themselves

Parents often ask me whether or not it's appropriate for them to "snoop around" their child's room, backpack, car, cell phone bills, e-mails, and so on. While it's important for a teenager to have a sense of private space, there is absolutely nothing wrong with "invading" that space if you have any suspicions at all that your child is engaging in morally and physically dangerous behavior. If our teenagers are making decisions that are harmful, we must step in and do everything we can to protect them from themselves. It's especially important for you to monitor your child's private space if there is an established history—short or long—of substance abuse. Remember, you are your child's parent, not your child's friend.

I Know a Teenager Who's Abusing Drugs and Alcohol—What Do I Do?

The temptation is to deny that the ugly reality of teenage substance abuse has hit someone you know and love. But disbelief only allows the problem to continue and worsen. In order to redeem a situation gone wrong and to restore our teenagers to physical, spiritual, and emotional health, the substance-abuse problem must be acknowledged and addressed. Experts agree that now, more than ever, teenagers need loving adults—moms and dads and youth workers—who are committed to addressing the reality of their teenagers' problems by taking five steps on the road to undoing what's been done.

Step #1: Take a Deep Breath

Here are three bits of advice to heed as you take a deep breath and prepare for the very difficult road that lies ahead:

- First, don't panic. Losing your cool, composure, or head will only make the situation worse.

- Second, don't feel guilty. Your first priority is to eliminate the influence of substance abuse on your child. Wallowing around in guilt, shame, and self-pity can paralyze you and keep you from taking the needed steps. Remember, your kids have the freedom to make their own choices. For whatever reason, they have made the choice to abuse drugs and/or alcohol.

- Third, love your child. Now, more than ever, he needs to know you're going to stand by and love him unconditionally—in spite of his bad choices. When I asked a former teenage addict to tell me the best thing we can do when we discover this kind of problem, he answered without hesitation, "Love them!"

Step #2: Confront the Teenager about the Problem

After catching your breath, develop a plan for confronting the student immediately with your suspicion or knowledge of the problem. Delay only allows a bad situation to get worse. As you prepare to face the teenager, keep three objectives in mind:

- First, don't confront him while he's under the influence of alcohol or drugs. Because your goal is to get him to listen, be sure he's in a frame of mind to hear and understand what you're saying.

- Second, don't confront him until you're calm. Because your goal is to eliminate the drug problem and deal with the heart issues that have caused it, you should avoid any possibility of coming across with the alienating tone of a preacher or police interrogator.

- Third, you want the confrontation to yield an admission of your teenager's problem and a desire to get help. Because denial is a common problem for people struggling with chemical dependency, a process of *intervention* might be required to break through and motivate the teenager to seek help. An intervention is a well-planned confrontation that involves some combination of family members, friends, and professionals. Speaking with care, love, hope, and concern, the team shares examples of specific incidents in which the user's behavior has caused negative consequences for themselves and others. If an intervention is necessary, it's important you get some training or enlist the help of a professional who can structure and facilitate the session.

Step #3: Secure the Help of a Qualified Counselor

While we may know our kids better than anyone else does, the scope of a teenage substance abuse problem requires a course of corrective action and treatment that goes beyond what we can handle on our own. Gary Oliver, a trained substance abuse counselor in Pennsylvania, offers some straightforward advice to parents: "If you see a rattlesnake in your basement, you may want to call someone who knows something about rattlesnakes."

The best thing to do for a teenager—and for yourself—is to go to your pastor or a trusted counselor for a referral to a competent individual or program with a proven record of successfully handling teenage substance abusers. Look for a counselor who takes into account the spiritual dimension of teenage addiction problems. In a day and age where many counselors view "religion" as a crutch, you'll want to be sure you choose a Christian counselor who sees God as the solution, not part of the problem.

In cases where teenagers continue to deny their problems, even after intervention, they'll probably refuse to see a counselor. When a teenager refuses help, parents should continue to address the problem by going to a Christian counselor for themselves. A trained professional will help parents discover ways to break through to a teenager who seems unreachable.

Step #4: Determine the Depth of the Problem

In *Helping Your Struggling Teenager* psychologist Les Parrott distinguishes four possible and common types of adolescent drug users:[595]

- The least severe type of user is the *Experimenter*. He uses drugs or alcohol up to four or five times in order to gain acceptance by the peer group or to satisfy his curiosity as to what the high is all about.

- The *Recreationist* uses drugs as an avenue to share a pleasurable experience with friends, rather than for the mood or effect of the substance.

- The *Seeker* has a use pattern that goes beyond sharing an experience with peers. She pursues an altered state of consciousness and regularly uses drugs or alcohol to achieve that effect.

- The most dangerous and advanced adolescent abuser is the *Drug Head*. He's addicted to drugs and can't live without them. The use of drugs to feel okay indicates a strong physical and psychological dependence.

A thorough initial evaluation should determine where a teenager with a substance-abuse problem falls on the severity spectrum. Then, and only then, can an effective and appropriate course of treatment be recommended.

Step #5: Get Treatment

A qualified professional will work with parents to recommend and prescribe a course of treatment that's appropriate to the severity of the substance-abuse problem. Teenagers with more severe problems should be directed to some type of ongoing treatment program.

- *Outpatient care* is a cost-effective way for teenagers to continue with the regular activities of their daily lives while addressing their substance abuse problems. Teens with early-stage substance abuse problems can reap great benefits from the routine of attending meetings, counseling, and lectures several days a week after school then going home to practice what they've learned.

- *Inpatient care* is a comprehensive approach to treatment recommended for teenagers who need intensive support, supervision, and education. By getting away from the normal routines and stresses of daily life, teenagers are able to focus on the recovery process with the 24-hour support of a team of qualified medical and counseling professionals in a protected environment.

Parents who want to secure the best and most effective treatment for their teenagers should look for some basic elements in a treatment program:

- *First, the program should place teenagers in Christian counseling designed to increase awareness of their addiction, get to the heart issues of the problems, improve their coping skills, and lead them to establish and pursue goals for drug-free lifestyles.* Because substance abuse is not just a physical problem, counseling must address the spiritual and emotional issues as well.

- *Second, the program should involve parents and the rest of the family in the counseling and recovery process.* Teenage substance abuse problems don't occur in a vacuum. Treatment centers should recognize that family members need help themselves.

- *And finally, the possibility of a relapse should be addressed through a good follow-up program.* By some estimates, up to 70 percent of the chemically dependent resume alcohol or drug abuse within one year of treatment. Teenagers should leave treatment programs with relapse-prevention skills, a support network, and scheduled follow-up counseling.

Getting Personal

Over the last few years, I've asked several former teenage drug addicts and abusers to write down their stories. They're gut wrenching to read, and they include long lists of the types of substances that were abused and how often. On the average, these former addicts began using during the junior high years and were alcoholics, addicts, or regular users by the time they reached high school. When asked why they turned to drugs and alcohol, they consistently mention their struggles with the difficult years of adolescence and parents who were detached or absent. Another common thread to many of their stories is that most come from upper- and middle-class homes where parents were oblivious to their kids' spiritual, emotional, and developmental needs.

What about you? Do you take an active role in your teenagers' lives? Do you model godly values and behaviors? Do you pray for them continually? If you do, you're more likely to have substance-free teenagers who move into healthy adulthood. If you don't, now is the time to begin.

When Adolescence Hurts: The Dark World of Teenage Depression and Suicide

11

I can't handle this sucky world any longer.

—FROM A 15-YEAR-OLD'S SUICIDE NOTE

Why are you downcast, O my soul? Why so disturbed within me?

—PSALM 42:5

Sadly, I've sat with numerous suicide survivors—the parents, siblings, and friends of teenagers who've taken their own lives. The common thread running through all of their stories is that the loved ones' deaths took them completely by surprise. Now most of them speak about their own experience in the hope that the epidemic of teenage depression and suicide will start to wane.

One person who speaks openly about suicide and how it's touched his life is Phil, a father whose 17-year-old son took his own life. Phil and his wife have put together a Web site, and the first page reads, "My name is Phil and last year I lost my son to suicide. He was only 17. If you were like me, chances are you don't know anything about suicide or noticing the warning signs...but I do now. My wife and I have put this site together for both adults looking for some information in how to prevent this from happening to their kids and also for teens looking for help."[596]

Phil and his wife understand the value of information in the prevention of depression and suicide. In this chapter, we'll examine the ugly reality of teenage depression and suicide. It's my hope this information will help *you* as you try to help the teenagers you know and love to have a spiritually and emotionally healthy adolescence.

Teenage Suicide Facts and Figures

Today, suicide is the eleventh-leading cause of death in the United States, and the third-leading cause of death among teenagers.[597] While suicides account for 1.3 percent of all deaths in the United

States, they make up almost 12 percent of all deaths among 15- to 24-year-olds.[598] Every two hours and 11 minutes, a person under the age of 25 completes a suicide.[599] Official statistics indicate that roughly 6,000 teenagers a year take their own lives, but that number is believed to be low, since many suicides are reported as accidents in an effort to protect a family's privacy or to secure insurance settlements. At times, a family will rearrange the scene to hide the suicide, and some will even go so far as to hide the suicide notes. In some cases, coroners will only report those deaths where a note is found as a suicide. In other words, the real number of teenage suicides is much higher than the official number.

The growing number and intensity of problems associated with passing through the teenage years have contributed to this crisis. The teenage years are already a period of storm and stress. Add to that the societal factors that have made adolescence more difficult, and a growing number of teenagers are thinking about or attempting suicide. It comes as no surprise that the rate of suicide among 15- to 24-year-olds has tripled since 1960.[600] Along with heart disease, suicide is the fourth-leading cause of death for five- to 14-year-olds.[601]

The teenage suicide crisis has led researchers and the government to examine the problem closely. Many studies and surveys have shown that suicidal thoughts and considerations are far more prevalent than anyone ever knew. One national school-based survey of ninth through twelfth graders found that during the 12 months preceding the survey, 16.9 percent had seriously considered attempting suicide, 13 percent had made a specific plan about how they'd attempt suicide, 8.4 percent had actually attempted suicide one or more times, and 2.3 percent had made an attempt that required medical attention.[602]

High school girls were more likely (21.8 percent) than their male peers (12 percent) to have thought seriously about attempting suicide during the previous 12 months, and they were more likely (10.8 percent) to have attempted suicide than males (6 percent).[603] While fewer boys than girls will attempt suicide, the success rate among the 15- to- 19-year-old age group is 4.4 times greater than that of girls.[604] The reason is that males typically choose more violent means such as guns and hanging. Girls typically choose more nonviolent methods such as an overdose of pills or carbon monoxide poisoning. The highest rate of teenage suicides in America is among white males.

Suicide "clustering" is a phenomenon that suggests that those with friends or family members who've committed suicide may "catch" the inclination to do the same. Several years ago, officials at one Pennsylvania high school canceled final examinations and the graduation ceremony after they learned of a possible suicide pact among the friends of a student who had shot and killed himself at home over Christmas. Some of these students had told others that they were planning on making the graduation a memorable one that nobody would forget. These clusters of suicides typically take place in middle- and upper-middle-class neighborhoods with a transient population. The lives of these kids are filled with numerous stresses, including high levels of divorce, two-career families, pressure to perform, and the absence of an extended family. In addition, their situations are often complicated further by frequent family moves or best friends moving out of town.

But don't be fooled. Suicide doesn't play favorites. Teenagers of every age, from every socioeconomic group, geographic area, and type of family situation have become statistics. Many of our teenagers are at high risk for suicide. As parents and youth workers, we must realize that the normal pressures of adolescence have coupled with societal factors to leave all teenagers at potential risk.

Teenage Depression Facts and Figures

The increasing intensity of peer, media, and family pressures has made the teenage years more difficult. The constant barrage of confusing messages and expectations can be too much of a burden for some teenagers to handle during the normal adolescent developmental shake-up, especially when parents are absent or ignorant of what's going on in their teenager's life. One study of students in grades six, eight, and 10 (average ages 11, 13, and 15) found that 18 percent of youths reported symptoms of depression.[605] Other studies indicate 20 percent of kids "have some sort of mental, behavioral, or emotional problem, and that one in 10 may have a serious emotional problem. Among adolescents, one in eight may suffer from depression."[606] Seventy percent of these kids don't receive any professional help or treatment for their problem.[607] Our teenagers are at risk for being more than down in the dumps. Teenage depression has reached epidemic proportions.

While not always the case, most suicides are preceded by a period of depression. A diagnosis of depression represents one of the major risk factors in the attempt and completion of teenage suicide. With that in mind, it's important that we take some time to look at, define, and understand the problem of teenage depression.

Depression has been called the common cold of emotional problems. The American Psychiatric Association reports that depression affects nearly one in 10 adults every year, with twice as many women as men.[608] Depression is more than the normal feeling of discouragement or feeling "blue" that we all experience from time to time—you can't snap out of it and move on with life. Feeling blue becomes like a black cloud affecting everything. A teenager is diagnosed with clinical depression when normal functioning is interrupted and professional counseling and help is needed.

Until the 1960s, researchers and other professionals didn't believe that depression occurred in teenagers. One reason was that teenagers don't react to depression the way that adults do. Their depression is often masked by behaviors that appear normal for someone going through adolescence (moodiness, anger, withdrawal, etc.).

Common Signs and Symptoms of Adolescent Depression

- Persistent sadness, tears, crying
- Fluctuation between silent apathy and excited talkativeness
- An inability to concentrate
- Persistent boredom
- Fatigue
- Feelings of guilt
- A major change in eating or sleeping patterns
- Withdrawal from friends and family
- Talk about running away from home

- Complaining about headaches and stomachaches
- Severe weight gain or loss
- Insomnia or oversleeping
- Declining grades and an unwillingness to work in school
- Truancy
- Rapid mood swings
- Lack of interest in regular activities (such as sports, church, music lessons, youth group)
- Pessimism about the future
- Expressions of helplessness, worthlessness, hopelessness
- Aggressive and rebellious behavior
- Preoccupation with death or suicide

Disordered Eating

Adolescent depression also manifests itself in a variety of eating disorders, including anorexia and bulimia. Almost unheard of 30 years ago, these potentially deadly, anxiety-related emotional sicknesses have reached epidemic proportions in our population, especially among preadolescent and adolescent girls. But don't be fooled—although the majority of cases have occurred in females, males are not immune. In fact, it's believed eating disorders now affect about 2 percent of males.[609]

The overwhelming nature of the stresses that lead to teenage depression and suicide are usually evident in textbook cases of anorexia and bulimia. Victims are typically overachievers. Their parents are also achievement oriented and often place lofty and unfair expectations on their kids in everything from academics to personal appearance. Many times parents will put up a façade of marital unity even though their marriage is on shaky ground. The mothers of anorexics and bulimics are many times demanding and perfectionistic, while fathers are busy with work and out of touch with family needs and concerns. Add to this our society's overwhelming and everpresent focus on fitness, beauty, and body shape, and the combination can be deadly.

Anorexia nervosa. This term actually means "nervous loss of appetite." Consumed by the irrational fear of being fat or overweight, the aim of the anorexic is to lose weight. Society's pressure to be thin and beautiful influences even the thinnest girls to look in the mirror and see themselves as fat. Jess, a 12-year-old with anorexia says her thighs are too fat. Even though people are constantly telling her that she's too skinny, she doesn't believe them. She weighs 105 pounds and would like to be 80 pounds. She exercises regularly in an effort to lose weight. If anorexia continues to progress, she will waste away to nothing and eventually die.

Today, it's estimated that anorexia touches between 0.5 percent to 3.7 percent of all females.[610] A growing number of males, including teenagers, are suffering from anorexia, too.

Signs and Symptoms of Anorexia

- Emaciation
- Loss of 25 percent of body weight
- No physical cause for weight loss (illness, etc.)
- Voluntary starvation
- Excessive exercise
- Depression
- Constant fearful talk about being overweight or too fat
- Dry skin
- Cessation of menstrual period
- Perfectionism

Bulimia nervosa. The goal of the bulimic is to eat large amounts of food without gaining weight. Bulimics consume food during binges that last anywhere from 15 minutes to eight hours, eating between 1,200 and 11,500 calories per binge. Fearful of gaining weight, the bulimic then purges the food by vomiting or using laxatives, enemas, or diuretics. Like the starving of anorexics, the binge eating of bulimics is often a response to loneliness, anger, pressure, or depression.

Most often diagnosed after age 18, it's estimated that bulimia nervosa has personally touched the lives of between 1.1 percent and 4.2 percent of females.[611] In addition, two to three percent of adolescents have bulimia nervosa.[612] Approximately 50 percent of those who've been anorexic will develop bulimia or bulimic patterns.

Signs and Symptoms of Bulimia

- Secretive binge eating
- Fasting
- Self-induced vomiting
- Laxative use
- Chewing but not swallowing food
- Irregular menstrual period
- Intestinal discomfort
- Fluctuating weight
- Tooth decay
- Irregular heartbeat
- Fainting spells

The potentially deadly nature of anorexia and bulimia classifies them as a slow form of suicide. Like suicide and depression, eating disorders are reaching epidemic proportions as their incidence continues to multiply and they affect age groups as young as seven years old.[613]

Self-Mutilation

Another alarming form of self-destructive behavior that's becoming increasingly prevalent is cutting. A growing number of teenagers are venting frustration through self-inflicted cuts, bruises, scars, and broken bones. Because those marks are usually outward manifestations of inward pain, one researcher has called self-mutilation "the voice on the skin."[614]

Self-mutilation has been around for a long time. And in the last few years, the curtain has opened wide on this once private behavior, as it's become more acceptable for kids to share their stories about self-abuse. After all, this is a generation that has embraced piercing, tattooing, and other types of body modification as fashionable forms of self-expression and style. In addition, the late 1990s even saw pop culture icons such as Marilyn Manson talk about and/or demonstrate self-mutilation for the emerging generations to see. More recently, the film *Thirteen* tells the story of a confused 13-year-old girl who cuts herself three times onscreen in scenes that are strikingly real and horrifying. Popular media culture has introduced self-mutilation to mainstream youth culture and a worldwide audience being raised by media.

Self-injurious behavior (SIB) or self-inflicted violence (SIV) has been defined as "the commission of deliberate harm to one's own body. The injury is done to oneself, without the aid of another person, and the injury is severe enough for tissue damage (such as scarring) to result. Acts that are committed with conscious suicidal intent or are associated with sexual arousal are excluded."[615]

Experts who study SIB classify the behavior according to three types:

- *Major self-mutilation* is the most extreme and rare form of SIB. It consists of acts like castration or limb amputation, and it most often occurs when an individual is psychotic or intoxicated.

- *Stereotypic self-mutilation* consists of regular and rhythmic acts such as head banging, eyeball pressing, and arm biting. It's most commonly seen among institutionalized, mentally handicapped individuals or those suffering with obsessive-compulsive disorders.

- The type of SIB most common among teenagers is *superficial* or *moderate self-mutilation*. Kids caught in this cycle of behavior cut their skin, carve their skin, burn themselves, interfere with the healing process, stick themselves with needles, or utilize other methods of inflicting physical damage on themselves.

Since SIB is still somewhat stigmatized and kept secret by many, accurate statistics on its prevalence are difficult to find. One recent study of graduate and undergraduate students at two Ivy League schools found that one-fifth of students say they have purposely injured themselves by cutting, burning, or a variety of other methods.[616]

What is known is that the average self-mutilator begins at age 14 and continues the practice, usually with increasing severity, into her late twenties. Among adolescents, the ratio of boys to girls who mutilate themselves is equal. Many teenagers and young adults who exhibit SIB are the ones you'd least suspect. For the most part, they're bright, intelligent, and generally appear "normal."[617]

We *do* know that for most self-mutilators the act is a personalized ritual. They will often describe a favorite room, preferred lighting, background music, and a list of objects regularly used. They abuse themselves in specific ways. Among those who cut, some slash themselves with long shallow strokes; others focus on making one or two very deep cuts. Those who are bone breakers often smash their limbs against a hard wall or hit themselves with a hammer or other hard object. One 16-year-old girl describes it this way: "I close all the shades to my room, light candles on my bed, and incense, rub my arm with alcohol, and cut away while I'm listening to music." Another writes, "Once I burned myself with my curling iron. Another time I cut lines down my face that looked like tears and a couple of times when I didn't have a razor I stabbed myself with a very sharp pencil." A 20-year-old says, " I slam my hands/arms against something cement with corners until I hear something crack, and I am convinced that I've broken a bone. These sessions take three to five hours. I have never failed to break a bone."

Prior to an act of self-mutilation, most feel a mounting range of negative feelings or numbness. If there is pain, it's usually felt minutes or even days after the injury. Those who report feeling pain also say that pain is "fulfilling"—the sensation they are actually seeking. And even though most self-mutilators can't explain it, they somehow know when to stop a session. Their need to inflict damage is somehow satisfied. Feeling peaceful and relieved, they pick up and move on with life until the need to damage themselves surfaces once more.

Typically, the first incident occurs during early adolescence, and the self-mutilator describes an overwhelming desire—seemingly out of nowhere—to inflict damage. Self-mutilation isn't usually something they've heard about elsewhere, nor is it something they initially discuss with others. In fact, many are surprised to learn there are others who do the same. Of course, the mounting publicity surrounding self-mutilation means that this is changing.

Those who tell the first-person stories say they harm themselves because "it makes me feel better." They describe periods of incredible emotional turmoil, anger, hate, and stress that are calmed by the cathartic act of mutilation. While SIB is dangerous, wrong, and abnormal, it becomes an effective short-term strategy for individuals who haven't learned healthy ways to cope with the problems and pressures of life. Second, others say the practice helps them feel "alive." They are reassured by their capacity to "feel" physical sensation rather than numbness. Third, others resort to SIB as a way to gain control of a chaotic existence. "Sometimes I just feel out of control," says a 19-year-old college student. "All the hurt and confusion, the loss and emotional pain, is transferred into something I can control and feel." This is especially true for kids who've been victimized by abuse. They see SIB as a way to exert their own power over their bodies in the midst of feeling powerless.

Some experts theorize that cutting and other SIB releases betaendorphins, which act as the body's own opiates, leading to feelings of pleasure or being high. As a result, some believe SIB is actually physically addictive. As in the case of drug addiction, the longer the habit is practiced, the more frequent and intense the "dosage" must be to achieve the desired effect.

Researchers who study SIB have discovered several factors common to the background of those who self-mutilate repetitively. Not surprisingly, most of those factors relate to the breakdown of family. Chaotic family conditions during childhood, physical and emotional neglect, and exposure to physical or sexual abuse have all been found to be reliable predictors of SIB. Those who cannot remember ever feeling "special" or "loved" by anyone as kids were least able to control their SIB.[618]

We can be sure that the stigma associated with SIB will continue to disappear as this generation's cry of confusion and self-hatred continues. In turn, SIB will become more pervasive as a "normal" and accepted coping mechanism among kids. If that happens, chances are good that SIB might continue to move so far into the mainstream of youth culture that kids who exhibit none of the classic SIB precipitating factors will cut themselves simply because it's fashionable. In addition, we can expect that increased "publicity" for cutting will plant the idea in younger and younger minds.

The Causes of Teenage Suicide

In an effort to escape the reality of a painful existence, many teenagers choose death—not because they want to die, but because they want to get away from life. What makes the ugliness of death more attractive than life? What are the factors that make life so painful? Typically, there is no one cause for teenage suicide. But teenage suicide is always the result of a three-step process: *"a previous history of problems compounded by problems associated with adolescence and finally, a precipitating event* (death, breakup, etc.) triggers the suicide."[619]

What follow are eight of the most common factors in teenage suicide and depression.

1. Developmental Factors

Life can get ugly if you're the biggest, shortest, fattest, or youngest-looking of your peers. The Horatio Alger Association surveyed high school students about the pressures they feel. Fifty-one percent feel pressure to look a certain way. Forty-two percent identified "loneliness or feeling left out" as a problem.[620] Our kids walk on self-image eggshells as they tiptoe through the barrage of changes they face during adolescence.

Because of the very nature of the adolescent period, teenagers are more vulnerable to stress than any other age group. Things that would never bother an adult can be devastating to a teenager. What we might write off as "silly" or "insignificant" might be monumental to our teenagers. When something as simple as a pimple on the face becomes a major stress producer, one wonders what might happen when teenagers face problems of a more severe nature.

The adolescent years are a time of change, pressure, crises, and a tendency for impulsive overreaction. Teenagers tend to center in on the crisis of the moment, and that crisis then exists at the center of their universe. Teenagers experience great emotional anxiety, as the world of self seems to change before their eyes. Growing through this period of questioning and uncertainty makes life hard enough. Add to that the remaining seven factors we'll discuss, and you'll begin to see why so many kids can't deal with the pressure.

2. Family Factors

It used to be that home was the most stress-free environment for teenagers. But the many changes taking place in the family have transformed the home from a stress reducer to a stress producer. Roughly three thousand kids a day see their parents' marriage end in divorce. Most of those kids believe the breakups were their fault. Sixty percent of the kids born in the 1990s will miss out on the stability of a two-parent home, since they'll spend at least part of their childhood living with only one parent. With rates of cohabitation and out-of-wedlock births on the rise, the situation won't be any better for kids born in the first decade of the 21st century. One Gallup Poll on teenage suicide found that among those who had attempted suicide or come close to attempting suicide, the number one reason for considering this drastic action was "family problems" or "problems at home."[621]

Situational family factors beyond anyone's control also contribute to adolescent stress, depression, and suicide. For example, many teenagers who attempt suicide have lost parents to death before the age of 12 or had a parent become chronically ill during their early teenage years. But there are family factors that are preventable. Nearly three-quarters of all suicide attempters come from unstable family situations characterized by divorce, separation, talk of divorce, an absent father, substance abuse, isolation, or lack of support.[622]

While observers might understand why a child from a terrible home situation would try to take her own life, family, friends, and neighbors of suicidal upper- and middle-class kids from seemingly healthy homes are frequently left looking for answers, too. There are three additional family factors that are often present in these "healthy" situations.

First is a lack of time spent with one or more parents and the resulting feeling of abandonment. Kids interpret lack of time and intimacy as rejection. Often teenagers who attempt suicide claim they can remember no adults to whom they ever felt close. Young males usually point to the lack of an effective father figure in the home. In many of these cases, the father has been physically present but emotionally absent and unwilling to provide spiritual direction.

A second factor is unrealistic parental expectations. Parental pressure to keep up the grades, stay involved in activities, earn money, and get ready for the right college is too much for some kids to handle. High achievers who have considered or attempted suicide report that the catalyst has been feelings of worthlessness, the pressure to succeed, and the fear of failure. The pressure to excel can be extremely destructive. Placing unrealistic goals and expectations on kids can literally kill them.

A third factor is a family history of depression and suicide. While there's no proven genetic link or biological predisposition to suicide that's passéd from one generation to the next, family environment and the examples of others can play an important role in a child's decisions about their own futures. Kids learn from their parents. If Mom and Dad model how to effectively handle stress in healthy ways, then chances are their kids will learn those lessons well. But if Mom and Dad are paralyzed by stress and have attempted suicide themselves, kids may learn that taking one's life is an acceptable way of coping. This truth became real to me when a depressed young woman phoned me for some counseling. Only in her twenties, she shared that her marriage was on the same destructive track as her parents', and when Marsha was a teenager, her mother chose suicide as a solution to her marital difficulties. This young woman told me, "My marriage is so bad that I have thought about coping in the exact same way my mother did."

If difficult, unstable, or broken family situations are a major factor in teenage suicide, then the exact opposite should also be true: Parents need to learn that kids are more likely to feel better about themselves and exhibit healthier reactions to stress when they're loved, nurtured, and cared for in healthy home situations.

3. Societal Factors

It's been said that all the knowledge humankind has accumulated since the beginning of time is only half of what we'll know in 20 or 30 years. This rapid accumulation of knowledge has been paralleled by changing morals, values, and lifestyles. Adults can only imagine what it must be like to grow up in today's world. Kids are finding it difficult to cope.

One of the societal causes of depression and suicide is the push to grow up faster. David Elkind talks about "the hurried child syndrome" and how kids who are pushed into premature adulthood are on a quick road to self-destruction. What they need is time to be kids. What they get are the pressures of the adult world that even many adults have difficulty handling. What results is stress. How they handle that stress varies. Many choose to escape the stress through withdrawal and substance abuse. Others go so far as to take their own lives. When kids are forced to be something other than kids, it can kill them.

A second societal factor is worldview confusion. A Christ-centered worldview offers meaning, hope, purpose, and direction for the here and now, along with the joyful expectation of eternal salvation. But today's world laughs at such an "outdated" way of thinking. A tragic result of our vast and rapid accumulation of knowledge has been our willingness to think of ourselves more highly than we ought. When man sees himself as the measure of all things, God is no longer necessary. The lifestyle of adult role models has combined with our teenagers' media to send a strong message: "You don't need God." The biblical worldview has been replaced with the hopelessness of nihilism.

Dostoyevsky wrote, "If God does not exist, everything is permitted. The most meaningful reality is individual freedom, its supreme expression suicide."[623] If our kids grow up learning that life is futile, empty, and leading nowhere, it makes sense that dying could become more attractive than living. Conversely, it should come as no surprise that teenagers who attend church are less likely to consider or commit suicide.

The third societal factor is the devaluing of human life. Our kids are growing up in a society where abortion has been legalized and normalized. Violence fills the streets and school hallways, as teenagers have killed each other over something as silly as a parking space or a pair of sneakers. They're aware of debates surrounding euthanasia and stories of physicians willing to help people take their own lives. To many, these issues are just the facts of life, rather than matters of right or wrong.

Two interesting polls show how American attitudes toward life are influencing our attitudes toward death. A Pew Research Center Survey asked adults, "Do you think a person has a moral right to end his or her own life under any of the following circumstances?" Those who answered *yes* include 53 percent when the person has a disease that's incurable, 60 percent when the person is suffering great pain and has no hope of improvement, 29 percent when the person is an extremely heavy burden on the family, and 33 percent when the person is ready to die because living has become a burden.[624]

Another poll asked adults, "If you were seriously ill with a terminal disease, would you consider suicide, or not?" Thirty-two percent said *yes.*[625]

The final societal factor is "generational angst." There's been much written about the collective pain and hopelessness of Generation X (those born roughly between 1961 and 1981). Also known as "busters," they believe they've been handed a "busted" world. By growing up in an era where there's no commonly held set of "oughts" and no overriding purpose for life, many in this age group have grown confused and frustrated by a life full of contradictions. They feel disconnected from family, friends, self, and God. In their book *Inside the Soul of a New Generation*, Xers Tim Celek and Dieter Zander say that the anger of their generation often expresses itself in three ways: They feel "alone," they feel "abandoned," and they feel "alienated."[626] When combined with the aimlessness of postmodern thinking, these negative feelings form a recipe for deep despair that often leads them to ask, "So what if I go ahead and disconnect myself from my life?"

Some culture watchers believe that this way of thinking hasn't carried over into the post-buster generations. Instead they see the emerging generations as being more hopeful and positive about life. While there's certainly some accuracy in these observations, I believe that any generation that fails to put its hope in Christ has embraced a false hope. While that false hope might be able to delay or hold off feelings of deep despair, that despair will ultimately surface. In other words, the emerging generations are still angst-ridden even though their angst may look different or hasn't surfaced fully. In reality, their hopefulness may in fact be normal youthful optimism that's characteristic of people in their age group.

4. "Lessness" Factors

Julie is an example of what can happen to a young person who has no hope. The first time I met her was one week after her second suicide attempt. I couldn't believe that this beautiful and gifted young college student would have any reason to want to end her own life. Appearances can be deceiving. I asked her to tell me her story. During the two hours that followed, she described her life by using several words that I hear from suicidal adolescents over and over again. These words make up what I call the "lessness" factors.

Julie was haunted by feelings of uselessness. She was the oldest of three kids, and her two younger siblings had excelled in academics and athletics. Julie struggled with both. She might have been able to handle the struggle better if her father hadn't put her down by comparing her "inferior" efforts to those of her brother and sister.

"He's always putting me down by telling me how I don't measure up. I feel useless," she said. As her father's words chipped away at her over the course of her high school years, Julie began to lose the little bit of confidence she had in herself.

Like other teenagers who are suicidal, Julie suffered from extreme loneliness. Julie's overwhelming sense of being alone had led her to pursue a promiscuous lifestyle, hoping a chain of sexual relationships would fill the void. She told me the exact opposite had occurred as her loneliness increased with each new sexual partner.

Related, but different from loneliness, was Julie's sense of alone-ness. In their book *A Generation Alone,* William Mahedy and Janet Bernardi say, "Aloneness is being alone and not being able to trust anyone...Aloneness is largely about fear. It stems from abandon-ment or neglect and leads to alienation from friends, family and society."[627] With each new unfulfilling relationship gone sour, Julie took another step down the dark corridor of aloneness. Aloneness is a significant factor in the suicides of kids who've been bullied.

It wasn't long before Julie's efforts to eliminate her loneliness led to feelings of worthlessness. She'd been treated like a piece of dirt for so long she actually started to believe she was one. She wasn't much different from the young teenage girl whose father constantly reminded her, "You aren't worth the price of the paper your birth certificate is printed on." The Gallup survey on teenage suicide found "feeling worthless" was a reason given by 18 percent of those who had attempted or considered suicide.[628]

Purposelessness was the next step in Julie's spiral into suicide. "Why am I here?" was a question she answered by saying, "For ab-solutely no reason at all." She saw no meaning for her existence.

Julie confessed she finally decided to kill herself because she could see her entire life funneled into one big bundle of hope-lessness. This is the greatest predictor of a person committing sui-cide. When they see no possible way out of the confusion, misery, and disappointment of life, death doesn't necessarily look *good,* but it looks much better than living. While Julie couldn't imagine how things could get any worse, she was convinced they wouldn't get any better either. This is one of the main differences between how adults and kids handle stress and depression. Kids have a greater difficulty dealing with the pain of living.

Julie's story is an unfortunate example of how feelings of "less-ness" can build during the difficult period of adolescence. In her case, as in thousands of others, the loss of meaning, purpose, and love led to a loss of hope—and almost to a loss of life.

5. The Revenge Factor

Many adolescents take their own lives in an effort to hurt or get even with someone who has hurt them. Rebellion against parents, the breakup of a romantic relationship, and divorce are common reasons for teenagers to choose suicide as a method of revenge.

6. The Publicity Factor

The shocking nature of teenage suicide means a teenager's self-inflicted death will usually be reported in the paper and become the talk of the school and neighborhood and community for several days.

Kids who've been driven to despair as a result of being shut off and left alone by family and friends long for love and attention. When someone in their school commits suicide, they see the student population focus their thoughts, discussions, and attention on that person during the days that follow. To them, they see that even though the person is dead and gone, he's having a high-profile moment in the sun.

Knowing full well that the publicity surrounding a completed suicide could open the door for many more attempts, school counselors usually mobilize to encourage those who might pursue such a course to rethink their plans. This is why so many schools work to avoid glorifying the deceased by not scheduling memorial services or assemblies in the school.

It's wise for youth workers and parents and educators to recognize the potential for a ripple effect following a teenage suicide. Andy Warhol once said that everyone is famous for at least 15 minutes; many kids see the "fame" bestowed upon a suicide victim and choose to find their 15 minutes of fame after their heart stops beating.

7. The Substance-Abuse Factor

Drugs and alcohol are a coping mechanism teenagers choose to deal with depression and stress. It's not unusual for alcohol and drugs to intensify depression, irrational thoughts, and feelings of hopelessness. For example, one study found "boys who drank alcohol and boys who were binge drinkers were about two-and-a-half times as likely to experience symptoms of depression, while those who abused intravenous drugs were about six times as likely to have symptoms of depression as boys who abstained completely.[629] Many who attempt suicide had been drinking or using drugs at the time. Alcohol is a depressant and the most common drug used by suicide attempters, followed by marijuana and stimulants. There's strong evidence suggesting the increased rate of substance abuse among teenagers over the last few decades is related to the dramatic increase in teenage suicides during the same time.

8. The Sexual Abuse Factor

As many as one in four girls and one in eight boys will be sexually abused by the time they reach the age of 18.[630] The probable effects of childhood sexual abuse on the millions of adult survivors include fear, anxiety, depression, anger, hostility, inappropriate sexual behavior, poor self-esteem, tendency toward substance abuse, and difficulty with close relationships. Sexual abuse combines many of the previously mentioned suicide factors into one big volatile bundle. It's no wonder so many victims choose death over a very painful existence. Eighty percent of young adults who've been sexually abused meet the diagnostic criteria for at least one psychiatric disorder at the age of 21, including depression.[631]

Keep a watchful eye. The presence of one or more of these factors in a teenager's life increases the risk for depression and suicidal tendencies or behavior. Stay alert so you can offer positive, hope-filled responses and support to your teenagers as they grow through the difficult years of adolescence.

Warning Signs and Cries for Help

Teenagers who attempt suicide give signs. It's estimated 80 percent of those who take their life communicate their intention to someone prior to the act. While they may not always communicate their pain and intentions with verbal clarity, the signs are there. But they may never be seen unless we know what to watch for.

In this section we'll examine five categories of signs and cries teenagers may give before attempting or committing suicide. Carefully read through the descriptions of these signs, realizing they'll usually appear in some combination before a teenager reaches the end of his rope.

1. Emotional Cries

Teenagers, by nature, can be moody. But not all of their moody behavior should be written off as just a part of the adolescent life stage. There are several unusual and extreme emotional cries for help that can clue us in to our teenagers' struggles with hopelessness, depression, and suicidal feelings.

The first emotional cry can be heard in the classical signs of depression we discussed earlier. If these symptoms continue for two weeks, then it's time to seek help.

Withdrawal from normal activities is a second emotional cry. When teenagers suddenly separate themselves from friends, family, objects, and activities that are normally a large part of their lives, trouble may be brewing. Depressed and suicidal teenagers may want to spend more time either alone or in their rooms.

The calm before the storm occurs when a teenager's spirits improve suddenly and dramatically after a period of deep and extended depression. Psychologists say this is a very dangerous time since the teenager's "peace" may actually exist because the decision has been made to take her own life. She's excited because she feels as though she's finally found the solution to her problems and the pain will soon be over. Parents should be very cautious when a teenager who has a history of depression appears to be dramatically and suddenly improved.

2. Physical Cries

Sometimes an observant eye is all it takes to discern that a teenager is depressed or suicidal. Here are some physical cries you might hear as a result of being aware of your teenager's physical demeanor and day-to-day habits.

- *Physical complaints* are sometimes heard from teenagers who experience depression and suicidal thoughts. Stomachaches, headaches, and constant fatigue are a common occurrence among teenagers who are finding adolescence and the pressures of their lives too much to handle.

- *A neglect of physical appearance,* characterized by sloppiness and poor personal hygiene, could be a way of saying,

"Why should I bother? Nobody cares about me anyway." Teenagers who feel worthless sometimes begin to look worthless.

- *A change in normal eating and sleeping habits* is also a sign of trouble. Suicidal teenagers will sometimes sleep more, eat less, and even develop one of the disordered eating patterns already discussed.

- Finally, *body language that shows an inability to concentrate* can be a sign a child is preoccupied with problems and depression. Slouching, staring off into space, and constant daydreaming may occur when the pain of what's going on inside drowns out an awareness of what might be happening in the same room.

3. Behavioral Cries

Teenagers who struggle with depression and suicide sometimes decide to become involved in some strange and frightening new behaviors.

- Becoming *accident prone* can be a conscious or unconscious attention-getting device for teenagers who desperately want someone to notice them. Teenagers who feel shut off from others find the attention they receive after an accident to be a form of immediate reinforcement. These cries for attention can also be cries for help.

- *Acting out* or other melodramatic behavior is another common attention-getter. I remember one girl who always acted as though the world was coming to an end. When she felt her friends were starting to ignore her, she'd quickly step on stage and respond like a terrible actress to some new manufactured crisis. It didn't take long for her friends to catch on to her act. As her fantasy world came crashing down, she'd move on to a new circle of friends who'd respond the way she wanted them to. Sadly, this was a cry to be noticed, loved, and cared for by a girl whose father had emotionally rejected her, leaving her depressed and feeling worthless.

- *A preoccupation with violence and unusually aggressive behavior* are clear signs something is wrong. Some suicidal teenagers will fight, yell, break things, and throw objects during increasingly frequent fits of rage. Some will be mesmerized by movie and television violence, renting and viewing violent films. Others will purchase or attempt to build weapons.

- *Self-destructive behavior and involvement in dangerous activities* are signs a teenager may have little or no regard for his personal safety or life. Many suicidal teenagers will live life on the edge by driving fast, playing dangerous games with weapons, or playing chicken with their cars and bikes. Any sort of high-risk activity of this type merits attention.

- *Promiscuous sexual behavior* is often an attempt to sedate strong feelings of failure and depression. Kids who see themselves as worthless, unloved, and rejected will look for acceptance and love through sexual intimacy.

- *Drug and alcohol abuse* has already been discussed as a factor contributing to suicide.

- *Sudden rebellious and disrespectful behavior* toward parents, teachers, and other authorities may indicate a teenager has decided to take his fate into his own hands, rather than listen to the wisdom and advice of those he may have respected at one time.

- *A drop in grades and increased truancy* are not uncommon when a teenager is preoccupied with so many problems that they find it impossible or undesirable to care about schoolwork.

- Teenagers who think about killing themselves will sometimes become *preoccupied with death*. They may write poetry or stories focusing on death or other morbid themes. Their musical tastes may change and lean toward an interest in music and media that portray and glamorize hopelessness and death. Their preoccupation with death may even lead them to dye their hair and dress in black.

- *Preparing for death* is a clear sign a teenager has decided to commit suicide. Many teenagers who've made the decision will begin to give away valued personal items to close friends or family members. They'll say good-bye and take care of other personal business. And they'll acquire the means by which they intend to kill themselves (rope, gun, pills).

- It seems strange that this last behavioral cry has to be mentioned, but the fact that many parents don't hear this loudest of all screams warrants its inclusion. *A suicide attempt* should not be brushed off lightly. Your teenager is crying for help and wants you to get involved in dealing with her issues and problems.

4. Situational Cries

Researchers and counseling professionals have noted there are numerous unpleasant life changes that affect teenagers more deeply than any other group of people because of the difficult developmental stage of adolescence. These events might precipitate feelings of failure, loneliness, depression, and suicide. Life becomes even more difficult if more than one of these circumstances are experienced at the same time.

A teenager might commit suicide after losing friends and social status following a family move from one community to another. Other situations include a romantic breakup, death of a friend or loved one, unplanned pregnancy, getting bullied, parents' divorce, or academic failure. Parents should be especially sensitive to the emotional needs of their teenagers during these times of personal crisis. Sometimes we falsely assume they'll be able to adapt to the change as well as we can. Don't forget we're adults, and they're still kids.

5. Verbal Cries

Parents who listen to their kids might be alerted to suicidal intent by the words they hear. A child who says things like, "I won't be a problem for you much longer," "Nothing really matters anymore," "It's no use," "I won't see you again," or "I'd be better off dead," may have already decided their fate.

Some have speculated that people who talk about suicide won't ever commit suicide. Don't believe it. It's only a myth. Most suicidal acts are preceded by some warning or cry. All of those cries and warnings should be taken seriously.

In the next two sections we'll look at the preventive and redemptive measures that loving parents can provide in order to help their kids deal with the stress of adolescence, depression, and suicide.

Preventive Measures

What follows are a number of preventive measures and approaches that, if consciously instituted in your home, will reduce the risk of depression and suicide by providing your kids with the strong foundation of a loving home and open lines of communication. (Note to youth workers: Much of what follows is easily transferable to youth ministry contexts.)

Preventive Measure #1: Do Your Best to Create a Stable Family

Teenagers who consider suicide talk about feeling alone, hopeless, and rejected. While these feelings will be experienced by most teenagers as they pass through adolescence, many who suffer from depression and suicidal feelings identify feeling alone, hopeless, and rejected *at home*. They're more vulnerable to having these feelings if they've been abused, have parents with alcohol or drug problems, or have a home life characterized by arguing, discord, disruptions, separation, absent father, or divorce. Nearly three-quarters of teenage suicide attempters report family problems.[632]

Fathers, God has given you the gift of your wife and kids. Mothers, God has given you the gift of your husband and kids. Your marital vows and commitment should be taken seriously. When Americans are committed to being uncommitted, you must be sure your marriage is in order. I've often heard couples in crumbling marriages say they're "staying together for the sake of the kids." While this has merit, I challenge you to go one step further. Don't just endure a difficult situation for the sake of the kids.

Rather, pray through your difficult situation and seek outside help with the intent of strengthening, restoring, and maintaining your commitment to each other. Your kids are smart enough to know when you're just hanging on until they grow up and leave home. They'll appreciate the positive model of a mom and dad intent on allowing God to empower them as they build and strengthen a marriage that lasts.

If you or another member of your family is guilty of abusive behavior, alcohol abuse, drug abuse, or violence, seek help immediately. If your family finds it easy to argue and difficult to communicate, go to your pastor or a qualified Christian counselor for help in improving communication skills in your home.

God created the family as the basic unit of society. It's the unit into which our kids are born, and in which they find their identity and are socialized and nurtured. God intended the family to be a place where each of us can find unconditional love, mutual caring, intimacy—a place where we can be ourselves without fearing rejection. When the family fails to function in this way, God's order is disrupted and people suffer. It's no coincidence that while the American family has been falling apart, the rate of teenage depression and suicide has been rising.

Preventive Measure #2: Lead Your Kids to Spiritual Maturity

God also created the family to serve as a place of spiritual nurture. One of the awesome tasks of parenting is the job of serving as signposts. Parents are to point their kids, by precept and example, to the God of the universe.

While Christians *do* get depressed and *do* commit suicide, rates of depression and suicide are lower among those with a sense of hope in the midst of trying circumstances. There's nothing that can replace the hope that comes from realizing one's created purpose to be in a relationship with God through Jesus Christ. One of your God-given tasks as a parent is to lead and nurture your kids into Christian maturity. This means that you, as a parent, must be growing in your faith and modeling the life of discipleship. As you live out a life characterized by faith in God, you will become a stable rock and point of reference for your kids as they travel the rocky road of adolescence. When parents work, with God's help, to genuinely live out a life centered on a faith in God that is integrated into all areas of life, their kids will learn by example to live out that same faith.

Preventive Measure #3: Model and Teach a Biblical Theology of Pain and Suffering

We live in a feelings-oriented and driven society where we grow up learning to avoid pain and pursue pleasure. Because we don't like to suffer, we tend to look for easy and quick solutions to our problems. Teenagers who commit suicide often do so because they've concluded that the quickest way to solve their problems is to end their lives. From the time our kids are young, we must be making a conscious effort to steer them away from these conclusions by teaching and modeling three simple truths about life in this world.

First, pain and suffering are an inevitable part of life. All of us will experience our share of physical and emotional pain. There's no escaping it.

Second, while pain and suffering are temporary, suicide is permanent. Kids need to know that suicide is a permanent end to temporary problems, and there are other ways to deal with those problems. Several teenagers who had actually attempted suicide shared these words with George Gallup:

- Suicide is *not* the answer...things are better after a while.

- It's not worth dying.

- Time heals everything.

- Taking my life solves nothing...Making some mistakes is definitely not the end of the world.

- It's a permanent solution to a short-term problem.

- Suicide is not the answer to anything. Life has its ups and downs, and you need to deal with them and move on.[693]

Finally, God is our source of strength in times of difficulty. On several occasions Jesus told his followers they could expect pain and persecution. The Psalms are full of the moans and laments of human suffering and emotional misery. But all of God's Word points to the fact that God does not leave us alone in times of trouble. In the midst of intense personal pain, the psalmist would write these words:

> Even though I walk through the valley of the shadow of death, I will fear no evil, for you are with me; your rod and your staff, they comfort me. —Psalm 23:4

> God is our refuge and strength, an ever-present help in trouble. —Psalm 46:1

> The Lord will keep you from all harm—he will watch over your life. —Psalm 121:7

Our parental example should teach our kids how to handle the difficulties life sends our way.

As we model the Christian way to handle pain and suffering, our kids will grow up learning they must place full reliance and dependence on God, even when they can't see the light at the end of the tunnel.

Preventive Measure #4: Spend Time with Your Kids

One of the greatest gifts we can give our kids is our time. Time fosters teenagers' openness and unclogs the lines of parent-teen communication.

A few years ago I attended a program on teenage suicide sponsored by a local high school that had experienced three student suicides in a matter of two months. Seated in the center of the room were a number of "suicide survivors"—relatives of young people who'd taken their own lives. At the end of the presentation one of these survivors, the mother of a young man who had killed himself, raised her hand and addressed the crowd. Her words to everyone: "Just be there for your kids."

Preventive Measure #5: Love Them for Who They Are

Too many teenagers grow up thinking the love of parents is merit-based, rather than unconditional. Praise and attention come only when the report card is up to snuff or when the child measures up in some other way. This is too much stress for any human being to handle. No wonder these kids rebel. And some find the pressure so great that it's easier to end their own lives than to live.

Let your kids be themselves. Encourage them to do their best. Let them know there's nothing that they can say or do that will make you love them less. Love them, no matter how they "play."

Preventive Measure #6: Develop a Network of Significant Adults

Teenagers need adults—besides their parents—to whom they can go and find listening ears, encouragement, and wise advice. Encourage your kids to develop friendships with Christian neighbors, pastors, church members, and youth leaders who will love them and invest time in their lives. If your child clams up and won't talk to you, ask him to talk to one of these other adults he knows and trusts.

Preventive Measure #7: Attend a Church That Models Christlike Love

Teenagers want and need the church to be in the business of supporting them as they pass through adolescence. Your teenagers need a church characterized by Christlike love, healing, openness, and compassion. If you're not attending a church like this, take steps to lead the church to this point or find one where this is already happening.

Preventive Measure #8: Encourage Involvement in a Positive Peer Group

Our teenagers need a place where they can fit in with their peers, where there is no pressure to wear a mask. The best place for teenagers to be themselves is in the positive peer atmosphere of a group of Christ-following friends who exhibit grace, mercy, and justice. Does your child have a group of friends in your local church that fits the bill? Be sure your church is actively committed with time, money, and other resources to provide a healthy youth group where teenagers can be themselves, be accepted, open up, talk, be heard, and receive sound biblical guidance.

Preventive Measure #9: Develop Friendships with Your Teenager's Friends

You can become a significant adult in the life of another parent's teenager. Take the time to get to know your kids' friends and work to foster an atmosphere of trust and openness with them. This will make it easier for them to come to you for guidance and advice when they're having problems. And your friendship with them will make it easier for them to come to you to tell you about the problems or trouble your own teenager is having. Good relationships with your kids' friends will open the lines of communication in ways you could never imagine.

Preventive Measure #10: Pray for Your Kids

Our teenagers will face numerous difficult situations, pressures, and choices on their way to becoming adults. They're crying out for parents who will be actively involved in their lives while placing them securely in the hands of God. Pray for your kids from the day they are born. Ask God to protect them from harm, guide them into making good decisions, and provide for their well-being. Ask God to open your ears and eyes to the needs of your children. Pray they'll grow up to experience the joy of the Lord, rather than the depression and suicidal feelings so many teenagers are living with today.

Redemptive Measures

What should you do in the moment of crisis when you realize your teenager is suffering from depression or suicidal feelings? There are six initial steps that can be taken to head off disaster so the crisis can be redeemed and the child led back to spiritual, emotional, and physical health.

Step #1: Know the Signs

Remember, 80 percent of those committing suicide signal their intentions through clear verbal clues or behavioral changes. By knowing and understanding the cries and clues mentioned earlier in this chapter, and by building a growing relationship with your teen, you'll be more aware of problems and sensitive to any changes that would signal problems.

Step #2: Take Threats Seriously

Any verbal or behavioral threats should be taken seriously until proven otherwise. Suicide is so ugly that most of us choose to live in denial, thinking the person making the threat isn't serious or is only trying to get attention. Don't look the other way. Instead, take whatever action is appropriate and necessary—immediately. Drop whatever you're doing and focus all your energies on your child and her situation.

Step #3: If You Suspect, Ask!

Are you suspicious about your teenager's behavior? Have the signs pointed to the fact that he may be suicidal? Then ask. Talking about suicide in a straightforward manner won't plant the thought in a teenager's mind, nor does it serve as a suggestion to go do it. Research points to the fact that "asking troubled students about any suicidal impulses appears to ease their distress and might make some of them less likely to try killing themselves."[634]

Have a heart-to-heart with your child. Ask, "Are you thinking about suicide? Do you have a plan?" This can be the first step to getting your teenager on the road to recovery and restoration. Suicidal teenagers are usually not fully intent on dying. Rather, they're waiting for others to step forward and lead them out of their depression. In effect, they're looking for a savior. Inviting them to talk about their feelings by asking good questions opens the door for them to see life as an increasingly attractive option.

Step #4: Listen and Encourage

Encourage the suicidal teenager to express feelings openly by listening intently to what he or she is saying. Don't act shocked or give in to the temptation to nervously respond by using clichés.

Don't say, "Oh, come on. Things aren't that bad. You really don't mean it. Everything will be okay. You're just overreacting." Be quiet and listen hard. When you do speak, don't react judgmentally. Rather, be open and direct in a very loving manner. Let them know you're there as a supporter, not a judge. And don't swear yourself to secrecy regarding their intent. The fact that they've spoken openly with you gives you the responsibility to take the necessary steps to prevent destructive action on their part.

Step #5: Do Something

Take action. Again, drop everything you're doing. This is the most important thing at this moment. If the person has secured the means by which to take her own life, remove it. Does he have a gun? Ask for it. Does she have a rope? Take it away. Does he have pills? Confiscate them. Does she plan to use her car? Get her keys. Don't leave him alone. Keep him with you at all times or get someone else to watch him while you go to get help.

Secure professional help. There are many good Christian counselors who have training and experience in helping suicidal teenagers. Be sure to find someone who comes highly recommended. Most suicidal teenagers are more than willing to talk to someone who can help them ease the pain of living. If your own child is the suicidal person, a good counselor will involve the rest of the family in the counseling process at some point. Decide to be open and vulnerable as that process unfolds. Listen willingly and intently for any behaviors or patterns you've adopted that may have contributed to the crisis. Take the counselor's advice to heart without being defensive. Remember, your child's life is far more important than your reputation.

In addition, make a deal with the suicidal person. Ask them to promise to call you anytime—day or night—if they begin to feel suicidal. This will open the door for you to intervene if suicidal feelings increase again. If the suicidal person is your own child, encourage her to call you at work or get you out of bed. Nothing is more important than your availability to her. Be willing to drop anything and everything to give and to get her the help she needs. Let your teenagers know you're so committed to them that you're willing to drop everything for their sakes at a moment's notice.

Finally, don't be afraid or hesitant to seek hospitalization. Again, a qualified counselor can assist with an assessment. Hospitalization may be required in those cases where you must step in to protect a child from himself.

Step #6: Offer Hope

A suicidal person is one who fails to see hope. The only true source of hope in this world is Jesus Christ. Minister to your child without preaching. Point them to the source of the peace that passes understanding.

Getting Personal

How are you doing in getting to know your kids? In what areas do you need to show them unconditional, committed love?

12

Especially for Parents: Helping Your Teenagers Find Their Places in God's Story

"Adolescents are nothing if not spiritual. Spirituality emerges in adolescence with a vengeance."

—EUGENE PETERSON[635]

"We proclaim him, admonishing and teaching everyone with all wisdom, so that we may present everyone perfect in Christ. To this end I labor, struggling with all his energy, which so powerfully works in me."

—COLOSSIANS 1:28-29

"So what are you hoping for...a boy or a girl?" Once the news got out that we had a kid on the way, my wife and I heard this question more times than I can count. If you're a parent, I'm sure you were asked that same question quite a few times, too. Even though expectant parents may secretly desire one sex over the other, most are too diplomatic to betray their preferences. Instead, they'll share this standard answer many times before their baby arrives: "We don't care if we have a boy or a girl—just as long as our baby is *healthy!*"

That parental desire continues long after we cradle our kids in our arms for the first time. On the days they were born, I held each of my four kids and wondered what it would be like for them to grow up in our rapidly changing world. Little did I know how much the world would change in the 25 years since I held my oldest child the first time. In hindsight, those changes make the questions I asked back then even more significant: *What kinds of choices will these little ones make as they grow up and pass through the earthquake of adolescence? What kinds of pressures will they face when they get to middle school and high school? Who will their friends be, and how will those friends influence my kids? Will my children buy into the negative messages that popular music and media will pound into them? Will they be a part of the minority who say no to premarital sex, substance abuse, depression, and the host of other problems that have woven themselves into the fabric of today's youth culture? Will they be healthy?*

Now that three of my kids have passed through their adolescent years, I've seen just how toxic the youth culture is and how vulnerable teenagers are to its influence. What I'd hoped and prayed for my kids didn't always happen. There were many bumps and bruises along the way. I messed up. They messed up. But together we learned about the reality of life as sinful and fallen people in a sinful and fallen world. Together we learned about God's amazing gift of grace.

Throughout this book I've challenged you to close—even eliminate—the cultural-generational gap between you and the kids. I've attempted to lead you into an understanding of the normal changes that kids face when they pass through adolescence. In addition to learning what's normal, your eyes have been opened to the changing world of 21st-century youth culture and how it's powerfully molding our kids. My goal has been to provide you with knowledge that will equip you to be a more understanding and effective parent or youth worker. It's my hope that you'll make use of this knowledge so when your kids are grown, you'll be able to look back over these years and say, "I was intentional about helping my kids face their teenage years and weather the storms and pressures of adolescence. I deliberately worked—with God's guidance—to help them make godly choices, to provide them with a healthy and close family, and to prepare them for adulthood as spiritually, emotionally, and physically healthy followers of Christ."

As we come to the end of our examination of youth culture, I want to reemphasize the underlying theme of this book and the most important aspect of our kids' lives: Their spiritual health. You see, it's not enough to feel as though we've been successful parents if our kids merely avoid the ravages of substance abuse or remain chaste during their teenage years. I believe with my whole heart that the most successful parents in the world are ones who determine that the spiritual well-being of their kids is top priority. When asked, "What are you hoping your little boy or girl will become?" these parents answer, "I don't care...just as long as they're *spiritually healthy!*"

As a father, I continue to learn that the process of leading our kids through adolescence and into spiritual health and maturity requires hard work. Each of my kids was created by God for a relationship *with* God. Humanity's sinfulness has undone what should have been and has therefore broken that relationship. Yet, the Bible tells the story of God's unfolding plan to provide us with a way back to that intended relationship through the life, death, and resurrection of his Son, Jesus Christ. As parents and youth workers, our primary responsibility is to share this reality with teenagers so they might find their place in God's story by becoming followers of Christ and living under his guidance in every area of their lives. If you're a parent who's ready to face this God-given responsibility to make the spiritual health of your kids your top parenting priority, then this chapter is for you.

In coming to an understanding of how to lead our teenagers to spiritual health, we must answer two foundational questions: *What is spiritual health?* And *How can I lead my kids to hear the still small voice of God—as God invites them into his story—when all the voices of youth culture are screaming in their ears?*

What follows are some of the principles I've learned as a fellow struggler in the parenting and youth ministry journey. The list isn't exhaustive, nor does following these suggestions guarantee that your kids will become followers of Christ. But based on what I've learned from the Scriptures and the experiences of those who've gone before, these suggestions are wise steps to take on the road to leading teenagers to spiritual maturity.

Just What Is Spiritual Health?

I grew up in a suburban Philadelphia neighborhood filled with boys. Our after-school hours and summer days were spent in search of adventure. Our greatest thrill was to indulge our exuberance by engaging in what seemed like risky escapades, chosen because they stretched the limits our parents had set for us.

One of the places we liked to go was a local apple orchard. This promised land was reached by a short bike ride over some back yards and through a small section of woods. When we were younger, we'd stand back and watch the big boys scale the eight-foot metal fence, run through the orchard, disappear over a hill, and come back with big red apples. However, eating the ill-gotten apple was only part of the reward. The real prize was making it back without the orchard keeper unloading a burst of rock salt from his gun into our rear ends.

While none of us had ever actually seen the orchard keeper or heard his gun fire (he and his gun were most likely an urban legend), we nervously cheered and feared for the guys all the same. We'd watch in awe as these heroes came back over the fence and proudly feasted on their apples. This ritual served as a neighborhood rite of passage to separate the "men" from the boys.

When I was finally old enough to go over the fence, I was confronted with a major dilemma: *Would I disobey my parents and step beyond the limits they'd set for me, or would I follow the crowd into the orchard?* While I can't remember my mom and dad ever telling me not to go into the orchard, I was smart enough to know that if I was ever caught, facing my dad would be much worse than running into the orchard keeper. As I look back on that day, I clearly remember three distinct feelings.

The first was of *safety and security* as I stood outside the fence. I was where I was supposed to be—right where I belonged.

The second feeling was one of being *torn in two* as I paused to straddle the top of the fence, trying to decide whether or not to continue on my journey. One leg hung on the side where the rest of me belonged, while the other dangled toward danger.

The third feeling came as I finally went over the fence and into the orchard. Strangely, it was nothing like the sense of freedom I'd expected. Instead, it was *an almost paralyzing sense of being where I didn't belong.* Even though I gave in to the pressure and ran for an apple, I wanted nothing more than to be out of there. And quite honestly, I didn't care if I ever went back in again.

The spiritual development and health of our teenagers is very similar to my experience at that apple orchard. My kids and your kids are spiritual beings who will grow up to fit into one of three basic categories that coincide with my experience of going over the fence.

The first category includes *those who give in to the voices of culture* that invite them to climb over. Shaped by society and its institutions, they find it easier to be where everyone else is, even though they don't belong there. They've opted out of playing the part they were created for in God's story. They grow to be adults whose personal sense of right and wrong hinges on what everybody else is doing. They refuse to live under Jesus Christ. Before long they get used to being in the orchard, and they eventually call it home. They have no interest in God or a place for him in their lives. They're *spiritually unhealthy.*

The second category of people is filled with *leg-dangling fence-sitters.* Unwilling to commit themselves to either side of the fence, they straddle the top and wind up living on both sides. When it's most convenient and easier to be in the orchard, they jump in. When it's to their advantage to be outside the fence, they stay out. Their habit of making decisions based on what's easiest or most convenient at any given moment leads them to lives characterized by a commitment to be uncommitted. They know they belong in a relationship with God. They've heard about the place they should hold in God's story. They know right from wrong. They talk about God, read their Bibles from time to time, pray out loud, and go to church. But their faith makes little difference in how they live their lives day to day. Their fence-sitting causes them to *forfeit their spiritual health.*

The last group of people are those who *understand why they were created and the roles they were made to play in God's story.* Even though it's not always easy, they go against the flow of the crowd and stay outside the fence. They're in vital relationships with the living God. Their commitment to God is characterized by a deep, passionate faith. They understand that Jesus came to usher in the kingdom of God and that their place in that kingdom is to live in obedience to Christ. Even so, their sinful natures still exist—they're often tempted to climb the fence, and they do make mistakes. But because their desire to love and serve God remains throughout their struggles, they never lose sight of the fact that

God has called them to lives *outside* the orchard. They've experienced the freedom of faith and obedience, and as a result—they don't ever want to leave. These teenagers will grow up as *spiritually healthy adults.*

Take a minute and think ahead a few years. Imagine your kids as young adults standing near that apple orchard. Where do you want them to be? Inside the fence, on the fence, or outside the fence? What do you want to see when you look into their eyes? Someone who has turned his back on God? Someone who only talks about God? Or someone who is committed to living under God's rule and reign? My greatest desire as a father is to see my kids standing outside the fence—not because I've said so, but because they know that's where they belong. I long for them to be spiritually healthy.

Jesus defines spiritual health and the spiritually healthy person during a discussion with a lawyer. He frames his definition in the form of a commandment: "Love the Lord your God with all your heart and with all your soul and with all your mind and with all your strength." And then he continues, "Love your neighbor as yourself" (Mark 12:30-31).

According to Jesus, living a life of spiritual health outside the fence is living a life of commitment. The first commitment involves focusing all that you have, are, and ever will be on loving God. The second calls us to serve God by loving others in the same way Jesus loves us.

Let me encourage you to make the spiritual health of your kids your goal by first making it your prayer. The next time you sit at the table with your family, quietly look at each of your kids. Think about God's desire to see your children realize their created purpose by loving him with all of their being. Silently pray for each one and watch what happens when, over time, God's will for the spiritual health of your kids becomes part of your will as you parent them through the adolescent years and into adulthood. I have often prayed, "God, please grow Bethany (Caitlin/Josh/Nathaniel) to love you with all of her heart, mind, soul, and strength. Give her the compassion and sensitivity to love others as herself. Give her the strength to say *yes* to you and *no* to going over the fence."

I'm convinced this is the most important, valuable, and necessary prayer we could ever pray for our kids.

I trust that reading this book has served not only to increase your knowledge and understanding of the world in which your kids are growing up, but that it's also raised your level of concern and prepared you for the reality of raising kids in today's world. After all, a lot of the teenage values, attitudes, and behaviors we've examined are horrifying. But the kids who stand the best chance to resist buying into those dangerous messages are the kids whose parents are committed to leading them to spiritual health and maturity on God's terms.

Leading Your Kids to Spritual Health

If you're convinced of your need to lead your teenagers to spiritual health, you may be wondering, "Okay, I understand the goal and what it looks like. But how can I point my kids to Christ and nurture their spiritual health in a culture that sends a different message and calls our kids to 'come and follow me'?"

I've asked numerous parents who've also struggled to raise spiritually healthy kids to pass on what they've learned—both from things they've done correctly, as well as things they've done incorrectly. And I've listened to a lot of advice—good advice, which I'll now pass on to you after making one thing clear: Even if parents do everything *right*, there's still no guarantee their kids will grow up to be spiritually healthy.

I know one family what that would define as a "strong Christian family." They shared devotions and wonderful times together while the kids were growing up; when all three kids were young, they indicated their desire to take their places in God's story and follow Jesus. Two continued on that path right into adulthood. But one son left his parents in pain and confusion as he retreated from his parents' faith and disappeared into the orchard. Devastated, the father said to me, "I never thought this type of thing could happen in a Christian home. I feel very helpless."

I don't know why God allows these things to happen. What I do know is God calls us to intentionally take the time to raise and nurture our kids in the Christian faith. Many who do this will see their kids grow into spiritual health and maturity. But I also know we can't force our kids to love, honor, and obey God. We cannot carry them kicking and screaming into God's kingdom. The Holy Spirit calls them to faith—we don't. They're human beings created by God with the ability to make their own choices. For many families, consistent spiritual nurturing doesn't bear fruit in the kids' lives until long after they entered adulthood.

Remember, spiritual growth is a process. We can never presume to know God's perfect timing. There will be situations where we just won't know how he's acting out his will. Sometimes God takes us through the desert of watching our kids go wrong as part of his plan to parent us and lead us to depend on him, our heavenly Father, all the more.

Throughout the rest of this last chapter, we'll examine four key elements necessary for raising spiritually healthy teenagers. As we do so, ponder the ways in which you can improve as a parent. And lest you forget, I make no claims to have it all together myself. I'm a fellow struggler.

Where I Am as a Parent

When my son Josh was just a little guy, we had a real battle with his transition from the infant car seat to the "big boy seat." Before we were even out of the driveway, we'd hear the click of his seat belt being unbuckled. It seemed as though he was unbuckling his seat belt every five minutes. "Josh, get your seat belt back on!" became our family's battle cry during even the shortest drives.

One day Josh and I were headed home after a trip to the mall. We were passing through an intersection just a few blocks from our house when I noticed a car coming at us from the left. It was traveling fast, and I knew it was going to run the stop sign. I immediately looked at Josh to see if he had his seat belt on. He did—a welcome sign that he'd followed our instructions. But I soon realized that wasn't all he'd learned from me.

In an effort to avoid a collision, I stomped on the brakes and skidded to a halt. As soon as Josh's doubled-over body snapped back to an upright position, I began to turn the incident into a little lesson called "this is why we tell you to wear your seat belt." But before I had a chance to say anything, Josh looked out his window and watched the other car as it continued on down the street. Then he shook his fist in the air and yelled, "You idiot!" I wondered, *Where in the world did he learn to talk like that to other drivers?* I knew he'd been spending a lot of time in the car with his mother—and then it hit me: He was responding to the other driver in a manner that he'd learned from watching...me.

All right, I'll admit it: I tend to regress a little when I'm driving. My son was only following the behavior modeled for him by his father. Today, Josh is a young adult. But over the years, there have been many occasions when I've reprimanded him for living out my bad example in his life.

Do you want your teenagers to grow up to be strong in their faith and able to handle all that our world throws at them? Then ask yourself, *What kind of example am I giving them?* Where you're at as a parent plays a more significant role in determining what your kids will become than any other factor. *Where are you standing in relation to that apple orchard? Are you outside the fence, on the fence, or inside the fence?* You've got to be where you want your kids to be because they'll follow your example and wind up right where you are. Better yet, you've got to be where you *belong* so your kids will learn that's where they belong, too.

In Deuteronomy 6, Moses shares God's plan for who should teach God's truths to succeeding generations and how they were to be taught: "These commandments that I give you today are to be upon your hearts. Impress them on your children. Talk about them when you sit at home and when you walk along the road, when you lie down and when you get up. Tie them as symbols on your hands and bind them on your foreheads. Write them on the doorframes of your houses and on your gates" (Deuteronomy 6:6-9).

Who should teach God's truths? Parents who have his commandments written on their hearts and gladly love God with their whole beings. Parents who prayerfully endeavor with God's help and by God's grace to integrate their faith into every nook and cranny of their lives. God, in his perfect wisdom and plan, has chosen to do his work through the family. God began with a family in Genesis, and he continues to use the family as the primary arena for bringing people to himself. And how are parents to teach? With a diligent commitment to teach and model wholehearted, single-minded devotion to God. When God's truths become the central, overriding interest and purpose in our lives, teaching them to our kids will happen almost unconsciously.

It's no mistake that our kids grow up to look, act, think, and be like us in so many ways. While similarities in physical appearance are inherited through the genes, our attitudes, values, and behaviors are passed from generation to generation by example. God made it this way. This is especially true when it comes to faith development and spiritual health.

After working with teenagers for several years, I heard someone say that in families where neither parent attends church regularly, only 6 percent of the kids will grow up to be faithful to Christ. If only Mom attends regularly, 15 percent will remain faithful. If only Dad is consistent in his attendance, only 55 percent remain faithful. But in those families where both parents model regular church attendance, 72 percent of their kids will remain faithful. My experience with teenagers and their families validates these figures. Granted, there's much more to spiritual health and vitality than church attendance. But those numbers speak volumes about the importance of parental example.

How do you measure up in this first necessary element for pointing kids to Christ in the 21st century? Here are some specific questions you can use to evaluate your own spiritual health and vitality:

- When my kids look at me, are they learning what it means to love God with all their hearts, souls, minds, and strength?

- Do they see me trusting God for guidance and wisdom as I plan the future, run my business, manage my home, and so on?

- Do they see me turning to God when I'm anxious, troubled, or ill?

- Do they see me living out my commitment to Christ by spending time reading and studying the Bible?

- Do they know that prayer is an important part of my life?

- Are they learning what it means to carry the cross and live a life of Christian discipleship?

- Do they see God is constantly central to my thoughts and actions or just on Sunday mornings?

- Do they see a faith that's integrated into every area of my life, including my relationships, my vocation, my spending decisions, my use of leisure time, how I play, and so on?

- Do they see me care for family, neighbors, friends, and the "lepers and outcasts" of the world?

- Are they learning to be compassionate and Christ-centered rather than insensitive and self-centered?

- Are they learning not to talk behind people's backs?

- Are they learning that God is the source of all they are and have, including the gift of salvation?

We all have wishes, dreams, hopes, and desires for what our kids will become. When you dream about your kids' spiritual futures, don't forget they're learning what place spirituality and faith should hold in their lives—from you.

Eugene Peterson describes it this way: "A parent's main job is not to be a parent, but to be a person. There are no techniques to master that will make a good parent. There is no book to read that will give the right answers. The parent's main task is to be vulnerable in a living demonstration that adulthood is full, alive, and Christian."[636]

What I Know as a Parent

If we're to live out our God-given calling to model and teach the Christian faith to our kids in a relevant manner, then we need to understand the cultural forces shaping the head and heart commitments of our kids. Only then can we teach them the value of using God's Word to navigate through the adolescent years and adulthood.

Over the years, my kids have made me aware of our cultural differences in a variety of ways. When they were young, it was their disbelief. Josh made me feel old when he discovered I didn't have rollerblades or a SuperSoaker when I was a boy. Caitlin informed me I desperately needed her help in choosing a wardrobe. Bethany couldn't believe my childhood was void of computers. Nate wondered what life was like back in the days when kids didn't have iPods. Now that they're older, they typically respond to my age with a telltale laugh and shake of the head. I know that in their young minds, my age automatically categorizes me as old and out of touch. But I don't have to stay in the dark when it comes to understanding their world. I can keep listening, looking, and learning.

The coming years will bring more changes as youth culture continues to snowball away from your own teenage experiences. This means you'll have to be more intentional about keeping up. I trust that reading this book will be only the beginning of your quest for youth culture knowledge. Continue the task you've begun because you need to know. (Be sure to regularly visit our Center for Parent/Youth Understanding Web site—www.cpyu.org—as it's updated daily with information and analysis on today's youth culture.)

How I Approach Parenting

I despise painting. There's no home-improvement task I hate more than spending my days on a ladder with a brush or roller in my hand. I'll do it when it needs to be done, but my endless grumbling and clock-watching betray my disdain for the job. I just want it to end.

I knew a mother and father who viewed raising their kids the same way. At first glance they appeared to be wonderful parents. They were not physically abusive toward their kids, and they gave them a lot of things. But they really weren't enjoying the opportunity they'd been given to raise their children. Several years ago I was standing with the father as our kids played together. He was complaining about how much it costs to raise kids, keep them clothed, help them with homework, run them from here to there, and anything else that required time or sacrifice. He looked at me and said, "You know, I can't wait until these bozos grow up. Then me and my wife are going to start having some fun. Bahamas, here we come!" I knew him well enough to know he wasn't joking. I felt bad for his kids, but I felt worse for him. His approach to parenting was terrible, and my guess was it wouldn't be long before his kids figured out what he really thought about being their dad. I've since lost touch with the man, but I've never forgotten his words.

Parents who hope to raise spiritually healthy kids in these challenging days must take a different approach to parenting. Instead of wishing the days, months, and years away (which at times is so easy to do), we should ask God to help us make the most of the time we have with our kids so we can do as much as possible to point them in the right direction.

Here are six elements that must be a part of our approach to parenting as we travel through the few short years we have with our children.

Our approach to parenting must be biblical. When scuba divers are down deep, it's easy for them to become confused and disoriented. Since water diffuses light, divers often find themselves surrounded by illumination, making it difficult to discern which way is up. Feeling weightless and lacking a sense of gravity also contributes to this confusion. The only way to distinguish up from down is to watch the direction in which their air bubbles travel. Divers who lose their sense of direction risk drowning if they trust their own senses more than their bubbles. They're taught early on that no matter how they feel, no matter what they think, their bubbles are always right.

I know a mother who's confused and disoriented. She desires to be the best mother in the world. Consequently, her shelves are filled with parenting manuals and books she's read from cover to cover. She's attended the many parenting seminars offered in her local schools and community. She even makes a point of going to other mothers to ask for guidance and advice. No doubt she's learned a lot. But she's the first to admit that after exposing herself to dozens of different parenting philosophies and techniques, she's felt mostly confused. She needs to learn that no matter how she feels, no matter what she thinks, no matter what subjective advice any book or parenting expert gives her, the Bible describes things accurately and clearly. Like the scuba diver's bubbles, the Bible is always right. Everything else must be evaluated in light of God's Word.

From the moment they're born, our kids need parents who tune themselves in to the most reliable source of parenting information and instruction. God has given us the Bible to guide us through these difficult and confusing days in our fallen world. Your approach to parenting should be informed by God's Word. Study the Bible with diligence on a regular basis. Discover how it speaks to the molders and shapers of contemporary youth culture. Uncover the character traits and attitudes God calls us to exhibit in our families and other interpersonal relationships.

On a personal note, I've found that my investment of time in knowing God's Word has been the very thing that's guided me through the deep waters of parenting. As I mentioned earlier in this book, I haven't been a perfect parent, nor have I raised perfect kids. We've experienced the blessing of suffering due to poor choices. While these times have been painful, they've also been times of great blessing as we've seen God be true to his Word as he parents us while we sometimes helplessly parent our own kids.

Our approach to parenting should be realistic. One of my most vivid baseball memories occurred on Father's Day in 1964. That was the day Philadelphia Phillies pitcher Jim Bunning—my hero—pitched a perfect game. Twenty-seven times the New York Mets came to the plate. No one made it to first base. Bunning was absolutely perfect, and he didn't allow any runs, hits, walks, or errors.

That day wouldn't have been so special if perfect games were commonplace. But they're very rare. There are times when years will pass before another major league pitcher throws a perfect game. Only a handful of pitchers have ever thrown nine perfect innings. And while there are hundreds of excellent pitchers who've never thown a perfect game—including many Hall of Famers—these "other" pitchers aren't awful by any stretch!

Why is it that so many of us feel like failures when we or our kids make a mistake? My guess is that we're disappointed because we expect ourselves and our kids to be perfect—a very unrealistic expectation. But even our gnawing sense of imperfection shouldn't keep us from being good parents.

Realistic parents pave the way for family closeness and build up their kids by parenting with grace. They aren't paralyzed by feelings of fear and inadequacy when they make mistakes. They know that since the beginning of time God has used imperfect people to carry out his plan. And they know he'll use them as they raise their kids—in spite of their imperfections. When I look in the mirror, I see inconsistency. When I look inside myself, I face the dark reality of my sinful nature. When I look at my kids, I see the same. I thank God for his incomprehensible grace!

Our approach to parenting should be prophetic. What image does the word prophet conjure in your mind? I would venture to say that for many in today's world, the image isn't very positive. Some immediately think of crazed and socially awkward religious zealots who stand on busy street corners holding homemade signs and muttering about the impending end of the world. Others think of televised news reports about charismatic cult leaders who serve as pied pipers to a small-yet-committed band of followers who've believed the "prophet's message from God."

Those who've read and understood the Bible know that throughout the course of biblical history, God called certain people to speak his truth in his name. The Bible includes both a written record of the utterances of these prophets, along with several books of prophecy. When these divinely called and inspired prophets spoke, their words were the commands and revelations of God.

When I suggest that our approach to parenting our children should be "prophetic," I'm certainly not suggesting we take on the role of the religious cult leader. Neither am I suggesting we function in the way that Old and New Testament prophets functioned. Instead, being prophetic in our relationships with our teenagers is an intentional effort on our parts of looking for opportunities to speak biblical truth into their lives and showing how God's Word and the Christian faith speaks and relates to all of life. It's the process of imparting godly wisdom to our teenagers.

How do we do this? First and foremost we should ask God to guide us regarding what, how, and when we communicate his truth. Unlike the prophets from biblical times, this doesn't mean we wait for God's Spirit to move in our lives in a way that provokes an utterance or new revelation. Instead we should ask God to guide us to the truths he's already spoken in Scripture, along with how and when to communicate those truths to our kids.

Don't ever forget: No nook or cranny in our lives lies outside of God's authority. The Scriptures speak to every teenage pressure, choice, problem, or situation that's already been discussed in this book, along with a whole lot more. Part of our God-given responsibility is to communicate what God has said regarding these matters. In this way, we become prophetic in our parenting as we help our kids hear and understand God's revelation and commands.

Our approach to parenting should be preventive. A working couple who just had their first baby came to visit us before deciding whether or not they wanted my wife to baby-sit their new arrival during the day. As we were getting to know each other, they asked to take a tour of our house. As we walked from room to room and around the outside of the house, they looked for safety hazards. The safety inspection was not complete until they'd gotten answers to all of their questions, "Will you put covers in the unused electrical outlets? Do you keep a gate at the top of the steps? Are the basement doors left open or shut? Does your dog like kids?" I must admit: Their endless stream of questions was starting to get on my nerves. But they wanted to be sure we'd take the necessary steps to protect their child from physical harm.

We all share that couple's concern for our own children's physical well-being. We tell our kids to stay out of the street, to look both ways, and to keep away from hot stuff. We want them to be wise to dangers so they'll avoid getting in harm's way. Parents who expect to lead their kids through adolescence and into spiritual health should also take preventive measures.

Our teenagers should be equipped to face life and all of its challenges. They need us to pass on the valuable information we've learned about life. We need to speak openly about the results of substance abuse, premarital sex, peer pressure, and materialism.

Another preventive measure is teaching our kids decision-making skills. There will come a time when they're out in the world without Mom or Dad at their side, and they'll be called upon to make some crucial choices. How will they know how to choose wisely if we haven't taken the time to teach them?

They also need parents who will instruct them about the relevance of the truths of God's Word and how it applies to all of life. A working knowledge of God's transcendent standards of right and wrong is the best dose of preventive medicine. The cultural realities we've discussed in this book are pervasive. Your teen will face most of these realities at some level during their teenage years—or perhaps even earlier. Your preventive influence must start now.

Our approach to parenting should be redemptive. How will you respond to your kids when they make a mistake or do something wrong? What will you say if your daughter turns her back on all that you've taught her and winds up sexually active and pregnant? What will you say if your son gets suspended from school for fighting? What will you do if you find drug paraphernalia in your teenager's room? What will you do if your daughter gets arrested for shoplifting? All teens face temptation, and all teens make sinful choices. The determining factor in whether or not a bad choice turns into a situation that gets better or worse will depend on your response.

Let me suggest that your goal should be to redeem these situations by turning a mistake into an opportunity for your teenager to become a more godly and Christlike person. I once heard author John White share his rule for parenting through (and redeeming) difficult situations: "As Christ is to me, so must I be to my kids." During his lifetime, White had ample opportunities to live out that rule in his relationship with a prodigal son. Don't write off your teenager as hopeless or boot him out of the family. Rather, treat him as you think your heavenly Father would treat you if you were the offending party. And in reality, there isn't a day that goes by that you aren't blowing it somehow. Believe me, I know. Paul Tripp reminds us of this truth:

> We need to face the fact that the harsh realities of the Fall are depicted in everyday family life. It is this humble admission that opens us up to one of the most wonderful functions of the Christian family. It is when we humbly face the reality of our falseness that we begin to seek and treasure the riches of the grace of the Lord Jesus Christ.

As we—parents and kids alike—face our need as sinners, the family becomes a truly redemptive community where the themes of grace, forgiveness, deliverance from sin, reconciliation, new life in Christ, and hope become the central themes of family life.[637]

I wondered how Mike would handle it when his 16-year-old daughter, Kate, told him she was pregnant. They were a Christian family, but over the last couple of years there had been some growing tension between Kate and her dad. But to be honest, her pregnancy was quite unexpected and shocking to me. How would her father, a church leader, react?

On the night Kate gave her parents the news, she sat with her parents at the kitchen table. They later told me they were shocked and disappointed that Kate had slept with her boyfriend. I asked Kate what her father said when she dropped the bombshell.

"He stood up, walked around the table, put his arms around me, and said, 'Kate, I love you. I want you to know that your mother and I will not stop loving you. We will stand behind you, and we'll love this baby together.'" She continued, "I never felt closer to my parents in my life. I love them so much!" A broken relationship and sinful behavior was on the road to being redeemed.

John Seel writes, "So what is Christian parenting? In short, it's loving our kids as God loves us. It's emulating the father of the prodigal son who loved him enough to let him leave and squander his inheritance."[638]

Our approach to parenting should be prayerful. David Bryant, director of Concerts of Prayer International and a leader in the prayer movement says, "The primary reason there is an acceleration of prayer [is that] we are becoming more and more of the conviction that we don't have the answers any longer."[639]

Parents, we need to pray for answers—answers to our questions about raising our kids and answers to our kids' adolescent questions and their deep spiritual longings for God. You see, our kids grow in the wisdom and nurture of God in spite of us, not because of us. Sure, they learn a lot from the examples we live, but it's ultimately God who gives them faith and leads them to spiritual health.

Paul's words became more real to me as I struggled to raise my kids through adolescence: "Do not be anxious about anything, but in everything, by prayer and petition, with thanksgiving, present your requests to God" (Philippians 4:6). Prayer is God's gift to us as we depend on him and his power to keep us on track as moms and dads.

What I Give as a Parent

Mark was a teenager who had everything—and nothing. I met him when I was speaking at a middle school retreat. From the moment I arrived at the camp, he followed me everywhere. It didn't take long for me to figure out that Mark had some deep needs that were eating him up. I pulled his youth pastor aside to find out what was going on with Mark.

This is what he told me: "Mark is longing for the love of an older man. He comes from one of the wealthiest families in our community. All the kids envy him because his father gives him anything and everything he wants. He has the nicest clothes, stereo, and television. Every summer he goes to a prestigious camp in New England. He's got it all—except his father's love. What the kids in our group from strong families don't realize is that trading places with Mark wouldn't be much fun at all."

For the rest of the weekend, I went out of my way to pay special attention to Mark. It was a bittersweet moment when I put my arm around him after we won a game of two-on-two basketball. I knew that my arm on his shoulder put a smile on his face because of the emptiness in his heart.

The most fortunate teenagers in the world are the ones who say they live with parents who give them everything. But the "everything" that teens so desperately want and need can't be paid for at the cash register at the local mall. There is no price tag on what they want.

Parents in strong, healthy families are givers, and by their giving they raise strong, healthy kids who find it much easier to make it through the adolescent years of change. Conversely, parents in weak, unhealthy families fail to give their kids the things they really need, and they abandon their kids to be molded and shaped more by their culture than by Dad and Mom.

While my list is certainly not exhaustive, here are the gifts you need to wrap up and give to your kids every day.

Give them unconditional love. Today the word *love* has been drained of its meaning by those who only refer to it as "made between the sheets." Our teenagers need parents who will help them rediscover the meaning of the word *love* by demonstrating it in the home. The New Testament word used for the kind of love kids need from their parents is *agape*, the same word used to describe God's love for us. Agape is the highest and noblest form of love because it's given in spite of the receiver. There's no condition on the part of the receiver that could turn the free flow of this love on or off. The lover looks past the other person's faults, bad habits, imperfections, and unwillingness to love them back and continues to love. It's a commitment to love the unlovable, even when they don't deserve it.

Have there ever been moments when your kids have been unlovable? I asked that question to a group of parents one time, and one man shouted out, "Yes! The time between ages 12 and 20!" Sometimes it's difficult to love our kids during the awkward years of adolescence because we may not get anything in return. But true love seeks no return. It just loves. And while your kids may not say it or show it, they want and need your unconditional love.

Give them your time. My friend Ron Rand has dedicated his life to encouraging and helping fathers spend time with their kids. A pastor, Ron was once like many men who become so consumed by their long list of to-do's that they forget what they must do. He writes, "Eleven P.M.—two hours later than I'd told Jennifer to expect me. Again. Our sons have been prayed with and tucked in hours before, but not by me. I'd been presiding at a church committee meeting. The night before it had been Evangelism team. And Monday? Absent again. What kind of father was raising my boys? He was busy, distracted, and absent most of the time. Everyone else's needs—everything seemed more urgent than being a daddy."[640]

Ron is not alone. There are moms and dads everywhere who get so wrapped up in all that they're doing that they forsake what they *must* be doing—parenting.

Juvenile probation officer Fred Green interviewed hundreds of teenagers on their way to juvenile detention centers. Most of them talked about family problems and dysfunction. Green put together a list of 10 things that the kids he interviewed say they wish their parents had done. These kids say, "DO NOT GET HUNG UP ON A JOB THAT KEEPS YOU AWAY FROM HOME. Fathers, keep in touch with your kids somehow. Mothers, cut the heavy social schedule so you can be home to supervise the kids."[641]

Ron Rand gives parents good advice when he challenges us to "learn how to spend effective personal time with each family member. Our families need both quality time and quantity time expressed in ways that matter."[642]

One lost piece of family time that we must recover is meal time. It's not surprising that recent research shows that "families who consistently dine together and focus on one another at mealtime are more likely to describe themselves as very satisfied with the closeness of their families. Further, families who make this commitment are more likely to say that their kids are less susceptible to participate in destructive behaviors such as drinking alcohol and feeling disconnected from their families."[643]

Give them your attention. Beth started coming to our church youth group when she was a sophomore in high school. Her parents divorced when she was young, and her mother had since remarried and had another child. I decided to get to know Beth, and I went to one of her high school field hockey games. When the game was over, I started to walk back to the parking lot as Beth joined the rest of her team for an after-game meeting. Just as I was about to get into my car, Beth ran over. She threw her arms around me and, with tears streaming down her face, said, "Thanks so much for coming to my game. I've been playing since I was in seventh grade, and you're the first person who's ever come to watch me play." I felt badly for Beth. I resolved then and there that my kids would never have reason to say, "Dad was never around."

Information collected from surveys of more than 90,000 seventh through 12th graders across the United States was analyzed to determine what factors increase and decrease the incidence of risk-taking behaviors of teenagers in several areas: Emotional distress, suicidal thoughts and behaviors, use of three substances (cigarettes, alcohol, marijuana), and two types of sexual behaviors (age of first sexual experience and pregnancy history). The results don't offer anything new or surprising: Kids are more likely to make good choices when they sense they're connected to and cared for by others, especially Dad and Mom. Kids who report connections with loving parents are less likely to suffer from emotional distress, less likely to have suicidal thoughts or behaviors, less likely to use violence, and less likely to choose to abuse illicit drugs and alcohol. The study "confirms the importance of time availability of parents for their kids."[644]

So parents, drop that newspaper, let the housework go, leave the laptop at the office, and pay attention to your kids.

Give them boundaries. Healthy families have rules and boundaries. Healthy kids grow up learning right from wrong, thereby giving them more of an opportunity to become responsible and obedient. And as they learn to live responsibly within the limits of their freedom, their parents will gradually expand those limits until they're able to live independently.

The Institute for Youth Development reports research findings that show the importance of establishing clear rules and boundaries:

> When supportive, caring parents do not have clear rules and consequences, teens are more likely to engage in risk behaviors. Households with 'hands-on' parents (25% of teen households) have teens at half the average risk of all teens. Yet, teens from households with 'hands-off' parents (18% of teen households) are at four times the risk of teens from households with 'hands-on' parents.[645]

I once heard it said that raising teenagers is like holding a wet bar of soap: Too firm a grasp, and it shoots from your hand; too loose a grasp, and it slides away. A gentle but firm grasp keeps it in your control. One of the greatest gifts we can give our kids is reasonable and loving boundaries.

Give them consistent discipline. Perhaps you've run into the same little boy I've seen in restaurants and stores all over the country. He gets around. He's usually with his mother and father, and he's telling them what to do. They always seem oblivious to the fact that he's out of control, but every once in a while they'll lash out at him with some threat that you'd think would make him behave. "Sit down! Shut up or I'll rip your arms off," his mother says. But in a matter of seconds, he's back to his old tricks; it seems everyone except his father and mother notice what he's doing. Yet, he keeps it up, and his parents keep threatening to discipline him. It never happens, and the boy knows it never will. If his life continues this way, this poor boy won't know how to discipline himself. He'll grow up and have trouble functioning in the adult world. What he needs more than anything else is parents who encourage his good behavior and correct his unacceptable behavior.

When we give our kids the gift of consistent, loving discipline, we're helping them learn self-control. Later, that same self-control will help them make responsible choices in life. That's why Fred Green hears juvenile offenders say they wish their parents would do the following: "SHAKE ME UP. Punish me when I first go wrong. Tell me why. Convince me that more severe measures will come if I transgress again in the same manner. CALL MY BLUFF. Stand firm on what is right, even when your child threatens to run away or become a delinquent or drop out of school. Stay in there with him and the bluffing will cease in 98 percent of the cases."[646]

The dictionary defines *discipline* as "training that corrects, molds, and perfects moral character." When your kids look back on their growing-up years, they'll thank you for taking the time to teach them that there truly is right and wrong in a world that works so hard to teach them otherwise.

Give them two listening ears. The Swiss psychologist Paul Tournier has said, "Every human being needs to express himself. Through lack of opportunity for it, one may become sick."[647] That's a good explanation of what is happening to so many teenagers today. They have so much to say, but nobody is there to listen.

My four-year-old friend Will loves to talk. Whenever I see him at church, he's frantically trying to keep up with his mom and dad. On several occasions I've watched Will tug at his father's trousers in an effort to get his dad's attention. "Daddy, Daddy, I have to tell you something!" Every once in a while, his father will glance down from his conversation with another adult to say, "Not now, Will. I'm talking." On one occasion Will wet his pants right there in the hall, even though he was telling his father he had to get to the bathroom. Do you know what his father said? He leaned over to Will and asked, "Will, why didn't you tell me you had to go to the bathroom?"

I've met a lot of teenage Wills. At times, they've been living under my own roof. But they try so hard to get their parents' attention only to hear, "Not now. I'm too busy!" Trouble comes and then the parents wonder, Why didn't you tell me? But they did try to tell their parents. Eventually these teenagers discover that their parents don't even have the time—nor do they care to listen. So they'll go somewhere else to be heard and clam up on the homefront.

Do you want to lead your kids to spiritual health? Listen to them. Drop everything you're doing, be quiet, get in their face, and let them talk. Respond in a way that lets them know you love them.

Colleen was often late for our youth group meetings. At first I was bothered by what I thought was her apathy. But I soon discovered that whenever she was late, it was for one of two reasons: Either she'd lost track of time while sitting and talking with her parents at the dinner table, or she was out in the church parking lot having a heart-to-heart with her dad. It should come as no surprise that Colleen was a great kid from a great family. Her parents had given her the gift of their undivided attention and listening ears.

Give them your willingness to admit your mistakes. Anyone who's grown up with a father in the house learns at a young age that there are three things that men find very difficult to say: "I'm lost," "I can't fix it," and "I'm sorry." You may laugh, but it's true.

All of us know when we've done something wrong, but it's hard to admit to ourselves and to others that we're capable of making mistakes. We've somehow come to believe that if we don't admit it, nobody will know. Or perhaps that admission is a sign of weakness. But I've learned that if anyone is going to notice what I do wrong, it's my wife and kids. I've also learned to swallow hard, go to them, and say, "I'm sorry. Would you forgive me?" I'm not nearly as consistent as I should be, but I know vulnerability is one of the greatest gifts I can give to my kids. The most convincing proof for me is the many conversations I've had with angry teenagers who feel cut off from their parents. Many of them have said, "You know what I can't stand about my dad (or mom)? He (she) thinks he's (she's) so perfect. He (she) can never admit when he's (she's) wrong."

By admitting our mistakes, we model the truths of the gospel, our need for a redeemer, and the life-giving freedom of forgiveness our children so desperately need to experience and understand. When we're vulnerable, we offer them an example of real faith that is credible.

Give them a spiritual heritage. When I was a teenager, I can remember lying in my bed and hearing the quiet whispers of my parents as they climbed into their bed and turned out the lights. Sometimes I could hear them whispering their prayers before they went to sleep. I would often hear them pray for me.

My parents' bedtime prayers taught me that God occupied center stage in their lives and in our home. Those prayers, combined with years of family devotions, spiritual discussions, and my parents' godly example, gave me a rich spiritual heritage that I hope to pass on to my kids and their kids.

Getting Personal

There's a little county airport a few miles from where I live that's home to a parachute club. Every Saturday and Sunday, dozens of men and women gather outside a trailer at the end of the runway to get ready for their jumps. Although I've never jumped out of an airplane (and it's not on my list of things to do before I die), I enjoy going to the airport and watching a few jumps.

I sometimes wonder if all the time these parachutists spend in preparation is really worth it. Before they ever step out of the plane, there are classroom lessons, simulated jumps from a small wooden platform to the ground, and numerous equipment checks. I've stood by and watched the concentration and care each jumper invests in untangling their cords and folding and packing their chutes. One by one they put them on, checking and rechecking every little latch and buckle. When they're finally ready, they climb into the plane and get ready for a 15-minute ride to the correct jumping altitude.

But any question over the value of all their prejump preparations disappears when those little black specks begin to fall away from the plane one by one. One careless mistake or oversight could lead to death. But hours of good preparation pay off in a successful jump that lasts a few short moments.

There's a sense in which this book has been about parachute jumping. It takes years and years of careful concentration and intentional, ongoing preparation to raise teenagers in today's world. I believe those of us who take the time to know the love of the heavenly Father, to know and love our kids, and to know how the world is influencing our kids will be rewarded with a successful "jump." No, there are no guarantees, and we're often blessed—yes, *blessed*—with rocky times that test and build our faith. But I can tell you from experience as a "jumper" who's experienced some very trying and hairy moments, our heavenly Father will help us through the few short years of parenting our adolescents. And as those precious kids jump from childhood into adulthood, we'll be able to hear them land with thanksgiving for a mom and dad who loved them and cared for them.

Parenting kids in this rapidly changing culture isn't easy. The pressures on our kids are big and powerful. The molders and shapers are loud and strong. The voices will continue to scream into our kids' ears, "Come and follow me." But next to the Almighty and All-powerful God of the universe, those forces are like a grain of sand or a speck of dust.

Maybe you have some little ones running around your house these days. I've learned firsthand that one day they're little, and the next day they're big. It won't be long before your little ones are big ones.

Or maybe your little ones are already big ones, and you're watching them take another step toward adulthood each day. Think about them and the many choices and pressures they face. Are you in touch?

It is my hope and prayer that the little bit of information and lessons learned in this book will give you a start. And with God's help, may you keep up the good work. May God grant you the grace you need to prepare, to pray, to understand your kids and their world, to parent, and to lead your kids to him.

God bless you.

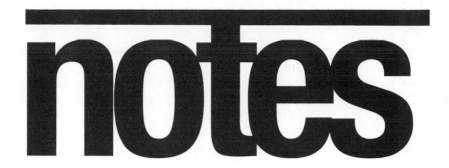

Chapter 1

1. Paul David Tripp, *Age of Opportunity: A Biblical Guide to Parenting Teens* (Phillipsburg, NJ: P&R Publishing, 2001), 19.

2. Tripp, *Age of Opportunity*, 19-20.

3. Peter Zollo, *Getting Wiser to Teens* (Ithaca, NY: New Strategist Publications, 2004), 168.

4. Chap Clark, *Hurt: Inside the World of Today's Teenagers* (Grand Rapids, MI: Baker, 2004), 108.

5. "Thinking with Computers," produced by the University of Arizona, 1991, videocassette.

6. John Stott, *The Contemporary Christian* (Downers Grove, IL: InterVarsity Press, 1992), 110.

7. Alister McGrath, *The Unknown God* (Grand Rapids, MI: Wm. B. Eerdmans, 1999), 120.

8. Stott, *The Contemporary Christian*, 39.

9. C. John Miller and Barbara Miller Juliani, *Come Back, Barbara*, 2nd ed. (Phillipsburg, NJ: P&R Publishing, 1997), 165.

10. John Fox, *Christ Jesus Triumphant*, quoted in Bernard Bangley, *Near To The Heart Of God: Daily Readings from the Spiritual Classics* (Wheaton, IL: Harold Shaw Publishers, 1998), 112.

11. John Fischer, *Fearless Faith* (Eugene, OR: Harvest House, 2002), 8.

12. Ibid., 14.

13. W. Bingham Hunter, *The God Who Hears* (Downers Grove, IL: InterVarsity Press, 1986), 12.

14. Stanley J. Grenz, *Prayer: The Cry for the Kingdom* (Grand Rapids, MI: Wm. B. Eerdmans, 2005), 23.

Chapter 2

15. Walt Mueller, *Engaging the Soul of Youth Culture: Bridging Teen Worldviews and Christian Truth* (Downers Grove, IL: InterVarsity Press, 2006), 113. For more information on culture, what it is, how to understand it, and the role it plays in the lives of teenagers, see Chapter 5, "Understanding Culture."

16. Clark, *Hurt*, 42-43.

17. Ibid., 59ff.

18. Ibid., 70.

19. National Association of State Boards of Education, *Code Blue: Uniting for Healthier Youth* (Alexandria, VA: 1990).

20. Dan Coats, "America's Youth: A Crisis of Character," Imprimis 20, no. 9 (September 1991): 2.

21. *Hardwired to Connect: The New Scientific Case for Authoritative Communities* (New York: Institute for American Values, YMCA of the USA, and Dartmouth Medical School, 2003), 8.

22. Jack O. Balswick and Judith K. Balswick, *The Family: A Christian Perspective on the Contemporary Home* (Grand Rapids, MI: Baker Books, 1989), 21ff.

23. David Elkind, *All Grown Up and No Place to Go,* (Reading, MA: Addison-Wesley Publishing Company, 1984) 115.

24. "Marriage and Divorce," National Center for Health Statistics, February 28, 2006, http://www.cdc.gov/nchs/fastats/divorce.htm (April 19, 2006).

25. "The State of Our Unions: The Social Health of Marriage in America" (Piscataway, NJ: The National Marriage Project, 2005), 18.

26. "U.S. Divorce Statistics," Divorce Magazine.com, 2005, http://www.divorcemag.com/statistics/statsUS.shtml (April 19, 2006).

27. "The State of Our Unions," 18.

28. "Helping Unwed Parents Build Strong and Healthy Marriages: A Conceptual Framework for Interventions, United States Department of Health and Human Services—Administration for Kids and Families, January 15, 2002, http://www.acf.hhs.gov/programs/opre/strengthen/strengthfam/reports/conceptual_framework/framework_chp1.html (April 20, 2006).

29. Frank F. Furstenburg Jr. and Andrew J. Cherlin, *Divided Families: What Happens to Kids When Parents Part* (Cambridge, MA: Harvard University Press, 1991), 11.

30. www.divorcereform.org/gul.html, 2002 (April 20, 2006).

31. "Marriage in America: A Report to the Nation" (New York: Institute for American Values, 1995), 8.

32. "Overheard," *Newsweek*, special edition, winter/spring 1990, 11.

33. Judith Wallerstein and Sandra Blakeslee, *Second Chances: Men, Women & Children a Decade after Divorce* (New York: Tickner & Fields, 1989).

34. Judith S. Wallerstein, Julia M. Lewis, and Sandra Blakeslee, *The Unexpected Legacy of Divorce: A 25-Year Landmark Study* (New York: Hyperion, 2000), xxiii.

35. David Popenoe, "Marriage Decline in America," May 22, 2001, http://marriage.rutgers.edu/Publications/pubMarriage%20Decline.htm (April 20, 2006).

36. "Preliminary Births for 2004," (National Center for Health Statistics, January 19, 2006), www.cdc.gov.nchs/products/pubs/pubd/hestats/prelim_births/prelim_births04.htm (April 20, 2006).

37. Ibid.

38. America's Kids: Key National Indicators of Well-Being 2005, (Washington, DC: Federal Interagency Forum on Child and Family Statistics, 2005), 9.

39. Popenoe, "Marriage Decline in America."

40. "Moving In: Teen Views on Cohabitation" (Princeton, NJ: The Gallup Poll, April 8, 2003), http://poll.gallup.com/content/default.aspx?ci=8128&pg=1 (April 20, 2006).

41. Wade F. Horn and Tom Sylvester, *Father Facts*, 4th ed. (Gaithersburg, MD: National Fatherhood Initiative, 2002), 15.

42. Wade F. Horn, *Father Facts* (Lancaster, PA: National Fatherhood Initiative, 1995), ii.

43. Horn and Sylvester, *Father Facts*, 15.

44. Ibid., 106-11.

45.   *Code Blue.*

46.   Maternal and Child Health Bureau, "Child Health USA 2002: Population Characteristics," http://www.mchb.hrsa.gov/chusa02/main_pages/page?14.htm (April 20, 2006).

47.   *The State of Our Nation's Youth: 2005-2006,* 32.

48.   Mark Robichaux, "Business First, Family Second," *The Wall Street Journal,* May 12, 1989.

49.   Tamar Lewin, "Sexual Abuse Tied to 1 in 4 Girls in Teens," *The New York Times on the Web Women's Health,* October 1, 1997, http://www.nytimes.com/specials/women/war-chive/971001_758.html (April 20, 2006).

50.   "Fact Sheet: Sexual Abuse of Boys," *Prevent Child Abuse America,* www.preventchildabuse.org (April 20, 2006).

51.   "The Facts on Kids and Domestic Violence," *Family Violence Prevention Fund,* www.endabuse.org (April 20, 2006).

52.   Walt Mueller, *Engaging the Soul of Youth Culture* (Downers Grove, IL: InterVarsity Press, 2006), 91.

53.   Gene Edward Veith Jr., *Postmodern Times: A Christian Guide to Contemporary Thought and Culture* (Wheaton, IL: Crossway Books, 1994), 196.

54.   "Americans Are Most Likely to Base Truth on Feelings," *The Barna Update,* February 21, 2002.

55.   George Barna, *Real Teens: A Contemporary Snapshot of Youth Culture* (Ventura, CA: Regal Books, 2001), 63.

56.   Marva J. Dawn, *Is It a Lost Cause?* (Grand Rapids, MI: Wm. B. Eerdmans, 1997), 23.

57.   "Youth Indicators 2005/Indicator 42: Arrests," *National Center for Education Statistics* page, 2005, http://nces.ed.gov/programs/youthindicators/Indicators.asp?PubPageNumber=42 (April 24, 2006).

58.   "Youth Indicators 2005/Indicator 49: Personal Safety," *National Center for Education Statistics* page, 2005, http://nces.ed.gov/programs/youthindicators/Indicators.asp?PubPageNumber=49 (April 24, 2006).

59.   *Youth Risk Behavior Surveillance*—United States, 2003 (Atlanta, GA: Department of Health and Human Services, Centers for Disease Control and Prevention, 21 May 2004), Vol. 53, No. SS-2, 6.

60.   Grant Wahl and L. Jon Wertheim, "A Rite Gone Terribly Wrong," *Sports Illustrated,* December 22, 2003, 71.

61.   Tom Weir, "Hazing issue rears ugly head across USA," *USA Today,* December 9, 2003, C1.

62.   *Youth Risk Behavior Surveillance*—United States, 2003 (Atlanta, GA: Department of Health and Human Services, Centers for Disease Control and Prevention, May 21, 2004), Vol. 53, No. SS-2, 6-7.

63.   *Youth Indicators 2005: Trends in the Well-Being of American Youth* (Washington, DC: U.S. Departments of Education and Justice, November 2005), 20.

64.   Ibid., 22.

65.   "Death Among Children and Adolescents," *Medline Plus* page, November 10, 2004, http://www.nlm.nih.gov/medlineplus/ency/article/001915.htm (April 24, 2006).

66.   David Blankenhorn, "The Good Family Man: Fatherhood and the Pursuit of Happiness in America," working paper for the Institute for American Values, symposium on fatherhood in America, W.P. 12, New York, NY, November 1991, 16.

67.   Jonathan L. Sheline, Betty J. Skipper, and W. Eugene Broadhead, "Risk Factors for Violent Behavior in Elementary School Boys: Have You Hugged Your Child Today?" American Journal of Public Health 84 (1994): 661-63.

68.   "Facts about Media Violence," *American Medical Association* page, 1997, http://www.ama-assn.org/ad-com/releases/1996/mvfacts.htm (December 16, 1997).

69. *Youth Risk Behavior Surveillance*—United States, 2003 (Atlanta, GA: Department of Health and Human Services, Centers for Disease Control and Prevention, May 21, 2004), Vol. 53, No. SS-2, 8-9.

70. Pippa Wysong, "Dark Moods," Current Health 2 (December 2005), Vol. 32, Issue 4, 14.

71. Christian Smith with Melinda Lundquist Denton, *Soul Searching: The Religious and Spiritual Lives of American Teenagers* (New York: Oxford University Press, 2005), 41.

72. Ibid., 110, 162ff.

73. Ibid., 115.

74. Ibid., 171.

75. To gain a fuller understanding of this fact and answers to common objections to realizing our place in this world with this posture, see my book *Engaging the Soul of Youth Culture: Bridging Teen Worldviews and Christian Truth* (Downers Grove, IL: InterVarsity Press, 2006), Dick Staub's *Too Christian, Too Pagan: How to Love the World Without Falling for It* (Grand Rapids, MI: Zondervan, 2000), John Stott's *The Contemporary Christian* (Downers Grove, IL: InterVarsity Press, 1992), and John Fischer's *Fearless Faith: Living Beyond the Walls of "Safe" Christianity* (Eugene, OR: Harvest House, 2002).

76. Tripp, *Age of Opportunity*, 159.

77. Elkind's thesis is addressed in his books *The Hurried Child* (Reading, MA: Addison-Wesley Publishing Company, 1981), *All Grown Up and No Place to Go* (Reading, MA: Addison-Wesley Publishing Company, 1984), and *Ties That Stress: The New Family Imbalance* (Cambridge, MA: Harvard University Press, 1994).

78. George Michael, "I Want Your Sex" from the album *Faith*, CBS Records, 1987.

79. "American's Have Commitment Issues, New Survey Shows," *The Barna Update*, April 18, 2006, http://www.barna.org/FlexPage.aspx?Page=BarnaUpdateNarrow&BarnaUpdateID=21 6&PageCMD=Print (April 27, 2006).

80. Tom Sine, "Will the Real Cultural Christians Please Stand Up," *World Vision*, October/November 1989, 21.

81. To learn more about how to approach youth culture cross-culturally, see my book *Engaging the Soul of Youth Culture* (Downers Grove, IL: InterVarsity, 2006).

82. James Youniss and Jacqueline Smollar, *Adolescent Relations with Mothers, Fathers, and Friends* (Chicago: University of Chicago Press, 1985), 49ff.

83. Merton Strommen, *The Five Cries of Youth* (San Francisco: Harper and Row, 1974), 34.

84. Merton P. Strommen and A. Irene Strommen, *The Five Cries of Parents* (San Francisco: Harper and Row, 1985), 68.

Chapter 3

85. Quentin J. Schultze et al., *Dancing in the Dark* (Grand Rapids, MI: Wm. B. Eerdmans, 1991), 87.

86. *Spin*, October 2005, 108.

87. Victoria Rideout, Donald F. Roberts, and Ulla G. Foehr, *Generation M: Media in the Lives of 8-18 Year-olds: Executive Summary.* (Kaiser Family Foundation, March 2005), 6.

88. Ibid., 23.

89. Lisa Sanders, "Study: Teen Girls More Likely to Multi-Task Media," AdAge.com page, November 29, 2005, http://adage.com/news.cms?newsId=46928 (November 30, 2005).

90. Ibid., 6.

91. Ibid., 8.

92. Joe Francomano, Wayne Lavitt, and Darryl Lavitt, *Junior Achievement: A History* (Colorado Springs, CO: Junior Achievement Inc., 1988), 93-95.

93. Schultze, et al., *Dancing in the Dark*, 12-13.

94. Ibid., 99.

95. Peter G. Christenson and Donald F. Roberts, *It's Not Only Rock & Roll: Popular Music in the Lives of Adolescents* (Cresskill, NJ: Hampton Press, Inc., 1998), 29.

96. Neil Postman, *Amusing Ourselves to Death* (New York: Penguin Books, 1985), 10.

97. James W. Sire, *The Universe Next Door: A Basic Worldview Catalog*, 4th ed. (Downers Grove, IL: InterVarsity Press, 2004), 17.

98. Charles Colson, *How Now Shall We Live?* (Wheaton, IL: Tyndale House, 1999), 14.

99. William D. Romanowski, *Eyes Wide Open: Looking for God in Popular Culture* (Grand Rapids, MI: Brazos, 2001), 47.

100. Walt Mueller, *Engaging the Soul of Youth Culture: Bridging Teen Worldviews and Christian Truth* (Downers Grove, IL: InterVarsity Press, 2006), 56.

101. "'Dimebag' Darrell Abbott," *Rolling Stone*, December 30, 2004–January 13, 2005, 28.

102. Christenson and Roberts, *It's Not Only Rock & Roll*, 37.

103. Rideout, et al., *Generation M: Executive Summary*, 7.

104. Peter Zollo, *Getting Wiser to Teens: More Insights into Marketing to Teenagers* (Ithaca, NY: New Strategist Publications, 2004), 264.

105. Elizabeth F. Brown and William R. Hendee, "Adolescents and Their Music: Insights into the Health of Adolescents," *Journal of the American Medical Association*, September 22, 1989, 1659.

106. Rideout, et al., *Generation M: Executive Summary*, 7.

107. Ibid., 10.

108. "The Digital Music Report 2006—Facts and Figures," IFPI page, January 19, 2006, http://ifpi.org/site-content/press/20060119d.html (May 10, 2006).

109. Christenson and Roberts, *It's Not Only Rock & Roll*, 192.

110. Ibid.

111. "2005 Commercial Piracy Report: Key Figures Summary," *IFPI* page, n.d., http://www.ifpi.org/site-content/press/20050623a.html (May 9, 2006).

112. Howard Polskin, "MTV at 10," *TV Guide*, August 3, 1991, 4.

113. Schultze, et al., *Dancing in the Dark*, 204.

114. "The Sayings of Chairman Bob," in Schultze et al., *Dancing in the Dark*, 192.

115. William D. Romanowski, *Pop Culture Wars* (Downers Grove, IL: InterVarsity Press, 1996), 222-23.

116. Lee Winfrey, "All Day, All Decade, MTV Rocks U.S.A.," *Philadelphia Inquirer*, August 4, 1991.

117. "How MTV Has Rocked Television Commercials," *New York Times*, October 9, 1989.

118. Christenson and Roberts, *It's Not Only Rock & Roll*, 64.

119. *Spin*, October 2005, 96.

120. Terry Lawson, "Wan Madonna Faces Press and 'Prejudice'," Lancaster (PA) *Sunday News*, January 17, 1993.

121. Laura Parker, "Florida Jury Acquits Rap Group," *Philadelphia Inquirer*, October 21, 1990.

122. Brown and Hendee, "Adolescents and Their Music," 1661.

123. "MTV Smut Peddlers: Targeting kids with sex, drugs, and alcohol," *Parents Television Council Report*, www.parentstv.org.

124. Christenson and Roberts, *It's Not Only Rock & Roll*, 217.

125. Ibid.

126. Michael Goldberg, "Madonna Seduces Seattle," *Rolling Stone*, May 23, 1985, 20.

127. "Talking with Madonna: The Unbridled Truth," *Newsweek*, November 2, 1992, 102.

128. "Our Lives, Our Music," *Rolling Stone*, November 26, 1992, 50.

129. Dean Borgman, *When Kumbaya Is Not Enough* (Peabody, MA: Hendrickson, 1997), 128.

130. Hans Rookmaaker, *Modern Art and the Death of a Culture* (Wheaton, IL: Crossway Books, 1994), 136 (italics mine).

131. Brown and Hendee, "Adolescents and Their Music," 1659.

132. *Implications*, 4, nos. 1 and 2, 121.

133. George Barna, *Real Teens: A Contemporary Snapshot of Youth Culture* (Ventura, CA: Regal, 2001), 27.

134. Quentin J. Schultze, *Redeeming Television* (Downers Grove, IL: InterVarsity Press, 1992), 43.

135. George Comstock, *Television in America* (Beverly Hills, CA: Sage, 1980), 123.

136. George Dessart, "Of Tastes and Times," *Television Quarterly* 26, no. 2 (1992): 41.

137. Comstock, *Television in America*, ix.

138. "Facts About Media Violence," *American Medical Association* page, 1997, http://www.ama-assn.org/ad-com/releases/1996/mvfacts.htm (March 24, 1998).

139. Rideout et al., *Generation M: Executive Summary*, 1.

140. Ibid., 10.

141. Ibid., 13.

142. "How TV Affects Your Child," *KidsHealth for Parents* page, February 2005, http://kidshealth. org, (May 16, 2006).

143. Chip Walker, "Can TV Save The Planet?" *American Demographics*, May 1996, http://www. demographics.com/publications/ad/96_ad-9605_ad/9605af03.htm (March 27, 1998).

144. "Americans Watch an Average of 15 Channels, Less Broadcast," *Cox Media* page, March 13, 2006, http://www.coxmedia.com/newsmore.aspx?ID=DA_793793 (May 16, 2006).

145. Comstock, *Television in America*, 4.

146. "Nielsen Reports Americans Watch TV at Record Levels," *Nielsen Media Research* page, September 29, 2005, www.nielsenmedia.com.

147. Rideout et al., *Generation M: Executive Summary*, 27.

148. "New Study Finds Kids Age Zero to Six Spend as Much Time With TV, Computers and Video Games as Playing Outside," *Kaiser Family Foundation* page, October 28, 2003, www.kff.org.

149. "How TV Affects Your Child," *KidsHealth for Parents* page, February 2005, http://kidshealth. org, (May 16, 2006).

150. "David M. Ewalt, "Dorm Rooms: 2006 vs. 1976," *Forbes.com* page, January 20, 2006, www. forbes.com, (May 17, 2006).

151. Maria Aspan, "Nielsen Will Start to Measure TV Habits of College Students," *The New York Times* page, February 20, 2006, www.nytimes.com, (May 17, 2006).

152. "Television Statistics," *KLSR TV* page, n.d., http://www.klsrtvefox.com/body_tv.htm, (May 17, 2006).

153. Rideout et al., *Generation M: Executive Summary*, 11.

154. Schultze, *Redeeming Television*, 77.

155. Richard Reeves, "The Networks Prefer the Low Road," *Philadelphia Inquirer*, March 9, 1989.

156. S. Robert Lichter, Linda S. Lichter, and Stanley Rothman, *Watching America* (New York: Prentice Hall Press, 1991), 301.

157. "U.S. Entertainment Industry: 2005 MPA Market Statistics," *Motion Picture Association of America* page, n.d., www.mpaa.org, (May 17, 2006), 13.

158. "2005 U.S. Movie Attendance Study," *Motion Picture Association of America* page, n.d., www.mpaa.org, (May 17, 2006), 1-4.

159. Ibid., 8.

160. Ibid., 11.

161. Zollo, *Getting Wiser to Teens*, 235.

162. "U.S. Theatrical Market: 2005 Statistics," *Motion Picture Association of America* page, n.d., www.mpaa.org, (May 17, 2006), 4.

163. "U.S. Entertainment Industry: 2005 MPA Market Statistics," 27-28.

164. Brian Godawa, *Hollywood Worldviews: Watching Films with Wisdom & Discernment* (Downers Grove, IL: InterVarsity Press, 2002), 187-88.

165. "Does Religion Shape Movie Viewing Habits for Teens?" *National Study of Youth and Religion* page, February 4, 2003, www.youthandreligion.org, (May 17, 2006).

166. "Teens who watch R-rated movies likelier to smoke, drink and use drugs," *The National Center on Addiction and Substance Abuse at Columbia University* page, August 18, 2005, http://66.135.34.236/absolutenm/anmviewer.asp?a+399&print=yes, (November 15, 2005).

167. Paul Gullifor, "Family Communication Patterns and Adolescent Use of Radio," *Journal of Radio Studies* 1 (1992): 1.

168. Rideout et al., *Generation M: Executive Summary*, 7.

169. Rideout et al., *Generation M*, 121.

170. "2004-2005 Radio Marketing Guide and Fact Book," *Radio Advertising Bureau* page, 2004, www.rab.com (May 18, 2006), 4.

171. Ibid., 8.

172. Ibid., 12.

173. Rideout et al., *Generation M: Executive Summary*, 10.

174. "2004-2005 Radio Marketing Guide and Fact Book," 35.

175. "Radio Today: How America Listens To Radio," (Arbitron, 2004), 12-13.

176. Larry Dobro, "Simmons Measures Teen Readers," *MediaPost's Media Daily News*, June 18, 2003.

177. Zollo, *Getting Wiser to Teens*, 369.

178. Rideout et al., *Generation M: Executive Summary*, 35.

179. Ibid.

180. Ibid.

181. Rideout et al., *Generation M*, 120.

182. "Key Facts: Tweens, Teens, and Magazines," *The Kaiser Family Foundation* page, Fall 2004, www.kff.org, 2.

183. "Mediawise: 10th Annual MediaWise Video and Computer Game Report Card," *National Institute on Media and the Family* page, November 29, 2005, www.mediafamily.org, 1.

184. "Study: Gamers Spend $700 A Year on Games," *MediaPost Publications* page, March 29, 2005, www.mediapost.com, (November 15, 2005).

185. Rideout et al., *Generation M: Executive Summary*, 36.

186. Rideout et al., *Generation M*, 110-11.

187. Ibid., 123.

188. Ibid., 126.

189. "Video Games Entice 4 Out Of 10 Americans," *eMarketer* page, May 17, 2006, www.emarketer.com, (May 17, 2006).

190. "Ziff Davis Video Game Survey: Mobile Gaming Doubles Again," *Ziff Davis Media* page, August 19, 2005, www.ziffdavis.com, (November 15, 2005).

191. "Report: In-Game Advertising to Double," *MediaPost Publications* page, April 18, 2006, www.publications.mediapost.com, (May 16, 2006).

192. "MediaWise Video Game Report Card," *National Institute on Media and the Family* page, November 23, 2004, www.mediafamily.org, 2.

193. "Mediawise: 10th Annual MediaWise Video and Computer Game Report Card," *National Institute on Media and the Family* page, November 29, 2005, www.mediafamily.org, 2.

194. "Teen-Rated Video Games Loaded with Violence," *Kids' Hospital of Boston Press Release,* March 11, 2004, www.kidsshospital.org, (May 22, 2006).

195. Ibid., 3.

196. Rideout et al., *Generation M: Executive Summary*, 36.

197. Ibid.

198. Don Tapscott, *Growing Up Digital: The Rise of the Net Generation* (New York: McGraw-Hill, 1998), 22.

199. Rideout et al., *Generation M: Executive Summary*, 10.

200. Ibid., 30.

201. Ibid.

202. Amanda Lenhart, Mary Madden, and Paul Hitlin, "Teens and Technology," Pew Internet page, July 27, 2005, www.pewinternet.org, i.

203. Rideout et al., *Generation M*, 30.

204. Ibid., 30.

205. Ibid., 113.

206. Ibid., 114.

207. Amanda Lenhart, "Protecting Teens Online," *Pew Internet* page, March 17, 2005, www.pewinternet.org, 121.

208. "U.S. marks new cell phone record in 2005," *InfoWorld* page, April 7, 2006, www.infoworld.com, (May 23, 2006).

209. "Almost Half of American Teens and Tweens Use Cell Phones, with Verizon Their Leading Provider, According to New Research from GfK NOP Technology," *PR Newswire* page, October 18, 2005, www.Prnewswire.com, (November 15, 2005).

210. Paul R. LaMonica, "Ringtones: The sound of money," *CNN Money* page, April 12, 2006, www.money.cnn.com, (May 23, 2006).

211. "Branded phones with bonus content and plenty of extras are going after Gen Y," *The Trendcentral Newsletter,* May 16, 2006.

212. "Ziff Davis Video Game Survey: Mobile Gaming Doubles Again," *Ziff Davis Media* page, August 19, 2005, www.ziffdavis.com, (November 11, 2005).

213. "Have iPod will travel," youthculture@today, Spring 2006, 12.

214. "As Consumers Continue to Take Legal Route, Online Music Market to Experience Healthy Growth," In-Stat page, March 15, 2006, www.instat.com, (March 28, 2006).

215. "Have iPod, will travel," 13.

216. Scott Van Camp, "OMG! Instant Messaging Is Becoming an Ad Vehicle," *Adweek*, November 2004, pN page.

217. Lenhart et al., "Teens and Technology," iii.

218. Ibid., iv.

219. "Teens Can Control Their Own Online Experience With Exclusive Content, Original Programming, and On-Demand Access to Their Favorite Content and Features," AOL Press Center page, February 3, 2004, www.media.aoltimewarner.com, (November 15, 2005).

220. "Top Trends In Communications: Third Annual Instant Messaging Survey," AIM page, n.d., www.aim.com, (November 15, 2005).

221. "Study: Kids revealing too much info online," *USA Today*, December 22, 2005, 8D.

222. Genoa Sibold-Cohn, "Teens travel risky Web superhighway," *Tri-City Herald* (Kennewick, WA), April 4, 2005.

223. "Dear Diary, Dear World," youthculture@today, Fall 2005, 19.

224. "Recent Statistics on Internet Dangers," Protect Kids page, n.d., www.protectkids.com, May 23, 2006.

225. The Center for Academic Integrity page, May 23, 2006, www.academicintegrity.org.

226. "Internet Addiction," Not My Kid page, n.d., www.notmykid.org, (May 23, 2006).

Chapter 4

227. *Entertainment Weekly*, February 9, 2006, 27.

228. *CosmoGirl*, October 2005, 83.

229. "Effects of Video Game Playing on Kids," *National Institute on Media and the Family* page, November 22, 2005, www.mediafamily.org, (December 7, 2005).

230. Ibid.

231. Joe S. McIlhaney, "Problems and Solutions Associated with Media Consumption: The Role of the Practitioner," *Pediatrics*, Vol. 116, No. 1, July 2005, 327.

232. Ayinde O. Chase, "Teen Gamers Shun Good Guy Roles," *All Headline News* page, October 30, 2005, www.allheadlinenews.com, (June 1, 2006).

233. Greg Toppo, "Study: A good man is hard to find—even in G-rated films," *USA Today*, May 3, 2006, 6D.

234. Quentin Schultze, *Winning Your Kids Back From The Media*, (InterVarsity Press ,1994, Downers Grove, IL) 149.

235. Mary Pipher, *Reviving Ophelia: Saving the Selves of Adolescent Girls* (New York: Ballantine Books, 1994), 184.

236. Donna Mitroff, "Prime-Time Teens: Perspectives on the New Youth-Media Environment," 2004, www.wtgrantfoundation.org/usr_doc/PrimeTimeMediascope2004.pdf, (June 2, 2006).

237. Karen Lee-Thorp, "Is Beauty the Beast?" *Christianity Today*, July 14, 1997, 31.

238. Nancy Etcoff, Susie Orbach, Jennifer Scott, and Heidi D'Agostino, "The Real Truth About Beauty: A Global Report—Findings of the Global Study on Women, Beauty, and Well-Being," *Commissioned by Dove*, September 2004.

239. Kristen Harrison and Joanne Cantor, "The Relationship Between Media Consumption and Eating Disorders," *Journal of Communication* 47(1), 1997, 60.

240. "TV, magazines affect viewers' body image," *USA Today*, May 4, 2006, 10D.

241. E.J. Mundall, "Soaps, Music Videos Linked to Teens' Body Image," *HealthDay* page, June 14, 2005, www.healthday.com, (November 15, 2005).

242. "Fact Sheet: Media's Effect on Girls: Body Image and Gender Identity," *National Institute on Media and the Family* page, September 6, 2002, www.mediafamily.org, (December 7, 2005).

243. "Wolves in Sheep's Clothing: A Content Analysis of Kids' Television," *Parents Television Council Special Report*, March 2, 2006, 1.

244. Ibid.

245. "MTV Smut Peddlers," 1.

246. "Kids, Adolescents, and Television," *Pediatrics*, February 2001, Vol. 107, Issue 2, 423-24.

247. "Kids and Media Violence," *National Institute on Media and the Family* page, February 27, 2002, www.mediafamily.org, (December 7, 2005).

248. National Association of Elementary School Principals, *Taming the Tube, an undated report*, Alexandria, VA.

249. "National Television Violence Study: Executive Summary," *Center for Communication and Social Policy* page, n.d., www.ccsp.ucsb.edu/nvts.htm, (June 2, 2006), 27.

250. Ibid.

251. Ibid., 26.

252. Mike Brunker, "Celluloid Carnage, Real-Life Rampages," *MSNBC Home* page, n.d., www.msnbc.com/news/127901.asp#Body, (April 3, 1988).

253. Lucille Jenkins, Theresa Webb, Nick Browne, A.A. Afifi, and Jess Kraus, "An Evaluation of the Motion Picture Association of America's Treatment of Violence in PG-, PG-13-, and R-Rated Films," *Pediatrics*, May 2005, Vol. 115, No. 5, 514.

254. "Study Finds 'Ratings Creep': Movie Ratings Categories Contain More Violence, Sex, Profanity than Decade Ago," *Harvard School of Public Health* page, July 13, 2004, www.hsph.harvard.edu, (November 15, 2005).

255. Gina Wingood, Ralph DiClemente, Jay Bernhardt, Kathy Harrington, Susan Davies, Alyssa Robillard, and Edward Hook, "A Prospective Study of Exposure to Rap Music Videos and African American Female Adolescents' Health," *American Journal of Public Health*, March 2003, Vol. 93, Issue 3, 437-38.

256. David Walsh, "Testimony Submitted to the Committee on Commerce, Science, and Transportation: Interactive Video Violence and Kids," March 21, 2000.

257. "Review of Research Shows That Playing Violent Video Games Can Heighten Aggression," *APA Online Site*, August 19, 2005, www.apa.org, (May 9, 2006).

258. David Grossman, "Trained To Kill," *Christianity Today*, August 10, 1998.

259. Personal e-mail from David Grossman, April 30, 1999.

260. Greg Toppo, "High-tech bullying may be on the rise," *USA Today*, April 11, 2006.

261. Calum MacDonald, "Teenagers are being desensitized to images of violence," *The Herald* page, 10 May 2006, www.theherald.co.uk, (May 16, 2006).

262. "Sons of Violence," *Psychology Today*, July/August 1992, 13; "Does TV Violence Cause Real Violence?" *TV Guide*, August 22, 1992, 11.

263. Ben Shouse, "Does TV Make Us Violent?" *Science Now*, March 28, 2002.

264. Miranda Hitti, "Media Violence Spurs Fear, Aggression in Kids," *Web MD* page, February 17, 2005, www.webmd.com, (November 15, 2005).

265. Brandon S. Centerwall, "Television and Violence: The Scale of the Problem and Where to Go from Here," *Journal of the American Medical Association 267*, no. 22 (June 10, 1992): 3061.

266. "Facts About Media and Violence," *American Medical Association* page, 1997, www.ama-assn.org, (March 24, 1998).

267. "AMA Survey Shows 75% of Parents Disgusted with Media Violence," *Baby Bag Online*, 1997, www.babybag.com/articles/amarele.htm (March 23, 1998).

268. Barry S. Sapolsky and Joseph O. Tabarlet, "Sex in Primetime Television: 1979 versus 1989," *Journal of Broadcasting and Electronic Media 15*, no. 4 (Fall 1991): 514.

269. L. Brent Bozell, III, "Just for the Smut of It," *Human Events*, November 29, 1996, 10.

270. "Number of Sexual Scenes on TV Nearly Double Since 1998," *Kaiser Family Foundation* page, November 9, 2005, www.kff.org, (November 9, 2005).

271. "Wolves In Sheep's Clothing: A Content Analysis of Kids' Television," *Parent's Television Council Special Report*, March 2, 2006, 1, 7.

272. Ibid., 14.

273. "MTV Smut Peddlers," 1.

274. Sapolsky and Taberlet, "Sex in Primetime Television," 514.

275. S. Liliana Escobar-Chaves, Susan R. Tortolero, Christine Markham, Barbara Low, Patricia Eitel, and Patricia Thiskstun, "Impact of the Media on Adolescent Sexual Attitudes and Behaviors," *Pediatrics*, Vol. 116, No. 1, July 2005, 3121.

276. Ibid., 317.

277. Escobar-Chaves et al., "Impact of the Media on Adolescent Sexual Attitudes and Behaviors," 317.

278. Ibid., 318.

279. Ibid., 317.

280. Thomas Patterson, *At a Theater Near You: Screen Entertainment from a Christian Perspective* (Wheaton, IL: Harold Shaw Publishers, 1994), 130.

281. Ibid., 132ff.

282. Brian Godawa, *Hollywood Worldviews: Watching Films with Wisdom and Discernment* (Downers Grove, IL: InterVarsity Press, 2002), 201.

283. Escobar-Chaves et al., "Impact of the Media on Adolescent Sexual Attitudes and Behaviors," 319.

284. Jerry Ropelato, "Internet Pornography Statistics," *Top Ten Reviews* page, 2006, www.internet-filter-review.toptenreviews.com, (July 26, 2006).

285. Escobar-Chaves et al., "Impact of the Media on Adolescent Sexual Attitudes and Behaviors," 319.

286. Ibid., 320.

287. "Sexuality, Contraception, and the Media," *Pediatrics*, January 2001, Vol. 107, Issue 1, 191.

288. Kelly Ladin L'Engle, Jane D. Brown, and Kristin Kenneavy, "The mass media are an important context for adolescents' sexual behavior," *Journal of Adolescent Health*, Vol. 38, Issue 3, March 2006, 186-92.

289. R.H. Durant, E.S. Rome, M. Rich, E. Allred, S.J. Emans, and E.R. Woods, "Tobacco and alcohol use behaviors portrayed in music videos: a content analysis," *American Journal of Public Health*, 1997:87, 1131-35.

290. "Kids, Adolescents, and Television," 423-24.

291. "Scientific Review Paper Finds Exposure to Smoking in Movies Is a Major Influence in Promoting Adolescent Smoking," *PR Newswire* page, December 5, 2005, www.prnewswire.com, (December 5, 2005).

292. "Teens Who Watch R-Rated Movies Likelier to Smoke, Drink and Use Drugs," *The National Center on Addiction and Substance Abuse* page, August 18, 2005, www.casacolumbia.org, (November 15, 2005).

293. Escobar-Chaves et al., "Impact of Media on Adolescent Sexual Attitudes and Behaviors," 306.

294. Ibid.

295. "Radio Daze: Alcohol Ads Tune in Underage Youth," *The Center on Alcohol Marketing and Youth* page, April 2, 2003, www.camy.org.

296. Ibid.

297. "Sexual Assault and the Media," *Stop Violence Against Women* page, February 1, 2006, www. stopvaw.org, (June 6, 2006).

298. "Domestic Violence is a Serious, Widespread Social Problem in America: The Facts," *Family Violence Prevention Fund* page, 2006, www.endabuse.org, (June 6, 2006).

299. Ibid.

300. "Media Education and Preventing Sexual Violence," *Media Education Foundation* page, 2003, www.mediaed.org.

301. Escobar-Chaves et al., "Impact of Media on Adolescent Sexual Attitudes and Behaviors," 318.

302. David Elkind, *Ties That Stress: The New Family Imbalance* (Cambridge, MA: Harvard University Press, 1994), 79.

303. Teresa Wiltz, "TV doesn't know what to do with functional families," *Sunday News* (Lancaster, PA), May 21, 2006, H8.

304. J. Francis Davis, "The Power of Images: Creating the Myths of Our Time," *Media & Values*, Winter 1992, 5.

305. Ibid., 6.

306. Michael Warren, "Storytellers Shape Spiritual Values," *Media & Values*, Winter 1992, 19.

307. Chip Walker, "Can TV Save the Planet?" *American Demographics*, May 1996, www.american-demographics.com, (March 27, 1998).

308. "New Study Links Television in Teens' and Pre-Teens' Bedrooms to Risky Behavior," *National Institute on Media and the Family* page, 2005, www.mediafamily.org, (May 9, 2006).

309. Ann Powers, "Mary J. Blige," *Blender*, May 2006, 58.

310. Deborah Prothrow Stith, *Deadly Consequences*, (New York: Harper Collins, 1991), 39.

311. Ted Baehr, "The Christian Film and Television Commissions: Why, What, & How," *Religious Broadcasting*, December 1991, 22.

312. "Violence on Television," *American Psychological Association* page, n.d., www.apa.org, (March 24, 1998).

313. Walt Mueller, *Engaging the Soul of Youth Culture*, 66.

314. Mike Yaconelli and Jim Burns, *High School Ministry* (Grand Rapids, MI: Zondervan, 1986), 37.

315. Mary T. Bassett and Sarah Perl, "Obesity: The Public Health Challenge of Our Time," *American Journal of Public Health*, September 2004, Vol. 94, Issue 9, 1477.

316. "Media Use and Obesity Among Kids," *National Institute on Media and the Family* page, July 12, 2004, www.mediafamily.org, (December 7, 2005).

317. "TV Watching and Sleep Problems," *Pediatrics for Parents*, Vol. 21, Number 2, 11.

Chapter 5

318. William D. Romanowski, *Eyes Wide Open: Looking for God in Popular Culture* (Grand Rapids, MI: Brazos Press, 2001), 19.

319. Albert M. Wolters, *Creation Regained: Biblical Basics for a Reformational Worldview* (Grand Rapids, MI: Wm. B. Eerdmans, 1985), 49ff.

320. Francis Schaeffer, *Art and the Bible* (Downers Grove, IL: InterVarsity Press, 1973).

321.   Brian Godawa, *Hollywood Worldviews: Watching Films with Wisdom & Discernment* (Downers Grove, IL: InterVarsity Press, 2002), 200.

322.   Ibid., 201ff.

323.   Quentin Schultze, *Redeeming Television* (Downers Grove, IL: InterVarsity Press, 1992), 167.

324.   To learn more about how to observe and listen to teenage culture by enlisting the methodology used by the apostle Paul, see my book *Engaging the Soul of Youth Culture: Bridging Teen Worldviews and Christian Truth* (Downers Grove, IL: InterVarsity Press, 2006).

Chapter 6

325.   Juliet B. Schor, *Born to Buy: The Commercialized Child and the New Consumer Culture* (New York: Scribner, 2004), 9.

326.   Sam Van Eman, *On Earth As It Is In Advertising: Moving From Commercial Hype To Gospel Hope* (Grand Rapids, MI: Brazos Press, 2005), 30.

327.   I am indebted to Dr. Bill Brown and Cedarville University for underwriting the cost of my trip to the *Kid Power Conference*. Dr. Brown and the University shared my vision for better understanding the world of youth marketing and generously offered the financial assistance to CPYU so I could attend the conference.

328.   Betsy Streisand and Richard J. Newman, "The New Media Elites," *The U.S. News & World Report* page, November 14, 2005, www.usnews.com/biztech/articles/051114/14media.htm, (August 18, 2006).

329.   "Scope U.S. 2004," *The International Council of Shopping Centers* page, 2004, www.icsc.org, (August 18, 2006).

330.   Schor, *Born to Buy*, 19.

331.   As quoted in Jean Kilbourne, *Can't Buy My Love: How Advertising Changes the Way We Think and Feel* (New York: Touchstone, 1999), 64.

332.   Schor, *Born to Buy*, 21.

333.   David L. Siegel, Timothy J. Coffey, and Gregory Livingston, *The Great Tween Buying Machine: Capturing Your Share of the Multibillion Dollar Tween Market* (Chicago: Dearborn Trade Publishing, 2004), ix.

334.   "Facts About Marketing to Kids," *The New American Dream* page, n.d., www.newdream.org/kids/facts/php, (August 25, 2005).

335.   Carolyn Bigda, "5 Ways to Protect Kids," *Money*, March 2005, 91.

336.   "Teen Spending Estimated to Top $190 Billion by 2006," *The Market Research Portal* page, April 12, 2006, www.marketresearchworld.net, (July 6, 2006).

337.   Susan Linn, *Consuming Kids: The Hostile Takeover of Childhood* (New York: The New Press, 2004), 1.

338.   Schor, *Born to Buy*, 23.

339.   Ibid., 24.

340.   Suzanne Martin, "Advertising to Youth: What Youth Want and What Advertisers Need to Know," *Trends & Tudes*, August 2006, 2.

341.   Linn, *Consuming Kids*, 42.

342.   Ibid., 183.

343.   Zollo, *Getting Wiser to Teens*, 51.

344.   Ibid., 50.

345.   Linn, *Consuming Kids*, 159.

346.   Ibid., 19.

347. Quart, *Branded: The Buying and Selling of Teenagers* (New York: Basic Books, 2003), 18.

348. To learn more about or view *The Merchants of Cool* in its entirety, log onto www.pbs.org.

349. Zollo, *Getting Wiser to Teens*, 107ff.

350. Ypulse.com daily update, September 6, 2005, www.ypulse.com, (September 7, 2005).

351. "Harris Interactive/Kid Power Poll of Youth Marketers: Summary Report," (Harris Interactive Market Research, 2004), 32.

Chapter 7

352. Kerry L. Bozza-George, "Resist the Pressure," *Current Health* 1, March 2004, 22.

353. Hayley K. Dohnt and Marika Tiggemann, "Body Image Concerns in Young Girls: The Role of Peers and Media Prior to Adolescence," *Journal of Youth & Adolescence*, April 2006, Vol. 35, Issue 2, 135.

354. Donald M. Joy, "Adolescents in Socio-Psychological Perspective," in Roy B. Zuck and Warren S. Benson, *Youth Education in the Church*, (Chicago: Moody Press, 1978), 95.

355. "Running in Place: How American Families Are Faring in a Changing Economy and an Individualistic Society: Highlights of Findings: Combating Negative Peer Influences," *Kids Campaigns* page, May 5, 1994, www.kidscampaigns.org (November 26, 1997).

356. Carol Shakeshaft, et al., "Boys Call Me Cow," *Educational Leadership*, October 1997, 22.

357. Jeffrey T. Lashbrook, "Fitting In: Exploring the Emotional Dimension of Adolescent Peer Pressure," *Adolescence*, Winter 2000, Vol. 35, No. 140, 747ff.

358. "Parents Could Have a Better Understanding about Teen Concerns," *Youthviews: The Newsletter of the Gallup Youth Survey*, October 1997, 2.

359. See David Elkind, *All Grown Up and No Place to Go* (Reading, MA: Addison-Wesley, 1984).

360. Dean Borgman, *Hear My Story: Understanding the Cries of Troubled Youth* (Peabody, MA: Hendrickson Publishers, 2003), 155.

361. Chap Clark, *Hurt*, 75.

362. Ibid., 79.

363. Ibid., 80.

364. Mary Elizabeth Curtner-Smith and Carol E. MacKinnon-Lewis, "Family Process Effects on Adolescent Males' Susceptibility to Antisocial Peer Pressure," *Family Relations*, October 1994, 462ff.

365. Laurence Steinberg, Anne Fletcher, and Nancy Darling, "Parental Monitoring and Peer Influences on Adolescent Substance Abuse," *Pediatrics*, June 1994, 1060ff.

366. Marcel Danesi, *Cool: The Signs and Meanings of Adolescence* (Toronto: University of Toronto Press, 1994), 41.

367. Lynn Minton, "Fresh Voices: 'How Do You Resist Peer Pressure?'" *Parade*, March 25, 1990, 16.

368. Peter Zollo, *Getting Wiser to Teens*, 58.

369. Ibid., 229.

370. Ibid., 82-83.

371. Hayley K. Dohnt and Marika Tiggemann, "Peer Influences on Body Dissatisfaction and Dieting Awareness in Young Girls," *British Journal of Developmental Psychology*, 2005, 23, 103.

372. Elkind, *All Grown Up and No Place to Go*, 24.

373. "London Teenager Bullied to Death," *AOL News*, October 2, 1997, personal e-mail (October 2, 1997).

374.   "Anabolic Steroids," *National Institute on Drug Abuse* page, n.d., www.teens.drugabuse.gov, (June 14, 2006).

375.   Joanne B. Eicher, Suzanne Baizerman, and John Michelman, "Adolescent Dress, Part II: A Qualitative Study of Suburban High School Students," *Adolescence* 26, no. 103 (Fall 1991), 679ff.

376.   Anita Smith, "The Power of Peers," *The Institute for Youth Development* page, 2004, www.youthdevelopment.org, (March 22, 2006).

377.   A.J. Hostetler, "Teen Killed for Pair of Gold Earrings,"Lancaster (PA) *Intelligencer Journal,* October 24, 1991, back page.

378.   Zollo, *Getting Wiser to Teens,* 54.

379.   I.T. Zwane, P.T. Mngadi, and M.P. Nxumalo, "Adolescent's Views on Decision-Making Regarding Risky Sexual Behavior," *International Nursing Review,* 2004, no. 51, 21.

380.   Carol Shakeshaft, et al., "Boys Call Me Cow," 23.

381.   Donna Eder and David A. Kinney, "The Effect of Middle School Extracurricular Activities on Adolescents' Popularity and Peer Status," *Youth & Society,* March 1995, 298ff.

382.   Mark Rafenstein, "How To Combat Negative Peer Pressure," *Current Health 2,* September 2002, Vol. 29, Issue 1, 29.

383.   "The Weekly Reader National Survey on Drugs and Alcohol," Spring 1995.

384.   "Girls More Likely to Drink Because of Peer Pressure," *Parenting of Adolescents* page, 2006, www.parentingteens.about.com, (June 12, 2006).

385.   "Peer Factors in Sex, Condom Use," *Family Planning Perspectives,* September/October 1994, 197.

386.   Nancy Dreher, "How Peer Pressure May Affect Decisions About Sex," *Human Sexuality Supplement,* September 2003, Vol. 30, Issue 1, 1-4.

387.   Nina S. Mounts and Laurence Steinberg, "An Ecological Analysis of Peer Influence on Adolescent Grade Point Average and Drug Use," *Developmental Psychology* 31, no. 6 (1995): 9121.

388.   "The State of Our Nation's Youth: 2005-2006," *The Horatio Alger Association* page, 2005, www.horatioalger.org, 65-67.

389.   Zollo, *Getting Wiser to Teens,* 57.

390.   George Barna, *Real Teens: A Contemporary Snapshot of Youth Culture* (Ventura, CA: Regal Books, 2001), 73.

391.   Lee Shilts, "The Relationship of Early Adolescent Substance Use to Extracurricular Activities, Peer Influence, and Personal Attitudes," *Adolescence* 26, no. 103 (Fall 1991): 615ff.

Chapter 8

392.   *It's Your (Sex) Life: Your Guide to Safe & Responsible Sex,* online guide produced cooperatively by MTV and The Henry J. *Kaiser Family Foundation,* 2005, www.mtv.com, (June 22, 2006), 5.

393.   Dean Borgman, *Hear My Story: Understanding the Cries of Troubled Youth* (Peabody, MA: Hendrickson, 2003), 329.

394.   "What the World's Teenagers Are Saying," *U.S. News & World Report,* June 30, 1986, 68.

395.   Zollo, *Getting Wiser to Teens,* 143.

396.   *The State of Our Nation's Youth: 2005-2006,* 65-6.

397.   "Youth Risk Behavior Surveillance—United States, 2005," June 9, 2006, Vol. 55, No. SS-5, *U.S. Center for Disease Control* page, www.cdc.gov (June 21, 2006), 19.

398.   Ibid.

399.   Ibid.

400. "Age at First Intercourse," *The Kinsey Institute* page, 2005, www.kinseyinstitute.org/resources/FAQ.html, (June 22, 2006).

401. "Teen Sex and Pregnancy," *Alan Guttmacher Institute* page, n.d., www.agi-usa.org/pubs/fb_teen_sex1.html, (October 23, 1997).

402. "The Truth About Adolescent Sexuality," *SIECUS* page, 2004, http://63.73.227.69/pubs/fact/fact0020.html, (June 22, 2006).

403. "Youth Risk Behavior Surveillance—United States, 2005," 19.

404. Alexandra Marks, "More Teens Have Sex and Fewer Parents Know," *Christian Science Monitor*, June 9, 2003, 2.

405. "Teen's First Sex Is at Home," *USA Today*, September 26, 2002, 8D.

406. "The Truth About Adolescent Sexuality."

407. Ibid.

408. "Teens and Sex," October 30, 2002, *Medical College of Wisconsin Healthlink* page, http://healthlink.mcw.edu/article/1031002177.html, (June 19, 2006).

409. "Youth Risk Behavior Surveillance—United States, 2005," 20.

410. "The Truth About Adolescent Sexuality."

411. "Teens break no-sex vows, study suggests: some say oral sex not sex," *Christian Century*, December 27, 2003, 14.

412. Ibid.

413. Lisa Remez, "Oral Sex Among Adolescents: Is It Sex or Is It Abstinence?" *Family Planning Perspectives*, November/December 2000, Vol. 32, No. 6, 298.

414. "With Males in the Mix, Federal Sex Survey Takes on Greater Importance," *Contemporary Sexuality*, December 2005, Vol. 39, No. 12, 4.

415. Sharon Jayson, "Teens define sex in new ways," *USA Today*, October 19, 2005.

416. Paul Ruditis, *Rainbow Party* (New York: Simon Pulse, 2005), 50.

417. "With Males in the Mix, Federal Sex Survey Takes on Greater Importance," 4.

418. Micael D. Lemonick and Carolina A. Miranda, "A Teen Twist on Sex," *Time*, September 26, 2005, 64.

419. Zollo, *Getting Wiser to Teens*, 241.

420. "Relationships: A Series of National Surveys of Teens About Sex," October 2002, *The SexSmarts* page, www.seventeen.com/sexsmarts, (June 21, 2006).

421. Barbara Dafoe Whitehead and Marline Pearson, "Making a Love Connection: Teen Relationships, Pregnancy, and Marriage," 2006, *The National Campaign to Prevent Teen Pregnancy* page, www.teenpregnancy.org, (June 19, 2006), 7.

422. Ibid.

423. "Fast Facts: Pregnancy Among Sexually Experienced Teens, Aged 15-19, 2002," 2002, *The National Campaign to Prevent Teen Pregnancy* page, www.teenpregnancy.org, (June 19, 2006).

424. "General Facts and Stats," May 2005, *The National Campaign to Prevent Teen Pregnancy* page, www.teenpregnancy.org, (June 19, 2006).

425. Ibid.

426. "Teen Pregnancy Rates in the United States, 1972-2000," 2004, and "Teen Birth Rates in the United States, 1940-2004," 2004, *The National Campaign to Prevent Teen Pregnancy* page, www.teenpregnancy.org, (June 19, 2006).

427. Ibid.

428. "U.S. Teenage Pregnancy Statistics: Overall Trends by Race and Ethnicity and State-by-State Information," February 19, 2004, *The Alan Guttmacher Institute* page, www.guttmacher.org, (June 19, 2006), 2.

429. Heather Boonstra, "Teen Pregnancy: Trends and Lessons Learned," *The Guttmacher Report on Public Policy*, February 2002, 7.

430. "General Facts and Stats."

431. Whitehead and Pearson, "Making a Love Connection," 8.

432. Ibid., 4.

433. "STDs—A Teenage Epidemic?" *The Youth Connection*, March/April 2004, 3.

434. Meg Meeker, *Epidemic: How Teen Sex Is Killing Our Kids* (Washington, DC: Lifeline Press, 2002), 12.

435. Harrell W. Chesson, John M. Blandford, Thomas L. Gift, Guoyu Tao, and Kathleen L. Irwin, "The Estimated Direct Medical Cost of Sexually Transmitted Diseases Among American Youth, 2000," *Perspectives on Sexual and Reproductive Health*, January/February 2004, Vol. 36, No. 1, 11.

436. Meeker, *Epidemic*, 31-32.

437. Ibid., 20.

438. Ibid., 99.

439. Whitehead and Pearson, "Making a Love Connection," 10-11.

440. Martha Kempner and Monica Rodriguez, *Talk About Sex*, n.d. [2005], The Siecus page, www.siecus.org/pubs/TalkAboutSex.pdf, (June 26, 2006), 9-10.

441. "Facts in Brief: Sexuality Education," August 2002, The Alan Guttmacher Institute page, www.guttmacher.org, (June 26, 2006).

442. "Siecus Public Policy Office Fact Sheet: On Our Side—Public Support for Comprehensive Sexuality Education," May 2005, Siecus page, www.siecus.org, (June 26, 2006).

443. White and DeBlassie, "Adolescent Sexual Behavior," *Adolescence* 27, no. 105 (spring 1992): 189.

444. Mary A. Ott, Susan G. Millstein, Susan Ofner, and Bonnie L. Halpern-Felsher, "Greater Expectations: Adolescents' Positive Motivations for Sex," *Perspectives on Sexual and Reproductive Health*, Vol. 38, no. 2, (June 2006): 84ff.

445. Chap Clark, *Hurt*, 123.

446. Guy L. Dorius, Tim B. Heaton, and Patrick Steffen, "Adolescent Life Events and Their Association with the Onset of Sexual Intercourse," *Youth & Society* 25, no. 1, (September 1993): 3ff.

447. Ibid.

448. "Dear Diary," *Psychology Today*, May/June 1992, 18.

449. White and DeBlassie, "Adolescent Sexual Behavior," 185.

450. Guy L. Dorius, Tim B. Heaton, and Patrick Steffen, "Adolescent Life Events and Their Association with the Onset of Sexual Intercourse," 3ff.

451. White and DeBlassie, "Adolescent Sexual Behavior," 187.

452. Ibid., 185.

453. Bethanne Black, "Teens and Sex: The Big Talk Isn't Enough," *USA Today*, January 4, 2002.

454. Ibid.

455. Ibid.

456. Renee E. Sieving, Marla E. Eisenberg, Sandra Pettingell, and Carol Skay, "Friends' Influence on Adolescents' First Sexual Intercourse," *Perspectives on Sexual and Reproductive Health*, Vol. 38, No. 1, March 2006, 13.

457. Mary Rucklos Hampton, Bonnie Jeffrey, Barb McWatters, and Pamela Smith, "Influence of Teen's Perceptions of Parental Disapproval and Peer Behavior on Their Initiation of Sexual Intercourse," *The Canadian Journal of Human Sexuality*, Vol. 14 (3-4), 2005, 107.

458. White and DeBlassie, "Adolescent Sexual Behavior," 184.

459. Whitehead and Pearson, "Making a Love Connection," 14.

460. "Virginity and the First Time: A Series of National Surveys of Teens About Sex," 2003, *The Kaiser Family Foundation* page, www.kff.org, (June 26, 2006).

461. Ibid.

462. "Youth Risk Behavior Surveillance—United States, 2005," 7.

463. Ibid.

464. Barbara VanOss Marin, Douglas B. Kirby, Esther S. Hudes, Karin K. Coyle, and Cynthia A. Gomez, "Boyfriends, Girlfriends and Teenagers Risk of Sexual Involvement," *Perspectives on Sexual and Reproductive Health*, Vol. 1, No. 2, June 2006, 77.

465. Kelly Ladin L'Engle, Christine Jackson, and Jane D. Brown, "Early Adolescents' Cognitive Susceptibility To Initiating Sexual Intercourse," *Perspectives on Sexual and Reproductive Health*, Vol. 38, No. 2, June 2006, 97.

466. Joan Kahn and Kathryn London, "Premarital Sex and the Risk of Divorce," *Journal of Marriage and Family*, November 1991, 845-55.

467. Ann Wharton, "How to Teach Teens About Abstinence," *Focus on the Family Citizen*, June 1988, 5.

468. Kristine Napier, "Chastity Programs Shatter Sex-Ed Myths," *Heritage Foundation* page, May 1997, http://www.policyreview.com:80/may97/thhome.html, (October 23, 1997).

469. Wade F. Horn and Jeffrey S. Trimbath, "Another reason for abstinence: The good news about abstinence is that more and more teens are adopting it as their personal standard," Lancaster (PA) *New Era*, May 22, 2006, 7.

Chapter 9

470. Rory Glynn, "Bargains, Flops in the World of Sports," *USA Today*, March 5, 1991.

471. David L. Siegel et al., *The Great Tween Buying Machine: Capturing Your Share of the Multibillion Dollar Tween Market* (Chicago: Dearborn Trade Publishing, 2004).

472. Susan Linn, *Consuming Kids*.

473. Schor, *Born to Buy: The Commercialized Child and the New Consumer Culture* (New York: Scribner, 2004), 9.

474. Alissa Quart, *Branded; The Buying and Selling of Teenagers* (New York: Basic Books, 2003), 16.

475. *Webster's New Collegiate Dictionary*, 10th ed., 717.

476. Rodney Clapp, "Why the Devil Takes Visa," *Christianity Today*, October 7, 1996, 19.

477. Schor, *Born to Buy*, 37.

478. Jon Pahl, *Shopping Malls and Other Sacred Spaces* (Grand Rapids, MI: Brazos Press, 2003), 65ff.

479. "Facts About Marketing to Children," *The New American Dream* page, n.d., www.newdream.org/kids/facts.php, (August 25, 2005).

480. Ibid.

481. Linn, *Consuming Kids*, 1.

482. Doris L. Walsh, "Targeting Teens," *American Demographics*, February 1985, 21.

483. Ibid.

484. "Teen Spending Estimated to Top $190 Billion by 2006," *The Market Research Portal* page, April 12, 2006, www.marketresearchworld.net, (July 6, 2006).

485. Zollo, *Getting Wiser to Teens*, 10.

486. Ibid., 16.

487. Ibid., 20.

488. Quart, *Branded*, 35.

489. Zollo, *Getting Wiser to Teens*, 13.

490. Ibid., 14.

491. "Americans Donate Billions to Charity, But Giving to Churches Has Declined," *The Barna Update*, April 25, 2005, www.barna.org, (July 7, 2006).

492. Ibid.

493. "Evangelicals Are the Most Generous Givers, but Fewer than 10% of Born-Again Christians Give 10% to Their Church," *The Barna Update*, April 5, 2000, www.barna.org, (July 7, 2006).

494. Olivia Barker, "School shopping goes pro," *USA Today*, August 23, 2004, 2B.

495. Rick Telander, "Your Sneakers or Your Life," *Sports Illustrated*, May 14, 1990, 36-49.

496. Kenneth S. Kantzer, "Ron Sider Is Mostly Right," *Christianity Today*, October 8, 1990, 21.

497. Robert Wuthnow, "Maladies of the Middle Class," *Princeton Seminary Bulletin* 13, no. 3 (November 1992): 296.

498. "Reflections," *Christianity Today*, October 23, 1995, 74.

499. John Stott, ed. by Timothy Dudley-Smith, *Authentic Christianity: From the Writings of John Stott* (Downers Grove, IL: InterVarsity Press, 1995), 242.

500. Edward Moran and Dana Pennett O'Neil, "Ball in the adults' court," *The Dallas Morning News* page, 2006, www.apse.dallasnews.com, (July 11, 2006).

501. Cliff Schimmels, *What Parents Try to Forget About Adolescence* (Elgin, IL: David C. Cook Publishing, 1989), 57.

502. Wuthnow, "Maladies of the Middle Class," 291.

503. Ralph E. Minear, *Kids Who Have Too Much* (Nashville, TN: Thomas Nelson, 1989), 10.

504. Paul Borthwick, Youth & Missions: *Expanding Your Students' Worldview* (Wheaton, IL: Victor Books, 1988), 148ff.

505. C.S. Lewis, *Mere Christianity* (New York: Macmillan, 1952), 120.

Chapter 10

506. *Rolling Stone*, March 4, 1999.

507. Lloyd D. Johnston, Patrick M. O'Malley, Jerald G. Bachman, and John E. Schulenberg, *Monitoring the Future: National Results on Adolescent Drug Use—Overview of Key Findings* 2005 (Bethesda, MD: National Institute on Drug Abuse, April 2006), 44-46.

508. Joseph Carroll, "Drugs, Smoking, Alcohol Most Important Problem Facing Teens," *Gallup Organization* page, 17 February 2006, www.poll.gallup.com/content/default.aspx?ci=21517, (July 17, 2006).

509. T. M. Nephew, G.D. Williams, H. Yi, A.K. Hoy, F.S. Stinson, and M. C. Dufour, "Surveillance Report #62: Apparent per capital alcohol consumption: National, state and regional trends, 1977-2000," *National Institute on Alcohol Abuse and Alcoholism* page, 2002, www.niaaa.nih.gov, (July 17, 2006).

510. Cyril Penn, "U.S. Wine Consumption Keeps Going Up," *San Francisco Chronicle*, January 19, 2006, F2.

511. Dean Borgman, "Alcoholism," *Encyclopedia of Youth Studies*.

512. Joyce Howard Price, "One-sixth of alcohol sales go to minors, study says," *The Washington Times*, May 2, 2006, www.washingtontimes.com, (July 17, 2006).

513. "Dangers of Alcohol Fact Sheet," *Partnership for a Drug-Free New Jersey*, 2006.

514. Lloyd D. Johnston, Patrick M. O'Malley, Jerald G. Bachman, and John E. Schulenberg, *Monitoring the Future: National Survey Results on Drug Use, 1975-2004*, vol. 1 (Bethesda, MD: National Institute on Drug Abuse, 2005), 272.

515. Johnston, et al., *Monitoring the Future: National Results on Adolescent Drug Use—Overview of Key Findings 2005*, 55.

516. Johnston, Patrick M. O'Malley, Jerald G. Bachman, and John E Schulenberg, *Monitoring the Future: National Survey Results on Drug Use, 1975-2004*, vol. 2 (Bethesda, MD: National Institute on Drug Abuse, 2005), 233.

517. *Overview of Findings from the 2004 National Survey on Drug Use and Health* (Rockville, MD: Department of Health and Human Services—Substance Abuse and Mental Health Services Administration, September 8, 2005), 121.

518. Joseph A. Califano, "Teen Tipplers: America's Underage Drinking Epidemic," remarks made at The National Press Club in Washington, DC, contained in Press Release from The National Center on Addiction and Substance Abuse at Columbia University, February 26, 2006.

519. *PRIDE Questionnaire Report for Grades 4 thru 6: 2004-05* Pride National Summary/Grades 4-6 (Bowling Green, KY: January 31, 2006), 3.

520. *PRIDE Questionnaire Report for Grades 6 thru 12: 2004-05 National Summary* (Bowling Green, KY: June 30, 2005), 3.

521. Ibid., 167.

522. Ibid., 168.

523. Ibid., 154.

524. Ibid., 151.

525. *PRIDE Questionnaire Report for Grades 4 thru 6: 2004-05* Pride National Summary/ Grades 4-6, 46-47.

526. Johnston, et al., *Monitoring the Future: National Results on Adolescent Drug Use—Overview of Key Findings 2005*, 64-66.

527. Price, "One-sixth of alcohol sales go to minors, study says."

528. *Morbidity and Mortality Weekly Report: Youth Risk Behavior Surveillance—United States, 2005* (Atlanta, GA: Department of Health and Human Services, Centers for Disease Control and Prevention, June 9, 2006), 5.

529. Ibid.

530. *Overview of Findings from the 2004 National Survey on Drug Use and Health*, 121.

531. "Traffic Safety Facts 2003 Data: Young Drivers," (National Highway Traffic Safety Administration: U.S. Department of Transportation).

532. "Measures of Alcohol Consumption and Alcohol-Related Health Effects from Excessive Consumption," *Centers for Disease Control* page, January 31, 2005, www.cdc.gov, (July 18, 2006).

533. Ibid.

534. "A Snapshot of Annual High-Risk College Drinking Consequences," *The College Drinking Prevention* page, September 23, 2005, www.collegedrinkingprevention.gov, (July 18, 2006).

535. "Kids Who Use Gateway Drugs Are at Greater Risk of Using Other Drugs," *The National Center on Addiction and Drug Abuse at Columbia University* page, 1996, www.casacolumbia.org, (December 11, 1997).

536. Ely Portillo, "Boozing takes toll," The (Johnstown, PA) *Tribune Democrat*, June 30, 2006, A-11.

537. "NIDA InfoFacts: Cigarettes and Other Tobacco Products," *The National Institute on Drug Abuse* page, July 2006, www.nida.nih.gov/Infofacts/tobacco.html, (July 17, 2006).

538. "Cigar Smoking Fact Sheet," *American Lung Association* page, November 2004, www.lungusa.org, (July 19, 2006).

539. "Smokeless Tobacco Fact Sheet," *American Lung Association* page, April 2006, www.lungusa.org, (July 19, 2006).

540. "NIDA InfoFacts: Cigarettes and Other Tobacco Products."

541. Ibid.

542. "Tobacco Product Advertising and Promotion Fact Sheet," *American Lung Association* page, April 2006, www.lungusa.org, (July 19, 2006).

543. "Smoking 101 Fact Sheet," *American Lung Association* page, March 2006, www.lungusa.org, (July 19, 2006).

544. "Tobacco Product Advertising and Promotion Fact Sheet."

545. "Smokeless Tobacco Fact Sheet."

546. Ibid.

547. Ibid., 274.

548. *Morbidity and Mortality Weekly Report: Youth Risk Behavior Surveillance*—United States, 2005, 10-11.

549. "Smoking and Teens Fact Sheet," *American Lung Association* page, April 2006, www.lungusa.org, (July 19, 2006).

550. "Smokeless Tobacco Fact Sheet."

551. Johnston, et al., *Monitoring the Future: National Results on Adolescent Drug Use—Overview of Key Findings 2005*, 51.

552. Ibid.

553. "Tobacco Product Advertising and Promotion Fact Sheet."

554. "Tobacco Information Overview," *Centers for Disease Control Tobacco Information and Prevention Source* page, n.d., www.cdc.gov, (December 8, 1997).

555. "Smoking and Teens Fact Sheet."

556. Johnston, et al., *Monitoring the Future: National Results on Adolescent Drug Use—Overview of Key Findings 2005*, 44.

557. Ibid., 48.

558. Johnston, et al., *Monitoring the Future National Survey Results on Drug Use, 1975-2004*, vol. 2, 35.

559. Johnston, et al., *Monitoring the Future: National Results on Adolescent Drug Use—Overview of Key Findings 2005*, 46.

560. Ibid.

561. Ibid., 44.

562. Ibid.

563. Jean Seligmann, "The New Age of Aquarius," *Newsweek*, February 3, 1992, 67.

564. Johnston, et al., *Monitoring the Future: National Results on Adolescent Drug Use—Overview of Key Findings 2005*, 44.

565. Ibid., 45.

566. Ibid.

567. "Generation RX: National Study Confirms Abuse of Prescription and Over-the-Counter Drugs," *The Partnership for a Drug-Free America press release, The Partnership for a Drug-Free America* page, May 15, 2006, www.drugfree.org, (July 17, 2006).

568. Jason Szep, "American kids getting high on prescription drugs," *Reuters News* page, March 17, 2006, www.go.reuters.com, (March 22, 2006).

569. Johnston, et al., *Monitoring the Future: National Results on Adolescent Drug Use—Overview of Key Findings 2005*, 45.

570. Ibid., 44.

571. *Morbidity and Mortality Weekly Report: Youth Risk Behavior Surveillance*—United States, 2005, 16.

572. Johnston et al., *Monitoring the Future National Survey Results on Drug Use, 1975-2004*, vol. 1, 355.

573. Ibid., 416-19.

574. Johnston, et al., *Monitoring the Future: National Results on Adolescent Drug Use—Overview of Key Findings 2005*, 45.

575. Ibid.

576. Ibid.

577. "NIDA InfoFacts: Methylphenidate (Ritalin)," *The National Institute on Drug Abuse*, April 2006, www.nida.nih.gov, (July 17, 2006).

578. Johnston, et al., *Monitoring the Future: National Results on Adolescent Drug Use—Overview of Key Findings 2005*, 45.

579. Ibid., 55.

580. Ibid., 44.

581. Johnston, et al., *Monitoring the Future National Survey Results on Drug Use, 1975-2004*, vol. 2, 230.

582. *Keep Kids Alcohol Free: Strategies for Action*, (Bethesda, MD: Leadership to Keep Kids Alcohol Free, April 2006), 1.

583. Johnston, et al., *Monitoring the Future: National Results on Adolescent Drug Use—Overview of Key Findings 2005*, 64-65.

584. Ibid.

585. "Nine of Ten Sites Do Not Require Any Prescription," *The National Center on Addiction and Substance Abuse* page, June 19, 2006, www.casacolumbia.org, (July 17, 2006).

586. Johnston, et al., *Monitoring the Future: National Results on Adolescent Drug Use—Overview of Key Findings 2005*, 67.

587. "Kids like cute creatures in beer ads, more likely to buy brand of beer, study suggests," *Pacific Institute for Research and Evaluation* page, October 17, 2005, www.pire.org, (July 12, 2006).

588. *National Survey of American Attitudes on Substance Abuse X: Teens and Parents* (New York: The National Center on Addiction and Substance Abuse at Columbia University, August 2005), 2.

589. "Smoking still cool in youth-rated movies," *USA Today*, July 18, 2006, 6D.

590. Judith H. Jaynes and Cheryl A. Rugg, *Adolescents, Alcohol and Drugs* (Springfield, IL: Charles C. Thomas, 1988), 13-22.

591. Laurence Steinberg, Anne Fletcher, and Nancy Darling, "Parental Monitoring and Peer Influences on Adolescent Substance Use," *Pediatrics*, June 1994, 1060ff.

592. "Adolescent Chemical Use," 2.

593. *PRIDE Questionnaire Report for Grades 6 thru 12: 2004-05 National Summary*, 146.

594. "1996 National Survey of American Attitudes and Substance Abuse II: The Parental Risk Factors," *The National Center on Addiction and Substance Abuse at Columbia University*, 1996, www.casacolumbia.org, (December 8, 1997).

595. Les Parrott III, *Helping Your Struggling Teenager: A Parenting Handbook on Thirty-Six Common Problems* (Grand Rapids, MI: Zondervan, 2000), 106.

Chapter 11

596. *#1 Teenage Suicide* page, www.#1TeenageSuicide.com, (April 18, 2005).

597. "Youth Suicide Fact Sheet," *American Association of Suicidology* page, February 12, 2006, www.suicidology.org, (July 24, 2006).

598. Ibid.

599. Ibid.

600. "Teen Suicide," *The Brown University Child and Adolescent Behavior Letter*, 2003.

601. "Youth Indicators 2005: Death and Causes of Death," *National Center for Education Statistics* page, July 2005, www.nces.ed.gov, (July 24, 2006).

602. *Morbidity and Mortality Weekly Report: Youth Risk Behavior Surveillance*—United States, 2005, 9-10.

603. Ibid.

604. "Youth Suicide Fact Sheet."

605. Gitanjali Saluja, Ronaldo Iachan, Peter C. Scheidt, Mary D. Overpeck, Wenyu Sun, and Jay N. Giedd, "Prevalence of and Risk Factors for Depressive Symptoms Among Young Adolescents," *Archives of Pediatric Adolescent Medicine*, August 2004, 760.

606. "Statistics—Adolescent Depression," *About Teen Depression* page, n.d., www.about-teen-depression.com, (October 4, 2004).

607. Ibid.

608. "Let's Talk Facts About Depression," *The American Psychiatric Association*, 2005.

609. "Male eating disorders may be on the rise," *USA Today*, May 12, 2004, 7D.

610. *Eating Disorders: Facts About Eating Disorders and the Search for Solutions* (Bethesda, MD: National Institute of Mental Health, 2001), 2.

611. Susan Ice, "Statistics," *Eating Disorders Coalition* page, 2006, www.eatingdisorderscoalition.org, (July 25, 2006).

612. Ibid.

613. Ibid.

614. Janice McLane, "The voice on the skin: self-mutilation and Merleau-Ponty's theory of language," *Hypatia*, fall 1996.

615. Ronald Winchel and Michael Stanley, "Self-Injurious Behavior: A review of the behavior and biology of self-mutilation," *American Journal of Psychiatry*, March 1991, 306.

616. Lindsey Tanner, "Survey shows high rate of self-abuse," Lancaster (PA) *Intelligencer Journal*, June 5, 2006, B5.

617. Jennifer Egan, "The Thin Red Line," *The New York Times Magazine*, July 27, 1997, 23.

618. B.A. Van der Kolk, J.C. Perry, and J.L. Herman, "Childhood Origins of Self-Destructive Behavior," *American Journal of Psychiatry* 148, (1991 no. 12) 1665-71.

619. *Educational Resources Information Center and the Counseling and Personnel Services Clearinghouse*, "Teenage Suicide: Identification, Intervention and Prevention," Highlights, fact sheet (University of Michigan: 1985).

620. *The State of Our Nation's Youth*, 65-66.

621. *The Gallup Organization, Teen Suicide: The 1994 Updated Survey on Teen Suicide*, 9.

622. *The Gallup Organization, Teen Suicide: The 1994 Updated Survey on Teen Suicide*, 9.

623. As quoted in R.E.O. White, "Nihilism," *The Evangelical Dictionary of Theology* (Grand Rapids, MI: Baker, 1984), 778.

624. Pew Research Center Survey, November 9-27, 2005, *The Polling Report* page, 2006, www.pollingreport.com/health2.htm, (July 26, 2006).

625. CBS News Poll, December 14-19, 2001, *The Polling Report* page, 2006, www.pollingreport.com/health2.htm, (July 26, 2006).

626. Tim Celek and Dieter Zander, *Inside the Soul of a New Generation* (Grand Rapids, MI: Zondervan, 1996), 25ff.

627. William Mahedy and Janet Bernardi, *A Generation Alone* (Downers Grove, IL: InterVarsity Press, 1994), 20ff.

628. The Gallup Organization, *Teen Suicide: The 1994 Updated Survey on Teen Suicide*, 4.

629. "Behaviors May Indicate Risk of Adolescent Depression," *National Institutes of Health* page, May 15, 2006, www.nih.gov, (May 23, 2006).

630. "Child Abuse and Neglect," *Medem Medical Library* page, 2000, www.medem.com, (July 26, 2006).

631. "National Child Abuse Statistics," *The Child Help* page, 2006, www.childhelpusa.org, (July 26, 2006).

632. Brad L. Neiger and Rodney W. Hopkins, "Adolescent Suicide: Character Traits of High-Risk Teenagers," *Adolescence* 23, no. 90 (Summer 1998): 473.

633. *Gallup Survey on Teen Suicide*, December 1991, 10.

634. Lindsey Tanner, "Study: Asking teenagers about suicide doesn't plant the idea," Lancaster (PA) *Intelligencer Journal*, April 6, 2005, B7.

Chapter 12

635. Eugene Peterson, *Like Dew Your Youth*, 90.

636. Ibid, 10.

637. Paul Tripp, *Age of Opportunity*, 66.

638. David John Seel, Jr., *Parenting Without Perfection: Being a Kingdom Influence in a Toxic World* (Colorado Springs, CO: Navpress, 2000), 37.

639. "Prayer: The 'Rising Tide' in Youth Ministry," *Network News of the National Network of Youth Ministries* 9, no. 3 (Fall 1991): 1.

640. Ron Rand, "A Challenge to Fathers Everywhere," *Princeton Theological Seminary Alumni/ae News*, Fall 1998, 6.

641. Fred Green, "What Parents Could Have Done," *Pulpit Helps*, November 1987, 19.

642. Rand, "A Challenge to Fathers Everywhere," 6.

643. "Families Who Make Dining Together a Priority Describe Themselves as Closer, More Connected and Less Likely to Raise Kids at Risk for Destructive Behaviors, TV Land & Nick at Nite Study Finds," *The Yahoo Finance* page, 29 November 2004, www.biz.yahoo.com, (December 2, 2004).

644. "Protecting Adolescents from Harm: Findings from the National Longitudinal Study on Adolescent Health," *Journal of the American Medical Association*, September 10, 1997.

645. "Parenting Keys for Success," *The Youth Connection*, October/November 2003, 6.

646. Green, "What Parents Could Have Done," 19.

647. Paul Tournier, *To Understand Each Other* (Atlanta, GA: John Knox Press, 1962), 17.

index